In the history of the SAS no one has ever matched Ken Connor's 23-year operational service with the Regiment. His career spanned from 1963 to 1986. He saw active service in four different theatres of war and became a Senior Instructor in a number of specialist departments, and was closely involved in the development of the Counter Revolutionary Warfare team and SAS VIP protection techniques. He also trained US personnel at the FBI Academy in Quantico, USA. With his unique record and extensive contacts, no one is better qualified to write the definitive history of the SAS.

GHOST FORCE

THE SECRET HISTORY OF THE SAS

KEN CONNOR

CASSELL

Cassell Military Paperbacks

Cassell
Wellington House, 125 Strand,
London WC2R 0BB

First published by Weidenfeld & Nicolson 1998
This Cassell Military Paperbacks edition 2002
Reprinted 2002, 2003

British Library Cataloguing-in-Publication Data
A catalogue record for this book is available from the
British Library

ISBN 0-304-36367-7

Printed and bound in Great Britain by
Cox & Wyman Ltd., Reading, Berks.

CONTENTS

List of illustrations   vii
Glossary   ix
Preface   xiii

Prologue   1
  1 Desert Warriors 1941–45   9
  2 Malaya 1950–58   22
  3 Jebel Akhdar 1958–59   56
  4 Return to the West 1958–63   87
  5 Brunei and Borneo 1962–66   118
  6 The Kennedy Assassination 1963   149
  7 Aden 1964–67   180
  8 Operation Storm, Dhofar 1970–77   219
  9 Northern Ireland 1968–97   262
10 Terrorism 1968–98   303
11 Iranian Embassy 1980   341
12 The Falklands 1982   356
13 Afghanistan 1982–89   415
14 Cold War 1945–90   427
15 Gulf War 1990–91   456
16 The Future   502

Appendix – Extracts from the Founding Principles
    of the SAS, laid down by David Stirling   527
Notes to the text   529
Bibliography   536
Index   545

ILLUSTRATIONS

1. The attack on Suez. *Source: Tony Ashton*
2. A paratrooper on SAS selection. *Source: TRH Pictures*
3. DLB and Johnny Watts on active service in the Jebel Akhdar campaign. *Source: Defence Picture Library*
4. A patrol recovering after a contact near the Sarawak/Sabah borders. *Source: Defence Picture Library*
5. Alfie Tasker – 'the Ancient Brit'. *Source: John Strawson, A History of the SAS*
6. 17 Troop, D Squadron on operations in Aden. *Source: Lofty Large*
7. An Indonesian senior NCO in a camp at Kalimantan. *Source: SAS Regiment*
8. Insertion methods practised in the mid to late 1960s. *Source: TRH Pictures*
9. Troops using the Grant Taylor method of shooting. *Source: Lofty Large*
10. In the Killing House in Hereford. *Source: Defence Picture Library*
11. Men returning from a four-month operation in Borneo. *Source: Ken Connor*
12. Part of the author's troop in Dhofar. *Source: Ken Connor*
13. The author in a sangar in Dhofar. *Source: Ken Connor*
14. The author and 17 Troop, D Squadron, training in Iran in 1970. *Source: Ken Connor*

15. A mortar being fired during Operation Storm. *Source: Imperial War Museum*

16. The results of the attack on the airfield on Pebble Island. *Source: TRH Pictures*

17. A Soviet barracks in East Germany. *Source: Graham Geary*

18. Soviet traffic regulators. *Source: Graham Geary*

19. An East German border guard in an armoured car. *Source: Ken Connor*

20. A Soviet artillery piece photographed on a training area south of Karl Marx Stadt. *Source: Graham Geary*

21. A 'Pink Panther'. *Source: TRH Pictures*

GLOSSARY

adoo: Arabic word for enemy

AWACS: airborne warning and control system

BDF: Botswana Defence Force

BG: bodyguard

casevac: casualty evacuation

CO: commanding officer

contact: engagement with the enemy

CQB: close-quarter battle

CR, CS: types of anti-personnel gas

Crabs: the RAF

CRW: counter-revolutionary warfare

CT: counter-terrorist

DF: direction-finding

DZ: dropping zone

E&E: escape and evasion

FAC: forward air controller

firqat: irregular troops comprising tribesmen of the Omani province of Dhofar

FMB: forward mounting base

FOB: forward operating base

Foreign Office: used throughout instead of its cumbersome full name, the Foreign and Commonwealth Office

14 Int: Fourteenth Intelligence Company

gaysh: Arabic name for the regular troops of the Sultan of Oman's armed forces

Glacis plate: front plate of a tank, where the armour is thickest

GPMG: General purpose machine-gun

GPS: global positioning system

Green Slime: Intelligence Corps

Head Shed: those in authority, often though

not exclusively officers. The expression originated in Malaya, derived from the watershed at the head of a river from which everything flows

hard dog: attack dog

humint: intelligence collected by human beings

jebali: mountain tribesman from the Omani province of Dhofar

LTD: laser target designator

LZ: landing zone

LUP: lying-up position

MID: Mention in Despatches

MSR: main supply route

NBC: nuclear, biological and chemical warfare kit

NCO: non-commissioned officer

net: radio network

NVG: night-vision goggles

OC: officer commanding

OP: observation post

PNG: passive night goggles

RPG: rocket-propelled grenade

RSM: regimental sergeant-major

RTU: return to unit, the fate of soldiers sacked by the SAS

Rupert: officer, not always derogatory

RV: rendezvous

sangar: fortified observation post, usually dry stone, often constructed by night in complete silence

SADF: South African Defence Force

SAF: Sultan's (Omani) Armed Forces

SARBE: search and rescue beacon

sat-coms: satellite communications

SBS: Special Boat Service

SEPs: Surrendered Enemy Personnel

siaseet: Arabic word, literally meaning political, but used to describe anyone suspected of being devious

sigint: signals intelligence

SIS: Secret Intelligence Services, also known as MI6, the covert arm of the Foreign Office. Took its present form at the end of the Second World War when the SOE was merged with MI6

SLR: self-loading rifle

SOAF: Sultan of Oman's Air Force

SOE: Special Operations Executive

SOF: (US) Special Operations Forces

SOP: standard operating procedure

SSM: squadron sergeant-major

Tacbe: tactical beacon

Tac-sat: satellite communications

TOS: Trucial Oman Scouts

PREFACE

I had several motives for embarking on this book, not the least of them the desire to tell the story of the Regiment as succeeding generations of SAS men have told it to each other.

I wanted to tell the hitherto untold story of the Regiment – except where continuing operations make that impossible – but also to give due prominence to the men who helped to shape the SAS and build the reputation it enjoys today. I didn't want the stories of the 'Old and Bold' to die with them.

The existing SAS histories written by people such as John Strawson, Tony Geraghty, Philip Warner and Anthony Kemp suffer from three constraints: they are all written by outsiders – though John Strawson had a distinguished career in other branches of the armed forces – largely rely on the testimony of high-ranking officers and can draw on little supporting documentation.

The lack of documents is in part a product of the Regiment's obsessive secrecy. John Strawson was given access to SAS documentation but the policy of shredding paper at the conclusion of covert SAS operations – which effectively means all of them – ensures that the written sources are less valuable than they would be in other circumstances.

Official reports on SAS operations do still exist, but they were written for external army consumption, often by officers who were not part of those operations, and are extremely unreliable records of events.

There are few other documents for historians to consult. Military and government papers which might shed some light on the Regiment's activities are often buried under the thirty-, fifty- or one-hundred-year rules.

The second constraint on writers is largely self-inflicted. Authors such as Hugh McManners in *The Scars of War* and Robin Neillands in *A Fighting Retreat* have used the stories of all ranks to convey something of the experience of war through soldiers' eyes, but, like the SAS historians, they would be most unlikely to seek a foot-soldier's opinion on overall military strategy.

Just as some general histories are written as if the story of monarchs, presidents, prime ministers and dictators is the whole story of mankind, so military history is almost invariably constructed from the opinions and recollections of senior officers and commanders-in-chief.

There are valid reasons for that honourable tradition. It is the correct approach to writing about almost every section of the armed forces. While the trogs slog through the mud, keeping their eyes on the toe-caps of their boots, the officers alone have the time to raise their eyes, scan the distant horizons and separate the strategic wood from the tactical trees.

The SAS is unlike every other section of the armed forces, however, and to place too much reliance on officers as sources is to give only a partial – in both senses of the word – account of the Regiment's history.

The SAS has its own long and honourable tradition: leadership is by merit, not rank. It also has another unique feature. Only the troopers and NCOs form a permanent cadre; officers are seconded to the Regiment for a three-year tour and then return to their former units.

The implications go far wider than the simple matter of who gives the orders on a patrol. There were – and are – many areas of SAS activity about which most, and sometimes all, of the officers remained in blissful ignorance. The only people with an overview of the Regiment's actions in the long term were the senior NCOs.

During my twenty-three-year service with the SAS I was fortunate enough to be one of those men and to be privy to some of the Regiment's most covert and clandestine operations, unknown not just to the outside world, but to 99 per cent of its officers and men too.

I have tried to tell the whole history of the SAS and also set it in its political context. Military histories often seem to regard political events as merely a footnote or a tiresome interruption to the main action.

Yet without an understanding of the external forces shaping Britain's post-war defence priorities and the way that the SAS came to be used as an integral part of British foreign policy, it is impossible to appreciate the true importance of the Regiment's contribution to the maintenance of Britain's power, influence – and affluence – in the modern world.

My debt to other writers and historians is acknowledged in the bibliography, but my personal thanks go to Sir Raymond Ligo, Sir Richard Evans and Syd Gillibrand, who all convinced me that I had a story to tell, and to George Rakonitz of Menlo Park, California, who finally persuaded me to get off my arse and write it.

The greatest debt of all, however, is to my peers in the SAS. From the re-forming of the Regiment in 1950 to the present day, many SAS men, from troopers to colonels, have shared their experiences and memories with me. Some are named in the text, others preferred to remain anonymous, but this book could not have been completed without their help.

Some of them are still serving with the SAS and their wish to see the story told conflicts with the Regiment's present foolish obsession with imposing monastic silence on its men in all circumstances. Like biographies of Howard Hughes, books on the SAS exist in a vacuum; the Regiment neither confirms nor denies anything written about it.

That policy has allowed several urban myths about the SAS

to be solemnly recorded by one 'historian' of the Regiment and then transcribed by others. More importantly, it has allowed the proud name of the SAS to be diminished by leaving unchallenged completely fictional accounts of the Regiment's operations masquerading as fact; *The Nemesis File* is only one example. It is one of the reasons why I was determined to write this book without the use of a pseudonym or a black bar obscuring my photograph.

In sharing their stories, those who served before, with and after me have helped me to write the true secret history of the SAS. This book is respectfully dedicated to them: ordinary men achieving extraordinary things.

Ken Connor, May 1998

PROLOGUE

We moved out at dusk. Thick cloud obscured the moon as we inched our way forward in near total darkness, straining our ears for any warning sound above the soughing of the wind through the long grass. It took us all night to cover nine miles. We got into position just before first light.

It was our first major operation for three months. We'd been holed up in our forward base from July to September, waiting out the monsoon. The radio was our only link to the main base on the narrow strip of Dhofar's coastal plain, sandwiched between the Indian Ocean and the sheer rock wall below the plateau. There were no roads; the only way in or out of the jebel – the mountain – was a foot-slog up the precipitous, rock-strewn track or a helicopter insertion.

In previous years we'd pulled back at the onset of the monsoon. This time we'd stayed, trying to maintain the pressure on the enemy. Although we were isolated, we were well armed: we had a twenty-five-pounder, a few mortars and plenty of machine-guns.

There was no officer with us. I ran the troop: about twelve men controlling two small groups of firqat – Jebali irregulars – totalling about 125 men, and two companies of Baluch, mercenaries recruited in Pakistan and Baluchistan, numbering about 150 men.

We communicated in Arabic. I was fluent in it and the

others had at least a working knowledge of the language. Although the firqat used their own tongue among themselves, they also spoke Arabic.

When the first full force of the monsoon broke, it was virtually impossible to patrol. Even when the worst of the rains were over, the south-west winds continued to lay a stifling blanket of low cloud, fog and drizzle over the jebel. Everything rotted in the warm, suppurating damp. Food was covered in mould; boots, webbing and clothing stank of mildew.

The adoo – the enemy – staged stand-off attacks, lobbing in a few mortars out of the mist and then running away before we could retaliate. We patrolled as best we could, but the poor visibility increased the sense of isolation and vulnerability.

As the weather at last began to break, the fog lifted. The jebel had been transformed. The parched brown dust, studded with clumps of thorn trees and outcrops of rock, had given way to a waving sea of tall new grass. Bony, long-horned cattle, half-starved before the rains, gorged themselves on the new growth.

Thin plumes of woodsmoke rose from the villages. The tightly grouped, round stone huts under their straw or tarpaulin roofs looked like clusters of fat mushrooms thrusting out of the rich, black soil.

The only people left in the villages, tending the cattle, were old men, women and boys. All the able-bodied men were involved in the fighting and it was quite usual to find some members of a family fighting for the Communists, while the others fought for the government.

With the weather now on our side, we wanted to impose ourselves on the area again. Our target was a village called Shaihait, about nine miles away. We were hoping to carry out a short, sharp action, so we took maximum ammunition and water, but very little food. I left the minimum number of men in camp, about thirty of the Baluch guarding the twenty-five-pounder crew, with one of our lads in charge.

My firqat bodyguard walked in front of me. If I was harmed, it was as if someone had killed or injured a member of his family. He looked after me very, very well.

Three hours before dawn, we halted on a ridge. Although we couldn't see it in the darkness, I knew that our target lay about three miles ahead. I left some of the Baluch there to establish a firm base, somewhere we could pull back to if necessary. Then the rest of us went forward, fanning out into our pre-planned positions.

The plateau was deeply scored with wadis – deep valleys, almost like rifts, with very steep sides. At the bottom there was thick scrub, as dense and impenetrable as jungle. The wadis held the only natural water on the mountain.

As soon as we hit the adoo, they would normally head for the wadis and get down among the scrub. We wanted to keep them on the mountain plain where we could bring everything we had to bear on them: mortars, machine-guns, the twenty-five-pounder, two 5.5-inch guns firing from the plain, and the Strikemaster ground-attack aircraft, nominally Omani but flown by RAF pilots.

I took up position on a slight rise on the near side of the village, closest to our camp, from where we could control the artillery and mortars – all the heavy stuff.

The remaining Baluch and the main body of the firqat deployed in ambush, while another group of firqat circled around and laid up on the far side of the village ready to move in at dawn, flushing out the enemy – if there were any there.

Everybody was in position, as far as I could tell, before the first faint streaks of red began to stain the sky. Our maps were unreliable and there were so many different groups involved, a total of around 250 people, I could only hope they had deployed correctly.

If something happened, we couldn't react until we knew where everybody was. If we got it wrong, incoming artillery would land on our own troops. There was lots of talking on the radio and you could taste the tension.

We lay watching and waiting as the faint light gradually strengthened. The low cloud was only sparsely broken and the air was already warm and humid. The rising sun showed red through the mist that still clung to the plateau.

The stillness and silence became oppressive, the only movement the flight of the birds. Then, just after first light, a large group of people left the village. They were moving directly towards us on the ridge – the wrong way – at right angles to the firqat and Baluch lying in ambush.

For a few moments, the low light and the mist shrouded their identity; even with binoculars and telescopes we weren't sure if they were villagers or adoo.

Then there was the crack of rifles and the answering chatter of a machine-gun as the firqat and adoo began exchanging fire. Adrenalin began to pump as the fire-fight erupted, the staccato notes of the small-arms fire underscored by the insistent bass of heavy weapons. On every side, bright muzzle-flashes pierced the mist.

In any fire-fight, you never hear the bullet that hits you, you just hear the crack of rounds passing close by and feel the splinters of flying rock. With a clear sky the sound dissipates, but with a cloud ceiling only a couple of hundred feet above our heads, we felt every shell and rifle round.

We were faced with total chaos. Everyone was on different radio nets. The SAS, firqat and Baluch each had their own, and there was also the command net. I was on two at once.

We were target-spotting from our vantage point and responding to the different groups on the ground who were clamouring for artillery support. We were also trying to keep the fighting away from the village. I didn't want anything happening near there. The firqat and SAS would stop working if the fighting moved too close to the village, but I had my doubts about the Baluch, who could be real bastards.

As the artillery and mortar rounds began falling, the crackle of small-arms fire was drowned by the thundering concussion of the shells. The first rounds were sighting shots. I redirected the fire and shells began to rain down on the adoo positions. The battle resembled something from the Western Front. Each shell-burst sent clods of dark earth hurtling into the air. Curtains of finer debris hung in the wind like smoke until pierced by the vivid flash of another shell-burst.

There was no sense of time passing. We were deluged with requests for artillery, mortars and covering fire while we tried to piece together a picture of the battle from what was coming over the net.

Patches of weak sunshine appeared through the smoke and dust. Praying that the mist wouldn't close in again, I stopped all the artillery and called up the Strikemasters.

There was only a couple of hundred feet of clear airspace beneath the cloud ceiling. We put a marker on the ground – a red flare – and then talked the Strikemasters in from there on to the target, shouting over the radio as they swept over our heads.

They swooped again and again, the screaming engines counterpointed by the roar of rockets and the dull crump of bomb-bursts.

Reports were starting to come in of adoo killed and I was praying that we didn't take any serious casualties on our side. If we had to bring in a casevac helicopter there seemed every chance that it would be shot down.

Without warning the jets wheeled away and disappeared back through the clouds, the noise of their howling engines fading to a faint rumble. Then the firing stopped. My ears were still ringing but I suddenly realised how quiet it was.

The brush with death had heightened every sense. As the stench of cordite blew away on the breeze, I could smell the damp grass, hear the birds singing and see the thorn trees etched against the sky. Far beyond our base, I could see the beginning of the vast sweep of the Rub al Khali, the Empty Quarter.

I dragged myself back to the job in hand and began taking in the reports from each group over the net. A couple of firqat had been slightly wounded but to my relief they were not badly enough hurt to need casevacing, even if they'd been willing to leave. We had enough ammo left to avoid the need for a resupply before moving out.

As I spoke on the net, my words kept catching in my throat and I realised I was very thirsty. I took a time check before sending a report of the action to our main base and realised why. It was 11.30. The contact had gone on for nearly six hours.

We'd had a little water, but no food since the previous night. Despite the pangs of hunger, food could wait until we got back to our main base. We had to reach it before last light. Without us it was only lightly defended and very vulnerable; the adoo could counter-attack very quickly.

We began to withdraw. We moved separately, 100 yards at a time, one group taking up firing positions to cover the next as they pulled back. We never moved together in case something happened.

As we reached the outer base, every returning group of firqat and Baluch added a contribution to a growing pile of Russian and Chinese weapons and ammunition belts. Unlike the farce and fantasy of American body counts in Vietnam, the rules were strict: no rifle, no kill.

We were all elated. The adoo had taken heavy casualties while we had only a few scratches, but, to my surprise, the firqat boss was rather subdued and aloof from the general excitement.

Then we got a report over the net. There was a pregnant woman in the village, long overdue. Some of the firqat were anxious about her. We were so elated we felt we could deal with anything now – another problem, let's sort it. I made the decision that we'd help her but I was not going to risk sending troops or a helicopter back to the village. The message went back: 'You bring the woman to us.'

We formed a defensive perimeter and waited. We were now up on the skyline, still in sight of the village, but three miles away. We watched through binoculars and telescopes as a procession in long, flowing robes came out of the village. It was like something out of the Bible.

There were six people, all men, carrying a stretcher on their shoulders. They were moving slowly but no one went to help them; it could have been a trap. There were 250 of us but we were going to stay put. They could come to us.

They took an eternity to reach us, moving like a centipede over the plateau. I started to think, Something is on here, and we were all getting very, very suspicious. I'd been in the troop ever since I joined the SAS – about twelve years then – and I knew everyone in it. None of them said anything; they just looked at me, the odd questioning glance.

When the stretcher party got closer, I could see the woman. She was very distressed and had a massive bulge. It was also obvious that she was far from young.

Everything was very tense as they reached the edge of our defensive ring. I sent our medic to do a quick check and he reported back that it seemed genuine. Some of the firqat were from the Shaihait area and they immediately got involved, helping to carry the stretcher.

The defensive perimeter was about 500 yards across. They carried the woman to a little hollow in the middle and laid her down. The medic took another look and confirmed that she really was pregnant – and then some. She was already extremely dilated.

The medic was fully equipped for battlefield trauma, but not childbirth. I hesitated a moment, then made the decision. I put everything on alert and requested the casevac chopper to bring in a medic team.

The pilot was not keen. The adoo had downed helicopters before with small-arms fire after lying up near a battle zone. I could hear the chopper coming from a long way off, flying above the cloud. As it came in I could feel the tension rising.

I kept thinking to myself, Christ, I hope this is right.

The medic team leaped out and the pilot was off again like a bat out of hell. I let out a sigh of relief as he disappeared back into the safety of the clouds.

Then there was just the distant, fading sound of the rotors. The birds began singing again but no one relaxed. The Baluch in particular were upset. If a helicopter could bring the medics, why couldn't it bring water and food? Why couldn't it have carried us back to base?

My troop number two, an Irishman, looked at me and grinned. 'You cunt.' I'd heard him say it often enough, but this time he just thought it.

The silence was broken by the sound of a baby crying. The tension evaporated in an instant. I smiled, the Irishman smiled, so did the rest of the troops. Even the Baluch lightened up.

We were all married, we all had kids, but it was more selfish than that: now the kid had been born we could all piss off back to our main base.

I turned to the firqat boss, who still seemed curiously detached. 'Isn't that wonderful?' I said in Arabic. 'A new life.'

He stood in silence, his expression unreadable. '*Allah kareem*,' he said, still staring out over the jebel. 'God is generous. He's replaced this woman's eldest son, one of the adoo we killed in the battle this morning.'

The author, Shaihait, Dhofar, 1974

1

DESERT WARRIORS
1941–45

Born in 1941, the Special Air Service was officially laid to rest in 1945. If Soviet military power and American economic muscle had been the ultimate engines of Hitler's defeat, British resolve and courage, even when alone in the face of overwhelming odds, had been the heart and driving force of that victory. It was ironic that the SAS, the force that best exemplified that spirit, was disbanded as soon as the war was over.

The Regiment formed by David Stirling had its origins in the Long-Range Desert Group operating against Italian forces in North Africa, and the commando forces raised in response to Churchill's urgings to hit back and 'Set Europe ablaze' after the disaster of Dunkirk.

Ten companies of commandos – 5,000 men in total – had been formed in 1940 to carry out hit-and-run attacks and intelligence-gathering. The first operation was a reconnaissance raid into northern France on 23 June 1940.

After the disintegration of the Italian armies in North Africa, the commandos were sent to the Middle East as part of Layforce, which aimed to take Rhodes as a stepping stone to a Balkan campaign. Instead, a series of defeats at the hands of Rommel's forces reversed most of the British gains and left them hanging on in North Africa.

David Stirling took part in three large-scale, seaborne operations by Number 8 Commando against German targets. The size of the operations made them impossible to conceal from enemy reconnaissance flights and, lacking the crucial element of surprise, the raids were all abortive.

The experience helped to convince Stirling that the way forward was small-scale raiding parties that could arrive at their targets undetected and assault communications, air-fields and dumps of ammunition, fuel and stores, all of which were vulnerable to surprise attack.

Stirling argued that instead of sending 200 men and high-value assets like ships or aircraft to attack an airfield, you could send a patrol of five (later four) men to accomplish the same task with a much greater chance of achieving surprise.

A group of 200 could then launch simultaneous attacks on twenty, thirty or even forty targets. Such attacks would have a twofold impact. The first effect would be the disruption and damage caused to the targets themselves. The second would be more permanent, forcing the withdrawal of battle troops to guard the installations, thus rendering the front-line forces more vulnerable to conventional attack.

Stirling envisaged groups of self-sufficient, versatile sol-diers, more intensively trained and better equipped than any others. They would reach targets by parachute, ship, submarine, vehicle or even on foot. He also insisted that the traditional chain of command be circumvented because it was both cumbersome and prone to leaks, which could compromise the security of the operations.

Although only a junior officer, Stirling's persistence and his burning faith in his ideas eventually saw him face to face with, first, the deputy chief of staff of the Middle East forces and later the commander-in-chief, General Auchinleck.

Despite presenting his ideas in 'one of the worst pieces of military writing ever submitted',[1] he found a receptive audience. Stirling was promoted to captain and given auth-ority to recruit men from Layforce and other British regiments in the Middle East. In July 1941 the SAS was born.

Although the initial establishment was only seven officers

and sixty men, Stirling's force was named L Detachment, SAS Brigade, to add further weight to an existing deception, aimed at convincing the enemy that a full airborne brigade was operating in the Western Desert.

Stirling set the highest standards from the start. He insisted on the right to RTU – return to unit, dismiss from the SAS – men who did not come up to standard at any stage of the training. He also required SAS discipline, in all aspects, to be as rigid as in his own former unit, the Brigade of Guards. It is virtually the only one of Stirling's principles which did not survive the transition to the modern SAS.

From the start the SAS role was strategic and not tactical. 'Firstly raids in depth behind the enemy lines, attacking HQ nerve centres, landing grounds, supply lines, etc; and, secondly, the mounting of sustained strategic offensive activity from several bases within hostile territory and, if the opportunity existed, recruiting, training, arming and co-ordinating local guerrilla elements.'[2]

The key unit for the SAS would be the patrol. The smallest army grouping had previously been an infantry section: eight to ten men, led by a corporal. The five- or four-man SAS patrol had no leader in the traditional sense and operated with a large measure of discretion and independence, on its own or in conjunction with other patrols.

Each patrol member was required to have one specialist skill and a broad spectrum of other skills, including navigation by day and night, weapons – both their own and the enemy's, for captured weapons were often put to use – demolition, signalling, first-aid and parachuting.

Missions were planned in direct consultation with head-quarters, bypassing staff officers who often had little grasp of the strategic role the SAS was pursuing and sought to divert it to minor tactical tasks best left to infantry. Security in planning, communications and operations was rigidly main-tained, protecting the integrity of the operation and the identity of the often confidential sources of intelligence.

Recruits – all volunteers – were put through a punishing physical training programme. Even those who passed that phase faced RTU at any time during the subsequent specialist training if their skills did not reach the required levels, or if their personalities made them incompatible with other members of the group.

Despite the intense preparations, the first operation by the SAS on 16 November 1941 – simultaneous airborne attacks on five airfields involving seven officers and fifty-seven other ranks – was a disaster. Strong winds blew the sticks of parachutists all over the desert. Only one group actually reached its target and all its men were killed. When the survivors of the other attack groups eventually emerged from the desert only four officers and eighteen other ranks remained alive.

That catastrophe did not shake the confidence of either Stirling or his supporters at HQ in his concept but it did see an end to airborne operations. All other subsequent insertions were made by vehicle rather than parachute. The SAS carried out long-range attacks on German forces and equipment, then disappeared back into the vast, empty reaches of the Western Desert.

The Special Air Service vindicated Stirling and Auchinleck's faith with a series of outstandingly successful raids in the Western Desert; the SAS actually destroyed more enemy aircraft than the Royal Air Force. As the war moved on, it operated with equal distinction, if less dramatic impact, behind enemy lines in the Mediterranean, Italy and northern Europe.

The last SAS operation of the Second World War, to disarm the German garrison in Norway, ended on 25 August 1945, ten days after the formal end of the war. On 5 October the Regiment was disbanded.

Seeking to save something from the wreckage, Brigadier 'Mad' Mike Calvert, by then the commanding officer of the Regiment, asked for opinions on the future of the SAS concept from a variety of colleagues. Major Roy Farran provided one of the most thoughtful replies.

His vision of a counter-insurgency role in small colonial struggles, even when not supported by sympathetic elements of the population, was prophetic; and against the whole weight of orthodox military opinion at the time, he also argued that nuclear weapons had actually increased the potential roles for special forces. Used aggressively, they could spread 'panic and confusion in the enemy's rear' as its forces retreated, and, used defensively, they could slow an enemy advance by harassing lines of communication.

In most cases, conventional wars between forces fighting from fixed positions rapidly reach a decisive point at which one side is brought to the brink of defeat; the Gulf War was a perfect example. In such a situation, losing forces armed with nuclear weapons will see no option but to resort to them. Had Saddam Hussein possessed nuclear weapons, there is little doubt that he would have used them.

In Farran's view, the use of special forces offered a potential escape from this near-inevitable escalation from conventional to nuclear war, either forcing the enemy to reassess its chances by a brief but ferocious attack, or buying time for political negotiations to take place by slowing an enemy advance.

A War Office study completed in November 1946 also concluded that special forces would have a number of valid roles in the fluid, fast-moving warfare of the future, distinct from the roles of both orthodox infantry and SOE-type intelligence operators. But the War Office saw the need for no more than a Territorial regiment to fulfil those future roles.

In 1947 the last remnants of the wartime Regiment, a handful of officers, were formed into 21 SAS (Artists) TA. A few other SAS veterans, unwilling or unable to make a part-time commitment, were named the Z Reserve. They would be available for call-up in a crisis, but would need intensive physical conditioning and retraining.

The subtitle of the TA regiment referred to the Artists' Rifles, recruited in 1859 from painters and other indi-vidualistic types. It had fought in the Boer War and the

First World War, but had been relegated to an Officer Cadet Training Unit in the Second. During the First World War they actually elected their own officers, a system that would have delighted modern SAS men as much as it would have horrified the traditionalists.

The only long-term contributions the Artists' Rifles made to the SAS were its cap badge – Mars and Minerva, still the title of the Regimental journal – a drill hall near Euston Station and a hut at the Bisley Ranges.

Twenty-one SAS was not much of a survival. The desert warriors had now been reduced to weekend soldiers, and part-timers could not maintain the levels of skill, fitness and training needed by special forces.

A conflict was already brewing on the far side of the world, however, which would lead to the rebirth of the SAS in a very different guise.

The war-weary British public had revelled in their victory for a short while, then turned their attention to the pressing problems of peace. From now on the first priority was to build a land fit for heroes at home, not pursue military adventures abroad.

The empire had actually grown as a result of the war through the occupation of territories as the Germans and Japanese retreated. When hostilities ended, British forces were in control of parts of Austria, Germany, Greece, Turkey, Libya, Indochina and the Dutch East Indies. Britain had also taken over the administration of Sarawak, the curious territory in North Borneo that had been run as a private fiefdom of the Brooke family – 'the white rajahs of Sarawak' – since 1841.

In previous eras some at least of those territories would have become permanent additions to the empire, but post-war Britain lacked both the appetite and the economic and military strength for new conquests. Even to hold the pre-war empire together was beyond its abilities.

Forty years before Indian independence Curzon had famously warned of the consequences of the loss of India to the empire. 'Your ports and coaling stations, your fortresses and dockyards, your Crown colonies and protectorates will go too. For either they will be unnecessary, as the toll-gates and barbicans of an empire that has vanished, or they will be taken by an enemy more powerful than yourselves.'[3]

The arch-imperialist Churchill had now been replaced as Prime Minister by Clement Attlee, however, and after the long and stubborn refusal to accept India's right to self-determination, Britain was ready to bow to the nationalist pressure.

Any lingering temptation to backtrack on earlier pledges was undermined by the questionable loyalty to the crown of the Indian armed forces. Gandhi had warned that 'Indian soldiers are not a national army but professionals, who will as soon fight under the Japanese or any others, if paid for fighting.'[4]

That they could no longer be relied on to fight for the British, even when paid to do so, was shown by the mutiny of the Royal Indian Navy in February 1946, which ended with 223 dead and over 1,000 injured.[5]

Attlee had already conceded the principle of early independence for India but, as unrest grew, the date for the formal British withdrawal was brought forward, and then advanced again. Plans for a measured and orderly transfer of power were thrown into disarray by a breakneck race against time – to get out before India exploded.

The bloodbath that followed independence in August 1947 was perhaps inevitable anyway, but British haste to be gone after almost three decades of prevarication did little to prevent it.

The death toll from the mutiny proved to be nothing compared to the 200,000 killed in the mayhem that followed Britain's chaotic and ultimately hasty abandonment of the empire's greatest glory.

Two other countries were also fast-tracked to independence. What had been granted to the increasingly rebellious Indians, many of whom had supported and even fought for the Japanese, could not in justice be denied to the Ceylonese, who had loyally supported the Allied war effort. Burma also had little strategic value to Britain and any struggle to hold it within the empire was widely thought not to be worth the candle. Another swift departure ensured that independence for Burma was also the prelude to a slaughter of ethnic minorities.

Neither the government nor the opposition had much interest in loosening their grip on the empire beyond that, in the short term at least. On his return to power in 1951 Winston Churchill was to trumpet that he had not become Prime Minister to 'preside over the dissolution of the empire', but even a reforming Labour government in broad sympathy with nationalist aspirations did not envisage a transfer of power without a long handover period, during which the states of Asia, Africa and the Middle East could be gradually prepared for independence.

What looked like sensible caution to the British could look awfully like imperialism under a different guise from a colonial point of view. Violence in India had led to independence and unrest had also compelled Britain to give up its UN mandate in Palestine in 1948. The emerging nationalist politicians drew their own conclusions about the value of force in persuading Britain to loosen its grip.

Much of the empire had been acquired to protect the trade routes with India, and countries in the Middle East had originally had little significance for Britain other than their strategic position near the Suez Canal and the Persian Gulf.

The increasing importance of oil (Britain consumed half of Europe's total pre-war imports) had changed all that, but in the face of widespread Arab hostility, Britain's ability to subjugate the region or buy stability through development was seriously impaired. 'The Arab mind is said to respect great power; the spectacle of Britain peering into an empty purse at the end of the war was certainly no invitation to Arab quiescence.'[6]

Other imperial territories whose pre-war value had been much less significant had also moved to centre stage. Even without India, the value of Malaya's exports of tin and rubber alone – it produced one-third of the world's natural rubber and over half its tin – was sufficient to ensure the maintenance of a British presence east of Suez.

The British ability to cling to these key parts of the empire was challenged not only by the loss of the Indian army, which had provided a huge reserve of troops for imperial duties, but also by Britain's changed economic circumstances. The unheard-of introduction of peacetime conscription eased the army's manpower problems a little, but solving Britain's financial problems was an altogether different proposition.

Britain had emptied its own pockets and pillaged the empire to pay for the war. In victory it was technically bankrupt, the world's largest debtor nation, in hock not just to America but to virtually every member of the empire as well. As John Maynard Keynes admitted, 'We threw good housekeeping to the winds,' and the country now faced 'a financial Dunkirk'.

The rapid demobilisation and contraction of the armed forces was not enough to offset the huge additional strain on Britain's already stretched resources imposed by the new National Health Service and social security system.

Attempts to subsidise British economic recovery with the dollar revenues earned by raw material exports from the colonies were only partially successful. One of the past requirements on countries within the empire – though it was not always rigidly enforced – had always been that they should be net contributors to the United Kingdom's balance of payments. Under Labour, expenditure on the empire was rapidly increased to fund the development that was the necessary first step to independence. The result was further pressure on Britain's battered economy, which faced the first of a succession of sterling crises.

Britain's economic plight soon forced it to hand over its military commitments in Greece – where a civil war had been raging since 1944 – and Turkey to the US, which, in contrast to British woes, had emerged from the war with its economic supremacy unchallenged.

The new world order was dominated by twin superpowers, an event predicted by American military planners well before the final defeat of Germany and Japan, who foresaw a change 'comparable indeed with that occasioned by the fall of Rome ... The United States and the Soviet Union will be the only military powers of the first magnitude ... Both in an absolute sense and relative to the United States and Russia, the British Empire will emerge from the war having lost ground economically and militarily.'[7]

The Soviet Union had been ravaged by the war but even with half its industry and agricultural land under German occupation, its military output had still been double that of Britain. With its territories restored and Germany and East Europe plundered for equipment and materials, its military and economic power could only grow.

That prospect caused alarm in London and Washington, but Stalin felt he had every reason to maintain his country's war-readiness. Churchill had despatched British troops to Russia in 1918 to intervene in the Russian civil war against the Bolshevik regime and many Western leaders had continued to display a marked preference for Fascism over Communism in the 1920s and early 1930s.

The wartime marriage of convenience between East and West had been summarily dissolved and Stalin had no need to look further than Saigon – where the conquered Japanese had been rearmed by the British to suppress the Viet Minh – to see the practical consequences of the strident anti-Communist line adopted by Churchill and Truman.

The Soviet Union had even more reason than France to

seek a permanent means of ensuring that Germany would never again be able to wage aggressive war. If the price of that was the occupation of Eastern Europe as a whole, it was a prospect Stalin could regard with equanimity.

Spurred by the perceived threat from the Soviet bloc, the US had only briefly adopted its traditional retreat into isolationism. By 1948 it was showing an appetite for matching its economic power with a world political and military role.

The Truman Doctrine and the Marshall Plan strengthened the US stake in Europe and the formal establishment of NATO – America's first ever peacetime military alliance – gave military expression to that commitment.

Western fears were rapidly increased by the first successful Soviet atom bomb test in August 1949 and the Communist seizure of power in China that autumn. Even before the outbreak of the Korean War on 25 June 1950, the US had rearmed and pressed ahead with production of the H-bomb.

Although their ideological standpoints were radically different, both the US and the Soviet Union were fiercely anti-colonial. The new United Nations also provided a forum in which emergent nations could add to the pressure on Britain to grant independence to its colonies; a General Assembly motion calling for a rapid end to colonialism was passed by ninety-seven votes to nil.

While professing to have no imperial ambitions itself, the US remained eager to demolish the last remnants of the British Empire. Roosevelt had made persistent attempts to prise Hong Kong from Britain's grasp during the war, first offering to pay the purchase price if Britain would sell it to Chiang Kai-shek's Chinese nationalists, then urging Churchill to 'give it up as a gesture of goodwill' and finally proposing to Stalin at Yalta that it be made an international free port.[8]

Vice-President Nixon on a visit to Asia made haste to reassure his hosts that 'we were not a colonial power, nor did we approve of the lingering colonialism of our European allies'.[9] Whatever its public statements, however, the economic ambitions and anti-Communist aims of the US soon coalesced into a policy that was at least neo-colonialist and neo-imperialist, playing the 'Great Game' of making and breaking rulers on the world stage.

Even in the Middle East, notionally conceded by the Americans as a sphere of British interest, there was covert US support for the Saudi royal family and continuing efforts to win concessions for American oil companies.

In parallel with the sweeping post-war political and economic changes, all previous military strategies had also been called into question by the evolution of air-power and the development of nuclear weapons.

The empire had been built on British domination of the high seas but it had been progressively diluted since the turn of the century when the famous 2:1 formula – twice the ships of the next largest power – had been abandoned. In the nuclear age, even if Great Britain could have afforded such naval power, it had become almost an irrelevance. The Second World War had offered conclusive evidence that air-power, not naval power, was now the vital element.

The British hold on the empire had also been sustained by bluff. Even at the height of Britain's power there had never been a time when it was strong enough to withstand two major colonial wars in different parts of the empire at the same time, or sustain a European campaign while fighting off rebellions elsewhere.

Fighting full-scale colonial wars against entire populations was out of the question for Britain and, as was soon to be evident, even the task of fighting small colonial uprisings was rapidly passing beyond its abilities. Each successful or inconclusive military challenge to British power anywhere in the empire merely invited further ones.

Unlike its old colonial rivals, Britain was willing to let go of its overseas possessions – eventually; but its great post-war dilemma was how to manage the break-up of the empire in a way that might hold the former colonies in some form of continuing relationship with Britain.

The Foreign and Colonial Offices were desperate to prevent a succession of former colonies becoming hostile, possibly Communist, states, but faced with this dramatically different world they could offer only two options.

The first involved the use of diplomacy, coupled with a judicious use of aid. While doing its best to hold back or slow the tide of nationalism, usually by locking up nationalist leaders, Britain encouraged moderate – i.e. pro-British – politicians. Officials also tried to model the institutions of the emerging nations – the parliaments, judiciary, armies and police – on those of Great Britain, and worked to persuade the colonies to swap the formal ties of empire for the looser bonds of the Commonwealth.

Where diplomacy alone was insufficient to control the rise of nationalism, the Foreign and Colonial Offices also showed a willingness to use the military option in key strategic areas. If our straitened circumstances no longer permitted the wholesale despatch of gunboats to quell uprisings or whip dissident warlords into line, British troops could still be used to damp down the bushfires of colonial rebellion.

India had been too vast and too far down the road to independence – with or without British consent – to be held back any longer. Burma had been too intractable and insufficiently valuable to be worth fighting for, but Malaya was a different case altogether.

When rebellion broke out there in 1948 there was no question of giving in to it. The insurgency was on a small scale, without mass popular support, and, in any case, Malaya was far too valuable an asset to be given up without a fight.

The battle to contain the Malayan insurgency developed into a prolonged colonial war. When it began to slide out of Britain's control in 1950, the Special Air Service, disbanded five years before, was reborn and put in the forefront of the fight.

2

MALAYA
1950–58

Two army trucks were parked on a dirt track at the edge of the jungle. A number of young soldiers stood around them in the sweltering heat. Their immaculate starched uniforms were already stained with sweat.

They kept peering into the darkness of the jungle, where the ground sloped down towards a swamp glinting among the tree-trunks. Their nervousness was almost palpable.

There had been no sound, no movement, not even a ripple on the surface of the water, yet suddenly a man appeared out of the swamp. He was as pale, haggard and emaciated as a concentration-camp survivor and the rags he wore hung loose around him, but his posture was upright and alert. He stood motionless in the shadows just inside the jungle, listening intently, the barrel of his gun tracking the path of his watchful gaze.

The soldiers around the trucks still had not seen him. He clapped his hands softly to attract their attention and then walked into the open, shading his eyes from the fierce sun, the first direct sunlight he had seen in three months.

He signalled behind him and another seven men emerged from the swamp and immediately went into a defensive screen around the trucks, taking up the best firing positions.

They communicated with each other in a strange mixture of signs and whispers, and were barely recognisable as soldiers. The clean and pressed soldiers stared at them with a mixture of revulsion, awe and incomprehension.

Everything the SAS men were wearing or carrying was soaking wet and they were filthy and unshaven, their faces white and gaunt. Their uniforms were ragged and their calf-length boots were torn, exposing their bruised and bleeding feet. The only things that looked cared for were their weapons, a curious mixture of sawn-off, pump-action shotguns, Patchet submachine-guns and jungle carbines.

They were totally at home in the swamp and jungle, carrying on their backs everything they needed to survive, as they harassed and fought the enemy who lurked there. What they did not have they did without.

Their daily routine in the swamp was beyond the imagination of the soldiers meeting them. They woke before dawn, packed their meagre belongings in the dark and lay motionless as the light strengthened, listening for movement. Then they began patrolling through the waist-deep water.

Leeches attached themselves to their bodies as they moved through the swamp and the air was cloudy with mosquitoes. Water snakes wriggled away through the murky water. Monkeys and birds passed through the sunlit canopy high above their heads, but the trees filtered out the sunlight and the floor of the jungle was in semi-darkness.

The soldiers paused constantly to listen, scent the breeze and scan the vegetation; in the swamps and jungles noise and smell were even greater giveaways than movement.

About two hours after first light they found a small dry area and made breakfast: a tin mug of tea and a biscuit and cheese, followed by the first cigarette of the day to dull the gnawing hunger pangs.

Then they moved on again. The swamp got deeper after rain in the hills and the only way to rest was to suspend the heavy packs on floating logs. Often a dead animal floated silently past as the debris of hundreds of square miles of jungle slowly settled into the mud of the swamp.

Lunch was another mug of tea and another comforting cigarette. Towards the end of the afternoon they hoped to find an island large enough for them to sling their parachute hammocks. If not, they slept or rested where they could.

After the evening meal of curry, rice and tea they changed into their spare clothing, which was only damp instead of wet. In turn, they stripped, cleaned and oiled their weapons, then lay awake listening until it was so dark it was impossible to see a hand held in front of the face. Then they fell into an exhausted sleep, knowing that tomorrow would be the same as today. Their only motivation was that if they were there, the terrorists had to move to another area or be killed.

This was their routine for twelve weeks, broken only by the monthly journey to the edge of the swamp to collect one day's fresh rations and another four weeks of tinned food.

Now that their patrol was at an end, they made an attempt to become like normal soldiers. They washed and shaved for the first time in three months, sharing a razor, and changed into their sleeping clothes, which were slightly less torn than the ones they were wearing.

One of them collected some swamp water in a mess tin and began to make a brew of tea. An army doctor, just arrived in Malaya and very conspicuous in his new uniform, rushed forward. 'Where did you get that water?'

The soldier jerked his thumb towards the swamp.

'But you can't drink it. It's polluted.'

The soldier gestured around. 'In case you haven't noticed, there's a shortage of taps around here. This is all there is. We've drunk it for the last three months.'

'Then none of you will live to see old age.'

His prediction proved to be correct. The cumulative effects of extreme hardship, inadequate diet and tropical disease have sent most of those SAS men to early graves.

D Squadron corporal, Telok Anson, Malaya, 1958

The Special Air Service formed by David Stirling in 1941 had been a highly mobile but conventional military force. The lineage of the modern SAS can be traced back more directly to wartime guerrilla forces such as the Chindits and Force 136.

In the long war in the jungles of Malaya the traditional SAS role was reversed. The 'terrorists' of the Second World War, using the weapons of assassination, ambush and explosion, became the counter-terrorists of the post-war period, the cutting edge of a post-imperial strategy designed to maintain Britain's role as a player on the world stage.

The insurgents in Malaya were veterans of the Malayan People's Anti-Japanese Army who had fought alongside the British Force 136 during the war. Although they were Communist, they had been supplied and armed by the British on the time-honoured principle that my enemy's enemy is my friend.

The friendship quickly turned sour. After the defeat of Japan, Britain granted the Malayan Communist Party recognition in reward for its wartime services – it had been banned before the war – and even awarded the OBE to one of its military leaders, Chin Peng, in the Victory Honours, but Britain showed predictably little interest in including the Communists in any discussions about Malaya's future status. A federation of the conservative, semi-feudal rulers of the Malayan sultanates, guided by British advisers, was Britain's preferred blueprint for the future.

Malayan stability was vital to Britain's own plans for economic recovery. Apart from the huge sterling balances Malaya had accumulated by the end of the war, it also had the ability to earn hard currency – dollars – through the export of rubber and tin. The British government had no intention of granting independence without first guaranteeing a pliable or sympathetic ruler.

Chin Peng, now newly installed as secretary-general of the Malayan Communist Party, was equally determined to prevent Malaya from reverting to colonial or neo-colonial status. He had seen India's long campaign of civil disobedience force Britain to grant independence on 14 August 1947 and watched Mao Tse-tung's People's Liberation Army sweeping towards power in China. Now the moment had come to overthrow colonial rule in Malaya.

A Communist-led campaign of strikes and civil unrest had been largely ineffectual but when it became clear that Britain had no intention of reaching any sort of accommodation, Chin Peng ordered his men back into the jungle. They took with them their British-supplied weapons and the substantial caches of arms and equipment they had liberated from the Japanese.

The 3,000 fighting men of the renamed Malay Races Liberation Army – all but a handful of them Chinese – set up bases in the familiar terrain of the jungle margins. They were supported by twice that number of clandestine supporters, the Min Yuen, who recruited new fighters and obtained supplies of food and arms for the combatants from the half-million Chinese squatters living in sprawling settlements near the fringes of the jungle. There was also a third grouping, the Lie Ton Ten, charged with carrying out attacks and assassinations in the towns and cities.

The insurrection began in April 1948 when the CTs – Communist Terrorists – launched their first strikes against rubber plantations, tin mines and police stations. At first the violence was directed against non-Communist Chinese and

Malays – foremen and overseers on the plantations – who were rounded up and shot in front of the other workers.

The first British victims died on 16 June, when three planters were murdered near Sungei Siput in Perak. The Malayan Emergency, as it was called, was declared two days later. Twelve years were to pass before it was finally rescinded.

The reason for describing it as an emergency rather than a war appears to have been purely financial: Lloyd's of London would meet insurance claims on the grounds of civil commotion, but not those arising from acts of war.[1]

Despite the previous civil disturbances, the insurrection had taken the British completely by surprise and the military response was very slow. When it did at length materialise, it was inadequate: six poorly equipped and badly trained Gurkha battalions, half of them just off the boat from India, were thrown into battle with very limited results.

Neither they nor the other British forces could operate effectively in the lowland swamps or the mountainous interior of Malaya. Outside the populated areas there were no roads at all and 90 per cent of the country was covered in primary jungle.

The tree canopy extended to a height of at least 200 feet above the ground. Below it the undergrowth rose no more than ten feet, but the canopy of trees and the dense, low-growing vegetation blocked the sun and reduced visibility on the jungle floor to a maximum of five yards.

Even though they were mostly village- and town-dwellers, the jungle held few fears for the Chinese CTs, who had fought the Japanese from the jungle margins, but the native Malays were very suspicious of it. They would not enter it unless they had to and were very doubtful of coming out of it alive.

The British forces showed little more confidence during their early jungle operations. Under the overall charge of Colonel Nicol Grey, the Commissioner of Police, they concentrated their efforts instead on protecting strategic areas – predominantly the tin mines and rubber plantations.

This effectively handed the initiative to the terrorists and in the following two years the insurgency grew in scope and scale, and enjoyed increasing support among the Chinese squatters. The CTs lost a claimed total of 1,000 men killed – though the body counts were of questionable accuracy – and a similar number captured in that period, but they inflicted heavy casualties too. Almost 1,000 civilians died, along with 300 police officers and 150 soldiers.

The British forces trying to contain the insurrection were part of a conscript army in which discipline was rigid in the extreme and the lower ranks were very badly treated. They had the wrong equipment for jungle warfare, the wrong weaponry, the wrong tactics and completely the wrong attitude.

British forces had been trounced in these jungles once before, within the memory of every soldier sent to fight there. A Japanese army half the size of the forces ranged against them had brushed them aside as they swept through the Malay peninsula to conquer Singapore in 1942. British incredulity at the humiliation being heaped on them was reflected when soldiers trying to make a last stand on the golf course were told that 'nothing could be done until the club committee had met'.[2]

The British soldiers in Malaya at the start of the emergency were no better prepared for jungle warfare than their peers had been in 1942. They were an army frightened of the environment in which they were working, mistrustful of the people with whom they were working, operating contrary to all common-sense methods of jungle soldiering, and reluctant to engage a seasoned enemy on his own ground and his own terms. They were also hampered by an unwieldy chain of command, with the colonial administration trying to referee turf wars between the army, police and Special Branch.

The British forces' idea of patrolling was to march or drive along a track at the edge of the jungle, practically inviting an ambush by the CTs, who could then melt back into the undergrowth. When attempts were made to pursue them, they were undermined by the army's poor navigation and even poorer maps, and by its lack of knowledge of even the rudiments of jungle warfare.

In conditions where the range of vision is never more than five yards, sight is much less use in the jungle than hearing and the sense of smell. Like any other creatures, men make noise when moving through the undergrowth and the smell of things like soap and toothpaste also carries a considerable distance. Yet the patrols that did venture into the jungle made enough noise to waken the dead and the regulations requiring every soldier to wash and shave every day were strictly enforced.

The British forces read such maps as they had in straight lines and needed to carry a lot of rations to survive for any length of time. Throughout the emergency conventional forces were restricted to operations of a maximum of fourteen days' duration, and even that limited span was only possible when their sole aim was to lie up in ambush.

The CTs had no such logistics problems. They were entirely at home in the jungle environment and travelled light, relying for their supplies on the local population, who often had every sympathy with their aims. Those who did not were intimidated, terrorised or killed.

It was obvious that the necessary first step towards defeating the terrorists lay in cutting them off from their sources of supply. The man charged with achieving that task was Brigadier 'Mad' Mike Calvert, whose arrival in Malaya heralded a long-overdue shake-up for the stagnant counter-insurgency campaign.

Calvert had commanded the SAS brigade in north-west Europe in 1945, but more significantly for the conflict in Malaya he had previously served for three years in Burma, operating for much of the time behind enemy lines with Colonel Orde Wingate's Chindits.

Like Force 136 in Malaya, the Chindits were special forces

trained in sabotage and guerrilla warfare, but, unlike the SAS, they operated in large groups. They were sent back into Burma after the British withdrawal in May 1942 and fought alongside the Karen hill tribes, who were offering the last armed resistance to the Japanese.

Calvert and his men learned from the Karen how to live and fight in the jungle. When resupply air-drops did not materialise, they survived for weeks on what the jungle could provide. They operated over the most severe terrain, and even when forced to abandon guerrilla warfare because of a shortage of arms, they remained behind Japanese lines gathering intelligence.

Calvert was sent into Malaya by General Sir John Harding, the Commander-in-Chief, Far East, with *carte blanche* to reshape the counter-insurgency strategy. He had great pull in elite circles and enjoyed Harding's confidence; as a result, when he asked for something, he usually got it.

Calvert spent six months in Malaya alongside police and army units and also made several solo reconnaissances into the jungle before producing two key proposals. The first was the separation of the terrorists from their sources of supply by the crude but effective means of moving the inhabitants of the kampongs into a number of fortified villages protected and policed by the army. It was a huge undertaking, requiring the resettlement of half a million people inside two years.

It was named the Briggs Plan in deference to Lieutenant-General Harold Briggs, the Director of Operations in Malaya, but the plan was largely Calvert's. It cut off the CTs from their primary sources of food but it was only a first step. They could still retreat deeper into the jungle and either grow their own food or force the scattered aboriginal tribes to supply them.

The only way to defeat them was to pursue them deep into the jungle and flush them out into areas where the army could bring their heavier firepower to bear.

An earlier attempt to follow the terrorists into their jungle hideouts had been made by a cobbled-together group called Ferret Force, composed of a mixture of regular soldiers and civilian veterans of the wartime Force 136. It was not a success and was quickly disbanded amidst rumours of very hard-line tactics and atrocities against the local population.

It was clear that no conventional British forces could take the fight to the CTs in the jungle but Mike Calvert's second proposal was the formation of a specialist force that was very far from conventional.

He had been forced to preside over the disbandment of the SAS at the end of the war and now seized the chance to recreate it, though he was careful to claim that it was a purely temporary expedient which could be wound up as soon as the conflict was over. Despite its name, the shape and tactics of the new force owed more to his service with the Chindits in Burma than it did to David Stirling's SAS.

Mike Calvert set up a base at Kota Tinggi near Johore and around 100 volunteers for the new force, the Malay Scouts (SAS), came there from regiments throughout the Far East theatre. A handful of them were veterans of the original SAS, the SOE, Force 136 and the short-lived Ferret Force. Many more were regular soldiers or men on national service joining to escape the 'bull' and the boring grind of normal soldiering. Many others came straight from military prisons.

Calvert was unworried by their origins, feeling that men who chafed under the rules and restrictions of a conventional regiment would be well suited to the unconventional force he was assembling. The new force attracted its share of boozers and brawlers, however, and its perceived indiscipline shocked many more traditional army officers.

Calvert's aim was to establish an elite, but there was little initial difference in the training methods, organisation or equipment from any other British regiment. There was not even a permanent cadre of men; all of them were seconded from other units.

What was different was their toughness. The type of person

who would now become a mercenary was then a natural recruit. These were vastly experienced and battle-hardened regular soldiers or national servicemen, mostly veterans of the Second World War and/or the Korean War, which broke out in June 1950.

They could already fight longer, stronger, harder and faster, but they now had to develop the ability to live in the jungle for months on end. It was a long, debilitating process. Some were defeated – more often by the jungle than the enemy – but the others learned how to exist there, constantly adapting, improvising and refining their survival techniques and jungle-fighting skills. Their contribution, both overt and covert, was to prove decisive in tilting the battle for Malaya Britain's way.

Initially there were just two squadrons – A Squadron and a purely administrative HQ Squadron – but they were soon joined by another group. The Territorial unit, 21 SAS, had been mobilised and despatched to fight in Korea, aiming to operate behind enemy lines using Jeeps, much as Stirling's original SAS had fought in the Western Desert during the Second World War.

They were already *en route* to Korea when the American Long Range Patrols and other US special forces operating in the same way were wiped out by the Koreans.

The deployment of the 21 SAS troops was hastily abandoned and they were then given the choice of returning to the UK or joining the Malay Scouts. Some of them went straight back home, the others diverted to Malaya. They formed B Squadron, but were immediately dubbed the Chelsea Chindits by the A Squadron cadre that was training them, a name that has stuck ever since.

Calvert then travelled to Africa to recruit an all-Rhodesian squadron on the straightforward but not necessarily accurate assumption that, as there was jungle in parts of that country too, Rhodesians would make good jungle soldiers.

Calvert now had a group of people that in army terms did

not exist. To get rations, equipment, weapons and ammunition you need to be a recognised regular army unit. Seizing the opportunity, he changed the name of the Malay Scouts and they were officially designated the Special Air Service.

While A Squadron was carrying out combat operations in the jungles of Perak, the new arrivals were taken to the base in the jungle near Johore to be trained by a small detachment of the HQ Squadron.

Calvert planned the training, based largely on his experience in Burma, and laid great emphasis on training with live ammunition, even using live grenades. His recruits could only escape the shrapnel by diving into the monsoon drains on the base. They also practised stalking each other through the jungle with air rifles, wearing fencing masks to protect their faces, a technique that is still used to train SAS recruits today.

The training was necessarily perfunctory, however, and the men of B Squadron proved to be an absolute shambles. They had come mentally and physically prepared to operate in a conventional war. Instead they found themselves required to fight in a totally unconventional jungle war, after the briefest and most rudimentary training from people who in many cases had little better idea than they of what was required.

Calvert had his unconventional force. The only thing now lacking was any unconventional skills. Selection for the SAS at that time owed more to Charles Darwin's theory of evolution than to any intensive training. They went into the jungle and those still alive when they came out again were in the Regiment.

Their range of skills was inadequate, the people involved were often unsuited to the type of operations they were trying to do and after sampling jungle operations many of them did not want to be there at all. Only a very small hard core of individuals were determined to make the SAS succeed.

The first two skills recruits had to acquire were signalling and navigation. Almost fifty years later, they remain the foundations on which all other SAS techniques are constructed.

The ability to signal was vital. In the early days communications were usually at squadron level and the smaller groups roaming the jungle had no contact with the rest of the army at all. The squadrons used voice radio, which was very erratic and unreliable in the atmospheric conditions in the jungle. The sets were also dauntingly heavy. The ones used early in the Malayan campaign weighed thirty pounds and also needed a dozen nine-pound batteries.

The Australian army was asked to provide Morse signallers who operated alongside the SAS men for a number of years until they had developed their own skills. As radios became more sophisticated, they were even sometimes issued at patrol level.

The ability to read and send Morse was not the only skill a signaller might need. Local conditions – mountains, trees, atmospherics, monsoon storms – sometimes made the signal so faint that a signaller might have to use a bow and arrow to fire an aerial wire up into the tree canopy.

Conventional straight-line army navigation was useless in dense jungle. There were no stars to be seen, no distant points on which to take a compass bearing. The only maps were taken from aerial photographs and were virtually worthless: they showed only the forest canopy.

The course of rivers changed or became almost invisible as they meandered through the swamps. In the wet season the rivers flooded huge areas; in the dry season some dried up completely and disappeared beneath the tangled vegetation. The obstacles to navigation were enormous and if you got lost and panicked, you died.

SAS men had to develop the capability to navigate by following the contours of the ground. They also had to do so without cutting their way through any vegetation. Using the few man-made tracks through the jungle was an open invitation to an ambush, but leaving any kind of 'sign' – a stem cut with a bush-knife, a footprint or even a bruised or broken leaf – might be enough to alert the enemy and turn the pursuers into the pursued.

To travel through the jungle without leaving obvious signs, patrols had to learn to use the animal tracks that snaked along the ridge lines or the river lines. Most of the tracks were covered with leeches waving like grass stalks in a breeze as they awaited their next passing meal-ticket.

Newcomers tried to work their way around them, but hard-bitten SAS men just walked straight on, knowing that no matter how hard you tried to avoid them there would still be leeches clinging to your body at the end of each patrol.

They crawled up your legs or dropped off the vegetation and worked their way through your clothing to the softest areas of the body: ankles, wrists, neck, ears, armpits, even the genitals. Something in their saliva numbed the skin as they bit you. You remained unaware of them until the patrol halted, when you found black, bloated leeches all over you. An SAS sergeant recalled one trooper who found eleven leeches, 'like a bunch of grapes', attached to his penis at the end of one patrol.[3]

Progress was painfully slow, constantly clambering over fallen trees, slipping and sliding down steep muddy slopes, fording swollen streams and rivers, wading through murky swamps or battling through tangled undergrowth. Worst of all was the thorn called nante sikkit – wait a minute – in Malay, which spread fronds for up to twenty feet in every direction. They were almost invisible among the other vegetation, as strong as steel wire and covered in vicious barbed thorns.

In the densest swamps and jungle a patrol might cover as little as 500 yards in a day, painstakingly holding the vegetation aside and then moving it back into place behind them.

A few Iban tribesmen had been recruited from Borneo to work alongside the still-born Ferret Force. They were head-hunters with filed teeth, heavily tattooed bodies and distinctive high-pitched voices; they were also magnificent jungle trackers.

More Iban tribesmen were now brought in and SAS men learned the skills of tracking from working alongside them. They learned to detect the faintest sign left by the enemy: broken bark, bruised vegetation, muddied water, urine traces on a bush, and even a footprint invisible to a casual glance but impressed through fallen leaves into the wet earth leaving a copy as clear as a carbon from a typewriter.

Even the absence of something could be enough. If a tracker was not feeling cobwebs on his face every few yards he knew that someone else had recently passed that way.

The Iban also learned from the SAS men, who trained them in the skills of soldiering to the point where they became a recognised British army unit, the Sarawak Rangers.

There was almost no other outside influence on the SAS jungle-warfare training. All their other skills were self-taught. If someone had a useful skill that the Regiment needed, then they taught the other people in the unit.

The key to the campaign was to deny areas of the jungle to the terrorists. This could only be done in two ways. One was to have your own troops there; if you're there, the enemy can't be. The other was to set explosive ambushes. Large areas of the jungle could then be left to police themselves. If someone triggered an ambush, the explosives would destroy them.

The terrorists used a similar tactic against the SAS, setting animal traps like pits lined with sharpened stakes, and pungees – heavy bamboo frames covered in spikes which swung down to impale any soldier unwary enough to trip the wire.

Sometimes patrols were lucky and walked straight through enemy ambushes without them being initiated. Unused to seeing British forces patrolling in twos and fours the CTs held their fire, assuming that the patrol was a recce group for a larger force.

On other occasions they were less lucky. When the traps were sprung quite a number of troopers were injured. The evacuation of casualties or people with illnesses took away scarce resources from the fight and was only undertaken in extreme circumstances. If the casualty could be treated in the jungle instead, he could return to the battle much quicker.

If anyone had a serious injury and needed to be casevaced, the only support aircraft available were the old Sycamore helicopters, which were highly dangerous and could not lift heavy weights. Working at altitude in the mountains, their safe working load was one fully equipped soldier.

Despite their drawbacks, they were flown very courageously by Royal Air Force pilots. SAS men found it significant that the helicopter pilots at the time were non-commissioned officers. It was believed, not entirely without justification, that commissioned officers would have been much less likely to risk valuable air assets to extract wounded soldiers.

Less serious wounds, injuries and diseases were treated by the patrol medics, who were all self-taught. Much of the impetus to acquire basic medical knowledge came from an incident early in the campaign when a soldier taking an early-morning crap was shot by a CT. The rest of the troop just heard a single shot and a high-pitched laugh from the CT as he ran away.

They discovered the reason for his laughter when they went to find the trooper. In jungle camp the latrine was a very basic affair, a deep pit with two logs laid across it and a 'straining bar' in front of it. The trooper had been shot in the arse and had then fallen into the shit-pit.

The CT undoubtedly caused the patrol more psychological and logistical problems by wounding the trooper than killing him. The other members of the patrol shared the CT's amusement until they realised that they were going to have to carry their mate several miles through the jungle to the roadhead.

That dangerous and back-breaking journey forged a determination to acquire the medical skills that would let them treat simple wounds and injuries *in situ*. The fount of all medical knowledge was 'Doc' who, despite his nickname, was not a trained doctor but had merely been an observant soldier in the Royal Army Medical Corps. He had some knowledge of medicine and taught anyone who was interested the rudiments of first-aid.

The large number of eager pupils may have been linked to an unexpected side-benefit of developing medical skills – the ability to use hypodermic needles to gain illicit access to the rum ration. It was in heavy stone jars and was only issued in extreme circumstances, for medicinal purposes. A long needle and a hypodermic syringe allowed access to the rum without leaving any sign on the cork. When the rum was to be officially issued, the medic replaced the missing spirit with water.

Malaria was held at bay by Paludrine tablets – catching malaria was an RTU offence – but other diseases contracted in the jungle were usually allowed to run their course. The unfortunate consequence was that if a soldier could not shake off the disease, it was already in a very advanced state when he was finally brought out of the jungle for treatment.

Many of the diseases caught by the troops deep in the jungle were new to medical science. Unsure of what they were dealing with, the army doctors came up with a novel solution to prevent the spread of these strange tropical diseases by isolating the sick men in the VD wards of various military hospitals.

For most of the men they were familiar surroundings. Such was the reputation of the Regiment at the time that whenever a man wearing SAS uniform approached a military hospital he was invariably sent to the VD ward without even being asked why he was there.

Apart from basic medical skills, the other essential, self-developed skill of SAS men was the ability to speak the local languages. Almost everybody who had spent some time in Malaya could speak at least a halting form of Malay, but several members of the Regiment also taught themselves the jungle dialects of the aboriginal Sakai tribe. Learning the language was not enough on its own, however. There also had to be a respect for the indigenous population and its culture.

The brutal treatment of the Chinese population by some regular army troops earlier in the conflict had scarcely helped the British cause. The SAS was determined that its own treatment of the different ethnic groups would help to win them over rather than alienate them.

The classic form of the SAS patrol was to evolve from these small, almost haphazard beginnings. Each patrol had a commander, a medic and a signaller, with a fourth man who often had a separate specialist skill but who was included mainly because it is better to operate in the jungle as a pair rather than as a single. Every member of the patrol would have at least a working knowledge of the local languages and one would be a skilled linguist.

The new Special Air Service made very tentative initial inroads into the jungle proper, but as the men grew more experienced and more confident of operating in the terrain, they were able to stay in the jungle longer and longer without relief or resupply.

Water is never a problem in the jungle; food always is. Dig a hole at almost any low-lying point and it will fill with water, but although the soil is fertile and there are fish in the streams, animals like wild pigs and deer, and wild fruit trees like the rambutam, actually to grow or find food in the jungle is a full-time job, as the terrorists were to find to their cost.

The key to the SAS being able to sustain long operations was their ability to carry sufficient rations. That meant the tinned food supplied to the rest of the army, for dehydrated rations were not introduced until the 1960s. A pile of tins on top of all the weapons, ammunition and other kit each trooper had to carry was a back-breaking load. Yet it was still a pitifully inadequate, starvation diet on operations that were progressively extended to three months.

A patrol entered the jungle carrying one month's rations and was resupplied each month with a single day's fresh rations and a further four weeks' supply of tinned food. After a resupply by air-drop the patrol would always move base camp because of the risk of compromise. Anything that could not be carried was either burned or buried.

Operations often exceeded the notional three months. The first patrol by D Squadron in October 1953, near the Sungei Brok River, lasted four months. Two men were killed in contacts with the CTs and by the time the squadron was relieved, half the members of the original patrol had already been lifted out because of exhaustion exacerbated by malnutrition and tropical diseases.

The Regiment operated in the jungle by going in at squadron strength, which could be up to forty people. They would set up a base – a jungle fort – to house the signaller and the squadron commander, who would maintain communication with headquarters.

From that base the four troops, varying in strength from six men to about a dozen, deployed to satellite bases, and from there in turn they would patrol their area of swamp or jungle. Sometimes they patrolled as a full troop, but in most cases they operated in smaller groupings, even down to individuals, for some of the more experienced and unconventional members of the Regiment preferred to patrol alone.

It is impossible to move through the jungle without leaving a track of some description. Once a patrol had found a track they set up ambushes or followed it, maintaining unrelenting pressure on the terrorists until they were either killed, left the area or surrendered.

In a few instances the roles were reversed. An SAS patrol finding itself heavily outnumbered often had to rely on quick wits and nerve as much as its military skill to get away. The sheer volume of fire that SAS men could generate was a valuable deterrent, tending to convince the enemy that they were facing a large force, not a handful of men.

On one occasion a small patrol encountered a very large enemy group. The patrol leader, a phlegmatic character known as Lofty 'The Gloom' Ross, immediately began shouting, 'Move up on the left, move up on the right,' as if he were also heading a large force.

While he was shouting, his patrol was backing off. The CTs deployed to confront them, but by then the patrol was safely out of range with only a few shots fired.

The rigorous routine developed of a three-month op in the jungle, followed by fourteen days' rest, recuperation and retraining, and then a return to the jungle for a further three months. This cycle continued for three years. At the end of it the SAS men were given something laughingly called inter-tour leave and allowed back to the UK for a one-month break, before coming back to start the whole grind once again.

They were living on the edge, and the need to release the tension generated by such long, strenuous and dangerous operations led to many alleged breaches of discipline when they came out of the jungle. Some were genuine, others were merely perceived as indiscipline by officers more accustomed to drill and regimental dinners than the dirty realities of jungle war. The SAS tradition of thinly veiled contempt for officers and others, including the administrative staff, who were not up to the job began in Malaya.

There was no shortage of friction, not only with the officers, but also between the squadrons and the army, among the squadrons themselves and between individuals within the same squadron. There were those who wanted to get the job done and others who just wanted a quiet life.

It was not surprising that the most frequent conflicts arose between the Chelsea Chindits and the maverick members of A Squadron, who were openly disparaging of the backgrounds, aptitudes and attitudes of the reservists. Although their lack of expertise in jungle warfare was not all their fault, most of the criticisms were well founded.

The gulf in understanding between them was illustrated by the comments of B Squadron's squadron sergeant-major, Bob Bennett: 'We had pretty good discipline in our squadron and it made things difficult all round when I was making my guys shave and do all the normal things soldiers do in camp while A Squadron seemed to just do as they pleased.'[4]

Shaving, of course, was one of the 'normal things soldiers do in camp' that was an instant giveaway in the jungle. Over the course of a few months the majority of the 21 SAS reservists returned to the UK. They were replaced by more rough and ready soldiers, better suited to jungle warfare.

The success of the army in protecting the mines and plantations, and of the Regiment in denying the terrorists the ground on the jungle edge, had gradually driven them deeper into the jungle. As the terrorists retreated, the SAS patrols followed them into their last refuges, the coastal swamps and the dense jungle of the mountainous spine of the country.

The only true jungle-dwellers in Malaya were the small and very scattered aboriginal tribes, who grew some crops but were mainly hunter-gatherers. In desperation, the terrorists linked up with them. Sometimes willingly, more often under threat, the aboriginals supplied the CTs with food.

SAS patrols were also making contact with the aboriginals, however, forcing the terrorists to move again. It became a constant pattern. One captured female CT admitted that her group had been forced to move eighteen times in the three months before her capture, during which time two of her companions had been killed in contacts with SAS patrols.

One of the most distasteful and hated parts of the SAS men's work was to carry the bodies of dead CTs out of the jungle so that they could be identified by the Special Branch. It was much easier all round if an Iban with the patrol was simply allowed to follow his tribal traditions and cut off the head instead.

Captured CTs were interrogated but otherwise well treated and many were persuaded to 'turn'. The gentle approach paid dividends and was in stark contrast to the policy followed by the CTs. In the dozen years that the emergency lasted, no captured British soldier or civilian was ever released alive.

SAS men speaking the language of the aboriginal Sakai tribes worked among them, using their newly acquired medical skills to treat their injuries and diseases, and primitive dentistry to remove rotting teeth. Cultural differences and the taboos surrounding childbirth meant that the midwifery skills they had acquired were rarely called upon.

The SAS troopers also helped the Sakai with simple construction projects while offering them military protection from the CTs. In return, they received priceless intelligence on the enemy and also recruited and trained indigenous forces from the tribes.

Malaya was the testing ground for the Regiment's signature 'hearts and minds' strategy, but it was in a very rudimentary form. Although the term was first coined by General Templer, the policy on the ground did not arise out of some complex and far-sighted plan from headquarters. It evolved slowly and gradually out of the basic good nature of the soldiers involved.

When the SAS policy of giving medical treatment and other forms of help to indigenous populations was proved to pay military dividends, it became an official policy and the wisdom of hindsight allowed people to claim that it had been planned from the start.

Hearts and minds could never have been fully effective in Malaya, however, due to the restrictions placed on the Regiment by the army command. SAS men were forbidden to enter the squatter villages on the margins of the jungle, where most of the Chinese population lived, existing on slash-and-burn agriculture.

When a patrol discovered a new settlement they had to bring in the Special Branch and the local police, who screened the inhabitants for terrorist suspects and then used whatever persuasion was necessary to move the rest to fortified villages.

There were no restrictions on SAS contact with the Sakai tribes deep in the jungle, and hearts and minds work with them proved its value. It may have been a means to an end, but over time genuine friendships developed between the SAS patrols and the tribes. The initial contacts were always tense, however, sometimes with good reason.

One SAS trooper made contact with an aboriginal tribe, unaware that the CTs had already convinced the tribespeople that the jungle forts and fortified villages were concentration camps, where they would be tortured and killed. The terrified tribesmen stoned the trooper to death.

Despite such setbacks, the new force had already proved its worth when its founder was invalided out of Malaya at the end of 1951, suffering from malaria and dysentery. Mike Calvert's methods had attracted as much criticism as praise and much was made of the indiscipline of those early SAS men, but as Colonel John Woodhouse remarked in a letter to the SAS Regimental Association in 1981, 'Calvert's comparison was that a building site can be a rough and mucky place until construction is finished.'[5]

In a rapidly deteriorating military situation, his job was to construct a force from scratch, in minimal time, to turn the conflict around. In that he was successful. Three squadrons – A, B and C – were operating in Malaya by the time he returned home, part of a 35,000-strong force of British troops confronting an estimated 8,000 guerrillas.

The army establishment made an attempt to rein in this unconventional unit by appointing a thoroughly conventional career officer, 'Tod' Sloane, as the new SAS commanding officer. He took the opportunity to withdraw the Regiment from jungle operations for a period of retraining, during which he removed what he saw as some of the wilder elements of the SAS.

That he did not remove them all was demonstrated a couple of years later when Lieutenant-Colonel Oliver Brooke's first action on assuming command was to RTU a senior NCO and sixteen troopers of B Squadron.

They had greeted his arrival – although it was more in celebration of Sloane's impending departure – by 'fragging' the Officers' Mess, blowing down one of the walls and sending a table full of drinks into temporary orbit. The incident said as much about the officer as it did about the perpetrators, but even Mike Calvert might have had trouble ignoring that infraction of the rules.

The Regiment's training and discipline were enhanced in early 1952 when John Woodhouse returned to England and set up SAS Selection. It took a particular type of arrogance to impose daunting minimum standards on newcomers to the Regiment when the serving members had not done Selection at all.

The endurance training was carried out in the Brecon Beacons, but the Selection course itself was administered from the Parachute Regiment's depot in Aldershot. That choice of location proved unfortunate: the Parachute Regiment made numerous attempts to absorb the SAS over the succeeding years.

In every other respect John Woodhouse produced the goods. His fearsome commitment to the highest standards of professionalism was demonstrated by the punishment he devised for a trooper who accidentally fired his rifle. To teach him the proper respect for weapons, Woodhouse removed the safety pin from a grenade and forced the man to carry it around with him for a week. His methods were extreme but they were ideally suited to producing the men that the SAS needed in Malaya.

Despite their reverses, the CTs were far from a broken force and claimed a notable scalp around the time of Calvert's departure. On 7 October 1951 they ambushed and assassinated the British High Commissioner, Sir Henry Gurney.

The new High Commissioner, General Templer, arrived in March 1952 with 'absolute ... civil and military power' conferred on him by Winston Churchill. He carried a carrot as well as a big stick, however, the offer of ultimate independence for Malaya – once the insurgency had been defeated.

As he admitted in a speech later that year, 'The shooting side of the business is only 25 per cent of the trouble; the other 75 per cent depends on getting the bulk of the people behind us.'[6]

To that end he pushed through measures to broaden the franchise to the ethnic Chinese, who had previously been denied the vote, installed Malay chief executives in every state and speeded up the formation of a Malayan army. Although the officers were initially seconded from British regiments, Malays were commissioned and fast-tracked towards command at company and battalion level.

Templer also further strengthened the counter-insurgency campaign, introducing financial rewards for defecting CTs and overseeing the expansion of the Special Branch to improve the flow of intelligence on the terrorists.

As they were steadily driven back and the campaign penetrated further into the deepest and most inaccessible parts of the jungle, the Regiment cast around for a way to remove the need for long marches into the heart of the jungle before an operation could begin.

Helicopter insertions were problematic. Even supposing a suitable landing zone could be found, the noise of the helicopter would alert the enemy to the operation before it had even begun. Instead, members of the Regiment were trained by the RAF to parachute into the jungle.

The only problem was that the RAF concept of parachuting required flat fields and short grass as a landing area. To jump into trees was not considered suitable. In its wisdom the army then used bombs and artillery to blast dropping zones, believing that the CTs would not be alerted since 'harassing fire' was already being rained down on unpatrolled areas of the jungle.

The SAS vigorously opposed the policy. They feared that the indiscriminate bombing of the jungle would create casualties among the Sakai tribesmen and make the job of hearts and minds all the more difficult. Their other objection was even more practical: it created extremely dangerous jumping conditions. Split trunks and branches like spikes lay in wait to impale the parachutists as effectively as any terrorist booby-trap.

The SAS objections were overruled and, as a result, when they were required to jump into these areas they deliberately steered into the tree canopy, preferring to take their chances there rather than land in the bombed area. Once this idea had taken hold, tree-jumping became a concept in itself. Experimental jumps were made, first into rubber plantations and then into primary jungle.

At first troopers carried lengths of knotted rope to lower themselves to the ground. This was later replaced with abseiling gear but it was far from foolproof and the tree-jumping technique remained highly dangerous.

In retrospect it was unfortunate that the first operation to make use of the technique, Operation Helsby in the Belum Valley in February 1952, was also virtually the only one to do so unscathed. Most of the subsequent tree-jumps resulted in injuries and sometimes deaths, as men broke their arms, legs and even backs after plummeting through the canopy to the jungle floor.

If the injury was sufficiently serious, a helicopter had to be called in to evacuate the casualty, compromising the whole operation. The casualty rate from tree-jumping was so high that practice jumps were outlawed and eventually the technique was abandoned, its demise hastened by débâcles such as Operation Sword in Kedah in January 1954, when three SAS men fell to their deaths.

Such large-scale operations were also not the best use of the SAS, whose specialist skills made them infinitely more suited to strategic tasks of hearts and minds, intelligence-gathering and deep penetration than tactical operations best left to infantry units.

The insurgents were in full retreat by the end of 1955, by which time a total of five SAS squadrons were operating in Malaya. D Squadron had been formed from volunteers serving with other units in the Far East and new squadrons from New Zealand and the Parachute Regiment were also brought in.

The New Zealanders arrived as replacements for the Rhodesians of C Squadron who, though brave and committed, were a questionable asset because of three basic flaws. Whereas the New Zealanders had been given intensive jungle training, the Rhodesians had been pitched into combat operations after the most minimal preparation.

They also proved unusually vulnerable to tropical diseases, which further reduced their efficiency, and the racial attitudes considered perfectly normal in white-ruled Rhodesia were a considerable handicap in hearts and minds work with aboriginal tribes. The once all-Rhodesian C Squadron was progressively diluted with Australians, New Zealanders and paras and eventually the last Rhodesians went home.

The increased manpower allowed a constant presence of troops in the heart of the swamps and jungle where the dwindling bands of terrorists were still active. Even with five squadrons operating, the number of terrorists killed or captured by SAS patrols remained modest, but the cumulative effects of the incessant pressure on the CTs had results far in excess of the bald figures. Many CTs were forced out of the jungle where they became vulnerable to the police and conventional forces, and many others abandoned the guerrilla struggle altogether. Some even left the country, fleeing across the border into safe havens in southern Thailand.

The number of 'White Areas' declared free of CT influence steadily increased and the monthly total of casualties from terrorist actions dropped into single figures. There were still stubborn pockets of resistance in the most inaccessible areas of swamp and jungle, and SAS troops remained committed on mopping-up operations until 1958.

Almost the last act in the Malayan Emergency was Operation Sweep, a joint operation by D and B Squadrons to eliminate a group of CTs led by Ah Hoi, an infamous terrorist hiding in the coastal swamp of Telok Anson.

Three troops of D Squadron parachuted into the jungle in February 1958 but one trooper's parachute became entangled in the tree canopy. As he tried to free himself, the branch gave way and he fell 200 feet to the ground, breaking his back.

An RAF pilot flew a daring mission to rescue him, bringing his helicopter in through a hole in the canopy so narrow that the branches were within inches of his rotors, and then holding the helicopter stationary just above the surface of the swamp as the injured man was put on board.

The noise of the helicopter had almost certainly alerted the terrorists, but the operation was allowed to continue. Three separate troops began patrolling through the swamps on either side of the Sungei Tinggi River. They found recently abandoned camps, elaborate constructions with armouries for making and repairing weapons, lecture rooms, cookhouses and dormitories, all built on stilts to raise them above the surrounding swamps.

There was plenty of other evidence of CTs, but there was no contact with the terrorists themselves until the tenth night. They were now reduced to living on the turtles and fish they could catch from the river and an SAS troop led by sergeant Sandy Sandilands – also known as 'the Bosun' because of his naval origins – was sent to patrol the river by night in rubber dinghies, scenting the air for the smell of cooking fires.

They duly spotted a group of CTs on the riverbank and opened fire, but armed only with shotguns the range was too great and the CTs escaped, leaving much of their equipment behind.

With the need for secrecy removed by the contact, a helicopter resupply was organised. Sandy and an Irish corporal, now armed with a rifle and a Patchet submachine-gun, had a second contact with two CTs not long afterwards. Using a floating log as cover, they approached close enough to kill one, but the other, a woman, escaped. In her haste she left a clear trail through the jungle which the SAS troop tracked to a hurriedly abandoned camp.

The CTs were now pinned in a small area of the swamp. Conventional forces threw a cordon around it and helicopters began overflying the area by day, searching for signs of the terrorists, as the SAS patrols tightened the noose on them.

Soon afterwards the woman terrorist, Ah Niet, appeared in a paddy field at the edge of the swamp. She had been sent to negotiate a surrender of the whole group. Her attempts to set terms were rejected but a couple of nights later the SAS received a signal that she had re-emerged from the jungle. The group was now willing to surrender unconditionally. As the SAS troop moved along the track towards Sekinchan, five terrorists stepped out of the paddy field and gave themselves up. They included the leader, Ah Hoi, who was disguised as a woman.

Ah Niet then offered to lead the SAS men to where another three CTs were waiting to surrender. On the way she demonstrated that they still had something to learn of jungle craft. She crossed the canal at the jungle edge without making a sound and expressed her horror at the noise the SAS men made in following her.

One of the three terrorists who surrendered to them in turn led the way to the Sungei Tinggi group, who also gave themselves up. The SAS unearthed several arms caches. To their astonishment they found that the weapons containers dropped to Chin Peng's forces during the war had been buried in the swamp and filled with oil, preserving the arms inside in perfect working order. Chin Peng's post-war terror campaign had been planned well in advance.

With the clearance of the CTs from their last refuge, the long war in Malaya was as good as over. The country had been granted its independence the previous year, 1957, under a government headed by Tunku Abdul Rahman, whose attitude to British tin and rubber interests was entirely acceptable to Britain.

Although the treaty of independence committed British forces to Malaya's external defence for the foreseeable future and regular troops remained in the country on mopping-up operations until 1960, the SAS had virtually put themselves out of a job by 1958.

They had paid a heavy price. Twenty-nine SAS men lost their lives during the conflict and there was a continuing toll of casualties long after the fighting was over as the hardships and poor diet exacerbated the effects of tropical diseases, many unknown at the time. When they fell ill there was no proper medical care – no trained paramedics and often no medevac system. Some of them died in the jungle, many more have gone to their graves prematurely, and few of the dwindling band of survivors will live to see old age.

The Malayan campaign had several significant consequences for the long-term development of the Regiment. The operations in the jungle forged the high degree of autonomy that SAS men now regard as routine. Regardless of rank, men had to work on their own.

There were not enough officers – even of low ability – to go round and NCOs did not rule by rank, but by ability. It was not unusual to have sergeants in a troop being led by a trooper. Whatever their rank, if someone had the ability they would lead.

An army colonel who came in by chopper to visit one troop was given an early demonstration of the point. He greeted the leader with the words: 'Are you in charge? What rank are you?'

'I'm a trooper, sir.'

The colonel did a double-take. 'But troopers can't command troops.'

'Oh, I don't know, sir, it's dead easy, really. I do a day's work, send a signal to HQ, and then the next day I do it again.'

The colonel could be added to the growing list of senior officers suspicious of or downright hostile to the SAS. It was to be a continuing problem for the Regiment, with frequent internal and external purges of the perceived unruly elements.

The problem was not solved until over twenty years later, when the storming of the Iranian Embassy silenced the Regiment's persistent critics. Even then there was only a grudging acceptance of the SAS within the army, which was exemplified by the lack of co-operation from staff officers during the Gulf War.

The SAS was operating quite openly in Malaya, but the campaign also saw the first use of covert or 'black' operations, using the Regiment's day-to-day operations as cover.

Two SAS covert operations wreaked particular havoc with the enemy. When Malayan prostitutes patronised by British forces began asking for payment in ammunition which then found its way to the rebels, the Regiment produced a typically inventive response.

British soldiers were encouraged to visit the prostitutes, paying for their services with doctored grenades which exploded when the pin was pulled and ammunition which killed the firer rather than his target. Fake messages and wads of currency were also left in known enemy letter-drops and safe houses, falsely implicating rebel leaders in treachery to their cause. Both actions took a heavy toll of rebel lives.

A counter-insurgency operation in dense jungle rendered the sophisticated weaponry of a Western army largely irrelevant. The use of air-power and artillery was ineffective and often counter-productive, and even machine-guns and high-powered rifles were normally of little use in the close-range contacts that occurred in jungle warfare.

The weapons and tactics needed were completely alien to the British army's normal mode of operations. Soldiers in Malaya were normally armed with the Number 4 rifle, but SAS experience showed that one of the most effective weapons in the jungle was a sawn-off, pump-action shotgun, a weapon more normally associated with bank robbers than professional soldiers. It was only superseded by the introduction of the self-loading rifle and the Armalite, which had the added advantage of automatic fire.

The SAS men's abilities to move through the jungle undetected, track an enemy from the faintest sign and trap and kill him like a hunter catching his prey were all self-taught or adapted from the skills of aboriginal hunter-gatherers.

Among its many innovations in Malaya the SAS also pioneered the use of helicopters and inflatable craft, but perhaps its most significant achievement was a psychological one.

The SAS had overcome the traditional fear of the jungle felt by Western armies and heightened by the humiliations at the hands of the Japanese during the Second World War. Now the SAS had at least partly laid that ghost in the same 'impossible' terrain.

For the first time in history, a unit from a Western army had defeated an indigenous force on its own ground and its own terms. It was the beginning of the belief both within the Regiment and in the wider world beyond that the SAS was as good as anyone, anywhere.

They learned one other vital lesson in the jungles of Malaya. The realisation that insurgencies could not be defeated by purely military means but only with a parallel awareness of the political dimension came early to the SAS. As in other facets of their operations in Malaya, their initial approach to the problem often lacked the sophistication of later campaigns but it laid the groundwork for what was to follow in other conflicts elsewhere in the world.

The exuberance over the British success in Malaya had to be tempered with a dose of hard realism, however. The CTs had never enjoyed the support of the Malay population as a whole. Their power base had been virtually confined to the half-million ethnic Chinese.

A guerrilla army operating with mass support was an entirely different proposition, as the British were already discovering in Cyprus and Kenya, and the Americans were to learn to such bitter effect in Vietnam.

In the heyday of the empire insurrections in the colonies were, in Lord Salisbury's words: 'but the surf that marks the edge and the wave of advancing civilisation'.

With Britain's limited means and shrinking world role, they were becoming instead the marks left by a retreating tide of power and influence. The SAS was destined to play the leading role in holding back that tide but as the Regiment prepared to return home from Malaya its future seemed far from assured.

There was a widespread belief in the upper echelons of the forces that conditions in Malaya were unique and that combat experience there was not readily transferable to other parts of the world. The Regiment had anticipated that argument and done its best to counter it.

Training in a wide range of other disciplines including demolitions, counter-interrogation techniques and work with the Royal Marines' Special Boat Section had been introduced in preparation for involvement in conflicts in very different regions, but the War Department remained unconvinced that the SAS had a future.

Its thanks for the tremendous contribution that the Regiment had made to the defeat of the terrorists in Malaya was to recommend that it should suffer the same fate it had met at the end of the Second World War – disbandment. There appeared to be no alternative gainful employment in sight for a bunch of hard-bitten jungle fighters.

Even while the fighting was still continuing, two of the four British SAS squadrons were marked for disbandment as a result of the government Defence White Paper of 1957. As the surviving two squadrons – A and D – prepared to pull out of Malaya twelve months later, there seemed no reason why they should avoid the same fate.

The immediate cause of the Regiment's salvation was an uprising in the Jebel Akhdar, part of the almost unknown Middle Eastern territory of Oman, but the underlying reason for the SAS deployment could be found in another conflict two years before.

3

JEBEL AKHDAR
1958–59

A group of dirty, bedraggled soldiers stood shivering in the darkest light before dawn. They had climbed the Jebel Akhdar, the Green Mountain. It was the highest mountain in the Gulf and supposedly unscalable. The last forces to conquer it had been the Persians 1,900 years before.

Although described as a plateau, the arid, rocky mountain was split by fissures, cliff-faces and hillocks. Stubborn patches of desert scrub clung to the bare, dusty rock.

It was a stark contrast to Malaya, where water was plentiful and the jungle hid them from the enemy. On this arid, desolate plateau the sun baked them all day and the nights were so cold that the water froze in their bottles.

In the jungle they had been able to work autonomously. Here they were operating cheek-by-jowl with officers they did not know. The enemy were numerous and their attacks frequent, but the SAS were slowly but surely gaining the upper hand.

The sweat from the brutal climb they had made was now cold on their backs as they waited for dawn. They were not surprised to be where they were; they expected to achieve the impossible. Now it was just a matter of doggedness, of seeing who could bear the hardships the longest. They knew with absolute certainty that it would be the SAS.

As the sky began to lighten with the first faint signs of

dawn, they became aware of a sentry outlined against a cliff-face ahead of them. He was about 300 yards away, guarding the entrance to a large cave, and still unaware of their presence.

The soldiers were intrigued. They surmised that the sentry was protecting other enemy soldiers sleeping inside. Everyone was instantly alert despite their tiredness. The adrenalin was starting to run. They were not over-endowed with ammunition and debated in hushed voices how to deal with the problem.

Drawing on the full authority of his rank, the young lieutenant – who went on to become one of the Regiment's most famous officers – insisted that the way to deal with the sentry was for the lieutenant to remove one of his socks, fill it with sand and use it as a cosh.

The troop corporal gave him a cynical look. 'I'll show you the best cosh to use.'

He picked up the 3.5-inch rocket-launcher, his number two fed in a rocket, and the corporal unleashed it into the mouth of the cave, blowing the sentry down the cliff-face.

The corporal glanced at the officer. 'That's the cosh that saves us all a lot of problems and stops you getting cold feet.'

The patrol moved cautiously forward, inching towards the cave. They pressed themselves against the cliff-face on either side of the entrance and the corporal threw in a hand-grenade as added insurance. Then the troop rushed in. The cave was not littered with bodies. It was full of large wooden chests, slightly battered by the blasts from the rocket and the grenade. A trooper lifted the lid of one of them very gingerly, feeling for booby-traps. Satisfied, he threw it wide open.

There was a stunned silence. The chest, like all the others in the cave, was full of gleaming silver Maria Theresa dollars. The cave was a treasure-house. This was wealth beyond the dreams of avarice.

Throwing down their packs, the soldiers dumped everything not essential to sustain their lives and began scooping armfuls of the dollars into their packs. They were laughing and joking, their eyes shining with excitement. Everyone was rich. Everyone was going to leave the army and retire to the south of France.

Then reality dawned. They suddenly became aware of how vulnerable they were in the cave. They went back outside, into the strengthening daylight, and took up their defensive positions.

Throughout the day the old chess game of war continued. They were sniped at and mortared, they attacked and they retreated. At the end of that long day they regrouped and drew back into the rock fissures that would give them cover and shelter for the night.

They realised that in the course of the day the wealth that they had gathered that morning had been thrown away, bit by bit, as the sheer struggle to stay alive took precedence. The dreams of riches and retirement faded and reality took hold. They had to win the war to continue living at all.

D Squadron sergeant, Jebel Akhdar, Oman, 1959

Britain had been the dominant power in the Middle East for well over a century, a grip that had been further extended by the end of the Second World War. Britain held the UN mandate in Palestine and British forces were stationed in Iraq, Jordan, Libya and at the massive military base at Ismailia in Egypt, where 75,000 troops occupied an area covering 3,600 square miles.

Britain enjoyed a corresponding influence on the governments of those countries, to the point where intractable heads of state would occasionally be forced to toe the British line or be removed and replaced. A degree of control was exercised over Iran through ownership of the giant Anglo-Iranian Oil Company and Britain also dominated the string of semi-feudal sheikdoms, emirates and Trucial States – named after the nineteenth-century truce imposed by the British on the pirates infesting the coast – running the length of the Gulf from Kuwait to Oman.

A combination of diplomacy and behind-the-scenes manoeuvres had loosened the French hold on Syria and Lebanon and led to independence on terms that suited Britain much more than France. Only the rulers of Saudi Arabia were firmly beyond British reach, lubricated by a massive flow of covert payments from the United States. In addition to wartime bribes often chan-nelled through the Aramco oil company, the Saudi ruler Ibn Saud also received a $25 million US loan and a $10 million payment for the lease of the airfield at Dhahran.[1]

Despite its weakened financial position, Britain had no intention of releasing its hold on the Middle East, as a report by the chiefs of staff made abundantly clear:

> The importance of the Middle East as a centre of Com-monwealth communications remains, and will remain, beyond question ... The primary task of the army ... will be to ensure the security of our Middle East base. Despite the possible risk of invasion of the United Kingdom by air, we consider the provision of forces to meet our requirements in the Middle East must be given priority over the anti-invasion role in the United Kingdom.[2]

The true importance of the region was not as a centre of communications, however, but as a producer of oil. Before the war the output of crude oil from the region had been a modest 335,000 barrels a day, putting it a distant fourth in the ranks of world production. That had swelled tenfold by the time of Suez, making it the leading oil-producing region after the United States itself.[3]

The chief producers were Saudi Arabia, the Gulf States, Iraq and Iran, but most of the oil was exported through pipelines running to the Mediterranean ports, making the security of the other Middle Eastern states equally crucial.

The Attlee government in Britain insisted it would deal with Arab governments as equals and would offer economic assistance in return for new military treaties to supersede those imposed in the 1930s. Attlee also expressed a desire to work with moderate nationalist forces rather than the conservative sheiks and sultans who had been Britain's allies in the past.

Despite the fine words there was to be little evidence of any of those three planks of his policy during his remaining years in power and even less under the Conservative government that succeeded him, and events during that decade dealt British interests in the Middle East an apparently mortal blow.

In the face of almost universal Arab hostility, Britain was reduced to clinging on to its last shreds of power and influence as a rising tide of nationalism – and a touch of American intrigue – threatened to sweep it away.

The first cracks in the façade of British power appeared inside twelve months as the Palestine mandate was given up in April 1948, in a way that managed to alienate both the Arabs and the Israelis. The twin promises of the Balfour Declaration, made in 1917, of 'a national home for the Jewish people', though 'nothing shall be done which may prejudice the civil and religious rights of the existing non-Jewish community', had proved to be mutually exclusive. The British washed their hands of Palestine and left the two sides to fight it out.

Israel's humiliating defeat of the Arab forces – the majority armed by Britain and in many cases British-officered – in the war that followed fuelled the growth of Arab nationalism.

Seven hundred thousand Palestinians fled to Jordan and Gaza and their slums and refugee camps became a lasting symbol of what the Arab world saw as British treachery.

Many of Britain's allies and clients – despite Attlee's democratic protestations still the conservative, often feudal sheiks and pashas – were shouldered aside by new leaders determined to put the control of Arab destinies in Arab hands.

The first serious alarm bells rang in Syria. Following coup attempts by Husni Za'im and Sami Hinnawi in the spring and summer of 1949, Colonel Shishlaki seized power in December of that year. The nationalist Prime Minister Mussadiq of Persia – swiftly renamed Iran – came to office less controversially, winning the general election in April 1951, but his expropriation of the Anglo-Iranian Oil Company's refinery at Abadan the following month set him on a collision course with Britain.

The previous year the American oil company Aramco had reached a voluntary agreement with King Saud to share royalties from the Saudi Arabian oilfields on a fifty-fifty basis. A similar deal would probably have been enough to secure Mussadiq's agreement, but neither the British government nor the Anglo-Iranian board of directors was in any mood for compromise.

A British naval task-force was put on stand-by but open intervention was eventually rejected under heavy pressure from the Americans, who feared a resulting civil war in Iran would open the door to the Russians. Instead, British personnel were withdrawn from the refinery at Abadan in the hope that the Iranians would not have the expertise to run it, and meanwhile the SIS – the Secret Intelligence Services, also known as MI6 – began working on a plot to overthrow Mussadiq.

The CIA later took over the lead role in the plan and in August 1953 Mussadiq was toppled and the shah restored to the peacock throne in a coup orchestrated from London and Washington. Ironically, given its refusal to consider such an arrangement with Mussadiq, the price to Britain of American co-operation was half the shares in the new consortium set up to exploit Iran's oil.

Britain had survived one serious test in the Middle East – at some cost – but the writing was now on the wall. Additional troops had been hastily despatched to Jordan in July 1951 after King Abdullah was assassinated. The intervention helped to preserve the Hashemite monarchy but the young King Hussein was not immune to the pressures of Arab nationalism. As a demonstration of his independence from British influence, he later peremptorily sacked 'Glubb Pasha' – Lieutenant-General Sir John Glubb – the commander of the Arab Legion for eighteen years.

Britain's attempts to maintain its power in Egypt only served to hasten the end of King Farouk, who was forced to abdicate in a coup by a group of young army officers, the Revolutionary Command Council. Although nominally led by Colonel Neguib, an altogether more substantial political figure was the driving force behind the coup and later assumed power in his own right.

As a young lieutenant, Colonel Gamel Abdul Nasser had witnessed the humiliating treatment of the Egyptian monarch in 1942 when the British ambassador ordered tanks to surround the royal palace to force King Farouk to appoint a pro-British government.

Another, greater humiliation for the Egyptian army came at the hands of the Israelis in the war that followed Britain's abrupt abandonment of the UN mandate in Palestine. It had an even more powerful formative effect on Nasser.

In an attempt to placate the ensuing wave of anti-British feeling, the royalist Egyptian Prime Minister, Mustafa al-Nahas, repudiated the 1936 Anglo-Egyptian Treaty in October 1951, five years before it was due to expire.

Churchill's instructions to his Foreign Secretary, Anthony Eden, were scarcely conciliatory. 'Tell them if we have any more of their cheek, we will set the Jews on them and drive them into the gutter from which they never should have emerged' – a threat that was to be realised five years later.[4]

Prime Minister al-Nahas's action was not enough to save him or Farouk's throne in the 1952 coup that brought Nasser's group of officers to power. A campaign of violence was then launched against the British in the Canal Zone. The linchpin of Britain's defence policy for the region was now under threat.

At the time, Britain had a substantial naval commitment to the war in Korea and its ground forces were embroiled in containing the insurrection in Malaya, the Mau Mau rebellion in Kenya and the developing troubles with EOKA in Cyprus, where even a force of 30,000 British troops and the widespread recourse to detention without trial could not subdue the rebels.

The commitment undertaken in 1954 to station four army divisions and the Second Tactical Air Force in Germany except when 'an acute overseas emergency dictated otherwise' was another massive drain on resources. British forces were stationed in Libya and Jordan, but they could not be used to attack another Arab country.

Even with the post-war reduction in the defence budget put into reverse, Britain simply did not have the troops or the economic strength to meet all its military commitments in the Middle East.

The military bluff that had sustained the British Empire throughout the twentieth century was increasingly being called, and Britain was forced to back-pedal by the new Egyptian regime. The Anglo-Egyptian Treaty of 1954 formalised the withdrawal of British forces from the Canal Zone, though it left open the theoretical option of troops returning to the base at Ismailia in the event of war in the region.

The decision to make Cyprus Britain's new Middle Eastern base of operations smacked of desperation. It suffered from two major flaws. Cyprus was now subject to the same nationalist fervour that had driven the British from Egypt and the attempts to deal with it proved equally ham-fisted.

Even more significant was the lack of adequate deep-water facilities, which made it unusable by Britain's Mediterranean fleet. That defect became apparent during the Suez crisis when the invasion force had to be marshalled and despatched from Malta. When the crisis was over Britain's base for Middle East operations was moved again, first to Kenya and then to Aden.

The Suez crisis was five years in the making, but the catalyst was the decision by the World Bank – the United States bank by any other name – to withdraw the offer of a loan to finance the Aswan Dam as punishment for Egypt's purchase of military equipment from the Soviet Union.

Nasser had tied his own prestige firmly to the construction of the dam, which had a huge symbolic importance for the country and his regime. His response to the rebuff was to announce the nationalisation of the Suez Canal Company on 26 July 1956. It was a calculated snub to Britain and the US, but it was no more an illegal act than the British Labour government's nationalisation of coal, steel, railways and the Bank of England ten years before.

Eden's government began immediate preparations for military action, but while the US had been perfectly prepared to antagonise Nasser, there was no hard evidence that it was willing to assist – or even acquiesce in – British attempts to topple him.

A secret agreement reached in the summer of 1946 allowed American B-29 nuclear bombers to operate from the giant base at Suez in the event of a conflict with the Soviet Union, placing the oilfields of the Caucasus within America's nuclear reach.[5]

When Turkey joined NATO in 1951 it provided the US with a number of airfields much closer to the Soviet Union. The development of the hydrogen bomb also made the use of the huge Suez base a questionable asset. The strategic requirement was now for a number of small, dispersed airfields rather than a monolithic facility that could be obliterated by a single Soviet nuclear strike.

Churchill had made an unsuccessful appeal for US military help in policing the Canal Zone against a wave of attacks in 1952. Lacking Churchill's charisma and reputation, his successor, Anthony Eden, can hardly have been more optimistic about the response four years later, but he was now irrevocably committed to bringing down an Egyptian leader he publicly compared to Mussolini.

He was also driven to make some sort of stand against the anti-British feeling breaking out all over the region. Glubb Pasha had been sacked by King Hussein of Jordan in March 1956 and a few days later the Foreign Secretary, Selwyn Lloyd, was abused and pelted with missiles by a mob in Bahrain.

The patronising belief persisted in British government circles that the Arab mind respected only power. If so, Eden was prepared to show them power on the grand scale – the largest invasion force assembled since the Normandy landings.

A covert plan for a simultaneous coup in Syria – possibly with US backing – to depose the pro-Nasser regime there was forestalled when the Syrian co-conspirators were exposed and rounded up, but in alliance with France and in secret collusion with Israel, Eden went ahead with the plan to invade Egypt.

Israeli forces swept across the Egyptian border at four in the afternoon of 29 October, their progress greatly helped by Nasser's immediate withdrawal of half his forces to counter the Anglo-French threat. The Israelis also launched a brief airborne attack into Jordan, while British forces at Aqaba blocked any possibility of a Jordanian counter-attack.

The next day, after the predictable Egyptian rejection of an Anglo-French ceasefire call that handed the Sinai to Israel, British bombers destroyed the Egyptian air force on the ground. To preserve the fiction that there had been no Anglo-Israeli collusion, however, the invasion force did not set off from Malta until the call for a ceasefire had been rejected. During the six days it took to reach Egypt, world opinion united against the invasion.

Meanwhile the Egyptians blocked the Suez Canal by scuttling ships in the locks and cut the oil pipeline to Syria, the two things the invasion had been designed to prevent. Military resistance was minimal as the British and French forces swept south, but the political climate was far less favourable to the invaders. The timing of the invasion to coincide with the American presidential elections on 6 November can hardly have been accidental, but in the event the distractions of campaigning did not prevent President Eisenhower from taking steps to whip Britain back into line.

British and American client states had clashed in the Middle East the previous autumn when Britain supported the occupation of the Buraimi Oasis by a joint force from Muscat and the Trucial States in defiance of the competing claims of the American-backed King Saud of Saudi Arabia. The Saudi claim to it was flimsy at best, but the action by Oman and the Trucial States provoked almost as much anger in Washington as it did in Riyadh.

A message was passed through intermediaries, informing Eden that the Americans considered Britain to have committed 'an act of aggression'. Suez provided the opportunity for a brutal demonstration of the new world order imposed by Washington. In the face of universal condemnation from the United Nations and under the enormous financial pressure of an American-orchestrated run on the pound, which wiped 15 per cent off the value of Britain's gold and dollar reserves in the month of November alone, British resolve cracked.

Chancellor of the Exchequer Harold Macmillan had previously threatened to resign if force were not used. As the American financial pressure started to bite, he underwent an overnight conversion from hawk to dove and began pressing Eden to withdraw. Eden dithered, further infuriating the

French who were perfectly happy to ignore the international opposition and press on to Cairo to overthrow Nasser, but finally he caved in and agreed to a ceasefire. The withdrawal of British troops began on 3 December, just as petrol rationing was introduced into a now oil-starved Britain.

It was an epochal moment. As the Israeli general Moshe Dayan remarked, for the first time Britain had to bring a war to an end at a time and place that was not of its choosing.

Suez was an unmitigated, unrelieved disaster for Britain. The operation never had any stated political aims; there seemed only to be a woolly assumption that Nasser would simply fade away as soon as the invasion force landed, allowing a more pliable government to be installed. The closest to a coherent statement of policy came in an aside from a French official: '*Il faut coloniser le canal ou canaliser le colonel.*'[6]

The British – the unchallenged past masters of world diplomacy – found themselves diplomatically isolated, uniting every shade of opinion against them. Eden also managed the near-impossible trick of alienating his only two allies in the venture. The French never forgave his vacillation, followed by his cave-in to US pressure, while Britain made no attempt to strengthen ties with Israel, the one country to emerge from Suez with nothing but gains.

Egypt had lost territory and suffered another military defeat by Israel, but the Great Power intervention had swung Arab opinion solidly behind Nasser and forced even the most conservative Middle Eastern rulers to take account of nationalist sentiment.

Even Britain's public enemy number one, the Soviet Union, made gains from the conflict. It distracted world attention from the Soviet invasion of Hungary and it allowed the Soviet leadership to brag – albeit inaccurately – that it was the threat of Soviet missiles that had made Britain withdraw.

The Suez affair was the last British resort to gunboat diplomacy. The most unreconstructed right-wing politicians now realised that British troops could no longer be used to overthrow governments or suppress the drive to national independence and self-determination – except with prior American approval.

The Foreign Office had watched the unfolding Suez crisis with horror. Over a century of painstakingly acquired alliance and influence, maintained by the use of patient diplomacy despite Britain's shrinking power, had been unravelled by a half-baked military intervention which was over almost before it had begun.

As the Foreign Office cast around for ways to repair the damage caused by Suez, it came to realise that the small-scale, covert deployment of British special forces was still possible, particularly in regions such as southern Arabia and East and Central Africa, where superpower rivalries were less intense and world attention more easily distracted or ignored.

In the right circumstances, used in the right way, special forces could be used to rekindle old friendships and alliances in the Middle East and ensure a continuing British influence in the region.

There was another straw the Foreign Office could clutch. American actions before and during the crisis seemed to have been aimed at supplanting Britain as the dominant power in the region. The US had undoubtedly dealt a huge blow to British prestige and influence, but there was a massive obstacle to American ambitions in the Middle East.

No President of the United States could afford to ignore the power of the Jewish lobby at home. The resultant unequivocal support for Israel made the US a pariah in most of the Arab world, despite huge handouts; by 1960 the US had made payments totalling $2,700 million to Middle Eastern states.[7]

The Foreign Office did not have to wait long to test its new policy. A series of shocks continued to reverberate around the Arab world in the aftermath of Suez as nationalist leaders, inspired and often armed and financed by Nasser, fought to change the political landscape of the Middle East.

A brutal coup by a group of Iraqi army officers in July

1958 overthrew the pro-British regime. King Faisal and all his family were murdered and his Prime Minister Nuri es Said – a thirty-year ally of Great Britain – was hacked to pieces in the street. Under its new rulers Iraq withdrew from the Baghdad Pact and forced Britain to quit its air-bases at Shaiba and Habbaniyah.

When nationalist unrest threatened Jordan too in August of the same year, Britain airlifted troops to Amman in support of the king, who, despite his earlier protestations, was only too grateful for British help. Crucially, this time Britain acted with the support of the United States and American troops were despatched to Lebanon at the same time to counter 'indirect aggression' from Egypt and Syria.

The claim rang hollow in the Third World, and the American and British actions aroused a fresh burst of condemnation in the UN, but the next British military intervention in the Middle East provoked no comment at all, for the simple reason that virtually no one knew it was taking place.

The Sultanate of Muscat and Oman, on the south-east of the Arabian peninsula, overlooking the narrow Straits of Hormuz at the entrance to the Gulf, was a very strict orthodox Muslim state in 1958.

It had been in alliance with Britain since the eighteenth century and although technically not even a British protectorate, the sultanate's external affairs were controlled by the British Political Resident.

He had no corresponding influence on internal affairs, however, and it was one of the most backward countries in the world. The dictatorial rule of the sultan was designed to maintain rather than change that situation.

Slavery had only been formally outlawed in other parts of the Gulf in recent history – Kuwait in 1949, Qatar in 1952, Aden not until the mid-1950s – but it continued in Oman until 1970 when the sultan was finally deposed.

The sultanate issued no money of its own. The currency

was the Austrian Maria Theresa dollar, still minted in Vienna for the sultan in its original, eighteenth-century form. There was less than a mile of sealed road in the whole country and the only cars were the sultan's private vehicles.

Schools and hospitals for the population of half a million were not only non-existent, but also forbidden by law. There was no electricity or mains water supply, and no postal or telephone service, even in the capital, Muscat.

A dusk-till-dawn curfew operated throughout the country and the Muslim Shariah laws were rigidly enforced. Hands or heads were routinely cut off and less serious crimes – such as smoking in the street – were punished with imprisonment in the notorious gaol, the Jelali. Villages that offended the sultan in some way would have their wells poisoned or filled in, a death sentence for the whole community.

With such a ruler it was unsurprising that unrest against the sultan had been festering since 1954, when it had flared into an uprising led by a tribal chief, Sulaiman ibn Himyar, in alliance with a religious imam, Ghalib ibn Ali, and his powerful brother Talib.

The sultan had won the first round of the battle, but Talib then fled to Saudi Arabia and raised a small army of expatriate Omanis. One hundred strong, they returned to Oman in summer 1957, infiltrating the country from the Empty Quarter, and recruited a further 400 or 500 men from among their fellow tribesmen.

A fresh uprising, covertly supported, supplied, financed and weaponed by Saudi Arabia, erupted in the mountains west of Muscat City. The rebel forces quickly established control of a swath of territory from their base on the top of the Jebel Akhdar – the Green Mountain. It was a 200-square-mile plateau in the central mountain massif of Muscat, over 7,000 feet above the coastal plain and guarded by 10,000-foot peaks. It dominated the roads linking the coast with the interior.

The sultan's army proved powerless to defeat or contain the insurrection and he appealed to Britain for help. The

British Political Resident then involved the Army of the Middle East. An infantry brigade seconded from Kenya in July 1957 restored order around the important inland town of Nizwa. The RAF also began regular bombing raids on the Jebel Akhdar, but attempted assaults on the rebel stronghold by two different British battalions both resulted in ignominious failure.

Talib's forces regrouped in the mountains and began a fresh terror campaign in mid-1958, descending from the Jebel Akhdar to attack army posts, ambush vehicles and terrorise the local population.

Even stiffened with men from the Royal Marines and the Trucial Oman Scouts, a British-officered army of Arabs and mercenaries from Baluchistan in north-west Pakistan, the sultan's army again proved unable to defeat the rebels. The Political Resident then deployed a squadron of Life Guards who tried to deter them by patrolling around the bottom of the jebel in armoured cars, but this only provided further targets. The rebels blew up the armoured cars with monotonous regularity, using mines supplied by the Saudis.

With the situation slipping dangerously out of control, the Political Resident decided on one last desperate gamble to keep the Sultan of Oman on his throne.

Two thousand miles away in the Malayan jungles, 22 SAS was reaching the end of a long and very successful campaign. The New Zealand squadron had already returned home and the para squadron had gone back to its parent regiment. Bravo Squadron, one of the founder squadrons, had also been disbanded and its troops absorbed into the two remaining squadrons.

Alpha Squadron and Delta Squadron in turn faced a very tenuous future and their commanding officer, Lieutenant-Colonel Anthony Deane-Drummond – nicknamed 'the Cupboard' because he hid in one for several days to avoid capture at Arnhem – was quick to seize the potential lifeline offered to him in October 1958.

The Political Resident summoned Deane-Drummond from Malaya for a conference in Aden with the Sultan of Oman's chief of staff, Colonel David Smiley, and Major Frank Kitson.

Kitson was fresh from anti-guerrilla success in Kenya with a policy of turning captured Mau Mau guerrillas against their former comrades. He advocated setting up a similar slush fund to bribe some of the rebels on the Jebel Akhdar into switching sides.

Smiley's preferred solution was an assault by four battalions, including a battalion from the Parachute Regiment or the Marine Commandos, but such a large-scale use of troops was politically impossible.

Both plans were rejected by the Political Resident, who preferred the direct but low-key approach advocated by Deane-Drummond. After a cursory survey of the terrain in which the SAS would be fighting, Deane-Drummond returned to Malaya, promising to deploy a squadron to Oman within a fortnight.

An unbending, ramrod-stiff career soldier, he was one of a succession of COs who had come to the Regiment to instil discipline and order. He was never entirely at ease with the hard-drinking, hard-fighting, semi-disciplined men under his command and would RTU people for the smallest misdemeanour. But he thought highly enough of their abilities to regard one squadron of SAS fighting men – notionally sixty-four, but in reality forty to fifty – as the equivalent on active-service operations of the four battalions – 4,000 men – that Smiley was seeking.

He immediately recalled D Squadron from mopping-up operations near the Thai border. After two days and nights of forced marches and headlong river journeys on improvised rafts, they reached base and began immediate work-up training for Oman.

Its value was limited by the very different nature of the terrain and conditions, but they did what they could to adjust, training in open areas during the full heat of the day and practising long-range marksmanship on the firing ranges.

On 15 November 1958 the seventy men of D Squadron – including its administrative personnel – left Malaya in two Beverley transports. The filed flight plan showed their destination as the UK. During the course of their journey, the squadron landed at Colombo in Ceylon and was then diverted to Masirah, an island off the east coast of Oman. Another decoy flight plan suggested that they would then be flying on to Aden and Khartoum.

The already long flight was further complicated by the continuing after-effects of Suez. Many Arab and Asian countries were still refusing British military aircraft permission to land or overfly their territory.

D Squadron eventually reached Masirah on 18 November. They changed planes, flew on to a dirt strip near Muscat and then deployed by truck to Bait-el-Falaj at the base of the Jebel Akhdar. On arrival they learned that forty-five out of the fifty British soldiers previously patrolling there had been evacuated because of heat exhaustion. Two of them had died.

The SAS men faced formidable problems in adjusting to a completely different type of conflict. In Malaya they had been able to dominate the area by their mere presence. Here they were heavily outnumbered. Jungle warfare ended at dark when movement became almost impossible, but in the desert war could be fought twenty-four hours a day.

In the jungle the limit of visibility was measured in yards and contacts with the enemy were at extremely short range. Although the barren, boulder-strewn mountainsides of Oman could have concealed an army – as long as they remained motionless – any movement could be spotted over huge distances.

Long-range weapons were needed, including sniper rifles and support weapons such as mortars, rocket-launchers and artillery. As virtually no artillery was available, air support was essential, particularly against superior odds.

In its own way, the terrain on the Jebel Akhdar was as

appalling as the swamps and jungles of Malaya. The sharp rocks ripped the SAS men's boots to shreds; they had to be supplied with new ones after just six weeks.

Visibility measured in miles combined with the ferocious daytime heat forced the SAS to reverse the pattern they had adopted in the jungle. Instead of patrolling by day and sleeping at night, they patrolled by night and then lay up in shade through the day, avoiding the worst effects of dehydration and heat exhaustion.

The sultan's military advisers scorned the plan, telling them that the nature of the terrain made night patrolling impossible; the SAS men tried it and proved them wrong.

Once more, all the skills they needed in this very different theatre of war were improvised or self-taught. Everything appeared to be against them succeeding but, as in Malaya, they developed their own momentum. They began frantic preparations, begging, borrowing and stealing suitable weapons and equipment from any available source.

They borrowed 3-inch mortars from the sultan's armed forces and took some of the .30 Browning machine-guns from the Life Guards' armoured cars to use in a ground role. The resident British troops in Bahrain sent down desert dress – brown khaki drill – but rather than camouflage them, it made the troops stand out against the rocky, predominantly black terrain. They had to daub the uniforms with black paint or boot polish to achieve the right disruptive pattern.

After a brief but intense period of training, D Squadron began carrying out aggressive reconnaissances to find ways on to the jebel. It was a formidable task. The only routes up to the mountain plateau were tracks and paths so narrow for most of their length that men could only climb in single file.

The tracks passed through steep ravines and narrow gorges – natural ambush points – and were always overlooked by high ground. In such terrain, a handful of determined fighters could hold off an invading force for months, inflicting heavy casualties.

During a month of patrols and sporadic skirmishes, several possible routes up the mountain were found. The most promising was a very ancient one. The Persian armies had been the last conquerors of the Jebel Akhdar almost 2,000 years before. They had followed a route up the north side of the mountain and had then cut steps out of a sheer rock-face to cover the last 200 feet to the summit. They lost a fearsome number of dead in the process but reached the top and put all the defenders to the sword.

Reconnaissance patrols from D Squadron rediscovered the route and found it unguarded; 16 and 17 Troops, which had deployed to the north of the jebel, then scaled the mountain under cover of darkness and reached the lower level of the plateau before dawn without firing a shot.

First light showed that the Green Mountain was about as fertile as Greenland. Apart from some very low-lying scrub and a few camel thorn trees, there was nothing but dusty earth and bleak, barren rock to be seen. The surface of the plateau was also far from level, interrupted by hills, valleys and precipitous wadis.

The SAS position was on one low hilltop but was overlooked from several higher ones. None the less, having reached the plateau, the SAS men decided to try and hold what they had. 16 Troop began building rough sangars while 17 Troop went back down the mountain, ready to bring up fresh supplies the following night.

Over the next few days they consolidated their position, bringing up more supplies and patrolling further on to the plateau. The rebels remained blissfully unaware that the outer wall of their citadel had been breached until a patrol led by Sergeant Herbie Hawkins set up an observation post on a hillock less than 2,000 yards from the enemy positions.

In the ensuing enemy attack, the patrol killed nine rebels and drove off the others. The hillock was immediately renamed Hawkins' Hump in honour of the occasion. In a subsequent assault on a rebel stronghold at Akhbat el Zhufar, just below twin peaks nicknamed Sabrina by the SAS after a 1950s sex goddess, the heavily outnumbered SAS men killed a further eight rebels in a ferocious contact and put the rest to flight.

Despite a fire-fight at ranges as close as thirty feet at times, there were no SAS casualties. The greatest danger to them came from their own rockets. Many were defective and fell well short of their supposed range, others failed to fire and had to be extracted – live – from the barrel of the launcher.

18 and 19 Troops were operating on the other side of the jebel at the same time and suffered the first SAS casualty of the campaign when a patrol came under heavy rebel fire. A very experienced SAS man, Corporal Duke Swindells MM, was shot and killed by a sniper.

To their anger, the troops later discovered that although Duke had died fighting for the sultan, the sole burial place available for a Christian in Oman was a cemetery in a remote cove only reachable by sea. Foreign sailors drowned off Oman's rocky coasts had once been buried there, but it had been disused for many years.

There had been no advance discussion about what would happen if the Regiment took casualties on the Jebel Akhdar; for psychological reasons, SAS men discounted the possibility of coming off second-best in any contact. Fearing the political consequences in the UK, however, the Political Resident had instructed the SAS commanders to avoid casualties at almost any cost.

It was an impossible instruction to reconcile with their orders to defeat the rebels and end the insurrection, but they did their best, often passing up opportunities to engage the enemy in situations they would normally have seized without a second thought.

Attacks were still made where conditions were absolutely favourable or where patrol leaders chose to ignore their safety-first instructions. On the same day as the battle of Hawkins' Hump, 18 and 19 Troops carried out an assault on a rebel cave on the southern flanks of the mountain, firing a salvo of 3.5-inch rockets into it.

Within ninety seconds of the attack, the SAS themselves came under sustained fire from rebel positions higher up the mountain. They were pinned down for a time but eventually withdrew under cover of an air-strike by RAF Venoms from Bahrain and covering fire from a Browning machine-gun.

18 and 19 Troops did not achieve a bridgehead on the plateau, retiring to their base at the foot of the mountain between patrols, and though 16 and 17 Troops had established a foothold, it was far from a secure one. Had the rebels realised how few men they were facing, they might easily have made a frontal assault and overwhelmed the SAS positions or cut their supply line and starved them out.

The frequency of the SAS men's aggressive patrols and the ferocity of their fire when in contacts may have made the rebels think they were facing a much larger force. That impression was unwittingly reinforced by propaganda broadcasts on Radio Cairo, claiming hundreds of British forces were dying in their efforts to conquer the jebel.

The rebels had a fearsome reputation and were equipped with heavy weapons – particularly mortars and .50 machine-guns – which outranged those of the SAS. But when it came to the crunch they were no match for disciplined professional soldiers – and the SAS were the most disciplined and professional of all.

Even after the conflict was over it suited some people – not all of them Omanis – to continue to portray the rebels as implacable, fearless opponents; the braver the enemy, the braver the man who fights him. But Lofty Large, a sergeant with 16 Troop, perhaps gave a more dispassionate assessment of the rebels' abilities after the assault on the Akhdar.

'Any shred of respect for their abilities evaporated that night. They might be great at long range, where they rarely did any harm anyway, but at close quarters – our favourite – they didn't want to know. Irrespective of numbers or reputations, they were now definitely on a loser. We knew it and I expect they did too.'[8]

For the SAS men on the plateau, resupply was now proving almost as much a problem as the enemy. The first RAF attempts at air-drops were largely unsuccessful. The SAS men watched helplessly as one entire air-drop drifted over the edge of the plateau and plummeted down the sheer sides of the jebel towards the plain thousands of feet below.

Other loads were simply dropped from far too high and smashed to pieces on the rocks. One contained mortar shells and phosphorus shells in the same pack. The phosphorus shells ignited and cooked the mortars, which then began exploding, blasting shrapnel in all directions.

The SAS had more success using a handful of donkeys to carry supplies up the mountain. Two hundred more donkeys were then recruited to bring up the food, water and heavy equipment. They were imported along with their handlers from Somalia.

It was a typical piece of War Office parsimony; the donkeys were well under half the price of those obtainable locally. When they arrived, the reason was immediately apparent: they were also half the size and could therefore only carry half the load of a local donkey – no more than fifty pounds. The SAS man accompanying each one invariably carried twice that amount. The donkeys were also lame, noisy, stubborn and unused to altitude and the diet of dates that the local ones thrived on.

After several frustrating days, one of the SAS troopers hit on a bright idea: instead of using them to carry food, the donkeys themselves would become the food. A donkey was slaughtered, skinned and roasted in front of its peers. From that moment on, a miraculous change came over the donkeys: they carried whatever load was put upon them and moved up the mountainside like athletes.

The bridgehead on the north of the Jebel Akhdar now looked secure but it was obvious that there were not enough

SAS men for the task of attacking and occupying the whole
of the plateau, including the rebel headquarters at Saiq. Only
forty of D Squadron's seventy men were battle troops. The
rest were support troops: signallers, mechanics, drivers, cooks
and clerks. Unlike every other regiment in the British army,
SAS support personnel – 'attached arms' in the terminology
of the Regiment – remained part of their parent unit. Drivers
were still attached to the Drivers' Corps and signallers were
still part of the Royal Signals.

Only men who had passed Selection were badged members
of the SAS; hence the question often asked to establish the
credentials of someone claiming to have served with the
Regiment: 'Were you *in* the SAS or *with* the SAS?'

The shortage of SAS fighting men was solved by recalling
A Squadron from Malaya to boost the strength. They arrived
in Oman on 9 January 1959, ready for the final assault on
the Jebel Akhdar.

A parachute-drop on to the top of the plateau was considered and quickly discounted, mainly because the troops
would do anything rather than parachute. Instead they
decided to use a route up the south side of the jebel, along a
steep ridge between the Wadi Kamah and the Wadi Suwaiq.
It was perilously steep and difficult, but, for that reason, the
rebels had left it only lightly defended.

As a deception, the SAS let their donkey-handlers know
that the main attack would be made from Tanuf, certain that
the information would be passed straight to the rebels.

The assault began on 26 January 1959. To reinforce the
deception, the whole SAS force formed up in a motorised
convoy and headed north from Tanuf, in full view of the
rebel observation posts on the Jebel Akhdar high above them.

As soon as night fell, the convoy did an about-face and raced
south again, running without lights to the start-point at the
foot of the jebel. After waiting half an hour for the moon to
rise, D Squadron started climbing the mountain at 8.30 that
evening. Every man was carrying around 120 pounds weight,

including 200 rounds of rifle ammunition, 250 machine-gun rounds, two 3.5-inch rockets, eight grenades, six phosphorous grenades and four rocket-propelled grenades.

It was a phenomenal load to carry on the level, let alone on a 7,000-foot climb. There was no real track to follow; the route lay straight up the mountainside. As they began labouring upwards, they heard the diversionary attack going in against Tanuf on the northern side of the mountain.

As they climbed higher and higher, the huge loads they were carrying began to tell. Men passed out on their feet and crashed to the ground. The others left them where they lay and plodded on towards the distant ridgeline.

At four the next morning they had reached the ridge, a false summit. It was some 600 feet below the main summit plateau, but it commanded the slopes and was the obvious position for the rebels' defensive line.

As they waited for the rest of the men to catch up, the first SAS troopers began building sangars, working in complete silence in the pitch darkness. The discovery of a pile of human excrement led them to a rebel .50-inch Browning machine-gun. To the good fortune – and considerable relief – of the SAS, the gun-crew were asleep in a cave.

The other SAS troops slipped silently by in the dark, leaving 16 Troop to dispose of the gun-crew and deal with any other machine-guns at first light, by which time the remainder of the squadron would be in position on the plateau.

Worried that the heavy-laden and exhausted troopers would not be able to reach the summit before daybreak, however, a group dumped their bergens and made a dash for the top with minimum weapons and ammunition, leaving the others to bring up the rest of the equipment.

To their own and the enemy's surprise, they arrived on the summit around 6.30, just as dawn was breaking. There were few rebel troops in the area, a further sign that the deception and decoy attack had been successful in drawing away many of the defenders.

D Squadron were too exhausted by the climb to do anything more than build rough sangars and hold their ground against an expected rebel counter-attack. As the sun rose, the sound of firing and explosions from the mountainside below them showed that 16 Troop had taken out the first machine-gun crew and were engaging another one.

The troops on the plateau then came under sniper fire, but their position was immediately strengthened by a pre-arranged air-drop of supplies a few minutes later.

The sight of hundreds of parachutes floating down through the clear mountain air must have told the rebels that their position was hopeless. The message was soon reinforced. With no artillery, the SAS called in air-strikes from Venom jet-fighters flying from Bahrain.

In the early part of the campaign they had fired blind but an RAF fighter ground-attack specialist – a former member of the Rhodesian SAS – had then been brought in. He joined the SAS forces on the plateau and directed the Venom aircraft in precision attacks on the enemy. The RAF also carried out indiscriminate bombing using Second World War Shackletons.

D Squadron were followed up the jebel by A Squadron, and once the two squadrons were established on the plateau there was only going to be one winner.

During the next night, patrols pushed further on to the plateau. One set up an observation post on a low hill overlooking a village. They spent all night getting into position, shivering in the night cold high on the mountain as they built dry-stone sangars to give them some protection from enemy fire.

Just after dawn a group of Arab women and children made their way out of the village to fetch water. They returned from the well a few minutes later, laughing and giggling as they carried the water in pails on their heads. They wore colourful clothes in vivid shades of green, quite unlike the normal black garb of Islamic women. The children running around them were naked. They walked along a small wadi, oblivious of the men watching from the hillock above them.

Although they were confident they had not been seen, the SAS men were on full alert. The group of women and children were immediately below them when there was a sudden burst of fire from another hill 400 yards away and rounds cracked against the stone walls of the sangar. In seconds a full-scale fire-fight had erupted as the SAS returned fire.

The women and children threw themselves to the ground and then scrambled up again, screaming and crying, and rushed off to hide in the nearest rocks. In the confusion and panic a small boy of about five or six was left behind, shrieking in terror at the deafening noise.

In the midst of the explosions, the crack of small-arms fire and the whine of ricochets, an SAS man raised his hands above the parapet of the sangar. He held his rifle in one hand, the other was open, palm outwards, in a gesture of surrender.

Shots still rang out as he slowly stood erect and then stretched out his free hand, pointing to the child. The firing from both sides slowly petered out. In the sudden silence he placed his rifle on the ground and walked down the hill to where the child still stood shrieking and crying.

The SAS man picked him up and tried to comfort him, but the child redoubled his cries, even more terrified by the appearance of this tall, powerful stranger, his face stubbled and streaked with grime.

The women peering from behind the rocks started to scream and shout as well, fearing that he was going to harm the child. Instead he hugged him close to his chest and carried him, still kicking and screaming, to where the women were hiding.

When the child was safely in his mother's arms, the man turned and walked back to the sangar. He turned to face the enemy and threw them a Guards' parade-ground salute. Then he picked up his rifle, held it in the air and very slowly disappeared from sight behind the sangar wall.

The instant he was back in cover the firing broke out again.

There was little more serious fighting. Over the next four days the SAS made further advances across the plateau and as they advanced, the enemy simply faded away.

Every village was abandoned. The rebel soldiers had fled and the inhabitants were hiding among the rocks a safe distance from their homes. The villages had been repeatedly strafed and bombed over the preceding days; hearts and minds was obviously not a phrase to be found in the RAF handbook.

The SAS closed on the rebel headquarters at Saiq, still expecting stiff armed resistance, but it too was deserted. The three rebel leaders managed to avoid capture by fleeing back into Saudi Arabia, but the insurrection was over. Huge quantities of weapons, ammunition, documents and supplies were found in the caves around the village.

The last sporadic fighting was over by 31 January. Apart from the death of Duke Swindells, the only serious SAS casualties from the whole operation came when a chance shot from a rebel sniper hit and detonated a grenade in a trooper's bergen. Three men from A Squadron were wounded, and two of them, Troopers Carter and Bembridge, later died of their wounds.

On 5 February the SAS was withdrawn from the Jebel Akhdar, its mission accomplished. To the undisguised fury of men who had just completed a hard campaign in some of the most demanding terrain on earth, they were then forced to spend the next few weeks doing 'flag marches' back on the plateau – a pointless show of strength to villagers who were already well aware of where power now lay on the jebel and a task that could easily have been performed by the sultan's own infantry.

Finally, in March 1959, the SAS squadrons packed their kit and returned home to England. For the first time in ten years there was no war to fight, but the lull before the next conflict broke out proved crucial to the future direction the Regiment would take.

*

After the collapse of Anglo-Arab relations provoked by the Suez crisis, the Jebel Akhdar campaign marked the beginning of the long love affair between the British and the Gulf States.

The whole operation was political in inspiration, conceived not by the War Office but by the British Political Resident. It was also completely clandestine. In both those respects, it set a pattern that the SAS was to follow in most of its future operations.

When Britain sent a full brigade, the 16th Parachute Brigade, to prop up the regime in Jordan in June 1958 it produced an outcry in the world's press, sensing another Suez in the making. The military intervention on the Jebel Akhdar in the same year involved just eighty fighting men, and passed virtually unnoticed.

The SAS involvement in Malaya had been quite open, even if certain operations were covert. The SAS presence in Oman was known only to a handful of senior military and political figures in Britain and those rulers of friendly nations that the Foreign Office chose to inform.

No public acknowledgement of SAS involvement was made until three months after the operation had ended, in a *Times* article based on information leaked by the SAS commanding officer Lieutenant-Colonel Anthony Deane-Drummond.

Eighty SAS men had been enough to conquer the Jebel Akhdar and end the insurrection, and while rebel fatalities ran well into three figures, the SAS lost just three men. To the Foreign Office it seemed a small price to pay to secure the sultan on his throne. He was one of Britain's less appealing allies – little more than a feudal despot – but every ruler in the hotchpotch of small sheikdoms and emirates that then made up the Gulf got the message. Britain would support them, fight for them and take casualties for them.

The political dividends were out of all proportion to the scale of the conflict. British blood was being spilled and British lives lost in defence of an Arab state. That blood sacrifice proved to be worth more than millions of pounds in aid or investment and the rewards from that one operation are still being reaped today.

Arms sales like the massive Al Yamamah deal – in which the Saudis equipped their air force with British Tornados, against fierce French and American competition – did not come about by accident. The seeds were sown years before.

The conflict also had an important immediate impact on the Regiment. As General Sir Frank Kitson later remarked: 'the most important effect of the campaign was that it ensured the continued existence of the Special Air Service'.[9]

British defence policy continued to be dominated by a belief in air-power and the nuclear deterrent as the panacea to cure all ills, but the Jebel Akhdar campaign had shown there was a continuing role for conventional forces, particularly in the low-intensity guerrilla conflicts that were an increasingly frequent feature of the political landscape.

Politicians who had virtually written off overseas armed intervention after the disasters of Suez began to have second thoughts. The covert use of the SAS had every attraction for them. It was cheap, efficient and successful, and if anything should go wrong it also had the supreme political virtue of being deniable.

Many of the lessons the SAS learned on the Jebel Akhdar were to be put to good use in subsequent Middle East operations. After the victory in the Malayan jungle, the campaign also reinforced the belief in the Regiment that SAS men could, would and should fight anywhere in the world, on equal terms with any enemy.

That was not arrogance or hubris. Over the previous decade those frightened young soldiers on the edge of the Malayan jungle had developed into battle-hardened veterans, with ten years of almost continuous warfare under their belts. They were self-taught and self-contained, with no need of recourse to the other sections of the army.

They knew they were not supermen but they were also aware that the vast majority of problems in the military are created by placing limits on the vision and imagination of troops. Freed of those restrictions, the SAS as a whole was able to achieve far more than the sum of its individual parts.

Over the first ten years of the life of the re-formed Regiment, they had proved that determination, physical endeavour, courage and daring could overcome all obstacles.

The SAS was now ready to return to Europe and make its unique contribution to one of the most successful armies of the modern era: the ultimate professionals in the newly professional British army.

4

RETURN TO THE WEST
1958–63

I was covered in frost, lying deep inside a bramble bush, on a freezing, dark November morning. It was not yet dawn but I could hear people talking and saw lights shining from the camouflaged tents.

I was very nervous but tried to stop myself shaking with the cold and the tension. I was surrounded by the enemy. I knew that if I was found, I would be interrogated, but it was too late now to escape. I was committed and would have to stay there for the rest of the day. With luck I would be able to exfiltrate and escape that night, but meanwhile I had to gain the maximum possible intelligence.

What am I doing here? I kept asking myself. I was not even in the Regiment yet, I was still under training.

The words of my instructor, the Bosun, ran through my brain. 'From now on go where the enemy least expect to find you and get as close as possible. The closer you get, the less they'll expect you.'

It had sounded good advice a long way from the action. It was rather less reassuring now that I actually found myself in the middle of an enemy base.

The previous night I'd seen lights in the distance. The other three members of the patrol and I had decided to split up and try to infiltrate the enemy camp. We arranged to meet the following night and pass on any intelligence gained to our headquarters.

I'd moved closer and closer. As I penetrated each layer of the defences, my confidence grew at the realisation that the impossible really was possible, until I found myself where I was now – and did not want to be.

Slowly dawn broke. Within six feet of me a table was laid for breakfast. This was completely alien to anything I had seen either in my old para unit or the unit I was trying to join, where breakfast – if there was any – was eaten on the hoof.

I raised my head a fraction and glanced around. I could see more tents, and sentries strolling in the distance, looking outwards. I was behind their backs. There was more movement as people started to come out of the tents. They were all officers. I realised that I was in the middle of a major headquarters.

Orderlies were laying out water for them to wash and shave and the field kitchen started up, making lots of noise. Before long I could smell sausages and bacon, toast and coffee. My mouth started to water. I had no food and my only equipment was my personal weapon, belt kit, map and compass. It was going to be a long, cold and very hungry day.

Suddenly an officer detached himself from a group and shouted for his orderly to come and clean his boots. He walked towards the bush and I was sure I would be seen. Directly in front of me, no more than six inches away, was a sawn-off tree stump. The officer plumped his foot down on it.

I looked up through the tangle of brambles and saw the three pips of a captain and the flash of the Coldstream Guards. His orderly came bustling across. He knelt down, his right knee within inches of my nose, and went to work with the boot-polish.

The officer surveyed the surrounding landscape like the Duke of Wellington at Waterloo, then said to the orderly,

'Keep your eyes peeled, Perkins, the bastards are out there somewhere.'

It was only an exercise, but the fundamental lessons the SAS was pumping into me were being learned: go where they don't expect you to be, stay for longer than they expect you to stay and get all the information you possibly can.

The author, Salisbury Plain, England, 1963

The campaign in the Jebel Akhdar had saved the Regiment's life – for the moment at least – but the SAS returned to England to find the armed forces in upheaval, still struggling to come to terms with savage cuts and changed defence priorities imposed by the new Macmillan government.

Suez had proved that Britain could no longer support sterling and fund the defence of a global empire. The attempt to sustain both aims merely put both at increased risk. Something had to give.[1]

That realisation forced Macmillan into a 'spontaneous conversion: after 1956, the advocate of empire and coercion stood four-square behind sterling and peace'.[2]

Eden's resignation in January 1957 had brought Macmillan to power and he took immediate steps to slash defence expenditure. In the five years to 1956 it had absorbed 10 per cent of Britain's gross domestic product. Macmillan's new Defence Minister, Duncan Sandys, was instructed to cut that by a third.

The chiefs of staff and their political protectors had fought off all previous attempts at comprehensive reform, either of their own services or of the defence establishment. Each service had its own secretary of state, and in this bedlam of special pleading a neutral and streamlined decision-making process was all but impossible.

Sandys's solution was to sideline the chiefs of staff. He

prepared his May 1957 White Paper, *Defence: Outline of Future Policy*, without even consulting them. When it was published he and Macmillan simply ignored their howls of complaint.

Sandys imposed swingeing cuts on manpower levels and equipment, particularly on the army, which was to be almost halved in strength from 690,000 to 375,000 men over the next five years. Conscription was abolished and overseas bases were closed. The wholesale reductions, including the disbandment of many units, meant that a huge overseas operation on the scale of Suez could never again be contemplated.

Sandys's most far-reaching reform, however, was to initiate moves to bring the three services under a single controlling body: the Ministry of Defence. The process he had begun was completed by Lord Mountbatten. As First Sea Lord he had vigorously opposed Sandys's plans for cuts in the Royal Navy. When appointed Chief of the Defence Staff two years later the naval poacher became a gamekeeper, forcing through the later stages of the ruthless reorganisation and centralisation of the MoD.

The reforms did not go far enough however. A further shotgun marriage would have greatly benefited the Foreign Office and the Ministry of Defence. Their policies impinged directly on each other, yet they have remained resolutely independent of each other from 1945 to the present day. The shambles of Suez and the withdrawal of HMS *Endurance* from the Falklands in 1981, which, at the least, contributed to Argentina's decision to invade, were just two of the occasions when the Foreign Office was either excluded from key decisions or ignored.

The Sandys White Paper also set Britain's defence priorities in stone. Secure in the knowledge that a test of an air-launched hydrogen bomb was about to be held – it took place at Christmas Island in the same month as the White Paper was published – Sandys reinforced the role of the nuclear deterrent as the cornerstone of British defence.

The original Strategy Paper advocating a shift to nuclear deterrence had been rapidly diluted under pressure from the navy and army chiefs of staff, who (rightly) saw it as heralding the virtual extinction of their own services.

As a result a compromise was reached and the bizarre assumption was made that the initial nuclear exchanges would not produce a decisive result, but would be followed by a period of 'broken-backed' warfare. This had far less to do with any military reality than with providing a continuing role for conventional forces to justify their share of the defence budget and support a top-heavy ratio of generals and admirals to troops. In an all-out nuclear conflict, the only realistic role for conventional forces would be helping to bury the dead.

Sandys took the nuclear policy a significant step further in 1957. The enforced climbdown over Suez had helped to reinforce the British obsession with an 'independent' nuclear deterrent. It had become a talisman, a virility symbol that would allow Britain to stand up to the bullies kicking sand in its wrinkled old imperial face.

Nuclear weapons were now to be not only the last line of British defence but also the first, even against an attack by conventional forces. The threat of nuclear devastation of an aggressor nation's own territory would substitute for conventional forces on the ground.

Sandys saw it as a cheap way to continue Britain's world role. Whatever the strategic considerations, the country's financial plight might well have forced him to the same conclusion, but the policy was deeply flawed.

The development of tactical, lower-yield nuclear weapons that could be used in 'limited war' had allowed proponents of a nuclear-first policy to argue that it could cater for any scale of conflict. This was manifestly untrue and skated over the real fear that any use of nuclear weapons, however tactical, would inevitably escalate into full-scale nuclear conflict.

It also ran counter to NATO strategy, which was shifting

to the idea of using nuclear weapons only in response to a nuclear attack. Instead a conventional 'forward defence' of Western Europe was planned along the River Weser in West Germany, close to the inner German border.

NATO planners had come to realise that a West Germany abandoned to Soviet invasion or nuclear destruction in the event of war had no great incentive for continuing NATO membership. It took British planners some considerable time to draw the parallel conclusions about Britain's remaining colonies.

The nuclear-first policy allowed for little gradation of response to provocation and ignored the political lesson from Suez that any unsanctioned British military action, including the use of nuclear weapons, would not be tolerated by the US.

Britain's policy was also increasingly called into question by its inability to maintain the necessary investment, as the financial economies from a nuclear-first policy rapidly proved to be illusory.

The technological complexity of the weapons and their delivery systems – and therefore their cost – had entered an endless upward spiral. Missile-firing destroyers, for example, now cost twice as much – £28 million – as the largest Second World War battleships.[3]

Military equipment took longer and longer to design, develop and commission. Along the way costs rose exponentially, and when delivery was finally taken the product had often already been made redundant by newer technologies. The first squadron of the strategic force of V-bombers came into service in 1955, but the rapid advances in missile technology had already rendered them obsolete.

If further proof were needed that Britain was already losing the arms race, it was offered just six months after Sandys published his 1957 White Paper. The Sputnik launch in October of that year threw the US into a blind panic at the (false) belief that the Soviets had opened a 'missile gap' on them, but it also emphasised how far Britain had fallen behind both superpowers.

That harsh reality was reinforced three years later, in June 1960, when the government was forced to admit it could no longer afford the cost of full membership of the nuclear club. The home-produced Blue Streak was cancelled and replaced by American-built Skybolt missiles. That decision in turn rebounded on Britain when the Kennedy administration axed Skybolt in 1962.

The Cuban missile crisis had put America and the Soviet Union on 'the brink of nuclear disaster and having looked over into it, seemed resolved never to approach it again'.[4]

In the wake of it, Kennedy was initially determined to reduce the potential for nuclear conflict by forcing Britain to give up its nuclear weapons. Only Macmillan's tacit threat to follow the French lead and withdraw from NATO persuaded him to change his mind.

Macmillan had mended fences with the US after Suez, granting permission for Thor missile silos to be constructed in the UK in 1957 and allowing US Polaris submarines to be based at Holy Loch on the Clyde from 1960 onwards.

Now Kennedy reluctantly agreed that Britain would also be given Polaris missiles, but only on condition that they were assigned to NATO. Macmillan extracted a face-saving formula allowing Britain to act independently in circumstances where NATO refused to take action. In practice, given Britain's dependence on the United States for the supply of warheads and missile systems, the British nuclear deterrent was about as independent of American policy as Rhode Island.

Britain's illusions of nuclear independence continued, however, and were even strengthened by Macmillan's role in helping to secure the partial test-ban treaty signed on 5 August 1963. His importance to the negotiations was not much greater than that of a dealer in a no-limits poker game between two billionaires, but Macmillan was so delighted with his contribution that he even thanked Kennedy and Khrushchev for 'helping to make the negotiations a success'.[5]

Sandys's attempt to balance the defence books had proved fruitless in both the medium and long term, doomed to failure by rising costs and by his refusal to reduce Britain's overseas commitments in line with them. The withdrawal from east of Suez finally forced on Harold Wilson's government in the next decade was a bridge too far for Sandys and Macmillan, but Britain's retreat from a world role could only be delayed, not reversed. The hammer and anvil of ongoing economic crises and the ever-rising cost of defence forced a series of progressively deeper cuts to the armed forces as Britain haltingly but inexorably gave up the last trappings of imperial power.

Although Britain was now irrevocably committed to fast-tracking all its remaining colonies to independence, counter-insurgency operations were a continuing – and growing – feature of the withdrawal from empire.

The obsession with a nuclear strategy had blinded many British politicians and military strategists to the continuing need for conventional forces to undertake such tasks, and the huge reductions in army manpower came at the very time when the nuclear threat was encouraging both East and West to adopt less overt uses of aggression in client and other states.

As the Foreign Office, if not the MoD, had realised, insurgency and counter-insurgency needed a rapier like the SAS, not the bludgeon of nuclear weapons, however low-yield they might be.

US Secretary of State Dean Acheson's comment in 1962: 'Britain has lost an empire, but not yet found a role,' was a few years out of date. By then the Foreign Office strategy was in place. Diplomacy backed by the covert use of deadly force were to be the twin arms of a policy to maintain Britain's power and influence in key strategic areas. The Sabre Squadrons – the fighting troops – of the SAS were to be the cutting edge of that policy.

*

The Regiment's A and D Squadrons had returned to the UK from the Jebel Akhdar in triumph, but any misconceptions about the heroes' welcome awaiting them were very quickly dispelled.

They had been totally at home in the jungle of Malaya and had come to terms with the desert of the Jebel Akhdar. After ten years away, they now had to adapt to another alien environment. Their newly allocated base, Merebrook Camp in Malvern, Worcestershire, was dilapidated even by army standards.

The site, once an emergency hospital, had been unoccupied since the war. The ground was low-lying and the camp and its decaying Nissen huts were regularly flooded. The toilets, baths and showers did not work, and the whole place was fit for nothing but demolition.

The living conditions added to the feeling of uncertainty and impermanence that had permeated the Regiment since its re-formation, but the Jebel Akhdar campaign had overcome at least some of the MoD's reservations and in 1960 the SAS was moved from Malvern to a former boys' training unit for the Royal Artillery, Bradbury Lines in Hereford.

A rare interlude of peace after a decade of war offered the chance to assess the present condition of the Regiment and its future direction – if it was to be allowed a future at all.

As the rebels in Malaya and Oman could testify, the SAS was already a formidable weapon, but it was a blunt instrument at the time. Its troopers were a bunch of grizzled veterans, brilliant soldiers, but rough, tough and unsophisticated.

Action was needed to develop further the unique potential of the Regiment. Its men would continue to be ferocious fighters when the occasion demanded but the primary function of the SAS would in future be intelligence-gathering.

In the three years before the uprising in Brunei that marked the start of its next spell on active service, the SAS was transformed into something like its modern form.

It was immediately apparent that the traditional regimental

way of doing things was not appropriate for a special forces unit. After a lengthy series of 'Chinese parliaments' – think-tanks involving all ranks of the Regiment – where a lot of midnight oil was burned, the regimental format was scrapped.

Each squadron was broken down into a headquarters comprising an officer, a clerk, a sergeant-major and a squadron quartermaster sergeant in charge of stores, and four sixteen-man troops. Each troop was in turn composed of four four-man patrols.

The ideal number in a patrol had originally been envisaged as five. The rationale was that if one man was wounded, three could not carry one, but four could. However, combat experience showed that the morale of a patrol was more important than their ability to carry a casualty.

Operating in small groups for months at a time, hundreds of miles from the nearest friendly forces, required complete trust and confidence between patrol members. An odd number of men in a patrol invariably left one as an outsider and on long operations that would have a potentially damaging impact on the patrol's morale and efficiency.

Having fought opponents inspired by political ideology in the jungle of Malaya and religious belief on the Jebel Akhdar, there was also a belief that SAS men needed some inner motivation to sustain them in their stressful, dangerous and isolated operations behind enemy lines.

Many officers made a point of attending church services, hoping their example would inspire their men to find God, but SAS men were too sophisticated – or too cynical – to swallow political or religious creeds.

Most of us shared the opinion voiced in 1781 by Private Jack Careless: 'Fine talking of God to a soldier, whose trade and occupation is cutting throats.'[6] One of the first army padres posted to the SAS had left shouting, 'This Regiment doesn't need a padre, it needs a missionary.'

Instead of religion, the Regiment's own creed became what

American cops call 'the buddy system'. SAS men formed a bond with the other members of their patrol that was as close as a family. The men of a four-man patrol – two pairs – would do anything for their mates: even die for them.

Having made the crucial decision after much soul-searching to adopt the four-man patrol, there was then a certain wry amusement when scarcity of manpower often meant that patrols became three-man rather than four.

The four-, sometimes three-man patrol was the building block from which everything else was constructed. It was the ultimate machine that could function anywhere in the world, in any environment and any type of terrain: arctic or desert, jungle or savannah, travelling by land, sea or air.

Each patrol consisted of a patrol commander, not necessarily the highest-ranking man in the group. The second man was a signaller, for there was no point in collecting intelligence unless you could transmit it. The third member had another skill such as demolitions, and the fourth was designated as a language specialist, although in practice most SAS men could speak at least one foreign language. One of the four – though never the signaller, a full-time job in itself – also doubled as the patrol medic.

Having established the right format, the Regiment then began an intensive training period. SAS Selection had already been introduced during the Malayan campaign but continuous training was also imperative if the Regiment was to progress and evolve, and not merely stagnate.

Selection was complemented by the establishment of training cells and intensive, highly specialised training programmes were introduced to refine existing skills and develop new ones. The two Sabre Squadrons were rarely in base together, for one or the other – and sometimes both – were almost permanently away on exercise, somewhere in the world.

In addition to advancing purely military techniques to previously unknown levels, SAS men also acquired expertise in a wide range of other skills including long-range communications, languages and paramedicine.

To practise their individual and collective skills the SAS would take on any task. One of the most infamous was a job demolishing factory chimneys in Coventry. The demolitionist in the Regiment loaded a pile of explosives on to a truck and took a team up there.

They blew down the first chimney with consummate skill. The only problem was that they also blew out every window in the adjoining terraced street. They rang Hereford for help and the rest of the boys turned up and spent several days perfecting an unexpected new skill, replacing all the broken windows.

Escape, evasion and counter-interrogation training was of rather more direct use. If general war against the Soviet Union was declared, the SAS would be operating deep inside Eastern Europe. In the event of capture they faced interrogation and torture. There was little doubt in anyone's mind then that sooner or later there would be a war, we would be operating in the Urals and we would be captured.

The Regiment took advice on counter-interrogation techniques from SAS members who had been captured in Korea while serving with their former units and even from the Bishop of Birmingham, who had also been interrogated by the North Koreans.

It had had a powerful effect on him. On leaving the army he had joined the Church, believing that the only way to beat Communism was with a greater faith. This caused some soul-searching in the Regiment, because the bishop was an impressive man and far from alone in his belief that you needed some creed to cling to during a very violent interrogation.

The theory that strong religious beliefs would help a man to resist Communist interrogators was not helped by the fate of Cardinal Mindszenty, the head of the Catholic Church in Hungary. After the Soviet invasion in 1956 the KGB subjected him to sensory deprivation and Mindszenty cracked within days, becoming one of the chief apologists for the Soviet action.

The creed the SAS chose to follow was the same as they relied on when patrolling in hostile territory. It was no good trying to plead to God, Queen or Country, or indeed the army or the Regiment. It came down to man to man, to not wanting to let down your mates in your patrol. All SAS men pledged to their mates that they would not crack for at least twenty-four hours after capture, and all escape and evasion plans were predicated on having that time.

For a couple of years the SAS did its own counter-interrogation training, then the Joint Service Interrogation Wing was set up as an extension of the Intelligence Corps. They had studied interrogation techniques and trained the army – on paper – in countering them. To be given living, breathing SAS men as interrogation subjects was a heaven-sent opportunity for them. They often wore Soviet uniforms for added authenticity and their treatment of their subjects was every bit as brutal.

They spent a great deal of time studying the Regiment, reading local and national newspapers, and any source of intelligence that would give them an edge in the interrogation. They could then unsettle a subject by gradually revealing more and more knowledge of his activities, suggesting that one or more of his colleagues was collaborating with them. They could also puncture his cover story that he was merely a medic or an infantryman by producing a newspaper photograph of him wearing SAS uniform.

If they could do it, the Soviet Union could certainly do it too. Part of the Regiment's defence from then on was to retreat further into monastic silence. The new emphasis on total secrecy extended to troopers' wives and families, and even other SAS men.

To ensure secrecy, SAS men were put into isolation as soon as a job was planned. The Sabre Squadron and all the necessary support personnel were separated from the rest of the Regiment and no home visits were allowed. Any persons attempting to breach the wall of silence were themselves held in isolation for the duration of the operation and then subjected to disciplinary action.

Need to know became the guiding principle in all operations. If you didn't, you didn't get told. Any breach of security, no matter how slight, was punished by an automatic RTU. One man was RTU'd simply because his wife was overheard telling someone, 'My husband's abroad at the moment.'

It was brutal and probably unfair, but it sent a powerful message.

The Regiment's public face was similarly silent. No information about SAS personnel or activities was released, no comments or public statements were made on anything and no photographs were permitted. The modern, slightly surreal development of this has been that no photograph of an SAS man, whether serving or retired, is ever published without a black bar obscuring his face.

Prevention by escape and evasion (E&E) was always preferable to the cure of counter-interrogation and the ability to evade capture with little or no kit was the supreme test of soldiering skill. The punishment for being captured was a trip to the interrogators for another gruelling session. Experienced SAS men were hard to capture on field exercises and, to keep the interrogators in work, arrangements were made to ambush patrols at their prearranged rendezvous (RV).

For years afterwards it was impossible to get an SAS patrol on exercise to give an accurate position over the radio. Patrol members would routinely fix a secret RV point, up to a mile from the one they notified, and they gave a very wide berth to any RV known to HQ.

Escape and evasion exercises became a regular pattern of Regimental life, taking place about once a month. Many of them were held in Denmark, where the Danes entered into them so wholeheartedly that they effectively closed the whole country down. The exercises were advertised on television and there were discussion programmes on what to look for, showing typical hides and bootprints.

It was like a forerunner of the TV show *Wanted*. Prizes were offered for information leading to our capture and the schoolkids were given a holiday to take part. It seemed like the whole population of Denmark was out combing every inch of spare ground. It was the ultimate test: you were good or you were caught.

During escape and evasion exercises the CO, John Woodhouse, would usually swap identities with one of the other ranks in the Regiment. His preferred swap was with Corporal Bert Perkins, who had been captured and interrogated for real while serving with the Gloucesters in the Korean War.

During one exercise the real John Woodhouse was captured and interrogated but maintained his cover as Corporal Perkins. At the end of it his interrogator remarked, 'I'm not surprised the Koreans let you go and it's no wonder you're still a corporal. You're as thick as a plank.' Sadly, history does not relate how Bert Perkins fared in his role as commanding officer.

Escape and evasion was important, but the development of close-quarter battle (CQB) shooting and combat techniques was arguably the most significant event in the history of the Regiment. It was a much neglected field, last used with any great expertise by Second World War commanders and other specialist troops.

The first close-quarter battle house was a sandbagged enclosure on the slopes of Mount Kenya. The Mau Mau rebellion was long since over by 1960, even though the state of emergency had only just been lifted, but D Squadron had been sent to Kenya on exercise, partly to establish what changes were needed to the jungle-fighting techniques used in Malaya to make them effective in African conditions.

At first they used the then standard method of shooting, the Grant Taylor system, in that first CQB house. Grant

Taylor was an American Office of Strategic Services instructor. The method he devised involved holding the pistol just below your navel, keeping it tight against the body, at right angles to the stomach wall and parallel to the ground. Holding that position, you jumped round to face each different target; if you were square on to it when you fired, you would hit the target just above the navel.

It soon became apparent that the method was not suitable for SAS purposes. On their return to Hereford a small group of soldiers was given the task of devising a new system and training programme. Over a very short time they created a more fluid, instinctive method of shooting and self-defence.

Under the SAS system the pistol is held at shoulder height with the arm extended and swept across the centre of the target. The pistol becomes an extension of the hand and the index finger which pulls the trigger points the way to the target. Anyone – young or old, male or female, right- or left-handed – could be taught to shoot accurately with the method; if you could point you could hit the target.

That one innovation had the most far-reaching implications for the future of the SAS. Almost overnight it made possible the change from a purely military force into a unit capable of carrying out all the covert and clandestine operations for which it is now world-famous.

Until then, the army pistol had been a purely defensive weapon. Only half a dozen were issued per battalion and they were carried only by senior officers and those – such as tank crews or pilots – operating in confined spaces that made a rifle impractical.

The SAS method made the pistol into an aggressive weapon, giving a trained user the ability to draw a concealed weapon and kill multiple opponents, even if they had already drawn their weapons and were covering you.

There were three basic modules in the training system: fitness, self-defence and shooting. SAS men were already extremely fit from their general training, but the pistol training developed hand and arm strength so that you could control the pistol at all times. It was a heavy piece of hardware and without that strength training it could drag your hand around even when you were not firing.

Self-defence was based on the use of multiple blows to create the space that allowed a person under threat to escape or draw his pistol and fire. It was used to build up the self-confidence needed to allow a situation to develop, knowing that whatever the outcome you were going to win.

The weapon was carried concealed in a quick-draw holster. There was nothing suitable on the market, so each of us made our own. It was worn under apparently normal clothing, but shirt buttons were purely decorative. Our shirts were actually fastened by press-studs, now superseded by Velcro. They could be ripped open and the pistol drawn in a second. Firing it took only fractions of a second more.

Everyone in the Regiment was issued with a pistol, which we then modified to suit our own particular physical characteristics. I had quite small hands so I reduced the size of the grip to allow me a firmer hold on the weapon. I also removed the sights, which were superfluous using this shooting method and hampered a quick draw. I smoothed down the profile of the weapon for the same reason.

Army pistols were not designed for left-handers, who previously had to learn to shoot with the wrong hand. Left-handed SAS men simply moved the safety catch to the other side of the weapon, allowing them to shoot with their natural hand. Army regulations forbade anyone but an armourer to carry out modifications, but we knew more about our weapons than any armourer and did the work ourselves.

The training took only ten days, but was designed to be very intense and required total dedication: you had to live it as well as do it. You practised indoors and outdoors, by night and day, beginning with a lot of dry-training using mirrors and then going on to fire well over 1,000 rounds as you perfected your skills.

The aim was to achieve 100 per cent accuracy, not in the sterile conditions of a normal firing range, but while being pushed, jostled and threatened, or while operating among crowds of innocent people.

In many circumstances we might have to move bystanders aside or use street-fighting techniques to clear a space in which we could then draw our weapon and fire, or make an escape, depending on the situation. We also learned how to roll with a push or punch, drawing our weapon as we did so.

For that short training period, everything we did – the way we walked down a street, got out of a car, entered a building or sat in a room – was conditioned by the fact that we could be attacked at any moment. Once we had learned the method, those habits stayed ingrained for ever. To this day, I carry out the drills without even thinking about them.

By the end of our training we had the confidence to deal with almost any scenario. Even an assailant pointing a pistol at our guts at point-blank range was not seen as a problem. We could knock his pistol aside, drawn our own weapon and shoot him before he had even had time to make the decision to fire.

It is no exaggeration to say that the new system revolutionised pistol shooting throughout the world. What had once been a purely defensive weapon – the last resort to try and get you out of trouble – was now used as an aggressive weapon, allowing you to go out looking for trouble in territory too dangerous for any conventionally equipped soldier.

That instinctive method of aggressive attack developed at the start of the 1960s was to become the backbone of all the subsequent plain-clothes bodyguard and counter-terrorist operations for which the Regiment became justly famous. It was the last major change in the evolution of the SAS. For all the sophistication of its modern equipment, the same methods are still used today both by the SAS itself and by the many SAS-trained forces throughout the world.

Two individuals deserve most of the credit, one for devising the method, the other for having the vision to see in it the potential to carve out a hugely influential world role for the Regiment.

We christened the man who invented the method 'the Master', in deference to the Kung Fu movies of the time. He was a thin, wiry Scot, barely five foot five inches tall. Born and raised in Edinburgh, he joined the Seaforth Highlanders as a national serviceman, but his early career was less than glorious: he was involved in three courts martial while on national service, including one in the Far East.

While in the military prison in Singapore he met a fellow inmate who had served with Ferret Force in Malaya. As soon as he was released, the Master volunteered to join the Malay Scouts that Mike Calvert was forming.

One of the founder members of the reborn SAS, he served until the 1970s and from the day he joined to the day he left, his career was unblemished. He retired as a staff sergeant, but was denied the long service and good conduct medal he richly deserved because of his courts martial almost thirty years before. He still teaches self-defence today and I long for the day when some yob tries to mug this particular OAP as he walks around Hereford.

As in so much else in the development of the supreme fighting force, the drive to create the new shooting system had come from the bottom not the top, but one of the finest and most forward-thinking officers the Regiment ever produced had the wisdom to see the value of what had been created and act on it.

The squadron commander, John Slim, later commanding officer of the Regiment itself, had given every encouragement to his men's relentless programme of re-evaluating old techniques and introducing new ones. He played the crucial role in marketing the new plain-clothes roles of the SAS, using his contacts and influence both in Britain and abroad.

He arranged a series of demonstrations at which initially sceptical army officers were won over, and used his family name and the contacts made while serving with the Aden brigade to lobby for the extensive use of the Regiment in its new roles of bodyguard training and counter-terrorism.

When the Master's group were developing the new method of shooting, they built a twenty-five-yard range from sandbags and railway sleepers on some farmland outside the confines of the camp at Hereford. It was used extensively for a number of years, infuriating the army staff officers, but bureaucratic hurdles were just more obstacles to be overcome.

The next development, following hard on its heels, was a permanent CQB house, soon christened the Killing House, where troops could train with the new shooting system, using live ammunition in realistic conditions. Sheets of thick rubber were hung over every wall to kill ricochets and the building could be blacked out completely and adapted to almost any conceivable scenario. It is still in use today and the £30,000 it cost to build is the best investment the British army ever made.

The Killing House had one slight design flaw, however. It was built right next door to the Regimental chapel, a further sign that organised religion was not high on most SAS men's list of priorities.

Sunday was just another working day, but there were constant complaints from the churchgoers as their services were disrupted by the bangs, thuds and explosions from next door.

Jungle warfare remained an important part of every SAS man's training, but each troop within a squadron began to specialise in a particular method of infiltrating enemy countries over every kind of terrain. Free-Fall Troop practised parachuting, Boat Troop used sea-entry by surface and submarine craft, Mobility Troop learned to infiltrate overland using vehicles and Mountain Troop practised infiltration in arctic conditions, through mountains and snow.

Although they now had a permanent home, the SAS men saw very little of it. Exercises were carried out in Europe, the Arctic, Asia, Africa and the Middle East. Troops were set different tasks to hone their infiltration skills and it was expected, indeed required, that they would be the best in any discipline they took up. As proof, SAS squads won events as diverse as the World Military Free-Fall Championships and the Devizes to Westminster Canoe Race. Others enrolled on the Alpine Guides course or navigated through the Libyan or Omani deserts in Land Rovers.

There were also many less formal tests of SAS men's infiltration skills. On one memorable occasion a trooper broke into the Operations Centre, then the ops officer's office and opened the top-secret safe. As proof of his success he left a trail of 'one-legged chicken' prints – like the arrows on a convict's uniform – leading through the Ops Centre and the office to the safe. Inside was a broken egg and the word 'Oops!' chalked on the inside of the safe door.[7]

The pursuit of excellence also had its darker side. In an exercise on Salisbury Plain in which a squad from the Regiment set a new high-altitude free-fall record of over 30,000 feet, one of the men, Corporal Keith Norry, was killed when his parachute failed to open.

The colonel of the Regiment at the time, also a free-fall parachutist, suggested that we all contribute a day's pay to purchase a regimental clock tower for the base in memory of Keith. None of us objected to the idea of a memorial or the contribution of a day's pay, but we were adamant that there should not just be one name on it, but the names of every SAS man who had died while serving with the Regiment.

A clock tower was duly erected, though in the light of the Regiment's uncertain future it was designed to be dismantled and moved to another site if necessary. The names of all the SAS men who had died in training or on operations were inscribed on the base and 'beating the clock' became the standard SAS euphemism for staying alive. Too many did not; well over 100 names are now engraved there.

Although the SAS demanded the highest levels of skill and dedication from its men, the commitment to excellence did not extend to pay. Many men were actually losing money by serving with the Regiment, having given up the rank they had achieved to join the SAS.

The rules were strictly applied; no matter what your rank when applying to the SAS, you had to revert to trooper on successful completion of the Selection course. For most soldiers and NCOs that meant a loss of rank and money. Paradoxically, the rules did not apply to officers, who were promoted and had an increase in pay on joining the Regiment.

The sole consolation for the other ranks was that officers were only passing through. They did a three-year tour and then returned to their former regiments. Only the troopers and NCOs were permanent fixtures in the SAS.

On passing Selection, the new SAS troopers were given a number of promises by the commanding officer. 'Rank: forget it, you're not getting any. Career: if you stay here, you won't have one. Pay: if you want money, you'll get none.'

Our loss of money and rank was called a disincentive incentive; if you really wanted to be there it didn't matter what the circumstances were, you would accept them. It was irritating to most of us but undeniably true. The SAS was *the* place to soldier.

Conscription had been abolished and the British army went fully regular in 1960 but it was still governed by national service attitudes. People were still forced to paint coal and cut grass with knives and forks, and once you signed on the dotted line you were committed. For those with enough nous, the only thing to do was get out, and one of the few places worth going was the SAS.

Having been notably unsuccessful at imposing strict army-style discipline in Malaya, the Regiment then took the novel stance of giving individual SAS men responsibility for their own actions. It proved a very astute move; there have been very few group disciplinary problems since then.

Unlike the rest of the army, discipline within the Regiment

was maintained by self-discipline, backed by peer pressure. The SAS remained virtually unknown, even within the armed forces, but it proved a magnet for gifted soldiers chafing under the petty restrictions, rules and regulations of the regular army.

The SAS then consisted of no more than sixty-five trained battle troops in two Sabre Squadrons – A and D Squadron. There was also a very small administrative group, but they were not allowed to wear the SAS beige beret and the distinction between badged and unbadged people was strictly maintained.

To be the best – if not the best paid – the Regiment would learn from the best, anywhere in the world. The SAS made use of civilian organisations with special skills, but also began training with special forces worldwide.

An exchange programme with US special forces was instituted in 1960. An SAS captain and a sergeant spent a year with the 7th Special Forces Group and two US soldiers came to Hereford.

The extent of the American commitment to their special forces was enormous. They had seen the potential and were investing heavily in it. But the US special forces had entered a period of massive expansion under Jack Kennedy's presidency and previous standards were being eroded. This led to an unfair comparison of the physical attributes of the British and Americans.

The 1962 Regimental visit to the headquarters of the US special forces at Fort Bragg, North Carolina, reinforced the SAS belief in the value of their own approach. Working in the swamps of Florida, the SAS men were passing in record times tests that the Americans thought impossible. The lesson that quality not quantity was the goal was obvious to the lower ranks of the SAS, but it was to be several more years before the Americans also reached the same conclusion.

The exchanges with US special forces continue to this day. There are always two members of the American special forces – one officer and one senior NCO – on detachment with the SAS. Charlie Beckwith, the man who led the raids into North Vietnam trying to free US PoWs, trained with the SAS. US special forces even went on active service with the Regiment during the Aden campaign and there are strong though unsubstantiated reports that some SAS men on exchanges with the Americans also went to Vietnam.

After the visit to America, Selection was refined still further and became a little more scientific, but the SAS still rigidly maintained the high standards that had always applied – except in one area.

The dominant feature of the new camp at Hereford was a huge drill square 800 yards long by 400 yards wide. It is hard to imagine anything of less use to the Regiment. SAS men did not and could not drill at all.

An attempt was made to rectify this terrible omission by sending some of the grizzled veterans from the Middle and Far East to do a drill course at Pirbright depot with the Brigade of Guards. Only one person passed it, an Irishman determined to show the Guards that being able to do drill was not beyond an SAS man.

His parting words to the Sergeants' Mess at Pirbright showed his true opinion of the value of his achievement: 'The Brigade of Guards is a luxury the British army can no longer afford.'

Many senior figures in the army held similar opinions about the SAS. The happy band of brothers, warts and all, were now the most battle-hardened, skilled and intensively trained fighting force in the world. But their self-confidence was tinged with the fear that the organisation they had built could yet be destroyed at the whim of some staff officer.

The hostility to the SAS did not all come from frustrated bureaucrats. A false notion exists – fostered by the officers – that they were in command of the Regiment. The truth is that it was run by the NCOs.

If there was a troop officer at all, he led only one of four autonomous patrols in the troop. Reports from the other patrols would pass up the line to the NCOs. They were the only people who knew the full picture. If they decided the officers needed to know something they would tell them; if not, they kept quiet.

The reason wasn't bloody-mindedness. Special forces operations require specialist skills; you need to be fully employed in special forces to understand how to do the job. For an officer from a tank regiment to come in and expect to run SAS patrols was as ridiculous as an SAS man joining the officer's regiment and expecting to drive a tank into battle.

Except on formal occasions like parades and regimental dinners, SAS men wear no badges of rank. It is a visual confirmation that leadership by ability and example, not rank, remains the SAS rule, but the idea that many officers are not only dispensable but sometimes even an impediment to the efficient operation of the Regiment is not one that was ever going to be popular with the average army officer.

The evolution of the Regiment's unique decision-making process was also a source of irritation to officers accustomed to having their orders carried out without question. But it was not just a by-product of the traditional hostility felt towards 'Ruperts' by battle-hardened NCOs.

David Stirling had laid the foundations of SAS democracy when forming the Regiment.

The SAS brooks no sense of class. We share with the Brigade of Guards a deep respect for quality, but we have an entirely different outlook. We believe, as did the ancient Greeks who originated the word 'aristocracy', that every man with the right aptitude and talents, regardless of birth and riches, has a capacity in his own lifetime of reaching that status in its true sense; in fact, in our SAS context, an individual soldier might prefer to go on serving as an NCO rather than having

to leave the Regiment in order to obtain an officer's
commission. All ranks in the SAS are of 'one company',
in which a sense of class is both alien and ludicrous.[8]

SAS democracy was not planned or imposed, however. It
evolved naturally out of experience in combat. It was
obvious – even to Ruperts – that men being asked to risk their
lives in dangerous actions would achieve their goals more
often if the teamwork essential to their success in the field
was reflected in every aspect of the operation, including the
planning.

The Chinese parliament allowed, indeed required, every
person involved in a task to contribute to the often heated
discussion about how it was to be achieved with the resources
available. No one was allowed to remain silent; if you did,
you lost the right to criticise afterwards. To say later, 'I knew
this wouldn't work' was to invite instant physical retribution;
if you knew it wouldn't work, why didn't you say so at the
planning stage?

Good officers realised the value of the Chinese parliament but not every officer was a good one. Over the first
ten years of the reborn Regiment's life a large number of
officers had served with the SAS. Very few of them had a
happy relationship with a semi-anarchic group of superb
soldiers who did not suffer fools. As those officers' careers
progressed onwards and upwards, they owed the Regiment
no favours and in many cases would have done it harm if
they could.

Many other officers who had come into contact with the
SAS had also been given short shrift. It took an unusual
officer to develop an affinity with people who only gave
respect to the individual, not the rank.

Some excellent officers served with the Regiment and commanded the absolute respect of their men, but they were a
very small minority. John Woodhouse and John Slim were
two of the finest special forces officers. Both rose to command

the Regiment but they did so at great cost to their own personal careers.

As far as the army was concerned, the SAS at that time was a cul-de-sac. Neither man was promoted beyond the rank of colonel and when their spell in command of the Regiment was over they were virtually forced to leave the army altogether; there was nowhere else for them to go.

There were a number of other outstanding officers but, like John Woodhouse and John Slim, officers who could get on with the SAS usually did not have a career beyond it and were not in a position to support it in MoD power struggles. In those circumstances, no matter what the past achievements and present standards of the Regiment, there was considerable paranoia about its future.

This led directly to the very harsh regime of RTU. The self-discipline that was the cornerstone of the SAS was the only means of preserving the Regiment. Every SAS man was already aware – or was rapidly made aware – that any indiscipline among the civilian population would probably be the last straw for the MoD. It was exactly what the staff officers, civil servants and stuffed shirts were expecting.

They believed that this strange Regiment over which they exercised minimal control would continue to act in Hereford as they had done on active service overseas. When they were not busy fighting the enemy, they would fight among themselves, get drunk, wreck property and upset the civilians.

The Regiment confounded its critics, however, and a strong mutual loyalty and affection grew between the SAS and the local population; hearts and minds work began at home. Hereford was a low-wage, rural community. SAS men had few opportunities to spend their wages when on active service overseas and when back in Hereford their disproportionate amount of cash and their great fondness for spending it was a significant boost to the local economy.

Many men from the Regiment married local women and became close to local families, and a strong bond also developed with the civilian staff working at the camp. Most of the people who came to work there when the Regiment arrived stayed till retirement. Some are still working there in one capacity or another.

There were one or two fraught moments in community relations. The Demolitions Training Wing at Bradbury Lines was sited in a wooden hut; indeed the whole barracks was built of wood. One of the training courses involved producing home-made napalm by boiling a mixture of petrol and soap flakes. It sounded more dangerous than it actually was, provided you took certain precautions.

On one occasion an officer new to the Regiment put the mixture on to boil without the necessary fire-fighting equipment to hand. The whole mixture erupted and set fire to the building, which had to be evacuated.

The local fire brigade arrived, bells clanging and lights flashing. They unrolled their hoses, connected up to the hydrants and began to fight what was now a very intense blaze.

The members of the Regiment watched with considerable interest from the far side of the massive drill square. One of the firemen wandered across and enquired why they were not helping to put it out.

'It's the Demolitions Wing,' one told him helpfully. 'If you knew what was stored in there you wouldn't go near it either.'

When the conversation was relayed to the other firemen, they all downed tools and ran across the square to enjoy the view from the same safe distance as the soldiers, leaving the fire to burn itself out.

Firemen excepted, the Regiment was now firmly accepted as a part of the local community, but its future was still far from secure. The reservations that senior army officers had about the Regiment were not shared by the Foreign Office. It was now well aware of the value of a ruthless, effective and unattributable weapon that could be used covertly and deniably anywhere in the world, in support of the British government's political aims.

The Foreign Office's plans to employ the SAS in altering the shape of the post-colonial world were now in place. If sympathetic rulers could be installed or maintained in power with the help of the SAS at minimal cost to Britain, former colonies or dependencies would then be virtually self-policing. The empire was fast disintegrating but British influence would remain through rulers who owed their tenure of office and often their lives to the SAS.

The first battle to be fought in support of this new strategy was with the military bureaucracy. The Soviet threat dominated military planning to the exclusion of all else and there were many staff officers who saw no role for 22 SAS other than deep penetration and reconnaissance behind Soviet bloc lines in Central Europe.

When – it was never if – the Soviet attack came, the regular forces on the Rhine would fall back to a prearranged defensive line and the Soviet forces would be targeted and destroyed by nuclear weapons.

The SAS troops would lie up in underground hides while the Soviet forces rolled past or even right over the top of them. Some would then help the targeting of missiles by reporting on Soviet installations and troop movements, while others would co-ordinate the 'stay-behind parties' in acts of sabotage.

The Territorial Regiment, 21 SAS, had been training exclusively for those tasks for some time and it seemed for a while that 22 SAS might be restricted to the same role; Britain was the only country using Territorials as its front-line special forces in the Cold War.

A second Territorial regiment, 23 SAS, had also been established in 1959. Twenty-one SAS remained based in London, while 23 SAS took in the north of England and Scotland. It was formed from the Rescue Reserve Unit and took on the role of M19, running the 'Rat Line' escape routes from Eastern Europe.

Although it was given the SAS name, 23 had no formal connection with the parent regiment for several years. It was largely a paper unit, but had one very considerable virtue in the eyes of the senior officers in 22 SAS. By adding it to the SAS establishment they became eligible for ranks that could not have been justified by the size of the regular Regiment alone.

The old threat of absorption by the Parachute Regiment was also raised again around this time, and had the future of 22 SAS been decided only by staff officers, on purely military grounds, the Regiment might not have survived in anything like its present form.

Fortunately the SAS was no longer a purely military force. Henceforth its use would be dictated more by political considerations than strategic requirements, and its orders were as likely to come from the Foreign Office or the SIS as the Ministry of Defence. The Territorials were left to continue to prepare for nuclear Armageddon, but 22 SAS focused on counter-insurgency.

As tensions continued to grow in the region, the Middle East looked the most likely immediate destination for the Regiment and desert training operations were stepped up.

Conflict was simmering in Oman and Aden – where RAF planes had already been involved in attacks on Yemeni-backed rebels – and an SAS squadron was also put on stand-by after Iraq massed troops on the Kuwait border and announced its annexation on 25 June 1961.

The threat was taken seriously – Kuwait supplied half of Britain's oil – but the announcement was premature. The despatch of a force of regular British troops from Aden and Kenya solved the problem without the need for SAS involvement.

D Squadron was then diverted on its way back from an exercise in Oman after trouble again flared at the Buraimi

Oasis, the scene of the confrontation between Oman, Abu Dhabi and Saudi Arabia in 1955. Encouraged by a nod and a wink from the Americans, a large Saudi Arabian force had occupied Buraimi in pursuit of its territorial claim.

In an attempt to deter them, two SAS troops – thirty men in eight trucks – were sent to the desert just east of the oasis with instructions to act like a large force. They drove their trucks to and fro at top speed until nightfall, creating a dust cloud that spread for miles, then lit dozens of campfires over a wide area of the desert, their glow clearly visible from the oasis. In the morning the Saudi troops had disappeared.[9]

Deception proved enough in that case, but the next call to active service required much more than mere bluff. To our surprise, the destination was not the deserts of the Middle East, but a return to the jungles of the Far East.

5

BRUNEI AND BORNEO
1962–66

We were hiding on the edge of a brown, swift-flowing river, just watching, listening and waiting. The only sounds were natural: the slap of water against the riverbank, the calls of birds in the forest canopy high above us and the distant cry of a hornbill.

The four of us had been there for ten days, communicating only in signs and clicks of our fingers and tongues. It was our third trip to the same area trying to verify intelligence reports of an Indonesian army camp upstream, so far without success.

Although the river was very deep and fast-flowing, we had crossed it to check the far bank for tracks and again we had drawn a blank. An Indonesian camp was usually revealed by the movement of canoes and supplies along the river, but in all the time we had been there the only things we had seen were local Dayaks moving up and down the river from the village just upstream.

We were close enough to hear the sounds of the village and smell the smoke of the cooking fires, and were very nervous because any compromise by the locals was almost certain to be reported to the Indonesian army. Our nerves were understandable; we were totally alone, deep inside Indonesia. The nearest help was back in Sarawak. If anything happened, we would have to sort it on our own.

I looked at each of the others' faces in turn, trying to read their expressions. They were pinched and thin with hunger and their eyes bulged from lack of sleep. I knew that my own face showed the same strain. I glanced down at my hands. They were black with dirt and scratched and torn from the barbed hooks of the nante sikkit thorns.

It was decision time. We had at least a five-day march back through the border to a pick-up point and our inconclusive report would almost certainly result in us being sent back to the same area again.

Blinky gave us his Chinese parliament look. 'Do we prove it or not?' There was only the faintest tremor in his usual calm public-school tones.

Ted and Tony looked at each other, then at me. We were all frightened, but we shrugged and said, 'Why not?'

Blinky gave a superstitious touch to the brim of his lucky jungle hat and then led us upstream towards the village. He carried an Armalite AR-15 captured from the Indonesians, the rest of us had SLRs.

We had cached our bergens. Apart from our weapons and ammunition, all we had with us were our belt kit, escape rations, search and rescue beacons, the medical pack and, most important of all, the patrol signal pack.

When we got very close, Tony and Ted took up firing positions while Blinky and I moved cautiously into the open, covering each other as we entered the village. After the relative coolness of the jungle, the sun was bright and uncomfortably hot.

It was deathly quiet. Then I spotted a villager through the window of a straw hut. He waved his arm at us and I waved back, not quite sure if the gesture was a greeting or a warning. Then I looked beyond him, through the pillars supporting the hut.

On the opposite bank of the river, the prow of a boat had just touched the bank. Four Indonesian soldiers stared back at me for an instant. I don't know who was more surprised. Then they leaped from the boat and ran up the bank.

Blinky and I both loosed off a couple of rounds, which went wide, then we hurried back to where we had left Ted and Tony. They were extremely agitated, not knowing what the shooting was about. We had a quick council of war and then Blinky led us back towards the cache of our heavier kit and what was left of our rations.

We were feeling quite smug because we'd got away with a calculated gamble and proved that there was a camp there. Then there was a horrific bang as an Indonesian outpost fired a mortar. A defensive fire pattern rapidly developed, with several mortars raining shells down around us and a number of heavy machine-guns firing on fixed lines.

Mortars are particularly terrifying – and dangerous – in the jungle. In an open battlefield some of the energy from the blast of a mortar bomb is absorbed by the earth in which it lands. In the jungle the bombs tend to detonate on the tree canopy and almost all the kinetic energy of the blast is retained by the torrent of shrapnel knifing downwards.

A lot of the rounds were dropping between us and the place we had left our kit. We had no choice but to abandon the equipment; we had to move before the inevitable follow-up from the Indonesians.

All we could do was head for the border with what we were carrying on our belts. It was not an easy decision to make. It was going to take us an absolute minimum of five days to reach the border – if all went well. We had only one day's rations each. If we missed the pick-up on the border, the only place we could head was the coast of Sarawak, 250 miles away through dense jungle.

As the defensive fire died down a little, we began to move away, trying to leave as little sign as possible. Behind us we heard a number of signal shots, the Indonesian army way of communicating between groups. The shots showed they were behind us, either side of us and trying desperately to get in front of us as well, to cut off our route to the border.

For the next five days the cat and mouse game continued. We had virtually no sleep and because of the risk of missing our lift-out at the border we had to conserve what little food we had. We survived on nothing but the two packets of cigarettes we used to kill our appetite.

Our escape kits contained benzedrine tablets – 'speed' – to help us keep moving as hard and fast as possible, but none of the patrol made use of them. Chased and harried through hostile territory by an enemy, fear was the only stimulant we needed.

Each night we transmitted to our base in Kuching to give them our approximate position and let them know that we were still heading for the pick-up point. On the sixth day we were given a final window. If we hit the landing zone before nightfall we would be picked up. If not we would have to head for the coast.

The deadline was imposed because of the danger of our communications being intercepted and decoded. The codes we used at the time were numerical blocks, but they were not one-time codes and were breakable by a reasonably sophisticated enemy over a short period of time. If we missed the scheduled pick-up, the RAF would not put its helicopters at risk to get us out.

By the grace of God we managed to stay ahead of the Indonesians, but we approached the LZ very cautiously, acutely aware of the danger of an ambush. Just before dark, a Wessex helicopter clattered in over the jungle and put down in the clearing. We dived into it and were whirled away in seconds.

We sat in silence for a while as the tension ebbed away. The crewman eyed us with ill-concealed distaste. We hadn't shaved since we went into the jungle, we hadn't washed or eaten for a week. We were soaked with mud and sweat, and stank to high heaven.

After a few moments the crewman slid the side door open again and sat with his head outside for the rest of the flight so he didn't have to smell the passengers.

We were flown to Kuching, to the headquarters of Major-General Walter Walker, the commander of the British troops in Borneo. It was pitch dark by then, but General Walker heard the helicopter landing and came across with a number of his staff officers to talk to the patrol.

The information we gave him pleased him greatly and he lost no time in demonstrating the fact. We didn't even pause to wash or shave. Within half an hour of landing we were down in the centre of Kuching, eating Chinese food and drinking Tiger beer, with the general's approval and at the general's expense. The money he loaned us that night has still not been repaid.

Ninety minutes before we had been deep in the jungle. The sudden contrast between the constant fear of our escape from hostile territory through the still, silent world of the jungle, and the bright lights, noise and normality of Kuching was very hard to handle.

Four human scarecrows settling down to dinner also attracted the attention of everybody in the area and upset the Royal Military Police patrols, but once more the general was our saviour. He had warned the MPs to leave us alone as we recovered from our arduous patrol in our own way.

Despite our hunger we could eat very little at first. Our stomachs had contracted so much that a few mouthfuls left us feeling full, but the taste of our first proper food in weeks was still wonderful.

As I pushed away my plate and signalled for another beer, I winked at Blinky. 'This is what makes soldiering worthwhile. You work hard, then play hard. You suffer and go short in the jungle, but when you come out the reward is there.'

It was my last patrol in Borneo before leaving for Aden, which made me a little smug. Blinky just smiled enigmatically and drained his beer.

Later that night I must have staggered into a taxi and got back to my bed. The next thing I knew I was being shaken awake by Blinky. 'Pack your kit. General Walker's so impressed with our report he's sending us back to lead an attack on that Indonesian camp.'

I was half laughing and half groaning with the weight of my hangover. 'You're making a mistake, Blinky. You might be going back there, I'm off to Aden.'

He gave an evil smile. 'That was yesterday, this is today.'

The author, Kalimantan, Indonesia, 1964

The initial conflict in Borneo was centred on the tiny state of Brunei on the north coast of the island, but the tense political situation in the region soon ensured that the insurgency spread across the whole of northern Borneo. The territory covered tens of thousands of square miles, rising from sprawling coastal mangrove swamps to the dense jungle of the mountainous interior.

Undeterred by the failure of its attempts to establish federations in the West Indies, Central and East Africa, the Colonial Office was now acting as midwife to Tunku Abdul Rahman's concept of a Malayan Federation, combining Malaya and Singapore with Brunei, Sarawak and North Borneo – now Sabah – which together occupied the top quarter of the huge island of Borneo. The other three-quarters was the Indonesian territory of Kalimantan.

Northern Borneo was separated from peninsular Malaya by well over 1,000 miles of ocean and though roughly half the population of the three territories was Malay, the rest were mainly Chinese and Dayak, with smaller populations of aboriginal tribes in the dense jungles.

Federation was being resisted by the minority populations and also by many of the Malays, but the initial unrest was sparked by the Sultan of Brunei's resistance to democratic elections and his unwillingness to recognise socialist parties.

Another powerful figure in Brunei, Sheik Azahari, had begun to recruit a guerrilla army, the TNKU – the North Kalimantan National Army. Their chosen name – Indonesia's preferred title for the territories of Brunei, Sarawak and North Borneo – indicated their affiliations.

They were armed and supplied by Indonesia, whose President, Achmad Sukarno, had ruled as a dictator since 1950. He had no reason to love the British, for his self-proclaimed Indonesian Republic had been stifled at birth in 1945 by British forces who had even recruited the recently defeated Japanese forces on Java to help control and disarm Sukarno's nationalists.

He had another powerful reason for destabilising the Malaysian Federation. He also had dreams of proclaiming his own federation – Maphilindo – comprising Malaya, the Philippines and Greater Indonesia, including the territories of northern Borneo. There were no prizes for guessing who would be the leader of this proposed South-East Asian superstate.

After a long campaign of subversion, Sukarno's forces had already staged a successful invasion of Irian Jaya – the former Dutch territory occupying the western half of the huge island of Papua New Guinea – in the summer of 1962. The impotent Dutch were forced to give official recognition to Indonesia's de facto rule on 15 August 1962, leaving Sukarno free to turn his attentions to the next territories on his list.

The rebellion broke out in Brunei itself on 8 December 1962. Government buildings and police stations were attacked by mobs and the Sultan's Palace and the British Residency were put under siege. There were also riots at the oil town of Seria and in Limbang in Sarawak, where many of the resident Britons were taken hostage.

The rebels made the crucial mistake of failing to take the

airfield in Brunei, however, and the uprising was quickly put down by Gurkhas, commandos and a battalion of the Queen's Own Highlanders who were all flown in from Singapore.

The defeated rebels then took to the jungle, basing themselves across the border in Kalimantan, where they continued to receive strong support from President Sukarno. On 20 January 1963 he formally declared a policy of 'confrontation' with the Malaysian Federation.

Although the guerrillas were now in the jungle, several thousand members of the so-called Clandestine Communist Organisation – as in Malaya drawn mainly from the ethnic Chinese – remained active in the towns. When spontaneous riots erupted in the main population centres of North Borneo and Sarawak, A Squadron of the SAS was immediately recalled from a winter training exercise in the Brecon Beacons and despatched from Hereford.

They arrived covertly in Singapore under the code-name Layforce 136. The local general, Poet Brown, then showed his intimate knowledge of jungle warfare by keeping them in Singapore to get a sun tan, because they were 'too white to go into the jungle'.[1]

The fact that anyone spending time in the jungle goes white as a sheet because of the absence of sunlight does not seem to have occurred to the general. An exception was made for the squadron signallers, who were sent straight to Brunei where their long-range sets were used for signals traffic with Singapore.

The rest of the squadron were given cash to buy civilian clothes so that they could enter Borneo covertly. Every man bought blue denim shirts and jeans, because that was the cheapest clothing available. The result was a party of identically dressed men who might as well have stayed in uniform.[2]

They were also given money to buy rations for use when deployed in Borneo until supply lines could be established. The same principles were applied: they bought the cheapest available food, tinned fish. Hearts and minds operations in

Borneo were essential from the start; if they didn't get on with the locals, they were going to be living on tinned fish for the foreseeable future.

Having conserved their cash with the prudence of thrifty housewives, the money saved was then spent in the time-honoured SAS fashion, on Tiger beer, before boarding the plane to Brunei.

Forces in Borneo were under the overall command of Major-General Walker, a 'fighting general' whose popularity with ordinary soldiers was only exceeded by his unpopularity with staff officers. As Templer had done in Malaya, one of his first actions was to establish a unified command over the troops, police and local government officials. Although Walker was a fanatical supporter of the Gurkhas he commanded, he was also an admirer of the SAS. The summons that brought the Regiment to Borneo originated with him.

The campaign came at the optimum time for the SAS, before the lessons learned in the jungles of Malaya had been forgotten. As usual, most of the army-issue jungle warfare equipment was totally unsuitable or rotted and fell apart in jungle conditions.

Fortunately there were enough experienced men in the Regiment to know what was needed. New equipment was made in the local markets by local craftsmen and paid for with the troopers' own money; having to use your own money to buy kit for active service was something of a first. Later, we also bartered with American and Australian soldiers for their jungle boots, which were infinitely better made than the British equivalents.

The preferred jungle weapon of most SAS men was now the American Armalite rifle, which was very light compared to the British army's self-loading rifle and also had the advantage of rapidity of fire over the first-choice weapon in the Malayan campaign, the sawn-off, repeater shotgun.

Armalites were so scarce, however, that at one stage there were only two available in the whole of Borneo, and one of those was the talisman of an officer strutting around a considerable distance from the front line.[3]

The cash-strapped British government had reluctantly purchased several hundred Armalites from the Americans for evaluation. Unfortunately they were given to a Guards Regiment serving in Malaya. While the fighting troops were crying out for them, the Guards, being Guards, delayed the issue of them while they attempted to develop drill movements with the unfamiliar weapons. As a result, the only Armalites available to the SAS were ones liberated from the enemy.

As a result most of us settled for SLRs in the early stages of the conflict, swapping them for Armalites as they became more widely available. Many lead scouts carried out a totally illegal modification to the SLR, filing down part of the firing mechanism of the weapon to allow it to fire on fully automatic as well as semi-automatic.

As soon as A Squadron arrived in Borneo it was broken down into four-man patrols and sent to the small towns in outlying areas. The orders were to impose curfews and restore order by patrolling up and down the main street like the Sheriff of Dodge City.

It was almost comical; most of the towns had a population of several thousand, yet they were supposedly being policed by four men who had only arrived in the country a few hours before.

That farcical deployment coincided with a period of 'phoney war' in which the insurgency subsided and staff officers back in Whitehall began making plans to redeploy the large force of British troops elsewhere.

It was a lull not an ending, and was broken when the insurgents based in Kalimantan began carrying out armed raids across the border. The first serious incident occurred on Good Friday, 12 April 1963. A party of 'guerrillas' – almost certainly Indonesian regular troops – crossed the border and attacked the police station at Tebedu, five miles inside Sarawak. Several policemen were killed.[4]

Until then, the British government had been more worried by the escalating conflict in Vietnam than the little local difficulties in Borneo and had been contemplating pulling troops back to Singapore. Instead, several additional battalions of regular troops were sent to help contain the threat, while the SAS withdrew and regrouped.

Controlled from 'the Haunted House' – the former Japanese Kempetai secret police headquarters behind the Sultan's Palace in Brunei Town – and later from a second base in Kuching, the capital of Sarawak, we were redeployed along the border in the classical Malaysian configuration: four troops in four separate locations.

The shortcomings of this strategy when applied to a different conflict were very quickly apparent. Each troop took responsibility for a section of the border, but in jungle so dense and terrain so difficult that a day's patrol might cover only a couple of miles, or even less, large areas were left unpatrolled.

To maximise our reach, the troops were further broken down into the Regiment's standard four-man patrols, searching the cross-border routes for the tracks of infiltrators. Contrary to established myth, the patrols were never spread along the whole border from the east coast of North Borneo to the west coast of Sarawak 800 miles away.

Initially we were concentrated in the border area broadly to the south of Brunei, between the Third Division of Sarawak and the Gap, a completely unpopulated area of dense jungle east of Pensiangan in North Borneo. That was where the maximum threat from the insurgents and their Indonesian backers in Kalimantan was focused. Their aim was to seize the corridor of territory from the border to the China Sea, capturing Brunei and cutting off North Borneo, which could then be subdued and also added to the Indonesian empire.

Even though we were only patrolling around a third of the whole border, some patrols had responsibility for vast sections that were impossible for four men to cover unaided, but we also enlisted the help of the local tribespeople through a hearts and minds campaign.

The tribes were fierce fighters and deadly with a blowpipe. Many had fought against the Japanese during the war and most longhouses were decorated with the shrunken heads of Japanese soldiers; we were glad that we became their friends, not their enemies.

We approached them with caution at first, since we had no way of knowing whether the tribes had already been suborned by the Indonesians. We would arrive, offer a small few gifts and then withdraw for a few days, sometimes after reinforcing the initial impression by a show of our own apparently magical abilities.

The favoured demonstrations were either the instant summons of a helicopter-borne force of heavily armed Gurkhas, through the magic of a radio message, or an air-drop of supplies for the local longhouse. The Kelabits promptly christened the aircraft 'the noisy bird that shits rice'.

We remained at arm's length from the village in the early stages of a hearts and minds operation, based in a hide a safe distance away, but once some degree of trust had been established the patrol would become part of the village's daily life.

We communicated in pidgin Malay, the lingua franca of the region, but many SAS men also learned the different tribes' own languages. We lived among them for weeks and months on end, sharing their huts and longhouses, and offering them medical treatment for their ailments and help with simple construction projects like improvements to their water supply. In return they supplied information which was passed back to the Haunted House. They patrolled the borders themselves in the normal course of their daily lives as hunter-gatherers and knew if any strangers were in the area.

One particularly dextrous SAS man rigged up a Heath-Robinson generator to provide the first electric light ever seen in the interior of the country, but the most lasting impact was made by the skills of the patrol paramedics.

One medic, Yogi Hollingsworth, was asked to treat a village headman's son whose temperature was going up like an express lift. Yogi found out that the boy had swallowed some sycamore seeds. He immediately asked for some eggs, separated the whites and forced the boy to swallow them, neutralising the alkali that was poisoning him. Within minutes his temperature started to drop and his life was saved. From that moment on, Yogi and his SAS colleagues were the lifelong friends of the entire tribe. Nothing moved in the border areas without us getting to hear about it.

In some extremely remote areas of the jungle there were no tribes at all, however, and the patrols had to cover the border themselves. We operated in very arduous conditions – as in Malaya, a mixture of primary jungle and swamp – and were resupplied by parachute-drop or very occasionally by helicopter.

Learning from the lessons of the Malay and Jebel Akhdar campaigns, SAS signals traffic was now totally Morse-based. The small patrol set gave an in-theatre capability with a range of several hundred miles; the larger troop set with a power generator had a range of several thousand miles. It proved a huge advantage, for the terrain and atmospheric conditions made other forms of communication a lottery at best.

The Gurkhas even had to abandon the standard operating procedure of standing-to every time an outpost failed to send its daily signal because there were so many false alarms caused by poor communications. The inevitable then happened. The significance of a missed signal from an outpost, Long Jawi, that really was under attack was not realised until too late. Four days later the survivors staggered into their base camp. Two Gurkhas, a Border Scout and a policeman had been killed.

A and D Squadrons had been rotating spells of duty in the early stages of the Borneo conflict, but a second active service operation began in Aden in 1963 and with only those two squadrons, the Regiment was very stretched.

One was permanently in Borneo, the other in Aden, with

minimal rest and recuperation periods. The interval between cross-border operations was only five days, of which three were spent debriefing the last patrol and briefing for the next one.

On normal border patrols you would remain in the jungle throughout the duration of your four-month tour. The interval between tours was only one month and the advance and rear parties would have even less. Specialists such as patrol commanders and linguists might go straight from one conflict to another. As an Arabist, I was sent straight to Aden from a tour in Borneo without any break at all.

It imposed a considerable physical and psychological strain on all the members of the Regiment, particularly the married ones. Many of us barely saw our homes for three years.

The continuous active service tours did have a cleansing effect on the Regiment, however. The peacetime soldiers melted away and the people who could not take the grind also left, leaving the Regiment lean, mean and ready for more.

The first phase of the Borneo campaign had been relatively quiet, with periods of routine patrolling punctuated by sporadic enemy raids over the border. The tempo of the conflict accelerated during the latter half of 1963 after the failure of President Sukarno's attempts to achieve his aims by diplomatic means.

After months of negotiations, it was agreed that the Malaysian Federation, due to be inaugurated at the end of August, would be delayed for two weeks while a UN-sponsored referendum took place in northern Borneo, offering the population the choice of federation with Malaya or Indonesia.

In an extension of the hearts and minds campaign, SAS troopers were told to use their influence among the tribespeople to persuade them to vote for union with Malaya. The region's geographical and cultural links were far stronger with Indonesia, but when the votes in the plebiscite were counted on 13 September 1963, the UN secretary-general, U Thant, announced that the people of Sarawak and North

Borneo had voted to become part of Malaysia.[5] Brunei opted for independence in its own right.

Furious at the rebuff, Sukarno refused to recognise the new Malaysian Federation, established just three days later, on 16 September, and ordered a sharp escalation of Indonesian attacks on Sarawak and North Borneo. At the same time, British properties in Indonesia were ransacked and the British Embassy in Jakarta was besieged, looted and burned to the ground.

Indonesian troops in company strength made repeated cross-border raids, aiming to push back British and Malayan troops enough to establish 'liberated zones'. An Indonesian force over 100 strong crossed into North Borneo on 29 December 1963 and attacked the Malay Regiment base at Kalabakan, near the North Borneo border town of Tawau. Twenty-seven sleeping Malay soldiers were either killed or wounded when the longhouse was machine-gunned by Indonesians firing up through the floorboards.

A series of raids into Sarawak followed in January 1964, including an assault on the airfield at Kuching, which was repulsed by the commandos.

Both of these raids were across areas of the border that were not then patrolled by the Regiment, but on the follow-up to the Kalabakan raid SAS patrols discovered the tracks of the infiltrators and deployed infantry into ambushes ahead of them. Of the 100 Indonesians who had attacked Kalabakan, ninety-six were killed or captured.

A brief, abortive ceasefire was then called at the instigation of the Americans, whom neither side could afford to offend, but peace talks proved fruitless and by March hostilities had resumed at an even higher level.

Indonesian attacks, often supported by heavy weapons, were frequent enough to raise fears of an all-out invasion. Kuching was particularly vulnerable because of its close proximity to the border. The Indonesian threat also extended beyond northern Borneo: sea and airborne raids were even launched against Malaya itself, though with little impact.

When Sukarno made the unwise prediction that he would destroy Malaysia 'by dawn on New Year's Day 1965',[6] a decision was immediately taken at the highest level to ease the pressure on Kuching by taking the battle to Indonesian forces inside their own country.

Denis Healey, Defence Secretary in the newly elected Labour government, gave his tacit support to the policy.[7] It was a brave decision, for his political neck was on the line if news of the cross-border operations leaked out.

Attempts were made to secure the border defences by building a chain of forts at key points, manned by infantry companies and protected by light artillery, mortars, Claymore mines and pungee traps.

Meanwhile the SAS formed the spearhead of Operation Claret, launching cross-border operations deep into Indonesia, locating enemy camps, lines of communication and weak spots. They were classical SAS tactics but had never been used in a jungle environment before.

The original area we had been patrolling, along the border south of Brunei, had now largely been pacified and most of the cross-border operations were launched into west Kalimantan, where the greatest concentration of Indonesian troops was massed, threatening Kuching.

British forces were allowed to cross the border by up to 3,000 yards – later extended to 10,000 – in attributable operations. This was partly to keep them within the range of supporting artillery fire if they were forced to retreat and partly to allow the excuse that the forces had only crossed the poorly defined border because of a map-reading error.

No restrictions were placed on the depth of penetration in covert SAS operations, other than the overriding imperative: not to get caught. They were mounted through one of the infantry bases, where the SAS patrol would normally wear the insignia and berets of the Royal Signals or Engineers, but everyone in the base knew who we really were.

The cross-border operations had a profound psychological effect on other army units. They watched the patrols come and go and were often called upon to fire artillery in support of them. It soon became common knowledge that British soldiers were deep in Indonesia, giving the enemy hell.

Even for those units occupied in a purely defensive role, the knowledge that someone, somewhere was taking the fight to the enemy was a huge boost to morale.

On cross-border operations we carried no identification and no equipment that could be identified as British army-issue. Even our boots had a different tread pattern. The only exception to the rule was that everyone wore dog-tags and syrettes of morphine around their necks. If they were killed, the dog-tags and morphine were removed and brought back.

The instructions not to discard any incriminating material, such as cigarette ends, in hostile territory were superfluous; the need to avoid leaving sign for enemy trackers ensured that nothing was ever thrown away.

The customary shortage of SAS manpower and fears about political repercussions at the UN if the scale and range of British involvement were known also led to a repeat of the Jebel Akhdar experience, with patrols instructed to avoid casualties at all costs.

Only the smallest Indonesian patrols were to be ambushed. If involved in an unavoidable contact with the enemy, the policy was 'shoot and scoot', engaging them only long enough to effect a withdrawal. The theory was fine, but the Indonesians could not necessarily be relied on to co-operate.

The criteria laid down by SAS headquarters for these patrols forbade anyone to carry more than thirty-five pounds in weight. This excluded weapons and ammunitions but included everything else: radios, medical equipment, search and rescue beacons, rations, sleeping equipment and spare clothes – which we never carried anyway.

The only expendable item was food. Very little could be carried and during the cross-border operations everybody was constantly hungry. The five-day period between patrols was the minimum necessary to regain some of the bodyweight lost in the jungle. We needed little encouragement to eat like pigs before each patrol but we invariably returned looking like victims of a famine, our clothes hanging off us.

Patrolling through the dense, near-impenetrable jungle was work for the brave only. The lead scout or point man had to navigate to keep the patrol heading in broadly the right direction and pick a way through the tangle of undergrowth without the giveaways of leaving sign, breaking twigs or rustling dry leaves.

While doing all that, he also had to be on permanent hyper-alert for the faintest hint of sound, smell or movement that might betray an enemy presence; but not so trigger-happy that he fired when startled by the sudden movement of a bird or animal. In a contact, the lead scout could be the only one even to see an enemy and if his reactions were not fast enough, he would be the first to die.

The lead scout covered the area ahead of the patrol as far back as the periphery of his vision. Number two looked right, number three left, and number four covered the rear, usually walking backwards.

The other members of the patrol had to maintain enough distance from each other to ensure they would not be hit by firing directed at the lead scout, or killed by the same mine or booby-trap. But they also had to be close enough to maintain contact and return fire if necessary, without hitting their own man in the back.

In a head-on contact – the most common kind in the jungle – the other three men fired semi-instinctively, often at targets they couldn't see. Their direction of fire was dictated by the actions of the lead scout – if he was still alive. The object was simply to lay down a short, concentrated barrage of fire, convincing the enemy that they faced a large force, then scoot as fast as possible away from the scene.

The gnawing, incessant tension of jungle patrols would

be brutally punctuated by 'sudden savage encounters, with victory or defeat often obscured initially by the tangled mass of dense undergrowth. Leading scouts walked on a razor's edge, only the fastest gun had any future.'[8]

One very raw junior officer, on his first patrol after completing Selection and jungle training, insisted on leading the patrol, even though he was the most junior trooper on it. During the patrol his life was saved by a burst of fire past his right ear. His number two, a sergeant, shot and killed an enemy that the officer, several yards in front of him, had not even seen.

On their return, the officer wrote the patrol report. He was awarded the Military Cross for his part in that patrol. The sergeant who had saved his life got nothing except the dinner the shame-faced officer then bought him.

Despite the dangers, the reconnaissance and ambush patrols were extremely successful, forcing the Indonesians to withdraw further from the border areas. As a result, we grew ever more daring and penetrated deeper and deeper into Indonesia.

Strangely we felt more secure deep in enemy territory than near the border. Most of the activity by the Indonesians and the British army was close to the border, where both sides laid defensive fire patterns. The odds on a chance contact with friend or foe were also very high. We used to cross the border and get deep into Indonesia as fast as possible, without leaving sign for enemy trackers to follow.

On a cross-border operation the distance travelled was far less important than the need to leave no indication of our presence. We followed the faintest animal tracks, which were virtually undetectable to an untrained eye.

We moved in complete silence, without damaging a single stem or leaf and measuring each footfall to avoid anything that might make the slightest noise. Even the absence of sound could be a giveaway; if the constant background noise of animal and bird calls was interrupted, it was a clear sign that something had alarmed the wildlife. It was not unusual to spend a whole day travelling just 500 yards, allowing maximum time to wait, watch and listen for the enemy.

Using animal tracks also had risks unconnected with enemy patrols, however. Unlike Malaya, where I once found myself face to face with a tiger on a jungle track, there were no big cats in Borneo, but there were other dangers.

A patrol making a fast withdrawal after an ambush of Indonesian forces found its way blocked by a rearing king cobra. A shot would have brought the Indonesian follow-up search down on their heads. The only option was to freeze and hope that the creature would not feel threatened enough to strike. After a tense few seconds, it lowered itself from its upright position and slithered away.[9] An Australian SAS lance-corporal was less lucky. He was gored to death by a bull elephant during a cross-border patrol.

Tribesmen also set animal traps, a sharpened bamboo stake fixed to a whippy sapling and triggered by a trip-wire. Most were set to kill wild pigs – at about knee height on a human – but they could cause a terrible wound and there was always the chance that the enemy would set similar, bigger traps to kill men.

Diseases such as dengue fever, scrub typhus and leptospyrosis – carried in the urine of the rats that infested every jungle camp – were also a constant worry. On cross-border operations, helicopter evacuation was only allowed in exceptional circumstances. No matter how ill, members of SAS patrols had to walk their way out.

The tension of every patrol was gut-wrenching; constantly alert for the faintest sound, smell or movement, watching for trip-wires, mines and booby-traps, straining to look through the vegetation, rather than at it, and knowing that at any moment the jungle could erupt with gunfire. Days would pass with nothing more than a few signs and faint whispers exchanged between us.

When we found a track we would assess the sign left by

enemy soldiers and either lie up to observe or ambush Indonesian patrols, or follow the track in the hope of discovering an enemy camp. To use the track itself was to invite an ambush or risk triggering a booby-trap. Instead we would make a series of loops through the jungle, aiming to intersect the track every few hundred yards. Each time there was the risk of hitting the defensive perimeter of the camp first, or straying into the sights of an enemy patrol lying in ambush on their own back-track.

There were no maps to help us; they were based on aerial photography and showed little more than an unbroken rainforest canopy. Even the details they did reveal, such as river courses, were often wrong. The jungle was similar to Malaya but the terrain was even more difficult: steeper and sharper, with razor-backed ridges and plunging ravines.

Slowly, painstakingly, SAS patrols pinpointed infiltration routes, enemy camps, tracks and resupply routes. We then led in infantry groups, usually two companies strong, to attack the targets or had them deployed by helicopter to ambush the enemy. It was classic jungle warfare and very successful; most of the insurgents were either killed or captured.

Only soldiers on their second or subsequent tours of Borneo were considered for these cross-border ops and in the beginning the Gurkhas – whose fearsome reputation was further strengthened in Borneo – were the only force used.

After the terrible stress and isolation of the reconnaissance patrols, the sight of so many heavily armed Gurkhas accompanying us into enemy territory was very reassuring – until we got into the jungle proper, where the noise they made frightened us witless.

SAS patrols also went deep into Indonesia to tap the telephone lines the Indonesians used for communications between army outposts. It was extremely hazardous. The lines were patrolled to try and prevent them from being tapped and there were several contacts between SAS troops and the Indonesian regular army.

Despite the instructions to minimise risks, casualties were unavoidable. The first three were victims of a helicopter crash in 1963, but four other SAS men were killed in separate contacts with Indonesian forces during 1964.

All SAS men promised each other that if anyone was hit in a contact we would make sure that they were dead before leaving them. It was all we could promise; there was no way a dead body could be brought back.

We would never abandon a wounded man, but if a patrol member was killed he had to be left behind. As soon as a lull in the fighting permitted, one of us would touch the body, take a pulse or do whatever was necessary to make sure that he was dead. Then we'd strip him of his equipment, and leave the body where it had fallen.

One of the dead was beyond our reach however. Trooper Harry Condon had been wounded and captured by the Indonesians. He was then tortured and murdered by an Indonesian army sergeant. His SAS troop offered blood money to the local highland tribes to kill the man responsible. The money was paid and we have no reason to doubt that the tribesmen kept their part of the bargain.

Although virtually unknown outside the armed forces, the SAS had now built a fearsome reputation within the army for its professionalism. Attracting recruits was not a problem; the difficulty lay in finding recruits good enough to do the business.

Our manpower shortage was eased by the arrival in autumn 1964 of a re-formed B Squadron, recruited mainly from bored regular soldiers with the British Army of the Rhine. Not long afterwards a new squadron, G Squadron, was formed, composed entirely of recruits from the Brigade of Guards, the Guards Independent Parachute Company. Many members of the existing squadrons were openly sceptical about the quality of this new squadron.

G Squadron was given a rudimentary jungle training

course, but the instructors were horrified to see that Guards officers on active service still had batmen to cook and clean for them.

When one of them was asked, 'What will you do if you come face to face with an Indo?' he replied, 'I'll wave my cheque book at him.' It was a joke, but only just.

They were eased into the conflict by being sent to cover the relatively quiet sections of the border, replacing SAS Sabre Squadrons, who redeployed to carry out Claret operations south of Kuching.

A full squadron from the Australian SAS and a half-squadron from New Zealand had also arrived in spring 1965, allowing the Regiment to step up its cross-border activity still further. Once more the SAS operations were secret and deniable; once more they were highly successful.

Even though we were now operating completely covertly, there were still deeper layers of secrecy; even Denis Healey was not given all the information about the Regiment's activities. The formal SAS role was to gather intelligence on enemy troop movements through hearts and minds operations. But other more aggressive activities went on.

The restrictions on us were eased a little further in the spring of 1965. We were now given *carte blanche* to cross the border, ambush enemy patrols and kill as many Indonesian soldiers as we could.

On one such operation a patrol followed the tracks of a group of Indonesian soldiers to their outpost and then carried out surveillance over a number of days. We discovered that the night sentry was a creature of habit. At first light each morning he would lay down his machine-gun and step away from his post to urinate. On the fifth morning it was the last thing he ever did. The outpost was overrun before his sleeping colleagues had even opened their eyes.

Other SAS groups also ambushed enemy patrols and attacked Indonesian river craft carrying troops and supplies.

One such raid, the Lillico Patrol, has entered the annals of the Regiment. The patrol was moving along a jungle track towards an apparently disused Indonesian camp when it was itself ambushed. Trooper Ian 'Jock' Thomson, the lead scout of the patrol, was hit by a burst of automatic fire that shattered his left thigh.

He fell almost on top of an Indonesian soldier lying hidden in a bamboo thicket but had the presence of mind to grab the rifle he had dropped as he was hit and kill him before the Indonesian could get off a shot.

Sergeant Eddie 'Geordie' Lillico had also been hit and lay on the track, unable to use his legs. Jock dragged himself over to Geordie and together they returned fire at the enemy. Mistakenly believing that Jock could still walk, Geordie then sent him back to bring up the rest of the patrol while he kept up a hail of covering fire.

Trailing his wounded leg behind him, Jock dragged himself along to a nearby ridge, then laid down a burst of fire at the Indonesians. It had the apparent effect of making them think that reinforcements were arriving and forced them to withdraw.

Jock bandaged his wound with a shell dressing, applied a tourniquet to his thigh and dosed himself with morphine, then continued to crawl along the track in search of the rest of the patrol.

Having seen the lead two men go down, the other two members of the patrol had withdrawn across the border to bring up reinforcements from the nearest infantry post. They returned to the area late that afternoon and, as light was fading, Jock heard the search party approaching and called to them. After an abortive attempt that night, he was lifted out by helicopter the next morning.

Geordie had dragged himself off the track and hidden in the bamboo. After passing out from his wounds, he regained consciousness to hear a search helicopter passing overhead. Realising it was pointless to use his rescue beacon because the crew would never locate him in the dense bamboo, he let it pass by.

He spent the night in the open and at first light the next day he began dragging his paralysed body up towards the ridge, a distance of some 400 yards. Weakened by his massive loss of blood, it took him until three o'clock in the afternoon to reach the ridge.

Once there, he fired some signal shots, but these only had the effect of alerting an Indonesian force. His shots were answered by burst of automatic fire from a few hundred yards away.

Geordie concealed himself as best he could while the Indonesian follow-up search combed the area for him. At one point he saw a soldier climb a tree forty yards from him. The man remained there for about half an hour, scanning the jungle for him.

The helicopter again passed nearby, but with enemy forces in the area, Geordie again could not risk using his beacon, which would only have drawn the helicopter into hostile fire. The enemy at last moved away as dusk approached and when the helicopter pilot, Flying Officer David Collinson, made his final search of the day – his nineteenth pass over the area – Geordie activated his beacon. He was found and lifted out before nightfall.

Both men survived their ordeal and their endurance and courage were officially recognised by the award of a Military Medal to Geordie and a Mention in Despatches for Jock.[10]

The patrol was one of the rare occasions when the SAS came off second-best in a contact with the Indonesians. More typical was a raid by Lofty Large's patrol on Indonesian craft using the Koemba River. They spent several days in hiding on the banks of the river, gathering intelligence on enemy movements and reporting it by radio to their base.

Many Indonesian craft were allowed to pass without being attacked as they waited for the 'big one' to hit. It prompted one of the patrol to remark, 'If we wait long enough the fucking *Queen Mary*'ll come up the river.'

The patrol finally ambushed a launch carrying Indonesian troops upriver towards the border. The boat was set on fire and sunk and there were no apparent survivors among the Indonesian forces.[11]

Unknown to them, a second launch carrying a number of senior Indonesian army officers had been coming upriver just behind the one attacked by the patrol. At the first sounds of gunfire they had pulled into the bank and remained undetected.

The patrol only discovered what a prize target they had missed twenty years later. A party of Indonesian officers visiting Hereford in the 1980s asked to meet the patrol that had come within a whisker of killing them.[12]

So many Indonesians were being killed in cross-border operations that a nervous Foreign Secretary called a halt to them for a while. While giving them casualties forced the Indonesians to pull back, he was worried that if we gave them too many, it might provoke a full-scale invasion.

After a few weeks' lull, we were given authority to restart Claret operations and the Indonesian death toll again began to rise. They could not sustain such losses indefinitely in the face of mounting domestic opposition to the war. The first signs of an end to the conflict came during September 1965.

A coup attempt by Indonesian Communists almost toppled Sukarno. He survived with the help of the army and began a savage purge of Communists; massacres occurred in different parts of Indonesia.

His generals had seen enough, however. A second, bloodless coup was launched and Sukarno was forced to yield power to General Suharto.

The general had no wish to continue a conflict he knew he could not win and opened negotiations with Malaysia in May 1966. Isolated cross-border raids by his forces continued, but it was now more of a ploy to win concessions at the conference table than in any real expectation of victory.

By August Suharto had made his peace with Malaysia. An Indonesian force still inside Sarawak was rounded up over the next couple of weeks and by 3 September 1966 the conflict was over.

The future of Malaysia – minus Brunei, which had opted for independence in 1963, and Singapore, which had withdrawn from the federation in September 1965 – was secure.

The use of guerrilla tactics to defeat an insurgency had proved hugely successful. As a delighted – and no doubt privately relieved – Denis Healey told the House of Commons, it was 'one of the most efficient uses of military force in the history of the world'.[13]

British forces had lost fifty-nine dead, the Indonesians an unknown number – unofficial estimates ranged as high as 10,000. All claimed kills had to be verified by an independent source, which often involved sending the Border Scouts to visit their relatives in Kalimantan to gather intelligence on Indonesian casualties.

The Indonesians were good soldiers – their special forces were US-trained and equipped – and by an irony that brought no amusement at the time, many of them had also trained at the British Forces Jungle Warfare School in Malaya. We sometimes turned that apparent disadvantage against them by second-guessing the contact and ambush drills they would use.

The Indonesians were also very brave, but the SAS, although not more brave, were more professional. Like the local tribesmen we used as surrogate forces, we were also more accustomed to working in the jungle. Indeed the British army at this time had arguably developed a level of expertise in jungle warfare that has never been equalled.

If terror attacks on the Indonesian army were one element in SAS success, Borneo also proved the value of a hearts and minds campaign offering medical treatment to the local tribes in their own areas. Hearts and minds had also been used in

Malaya, but there it had been improvised rather than pre-planned, and was based on the forced movement of the indigenous population into protected villages.

Borneo was the proving ground for a true hearts and minds campaign and, with one exception, it would play a vital role in all our future overseas operations.

Our success pointed up the failures of the American approach in Vietnam at the same time, where attempts to carry out hearts and minds operations were deeply flawed. Few American forces made the attempt to live among and befriend the indigenous population, speaking their language and eating the same food. Instead they carried out hearts and minds operations like commuters in nine-to-five jobs. They travelled into the area in the morning but then withdrew to their bases at night, leaving the field to the Viet Cong.

The US experience in Vietnam proved the emptiness of the macho boast of one American officer, 'Get them by the balls and their hearts and minds will follow.'

The American inability – or refusal – to distinguish between combatants and civilians in Vietnam led to the brutal treatment of whole sectors of the population, ranging from the horrors of My Lai to the carpet-bombing and defoliation of huge areas of the country.

The consequences included an unbroken flow of recruits and widespread popular support for the insurgents. In the long term, the only thing that followed American attempts to get the Vietnamese 'by the balls' was the humiliating defeat of the US forces.

By contrast the SAS formed strong bonds with the indigenous tribes in Borneo, and, as elsewhere, our hearts and minds operations led to significant and lasting improvements in their quality of life. Unlike the Indonesian forces, the tribes of North Borneo still have good memories of our time among them.

The initial SAS role of deep penetration and intelligence-gathering in Borneo had involved relatively little direct conflict with the enemy, but General Walker, the Director of

Operations, still rated seventy SAS troopers 'as valuable to me as 700 infantry in the role of hearts and minds, border surveillance, early warning, stay behind and eyes and ears with a sting'.[14]

If anything, that was an understatement. Rather than merely responding to terrorist incidents, the intelligence gleaned by the SAS enabled him to deploy his troops where they would be proactive rather than reactive.

The Indonesian-backed rebellion had given the SAS the chance to demonstrate the value of its reorganisation and its newly acquired skills against subversion and terrorism. It was spectacularly successful; the insurrections failed and when the Indonesians resorted to the use of their own regular army troops they were roundly defeated.

The Sultan of Brunei was also secured on his throne and the financial value of the loyalty to Britain shown by the sultan and his heirs – which remains just as strong over thirty years after the event – cannot be exaggerated.

There were many acts of individual bravery during the campaign – a Gurkha soldier won a Victoria Cross on one operation conducted by an SAS patrol, based on information they had collected – but the fighting skills of SAS troopers were not reflected in their own tally of medals.

Gong-hunting has always been a subject of scorn in the Regiment, but if medals are to be awarded it is important that they are seen to go to people who deserve them. The way in which decorations were awarded during the Borneo campaign was very contentious.

The notional establishment of each SAS squadron was one major and four captains, but squadrons were never fully staffed and were further depleted on active service when officers had HQ liaison and other duties which kept them out of the field.

As soon as officers joined an SAS squadron in Borneo, they were sent into the jungle on a quick loosening operation and then taken out of the active service role. The policy meant that on many operations a four-man patrol was led by a corporal or sergeant, with an officer tagging along, learning the ropes. Although he had no contribution at all to make to the conduct of the patrol, he was nominally in charge of it, since, in army terms, a corporal can't command a captain.

There were a number of occasions during the Borneo campaign where officers were awarded Military Crosses, despite being the junior person in the patrol. My sergeant, Blinky, was given an MID – a Mention in Despatches – for leading his patrol on four solid months of cross-border operations. More than one officer got a Military Cross for one patrol. The fact that the person compiling the report on the patrol was the officer may have had some relevance.

The practice continues to this day and has devalued the award of medals in the SAS. There is no way of determining whether the individual really earned a medal or was merely along for the ride when someone else earned it for him. It wasn't a major issue – we usually had more important things to worry about – but it did arouse some comment.

The cost to the Regiment of the victory in Borneo was much higher than mere medals forgone. Several men were killed, but, as in Malaya, SAS men also paid a price beyond the level of battlefield casualties. The result of long-running jungle operations, exacerbated by a poor diet based on completely unsuitable rations, was that many members of the Regiment developed obscure tropical diseases. Some were debilitating; some were life-threatening.

For the first time, I also saw SAS men suffering from post-traumatic stress disorder in Borneo. A couple of veterans from the Malayan conflict, men of indisputable courage, both developed a limp which prevented them from going on operations. It was almost unheard of in an era when psychosomatic complaints and mental illness were not even discussed, except in the most scathing terms.

They were as baffled as we were when they tried to explain that they were limping and could not stop. We just accepted that there was something wrong and that it could all be cured with a crate of Tiger beer.

Looking back, I realise the enormous mental stress they were under. You can only go to the well of courage so often before it runs dry.

6

THE KENNEDY ASSASSINATION
1963

The heat was stifling. The waters of the Gulf looked as hot and heavy as molten lead. Even in mid-morning, the temperature in the dusty streets was already climbing well past the 100°F mark and the humidity was almost 100 per cent. Despite the heat, the crowd showed no impatience as they awaited the arrival of the ruler's motorcade.

A mixture of policemen and recent recruits to the newly formed army lined the roads through the humble town, now the capital city. Their chests were puffed with pride, their rifles gleaming, but their pressed and starched uniforms were already sweat-stained and wilting.

They were surrounded by many thousands of people, dressed in flowing robes and sandals and wearing a multitude of colourful headdresses, all waiting to greet the ruler and his guest, the head of state of an adjacent country arriving to add his recognition to the newly formed state.

The British government had two abiding interests in the country: to maintain stability in the region and preserve the current very pro-British ruler in power. In furtherance of those interests, a small team of us had been in the country for almost nine months, supporting the ruler as we trained a team of bodyguards to ensure that he did not leave his throne in the same way that he arrived on it – by displacing his half-brother in a coup.

We had selected a group of the ruler's tribesmen and

trained them in the arts of bodyguarding, from shooting and explosives, to countersurveillance, communications and paramedicine. Up to that time such skills had been considered far beyond the scope of these Bedou desert-dwellers, but they proved to be remarkably receptive.

Many of them were unable to read and write, but far from being a handicap that turned out to be a tremendous asset, for they all had the gift of almost total recall. I became aware how tales, fables and stories had been remembered and handed down over millennia, preserved in the minds of the Bedou.

Once we had completed the basic training, we acquired a range of vehicles for the ruler and his bodyguard teams. Pride of place went to a new Rolls-Royce, the first in the Gulf. The ruler was incredibly proud of it but used it very rarely. There were no hard-topped roads in the country and like all rulers of Bedou tribes at the time he was a humble man, more used to a tent in the desert sands than the trappings of power.

The three of us – myself, Mick, a short, slight, volatile Scotsman whose dark looks suggested his roots were in the back streets of Naples not Dundee, and Apa Macham, Malayan for 'How's it going?', his nickname from the Borneo campaign – would be flying back to rejoin our squadron in a cold, dark and wintry Hereford the next morning. We had done our job and the ruler's safety was no longer in our hands.

To maintain our cover we were wearing the badges of rank of captain or lieutenant in the newly established local defence force and were dressed in its sand-coloured uniform and desert boots, a grey belt with a chrome buckle and a grey and white shamagh, held in place by a black haql, pinned with a shiny brass badge.

We exchanged small-talk as we waited but our nerves were obvious. We had handed over the whole of the running of the royal visit to the people we had trained and could no longer have any direct influence if an incident occurred.

We would have been much happier with a more direct involvement in protecting the two rulers during the visit. That had been vetoed by the British ambassador and the ruler himself, however. This was his show and his own people would protect him.

If they reacted to any incident as they had been trained, there would be no problems. If one person got it wrong, however, the outcome could be catastrophic for British interests in the region and terminal for our SAS careers.

I took another anxious glance around the crowd. Everyone appeared happy, out in force to support their new ruler, but I knew that there were strong undercurrents beneath the surface. The deposed ruler's half of the tribe remained angry that their time at the top table had come to an end and the patronage they had enjoyed for many hundreds of years had ceased.

There was also another incalculable factor: the presence in the country of a sizeable body of displaced Palestinians, uprooted from their homeland by the expansion of Israel. Their fury at becoming the gypsies of Arabia was further fuelled by their belief that the Bedou on whom they now depended were their inferiors. If their hunger for a Palestinian state could not be satisfied within the boundaries of Greater Israel, there seemed no reason why they would not try to stage a takeover of one of the Gulf sheikdoms.

The British mandate in Palestine had ended with the creation of the state of Israel and the Palestinians still regarded the British as the architects of their misery. They had already learned the value of terrorism in promoting their cause and were also well aware of the pro-British stance of the new ruler and his royal guest.

In the view of ourselves and the intelligence analysts there was a definite threat of an assassination attempt and the obvious time to carry it out would be when the two rulers were together.

Suddenly there was a stir away to our left like the ripple of a Mexican wave. The crowd started craning their necks to see what was happening and I could hear the sound of the approaching motorcade. It was travelling slower than we would have liked; the ruler had obviously insisted that his subjects got a good look at himself and his guest.

The crowd broke into spontaneous applause as I saw the lead car, a Mercedes, followed by the unmistakable shape of the Rolls-Royce. Even from a distance of 200 or 300 yards I could clearly see the two rulers in the back, both dressed in white and gold traditional robes, and looking the picture of Lords of the Desert as they waved to the crowds.

The bodyguards rode with them and in the lead and back-up cars, their eyes scanning the crowds for threats. Beneath their flowing robes was a hidden arsenal of weapons which could be drawn and used in split seconds.

When the lead car was fifty yards from where I was standing, a figure dashed out of the crowd towards the Rolls-Royce, holding something in his right hand. He moved too quickly for the guards in the leading car to react.

I froze. The man was almost within touching distance of the slow-moving Rolls-Royce. I was terrified that the driver would stop, but he reacted in exactly the way we had practised countless times in training and was accelerating even as the man stretched out his hand towards the door.

The car leaped forward. It hit the man, who rolled slowly along the flank of the Rolls-Royce. He fell to the ground as it picked up speed, still followed by the back-up car with the rest of the bodyguards.

We sprinted along the road with the police to arrest the man, who was picking himself up from the road, covered in dust. Between grimaces of pain, his face was wreathed in smiles. He held out a battered rose and said in Arabic, 'I was only trying to give our beloved ruler a flower.'

The author, Arabian Gulf, 1968

The re-formed SAS had built its reputation on its success in counter-insurgency operations. What guaranteed its long-term future, however, was counter-terrorism – both direct operations against terrorists and the training of bodyguards and elite forces in techniques to prevent or counter terrorist attacks.

One of the most notorious incidents of the twentieth century was the catalyst for the change. The assassination of John Fitzgerald Kennedy on 22 November 1963 sent shock waves around the world.

Foreign Office officials in London no doubt shared the general feelings of distress and revulsion at JFK's tragic fate, but it is the nature of career political officials to adapt swiftly to changed circumstances. They were shrewd enough to see in that one cataclysmic event an unprecedented opportunity to extend Britain's sphere of influence.

Help in suppressing internal conflicts or in the provision and training of bodyguards was the most direct route to influence with heads of state but until 1962 only the superpowers – the United States and the Soviet Union – provided bodyguard training for their friends and allies.

The rulers of British clients and allies were less well protected. Even the Queen did not have a bodyguard, just an unarmed police superintendent, who used to wander round with her instead.

The SAS had already formed a Bodyguard Training Team in 1962. It was another example of the Regiment seeing a niche and exploiting it. The SAS men pioneering BG – bodyguard – training started from scratch. They wrote the rules and began the evolutionary process that has led to the sophisticated BG training offered today.

The first to benefit was not the Queen, however. Prince Philip vetoed the use of bodyguards and was only persuaded to alter his stance when Prince Charles and Princess Anne entered their teens. The SAS BG team then trained the officers of the newly formed Royalty Protection Group and the Royal Military Police, who guarded the Queen and other members of the royal family. Both groups received their initial training at Hereford and the Royalty Protection Group still return regularly for retraining.

Whatever the attitude of our own rulers, there was no shortage of BG opportunities overseas. We aimed to provide a pool of highly trained SAS bodyguards to protect friendly heads of state, while preparing their own forces to take over the role.

BG training gave the SIS an extra lever in countries where Britain already had a strong presence, but access to states in rival spheres of influence was proving almost impossible to achieve until the events in Dallas threw the doors wide open.

John Kennedy's assassination not only traumatised America, it had a powerful effect on the heads of state of its allies too. Being surrounded by American-trained bodyguards when the American President had just been shot dead in front of his own helpless bodyguards suddenly did not seem the best idea in the world.

The Foreign Office could hardly believe its good fortune. The assassination had given it the means to maintain and extend British influence for a minimal outlay of expenditure and personnel. Showing a panache and entrepreneurial spirit that is almost entirely lacking in the Foreign Office today, it lost no time in sending the SIS to knock on the doors of those troubled heads of state, offering to send the SAS to train or retrain their bodyguards.

Not every head of state was given the opportunity, however. Those thought to be beyond British influence were excluded from the BG training programme. None of the leaders in

Aden, for example, then the main British base in the Middle East, was favoured with BG protection, since the SIS regarded them all as expendable.

In the context of a head of state, bodyguarding requires armed close protection, supplemented by uniformed help – royal guards, armed police, or whatever – and roaming external surveillance teams. The BG team's effectiveness hinges on the extensive use of surveillance of all known places that the principal might use, and requires complete vigilance and complete confidence in every one of the chosen bodyguards.

The other key requirement is to have the best available sources of intelligence and make the best use of the information gathered. In the normal course of events intelligence officers interpret the raw data and their analysis is invariably flawless – in retrospect. They'll always tell you after the event that they knew exactly what was going to happen, but their motivation to get it right when it counts – in advance – is insufficiently strong. Even if they get it wrong, they're not going to be among the dead bodies.

The only way to ensure that the maximum value is extracted from intelligence is for it to be evaluated and interpreted by the bodyguards themselves, because they're the ones who are going to carry the can. It's a fundamental change for military brains to assimilate, but it's the only way of ensuring that the bodyguards are proactive and pro-responsive, rather than passive targets for potential attackers.

The techniques taught by SAS BG trainers in the field were also based on the use of smaller numbers than the Americans. As in so much else, the American solution to a security problem was often to throw piles of money and men at it, but the phalanxes of security men surrounding President Kennedy had not been enough to protect him.

All the people involved in SAS BG training had very recent operational experience of attacking targets. It was put to good use when the poachers turned gamekeepers and began defending targets instead of attacking them.

Operational experience taught us that from an attacker's viewpoint even a large number of armed bodyguards was not an insuperable problem. Once we had established their numbers and routine through reconnaissance and surveillance we could pinpoint the weaknesses in their defences and exploit them to get at the principal. We were worried, however, if we couldn't identify the bodyguards in the group of people surrounding a target.

The Americans would surround their principal – their President or one of his senior officials – with squads of hatchet-faced, crew-cut, gumchewing Secret Service men, whom you could spot from miles away. Our aim and that of the men we trained was often to melt into the surroundings, carrying out 'offensive surveillance' to identify attackers before they could identify us.

An armed attack will always be preceded by a surveillance phase. If the BG team's counter-surveillance techniques are good enough, the principal becomes a near-impossible target. You can't provide close body protection using only the offensive surveillance system, but a really good BG team should never reach the stage where it's having to do so anyway. Its main job is to prevent an attack ever being mounted.

A cowboy in a Hollywood movie may be able to kill a man with every bullet he fires from his six-shooter, even at a range of half a mile, but real life is nothing like that. The true effective range of a pistol is only ten to twenty yards. The bullet travels a lot further, but actually to hit a target you need close range, great skill and plenty of practice. You need less skill with a Kalashnikov, but you still have to be within thirty to fifty yards, and you still need a lot of practice.

Attackers don't want to be at close range because it decreases their chances of getting away. That's why assassination attempts have usually been made using bombs. The attackers' second choice would be a longer-range weapon like a rocket-launcher – particularly against armoured cars.

They need to choose a specific place for an assault, however, at a specific time. If the BG team is using the correct anti-surveillance and counter-surveillance procedures, the attackers can only make their move at massive risk to themselves. Attackers give unconscious signals: hand and eye movements, and body language that distinguishes them in a crowd and can be identified by a vigilant bodyguard.

If the BG team is doing its job, the principal does not even need to wear ballistic protection – body armour – though it is usually carried nearby, just in case. One of the bodyguards of a head of state often carries an overcoat, whatever the weather. The coat contains the ballistic protection.

Ninety-nine per cent of the BG team's work is avoidance. While adopting stringent counter-surveillance and anti-surveillance procedures, the team also has to keep the principal out of danger zones and prevent him from adopting potentially dangerous routines, like always leaving his residence at the same time, by the same gate.

A top-class team has the ability to remove the head of state from much potential danger using nothing more than logic and risk management. If you are using the right surveillance and counter-surveillance procedures you can move the principal away from the places where he is normally seen, leave his state robes, his bulletproof limousine and his armed convoy at home, and send him out in a second-hand Datsun with a small group of bodyguards. Even if he's spotted by a member of the general public, they'll just do a double-take and say, 'That bloke's the image of President X. I wonder who he is.'

Public engagements break all the rules by which bodyguards would normally like to operate, for attackers know that their target will be at a predetermined place at a predetermined time. The use of decoy cars and doubles – which Saddam Hussein does extensively – can only deflect part of the threat, but in a public engagement you have access to the whole paraphernalia of the state, which makes the job relatively easy.

In the 1 per cent of cases where attackers launch an assault despite the risks to themselves – a suicide bomber, or the Egyptian troops who gunned down their own ruler, Anwar Sadat – the SAS-trained BG team relies on its speed of reaction and ability to shoot faster and more accurately than its opponents.

Training a team to that level of skill was by far the hardest part of BG training. It was definitely not a short-term, in-and-out job, even when working with people who were supposedly well trained. At one point we trained a BG team in a European country. The men were a mixture of serving policemen and civilian bodyguards. All were armed and when we questioned them about their proficiency with their weapons, their answers suggested that they already had a reasonable standard of training.

Just to be on the safe side, however, we carried out a simple test on the first day on the live firing range. The results were indescribable. The safest place for any attacker would have been in front of the target, for that was the only part of the range they seemed unable to hit.

Their incompetence was by no means unique. An assassination attempt on the Sultan of Oman, Sa'id bin Taimur, by his own bodyguards in 1966 had failed because such was the psychological pressure on them that even at a range of a few feet not one of them managed to hit the target.

From our SAS experience, we knew that training men to a high standard of skill with their weapons took two weeks' intensive training and 1,500 rounds. Building their confidence in their ability to use the weapons effectively in real emergencies could take years.

Even when the BG training was complete we would make periodic reassessment visits, for no matter how good the BG team, its efficiency will decrease over time. The only way to combat that deterioration is by reassessment, followed by retraining.

It's no disgrace; SAS troops are regularly rotated between

operational assignments and periods of retraining both in Hereford and overseas. This not only reduces the problem of 'burn-out' and resharpens their skills, it also gives other SAS men the chance to benefit from the returning troopers' knowledge and up-to-date experience of conditions in the current theatre of operations.

The money and manpower available to the US Secret Service is so huge that they can afford to rotate their people over a constant cycle of duty, leave and training. Other heads of state in less affluent countries may not have the resources to fund that level of retraining, but without at least some rotation the BG team will get stale, slack and careless and at that point their principal's life will be hanging by a thread.

The SAS approach was not only the best method of BG protection, it was also the most cost-effective. We believed that in most cases a potential threat could be countered most effectively by a small force of bodyguards, providing that they were well trained and well organised – which almost invariably meant that the BG team had to be administered by an SAS man.

With a Briton running his personal security, the country's ruler had a powerful incentive to maintain cordial relations with Britain, though of course no Foreign Office official would ever have been indelicate enough to remind him of that in such stark terms.

The testing ground for SAS BG training was Kenya, where we began training Jomo Kenyatta's bodyguards in 1962, a year before the assassination of Kennedy. The timing was fortuitous, but fortune favoured the brave, as it usually does.

Kenya was about to be granted independence, but even before it had assumed power Kenyatta's regime was threatened both by tribal feuding and by the presence of Somali insurgents infiltrating across the northern border.

With Foreign Office approval, the SAS sent a training team to Kenya in late 1962. It was one of a number of extremely covert operations the Regiment carried out on the East

African mainland around the same time, for we were also training the fledgling counterparts of the SIS in Kenya, Uganda and Tanganyika.

These operations were so sensitive that they had no official authorisation. The SAS men involved were posted from the UK to Aden and their onward destinations were never revealed.

The SAS team in Kenya had three aims: to train bodyguards to secure Jomo Kenyatta in power; to train the Kenyan General Service Unit – a euphemism for the secret police – in counter-terrorism and intelligence techniques; and to train a unit to operate in northern Kenya against the Somali insurgents.

The Kenyan operation involved a substantial investment of manpower and money, emphasising the importance that the Foreign Office placed on the country, which was seen as the model for other former British colonies in Africa.

Jomo Kenyatta had formerly been virulently anti-British, his hatred fuelled by a seven-year term of imprisonment during which, it was alleged, his gaolers had 'plied him with cases of brandy in the hope that he would drink himself to death'.[1]

Although the extent of his own involvement in the Mau Mau uprising was open to question, Kenyatta's Kikuyu tribe had been its source and the chief victim of the repression it provoked.

It was one of the 'last authoritarian excesses of British imperialism, complete with concentration camps and gallows',[2] in which over 1,000 Kikuyu were hanged, 430 prisoners were shot 'while trying to escape' and 150,000 were imprisoned in concentration camps.[3]

Only three years before independence Jomo Kenyatta was still being described by the governor of Kenya as 'the African leader to darkness and death'.[4] In turning to Britain for help as his country moved towards independence, Kenyatta showed a capacity for forgiveness – or a calculated pragmatism – that would have been beyond many a professedly more sophisticated British politician.

The SAS-trained bodyguards who helped to keep him in power also greatly increased his affection for Britain. He survived the turbulent times that saw many other African heads of state toppled, and held power for many years before dying of natural causes.

The benefits to Britain were not confined to improved relations and trade with Kenya. The SIS even used the Kenyan BG training as a reference when they were trying to sell other jobs. They had a good product and a very effective sales pitch to foreign rulers: 'We can look after you better than the Americans. They couldn't even protect their own President. We trained the presidential bodyguard in Kenya and, unlike Kennedy, Jomo Kenyatta is still alive and in power.'

The sales drive was highly successful. Over the next few years we trained bodyguards and elite troops for many other heads of state.

Britain sometimes created the heads of state as well as protecting them and BG training was used to particular effect in the Middle East, where the SIS was playing the great game of making and breaking rulers. In the process it was disregarding history and traditions going back many thousands of years to mould the Gulf sheikdoms into states acceptable to Britain.

Sultan Qaboos in Oman was protected by an SAS bodyguard after the coup which removed his ailing father, Sultan Sa'id bin Taimur. A British-inspired coup also deposed the feudal Sheik of Abu Dhabi, who had greeted the first discoveries of oil in this territory with a demand to be paid his royalties in Indian rupees, the currency used in most of the Gulf states at the time.

His fortune was stored in his tent and as the mound of bales of rupees grew larger rats began to eat their way through his fortune. When the amount stored in his tent had risen to over £1 million, he was toppled and replaced by his brother,

Sheik Zaid, who promised to use the money to build roads, hospitals and schools.

The SAS was immediately sent in to train a group of local forces as bodyguards for the new sheik, who has remained a loyal British ally ever since.

BG training was almost always done in-country and not in the UK. The policy preserved the security of the Regiment's Hereford HQ and also enabled the SAS BG trainers to assess local conditions.

The strict rule was only broken on three occasions, each time reflecting the importance the FO attached to the regime in question. The first foreign troops ever to be trained in Hereford were the Royal Guard from Abu Dhabi in late 1969.

There was no military necessity for their visit – we had already trained them in Abu Dhabi – but it was a political gesture to the ruler, demonstrating the high priority that the Foreign Office put on relations with his regime.

In 1970 the Shah of Iran's bodyguard became the second foreign group to visit Hereford. The shah had been an American client ever since the CIA-backed coup that had restored him to the peacock throne, but his relationship with his prime ally was deteriorating. The American obsession with Vietnam left them little time for distractions in the Middle East, even though the shah was only able to maintain a precarious hold on his country by the use of an iron fist.

The Foreign Office saw the chance to exploit his increasing impatience with the Americans by inviting his bodyguards to Hereford, and the shah undoubtedly had his own political agenda for the visit. It sent a strong message to the US: 'If you don't start paying more attention, the British will get my arms business.'

If the message was received, it was ignored, and not long after the shah's bodyguards returned from Hereford, Vickers made a big defence sale to the Iranian armed forces. There was no way of proving that the two events were related, of course, but in the absence of any evidence to the contrary, it remains a reasonable supposition.

Soon afterwards, a group of eight officers from King Hussein's Jordanian Royal Guards came to Hereford. The Royal Guards were and probably still are by some distance the best-trained and best-motivated bodyguards in the Middle East, even including the Israelis.

I was involved in their eight-week training course, concentrating on the high-risk scenarios that King Hussein always faced in his volatile kingdom. The day after they returned to Jordan there was a terrorist attack on the king.

As his convoy was driving near Amman, it was ambushed by thirty-two Palestinians armed with AK47s. They opened up on the convoy, peppering the king's car and killing several of the escort.

One of the Royal Guards we had trained, a captain, was commanding the escort, which meant he travelled in the front passenger seat of the king's car. He immediately jumped into the back seat, shielded the king with his body and pushed him out of the car into a ditch at the side of the road.

The two men then engaged in their own private fight as the king tried to stand up and return fire at the terrorists with his pistol. The king was a brave man, but the captain was reacting in the way he had been trained at Hereford. His job was to keep the king in cover and protect him with his body while the rest of the escort dealt with the attackers.

The struggle went on for several minutes. Then reinforcements arrived and the surviving Palestinians fled. When the captain finally allowed him to stand, the king cashiered him on the spot. He had no understanding of the Royal Guards' training; all he knew was that the captain had made him look a coward, hiding in a ditch while his escort were being killed and wounded.

The officer accepted his fate, went back to the barracks and packed his kit, but the next day he received a summons to the palace in Amman. King Hussein was anything but a fool and, having calmed down, he realised that he owed the man his life. The cashiering of the captain was immediately revoked and, instead, he was promoted.

With the three exceptions of Abu Dhabi, Iran and Jordan, all other BG training jobs were done in the relevant country. Such was the demand that within a very short time the Regiment had to form a Bodyguard Cell in Hereford to train additional SAS BG instructors.

The number of potential customers was virtually limitless, for the accelerating process of decolonisation by the remaining European imperial powers – Britain, France, Belgium and, eventually, Portugal – created an avalanche of new states with vulnerable regimes.

Britain's long-running Conservative administration had been a reluctant convert to decolonisation, for the dreams of empire remained alive in some sections of the Conservative Party, if often cloaked under suitable camouflage.

'The imperialist idea itself survived under altruistic guises proper to a world where the United Nations kept a sharper eye on overt exhibitions of colonial power, and where the emergence of the Cold War enabled many things once done in the name of plain imperial defence to be attributed to a desire to preserve global freedom.'[5]

It took the cold wind from Suez to blow away most of those lingering imperial pretensions, just as the Macmillan government's review of future policy options was confirming the shrinking value to Britain of the colonies.

The end of the Korean War had signalled the end of the world bull market in commodity prices. British colonies that had been running surpluses in their trade with the United States – and thereby helping to ease the mother country's financial problems – started the long slide into deficit. As they did so, their value to Britain diminished accordingly.

The policy of milking the empire while Britain's domestic economy revived had failed. Lacking the ability to fund significant economic development in the colonies, Britain could only offer political concessions instead – no guns, no butter, just independence.

A Conservative policy statement had talked of steering nations along 'the road to self-government within the framework of the British Empire' – something of a contradiction in terms. Speaking about Cyprus in 1954, junior minister Henry Hopkinson back-tracked even on that vague promissory note, warning that 'Certain territories in the Commonwealth ... can never expect to be fully independent.'

Yet Hopkinson's speech was almost the last time that the supreme Conservative article of faith – the preservation of the empire – would be publicly expressed.

Macmillan had been no evangelist for self-determination in the colonies, but he was shrewd and pragmatic enough to see that the cost in human and economic terms of trying to hold back nationalism in Africa – the last bastion of empire – was now too high for Britain to meet.

Attempts were still made to channel the desire for independence in ways acceptable to Britain. With varying degrees of subtlety, the message was given to newly independent and soon-to-be-independent nations that it was not in their financial interest to antagonise the source of funding for much of their development programmes.

Efforts to hold back independence movements by force of arms – of which Suez was the prime example – also continued throughout the rest of the 1950s, but by the end of the decade all but a handful of Monday Club right-wingers were, like Macmillan, ready to acquiesce in the final dissolution of the empire.

At the same time, Macmillan was strengthening British links to Europe. Britain was not one of the six founder-members of the European Economic Community (EEC), set up by the Treaty of Rome in 1957, but it joined the European Free Trade Association (EFTA) at its inception two years later.

Macmillan then announced in 1961 that Britain would apply for EEC membership. Without bothering to consult his other European partners, French President Charles de Gaulle rejected the first British application, largely on the basis that the British withdrawal at Suez had demonstrated that it was nothing but an American client state and therefore a potentially disruptive influence inside the community.

He was also suspicious of Britain's continuing links with its former colonies, calling Britain 'insular, maritime, bound by its history, its political, financial and trading systems to many and distant countries'.

Commonwealth members knew that neither Britain's history nor de Gaulle's opposition would change the direction of British policy, however; the economic special relationship with the Commonwealth was clearly coming to an end.

That economic blow was immediately followed by a political one, the 1962 abandonment of 'common citizenship', which, though pandering to the anti-immigrant vote at home, was also widely seen as Conservative retaliation for bad – i.e. independent – behaviour by the former colonies.

The leaders of the New Commonwealth showed few signs of repentance, and no amount of bad behaviour could now reverse the headlong process of decolonisation.

Macmillan had remarked in 1942 that the colonies were 'four or five centuries' behind Britain. 'Our job is to hustle them across this great interval of time as rapidly as we can.'[6] Less than twenty years later he had decided that they had all caught up enough to be set free.

It had taken India twenty-eight years from the Government of India Act in 1919 to achieve independence. Most of those wishing to follow in India's footsteps had to fight, or tolerate a period of transition that might stretch to a decade and usually involved the imprisonment of those – such as Nkrumah and Kenyatta – who would ultimately become their leaders.

Now all that was over. The process of separation was conducted with almost indecent haste. A change of government in 1964 made no difference. As the new Secretary of State for

Colonial Affairs, Anthony Greenwood, cheerfully admitted, his main aim was 'to do myself out of a job'. By 1966 he had succeeded.

Having once been damned by the US for the slow pace of independence for the colonies, Britain was now damned again for the speed of dissolution of the empire. It was then damned a third time if the newly independent colonies took a neutral or anti-Western line. Praised by the US for its anti-Communist operations in Malaya, Britain now stood accused of the ultimate crime of 'losing' several of its other former colonies to Communism.

Arab, Asian and African leaders were often too suspicious of Western attempts to prolong colonialism and too aware of racial discrimination in Western countries to join the anti-Soviet front that the US was constructing. But the belief, expressed most strongly by India, that joining military alliances merely increased the chances of war in their own regions did not play well in Washington, which had no time for shades of grey in its crusade against Communism.

Despite the best intentions, many of the new states – especially in Africa – were chronically unstable. For that the European powers, and the British in particular, had to shoulder most of the blame. Boundaries usually based on the competing claims of the imperial powers and drawn without reference to ethnic, cultural or sometimes even geographic factors could have been redrawn before independence.

Instead the chance was missed. The subsequent explosion in numbers of small, independent states, with illogical boundaries, barely formed institutions, and a population often composed of warring tribal factions, was a recipe for disaster.

After the often bloody struggles for independence, lingering ethnic and tribal differences created a second wave of conflict. The Congo, granted independence by Belgium in July 1960, was immediately involved in a vicious war with the secessionist state of Katanga. Biafra's attempts to secede from the Nigerian federation resulted in an even more bloody struggle. The upheavals in Zaire, Rwanda and Burundi continue to the present day.

In Britain's haste to be gone from its remaining colonies the original attempts to implant British-style democratic institutions were rushed, botched or abandoned altogether. The one institution that usually survived the transition to independence undamaged was the British-trained army, and as a result the armed forces were often the only bodies that were sufficiently organised to run the new states.

Prior to the First World War, no country outside Latin America had been under military rule.[7] There were times in the 1960s and 1970s when it seemed that almost no country in Africa was not.

Even where the army did not assume control, one-party regimes were almost guaranteed by the country's former colonial status, in which opposition to the imperial power had been the major, and often the only, issue.

The absence of any meaningful democratic channel for opposition to the new regimes only made instability, insurgency and civil war more inevitable. Governments maintaining the most fragile hold on their turbulent countries were an open invitation to armed intervention.

All-out nuclear warfare between the Soviet Union and the United States was too terrifying a prospect for all but a handful of zealots on both sides to contemplate. Insurgency or conventional war between their client states became the preferred option.

Except in their euphemistic role of 'military advisers', American and Soviet forces were only directly involved in a handful of Cold War conflicts, notably Korea, Vietnam and Afghanistan. Instead, the superpowers slugged it out by proxy. They poured a torrent of arms into the Third World, fomenting insurrections, engineering coups and ensuring that any splinter group in any country would be certain of arms and support from one side or the other.

Throughout the 1960s and 1970s there was scarcely a Third World region that was at peace, as conflicts raged across the globe. The Sino-Indian War of 1962 was overseen by the UK with the aid of photo-reconnaissance flights from Bahrain. There were also wars between India and Pakistan in 1965 and 1971, the endless and escalating conflicts in South-East Asia and the regular volcanic explosions of hostilities in the Middle East.

There were internal wars in Central and South America as a succession of US-backed military regimes suppressed every trace of dissent in their own countries, but the most sustained and wholesale epidemic of violence was that destroying every hope of peace and prosperity in the newly independent continent of Africa. There was no country anywhere in the entire continent that was not scarred by some form of insurgency, military coup, war or civil war.

The Commonwealth Conference in Lagos in early 1966, intended as a triumphant affirmation of the new Africa, was barely over before the revolt of the Nigerian army. Premiers of the north and west regions were murdered and the Prime Minister of the federation was kidnapped and later found dead. Less than a month later President Nkrumah of Ghana was deposed by a coup on 24 February while he was on a visit to Peking.

Anxious African rulers knew that even a small handful of armed men could sometimes be enough to overthrow their fragile governments. By the same token, however, an equally small number of armed men could prevent or reverse it. The SAS, both through our personal involvement and through the bodyguards and special forces we trained, offered a way to lessen the risks for those rulers.

Countries anxious to refuse the poisoned chalice of help from either the US or the USSR, and the ensuing threat of destabilisation and overthrow by the rival camp, increasingly sought British help. Once the arch-imperialist ogre, Britain was now seen as much the lesser of the available evils. As instability and insurgency threatened more and more regimes, the queue for SAS BG training grew longer and longer.

Where BG training alone was insufficient to contain the threat, SAS troops took direct action, acting alone or leading in infantry along previously surveyed infiltration routes to foil coup attempts or put down insurrections.

In 1964 alone, Britain was forced to intervene to protect the governments of Kenya, Uganda and Tanzania in turn, after each was threatened by an army mutiny.

There was one African country where the SAS refused to become involved, however. As a result, a revolt that the Regiment might have nipped in the bud grew into a crisis that all but destroyed the Commonwealth.

For the first dozen years of its existence, the Commonwealth had meandered along like some gentlemen's club. The membership rules had been relaxed sufficiently for one or two of the more decent types of native to be admitted, but it remained an organisation where the rulers of Britain and the white dominions could get together and enjoy a few chotah pegs while reminiscing about the good old days.

The steady increase in independent Asian and African members changed all that. By 1960 the white nations' Commonwealth majority had been ended. From now on it would dance to a very different tune.

British economic and strategic relations with the white dominions had undergone a similar change. Canada, Australia and New Zealand increasingly looked to the USA as their principal military ally and to the US and the Pacific for their export markets.

British companies retained substantial investments in South Africa and Rhodesia but neither that, nor the emotive arguments about 'kith and kin' deployed by the white supremacists among the white settlers of Kenya and Southern Rhodesia and their apologists on the right wing of the Conservative Party, could obscure the fact that black Africa was assuming a far greater significance in Britain's political and economic calculations.

Harold Macmillan made the first public acknowledgement of the new realities in his 'winds of change' speech in 1960 – recycling a phrase from a speech by Pandit Nehru in 1947[8] – but it was only the public confirmation of a policy decision that had already been made.

He chose the hostile forum of the South African parliament in Cape Town to signal the sea-change in his own and his country's attitude to African nationalism. His speech came on 3 February 1960 at the end of a month-long tour of Africa. Significantly, he was the first serving British Prime Minister ever to visit the continent that Britain had dominated.

'The most striking of all the impressions I have formed ... is of the strength of this African national consciousness. In different places it may take different forms, but it is happening everywhere. The wind of change is blowing through the continent. Whether we like it or not this ... is a political fact.'

The South African government emphatically did not like the icy blast but white opinion was no longer the dominant factor in the Commonwealth. Open conflict broke out between South Africa and the New Commonwealth members.

The final rift came in 1961 – the year after the Sharpeville massacre – when South Africa became a republic. By the rules of the Commonwealth it had to reapply for membership. Canada and the Afro-Asian members united against it, and Britain too made it clear that in the event of a dispute, its sympathies – and its commercial interests – lay in supporting black Africa, not white South Africa.

When it realised which way the winds of change were blowing, South Africa withdrew its application and retreated into its apartheid laager. It was followed there two years later by Rhodesia, provoking a crisis that pushed the Commonwealth to the brink.

Under British rule, minorities had been freed from:

> the necessity of bringing their attitudes and ambitions
> into line with their own real numerical strength; freed,
> that is, from the need to accommodate, adjust and
> compromise . . . In Ireland, in Palestine and in Rhodesia
> there were settler communities (Protestant, Jewish,
> European) which only existed as dominant races
> because of Britain's artificial suspension of the natural
> course of events . . . In this way, at least three of the
> world's main trouble spots in the 1970s could be
> directly debited to the account of the British empire: to
> its inevitable interference with the natural evolution of
> smaller, weaker countries.[9]

Rhodesia – Southern Rhodesia, as it had been called under
imperial rule – had, with Northern Rhodesia and Nyasaland,
been part of the Central African Federation, set up in 1953 as
part of a Colonial Office vogue for federations of colonies.
It made some economic sense, but few blacks shared the
patronising opinion expressed by the Colonial Secretary in
1957: 'It is good for you, and you must accept it.'[10]

The federation was doomed to failure, perceived by the
black majority as a further devious attempt to prolong
imperialism by other means. 'Federation means the domination of Southern Rhodesia; the domination of Southern
Rhodesia means the domination of the settler; the domination of the settler means the perpetuation of racial
inferiority.'[11]

Unrest in Nyasaland was so great that policing it was
absorbing one sixth of the entire colonial budget and the
counter-measures used meant that 'Nyasaland has become,
doubtless only temporarily, a police state.'[12]

The federation was finally dissolved on the last day of 1963;
Nyasaland became independent as Malawi and Northern
Rhodesia as Zambia. The status of the remaining part of the

federation, which kept the name of Rhodesia, proved far more difficult to resolve.

The difference came down to one thing: the size of the white minority. Southern Rhodesia's 210,000 whites were a very substantial bloc, even though their numbers were dwarfed by the population of over four million blacks.

Nyasaland and Northern Rhodesia both had negligible populations of white settlers. That did not mean that their views were in general any less extreme than their peers' in Southern Rhodesia, but it did ensure that they were not in a position to give them political effect.

One settler summed up the difference. 'I had a friend from Northern Rhodesia down here the other day, who said what a relief it was to see a really good flogging again. He told me: "You known up in Northern Rhodesia, if you raise your hand against one of these chaps, he drags you off to the police station." '[13]

There was no danger of that happening in Southern Rhodesia, as long as the white minority 'made their own laws, were judged in their own courts ... mobilised their own defence forces, were under the jurisdiction of their own police',[14] just as they had since 1923. They had too much to give up, for they enjoyed a standard of living that was luxurious even by normal colonial standards; only Beverly Hills had more private swimming pools than Salisbury.

Before agreeing to grant Rhodesian independence, the Conservative government in Britain insisted on adherence to the 'Five Principles'. These required 'unimpeded progress' towards majority rule, an immediate improvement in the political status of Africans, progress towards the ending of racial discrimination and an undertaking that there would be no 'retrogressive amendment' of the constitution after independence. The fifth principle gave the British government the right to satisfy itself that the constitutional basis for independence was acceptable to the whole people.

The incoming Labour government also adopted the Five

Principles, and later added a sixth, requiring that 'regardless of race', there should be no oppression of the majority by the minority, or vice versa. There was never the slightest chance that the white Rhodesians would accept any, let alone all, of them without a fight.

Ian Smith's newly formed Rhodesian Front had their own principles to uphold. The constitution they proposed offered an insultingly small place for representatives of the black majority in a white-dominated parliament. There were vague promises of further advancement for blacks at some unspecified time in the future.

It was nowhere near enough to satisfy Britain, but it was the message Smith's white electorate wanted to hear. The Rhodesian Front won all fifty seats reserved for whites in the May 1965 general election; black representation was limited to fifteen seats.

Harold Wilson returned from fruitless talks in Salisbury at the end of October 1965 warning that 'There should be no delusions in Rhodesia about the ability and determination of the British government to deal with the utmost firmness with an act of rebellion.'[15]

On 11 November 1965 Smith called his bluff with a Unilateral Declaration of Independence – UDI – 'echoing in every line the American Declaration of Independence in 1776'.[16] It was an appropriate echo, for UDI was the first revolt by white settlers against the imperial power since the American Revolution.

Black African leaders immediately began pressing Wilson for armed intervention to bring the settlers to heel. His first reaction was to use the SAS and 39 Brigade, based in Aden, to put down the illegal regime. What stopped him was a near-mutiny in the Regiment.

D Squadron were given air photography of dropping zones, lying-up points and targets in Rhodesia, but when we asked the location we were told that it was not Rhodesia, but somewhere else in Africa. We had already realised that there was a strong possibility of being sent there and the attempt to pull the wool over our eyes was strongly resented.

The hostile response led to a highly secret poll being conducted among the SAS troopers based in Aden. The question was simple: 'If the order to go to Rhodesia is given, would you be willing to fight?'

A substantial majority said, 'No.'

They were well aware that a refusal to obey a direct order would have been treated as mutiny and made it clear that if the order was given, they would go. They made it equally clear that in those circumstances they would not fight, but would lie up in the bush, taking no part in hostilities.

There may well have been instances of racism elsewhere in the British army, but there was no sympathy for the policies of the Rhodesian regime within the SAS. Hearts and minds work in the jungles of Malaya and Borneo had forged a strong respect among SAS men for the culture and survival skills of indigenous tribes; even if the relationships were driven by military necessity, genuine friendships were formed none the less.

The gruelling process of Selection also helped to eliminate any notions of racial superiority in SAS men. What was important was not that you were black or white, but that you had passed Selection and were a badged SAS man. Maori soldiers with the New Zealand SAS had proved themselves to be some of the finest trackers and jungle fighters around and the Fijian contingent were among the most respected and highly valued troopers in the Regiment.

What made Rhodesia different was that a squadron of Rhodesians, C Squadron, had fought alongside the SAS in Malaya. Although they had not taken part in the subsequent campaigns in the Jebel Akhdar and Borneo, the Rhodesians had recently held a joint exercise in Aden with their British counterparts, and remained very much a part of the Regiment's extended family.

UDI forced both sides to sever their links, but having

fought with them as friends and colleagues, no British SAS man could stomach the thought of fighting against them as enemies.

Our refusal to go not only deprived Harold Wilson of his most potent weapon, but also carried the threat of sparking a wider revolt among British troops. Such was the regard for the SAS among the rest of the army by this time that the knowledge that we had refused to fight in Rhodesia would have also made 39 Brigade's participation very questionable.

Wilson eventually ruled out the use of force altogether, but his public rejection of the military option in favour of economic sanctions brought the Commonwealth close to implosion.

Ghana and Tanzania broke off diplomatic relations and many other black African states only remained within the Commonwealth because it gave them a platform for relentless criticism of the British failure to curb Rhodesia. A Zambian diplomat's description of Britain as a 'toothless bulldog' was one of the lesser insults hurled in its direction.

Black suspicions that a racist heart was beating beneath Britain's urbane exterior were fuelled by the British financial stake in apartheid: 58 per cent of all foreign investment in South Africa by 1970 was in sterling.[17] The Heath government's resumption of arms sales to South Africa in the following year merely seemed further confirmation.

Wilson had tried to justify his non-interventionist policy at a stormy Commonwealth Conference in Lagos. 'It was all very well to speak of military intervention and of gunboat diplomacy, but this was not the nineteenth century and Rhodesia is a land-locked state.'[18]

His explanation found no favour among his hostile audience, whose anger was heightened by the realisation that, despite its forty-nine members, comprising one-quarter of the world's population, the Commonwealth was impotent to bring to heel a tiny rump of embattled white settlers.

The unrest of African leaders over Rhodesia was also

heightened by their fears of the instability of their own regimes, in which many saw – or thought they saw – the hand of Western governments.

Fears of another Suez fiasco may have helped to stay Wilson's hand, but his rejection of armed intervention also reflected British impotence without the rapier thrust that only the SAS could provide. He was afraid of being sucked into another prolonged colonial war and was also very aware of the risks of creating rifts in opinion at home and provoking a wider conflict if South Africa intervened on Rhodesia's side.

His analysis was flawed, however, and he and his advisers ignored Smith's own real doubts about the willingness of Rhodesian forces to fight against British troops, and forgot the lessons that Britain had learned in Malaya and Borneo.

SAS experience in those conflicts had shown that insurrections by small, unrepresentative sections of the population, particularly when largely confined to one minority ethnic grouping, could be contained and defeated, even when an outside military power became involved. Whether victory could also be achieved without the Regiment that had played the critical part in those two campaigns was another question.

Had the SAS gone in, it would not have been to wage open warfare. Our ability to pinpoint and destroy key strategic targets, particularly the railroad, would have deprived the Smith regime of its main sources of revenue very quickly and brought it to its knees. The Rhodesian armed forces were among the best in Africa, but they would have been reduced to chasing very small raiding parties of SAS, which they might well never have found.

Wilson's claim in January 1966 that the use of economic sanctions without military force might bring the rebellion to an end 'in a matter of weeks rather than months' was to haunt him for the rest of his career.

Given that three of Rhodesia's neighbours, South Africa and the Portuguese colonies of Mozambique and Angola, were openly sympathetic to Smith's regime, sanctions were unenforceable. Even the United States, which still had its own potent problems over segregation, breached sanctions by refusing to stop imports of Rhodesian chrome.

The clamour from the New Commonwealth for Britain to do something, anything, to overthrow Smith's regime did not slacken, but it was to be twelve years before Rhodesia was brought to heel. The instrument of its downfall was not sanctions, but armed intervention, in which Britain played no part.

The guerrilla forces of Robert Mugabe's ZANU and Joshua Nkomo's ZIPRA, operating from within Rhodesia and from across the borders of Zambia and, after 1975, Mozambique, wore down Smith's forces and eroded his regime's economic base; by 1979 the cost of fighting the civil war was absorbing half of Rhodesia's GDP.

The rise and fall of Smith's fortunes can be tracked from the movement of white settlers. Between 1967 and 1973, when the regime thrived despite Wilson's bluster and his attempts to enforce sanctions, 39,000 new white immigrants arrived in Rhodesia. It is safe to assume that none was going there to campaign for black majority rule.

Between 1977 and 1980, when the deteriorating military situation finally forced the Rhodesian Front to come to terms with the black majority, 48,000 whites left the country.[19]

Among the new white immigrants in the early years were a number of former SAS soldiers, now working as mercenaries. They were at the heart of the very aggressive cross-border raids carried out into guerrilla refuges in neighbouring countries during Rhodesia's long civil war. After the Smith regime was finally toppled, they moved on to South Africa and carried out similar operations against ANC guerrillas from there.[20]

Smith's attempts to buy himself more time by making a deal in 1978 with 'moderate blacks' – supporters of ZANU and ZIPRA chose another term for them – were largely unsuccessful. The Lancaster House Agreement brokered by the new British Prime Minister, Margaret Thatcher, ended the fighting.

The subsequent election on 19 April 1980 was the last major act of British decolonisation. To Margaret Thatcher's horror, it resulted in an emphatic victory for Robert Mugabe's ZANU party, which has held power ever since.

The civil war in Rhodesia cost over 20,000 lives. It might have been averted by a rapid intervention by the SAS immediately after UDI, when many members of the Rhodesian administration and security services were uncertain whether their loyalties lay with the crown or a regime whose actions were 'illegal, probably treasonable and unrecognised internationally'.[21]

The refusal of SAS men to fight against their own comrades forced the Wilson government to reject armed intervention. By contrast, a coup in Uganda at almost the same time was put down immediately.

Another coup attempt in Tanzania was put down by the Royal Marines. Such was the secrecy of the operation that the marines were told that they were going on an exercise.

As a result they did what they did on every exercise and loaded their weapons with blank ammunition. Had a firefight broken out, this could have presented them with a considerable problem but, being British, they decided to bluff it out. In the event their mere presence was enough to frighten the rebels into surrendering.

7

ADEN
1964–67

The late afternoon shadows were lengthening as the Wessex helicopter skimmed over the floor of the wadi. As the downwash from the rotors began to stir dust-devils from the sand beneath us, the pilot eased the helicopter a few feet higher.

The distinctive smell of guns, dust and heat permeated the bare metal interior of the Wessex, where nine of us squatted on our haunches, the full complement of a troop that should have been sixteen strong.

We were tired after working up to the operation all day, co-ordinating artillery and air support and practising drills with the fighter ground-attack aircraft. There had been no time for rest. As soon as the training was finished, we were into the helicopter and away, but as we approached our landing zone, the tiredness was forgotten and the adrenalin began to flow.

We were well aware of the enemy's capabilities. They were well armed and very mobile, often covering more than 50,000 yards in a day. They always moved by day and attacked at night and were fearless fighters, helped by their intake of qat, the local narcotic.

We knew from previous contacts that when the enemy moved the front man carried a rocket-launcher. Immediately he suspected the presence of British troops he would loose off a rocket in their direction.

Our bergens were loaded for a ten-day operation and were almost impossible to lift. We had to carry all our own water; going down into the villages to collect it from a well was not an option. We had five gallons of water each, four pints a day. Despite the intense heat, it would have to do; it was the maximum we could carry.

The troop had two Bren guns and each man was carrying four magazines for each one. We had Claymore mines and our personal weapons, a mixture of self-loading rifles and AR15 American Armalites. We also had medical kits in case we took casualties, binoculars and telescopes for daylight observation and flares for illuminating targets during night ambushes.

There were command radios, large sets enabling us to speak directly to base. We had further sets to control artillery, small VHF radios for controlling fighter ground-attacks, fluorescent panels and smoke grenades so they could identify our own positions.

We had a co-ordinated fire plan involving 155mm guns with a twelve-mile range, and in anything more than the briefest contact with the enemy, the army would lift in 105mm artillery pieces with a range of 12,000 yards. The primary support was the RAF Hunters, however, a flying fire-support system operating from Khormaksar airfield.

In this campaign, war was a twenty-four-hour, round-the-clock business. The operation would mean ten days of little sleep and constant adrenalin-buzzing, nerve-jangling alertness. We were going in as part of a deception using the collection of a group of Federal Regular Army troops as cover for our own insertion. Past experience had taught us that when government troops pulled out, the enemy very quickly moved in to reassert their influence.

The howl of the engines dropped and the thudding beat of the rotors changed in pitch as the helicopter slowed. Trying not to raise too much dust, we threw out our bergens and jumped after them in a rolling drop-off as the Wessex flew three or four feet above the ground.

As the last man cleared the door, the helicopter soared upwards. There was no time to worry if we had been spotted by the rebels on the mountain plateau high above us. Even though the sun was sinking towards the horizon, fierce heat was still baking the ground.

We hid our bergens among the rocks and then made a dash for the top of the nearest ridge, the favourite avenues of movement for the local Arabs.

We put together a quick linear ambush. The Ancient Brit took the uphill side, armed with the Bren gun. As the Arabist who would challenge anyone coming down the ridge, I was next to him. The rest of the troop spread out below us.

I lay in the cover of a large rock, gasping for breath from the exertion of the climb up the ridge. As soon as it was dark enough to move we would be marching all night, staggering under the weight of our bergens, and then scaling a steep mountain. For the next ten days we would repeat the climb before daybreak every morning, then move down from it at night to ambush the enemy.

I was staring blankly into space, marshalling my thoughts, when I heard the Ancient Brit mutter, 'I don't believe it.'

I rolled on to my stomach, grabbed my Armalite and glanced past him. Two Arabs were coming down the ridge. The front one carried a rocket-launcher over his right shoulder, the other, a few yards behind him, held an AK47. Local tribesmen usually carried the old Lee Enfield Number 4 rifle. I was 99 per cent certain that these were enemy.

I threw a couple of pebbles to alert the rest of the troop but they had already switched on.

I heard the Brit's faint whisper. 'When they get close enough, challenge them.'

When they were only six or seven yards from me, I shouted in Arabic, 'Halt. Raise your hands or we'll fire.'

Out of the corner of my eye I saw the one with the rocket-launcher immediately spin half-left. The knuckles of his trigger finger started to whiten, but before he could fire there were a couple of taps from the Bren gun and he collapsed in a heap.

The other man tried to leap from the track but again the Bren gun chattered. The impacts hurled him backwards. He sprawled over the rocks and lay still.

The only person who had fired was the Ancient Brit. As the echoes from the last burst faded away, he said quietly, 'That was for Robin, you bastards.'

He sat motionless for a moment, his arms folded across his barrel chest, the wind ruffling his mane of blond hair.

He had been on an infamous patrol in the Radfan when his troop were cut off. They had been subjected to a horrific, day-long attack and two of his friends had been killed. The rest of the patrol escaped, leaving the men's bodies behind. The enemy had cut off their heads, which were subsequently taken to a town in North Yemen and paraded around the streets. This was the Ancient Brit's revenge.

As soon as the Arabs went down, the troop went into all-round defence. Willy contacted the base and we alerted the artillery in case there was a follow-up. The status of the Hunter jet-fighters at Khormaksar was also heightened to immediate alert as we awaited any reaction. The enemy usually fought very hard for the bodies of their comrades.

After thirty minutes, just before dark fell, the Boss at HQ decided to pull us out. The Wessex that had dropped us off came back for us. We threw in our kit, the two bodies and their weapons and then flew back in triumph to Habilayn, the up-country army headquarters.

We were greeted like heroes. The base had been attacked innumerable times without coming to grips with the enemy, so the sight of us returning with two bodies sent the OC into ecstasies. He commandeered a Sergeants' Mess, laid on free beer and promised us that instead of a ten-day operation in the hills we would have ten days' rest and recuperation in Aden Town.

We got heavily into the drink and some time during the evening an argument developed between the officer commanding the squadron and a couple of the troopers. As it rapidly escalated into a shouting match, everyone not involved moved away. Before long punches were being thrown. By this time I was standing near the entrance to the Mess, leaning against the bar. The orderly sergeant in charge of the Mess tapped me on the shoulder. 'If you lot don't stop fighting I'm going to get your OC to sort this out.'

'You'd better go and get him then, he's the one taking the hammering.'

The author, Radfan, Aden Protectorate, 1965

Aden – now Yemen – had once been little more than a coaling station on the empire route to India. It had been acquired in 1839 as a by-product of the East India Company's attempts to stop pirates based there from raiding its ships. Governed by the Indian administration, Aden had grown into a major trading port, a natural calling point for all sea traffic between Europe and the Far East.

Every nationality under the sun seemed to be represented there, but it was far from a pleasant place to live. Aden itself was eighty square miles of bare rock cooked by a sweltering, humid climate. Around it stretched a barren hinterland of over 100,000 square miles of desert, acquired during the 1920s and 1930s, the last territories to be added to the British Empire.

This ramshackle grouping of twenty-five sultanates, sheikdoms and emirates was formerly divided into the Eastern and Western Protectorates of Aden. Between 1959 and 1963 the Western Protectorate and the Crown Colony of Aden were cobbled together as the Federation of South Arabia in an attempt to bolster the port of Aden in its strategic position at the entrance to the Red Sea.

It had become the focus of British civilian and military administration for the Arabian peninsula and East Africa. With Britain's previous regional headquarters at Suez, Cyprus and Kenya now either unavailable or unsuitable, Aden was also the centre of Colonial Office administration and the headquarters of Middle East Command for the army, navy and Royal Air Force.

As recently as 1960 a substantial investment in new barracks, docks and airstrips had been authorised, in the belief that Britain would be in Aden for at least another twenty-five years.[1] Within three years, unrest and insurgency in Aden made that scenario look wildly unrealistic.

It had been a trouble spot for decades. The RAF had dropped sixty-six tons of bombs and fired 247 rockets as far back as 1947 to punish caravan raiders and end an inter-tribal war.[2] Ten years later the RAF were again called into action, strafing Yemeni artillery positions after they had shelled targets in Aden. As the situation deteriorated over the next few years, British ground forces became more and more involved.

Aden and the other parts of the Arabian peninsula under British influence at the time were little more than fiefdoms of the political officers of the Colonial Office and Foreign Office, all of whom remembered the success of the Jebel Akhdar operation by the SAS.

They had undue influence on military activity, however, controlling it through their monopoly of intelligence. They retained central control, and decided what information would be passed down to the forces on the ground in Aden. They had learned the lesson from the CIA and it created similar problems to the American campaign in Vietnam. The Political Residents, spooks and spies were at the top of the pecking order, the military came right at the bottom.

The American motivation for fighting the Vietnam War was in large part the 'domino theory'. If Vietnam was 'lost to Communism', American military strategists believed that Cambodia, Laos, Thailand and the other South-East Asian states would follow.

The Middle Eastern version of the domino theory envisaged a succession of Communist or national independence movements rolling up the Gulf states one by one. The first to fall was North Yemen, when an army coup in September 1962 deposed the imam, Al Badr, who had assumed power on the death of his father less than a week before.

President Nasser of Egypt, who was vigorously exporting Arab nationalism throughout the region, promptly sent a huge force – almost an army of occupation – to support the republicans in the ensuing civil war against the royalist forces loyal to the deposed imam.

Helped by the Egyptians and Russians, North Yemen was now funding and fomenting the insurrection in Aden. After that would come Oman, opening the way to the oil-rich Trucial States, sheikdoms and emirates further up the Gulf, and ultimately the richest prize of all, Saudi Arabia. That was the theory at least.

Serving British soldiers had been trying to stem the advance of the North Yemeni-backed rebels, but it was already looking a lost cause by the time an emergency was declared. The catalyst was an incident on the morning of 10 December 1963. A terrorist threw a grenade at the British High Commissioner, Sir Kennedy Trevaskis, as he was about to board a plane at Khormaksar airfield to fly to London for a conference on the future of Aden.

He escaped unhurt, but two people were killed, including the Senior Political Officer, George Henderson, who threw himself forward to shield the High Commissioner and took the full force of the explosion.[3] Fifty people were also wounded. The state of emergency was declared later that day.

The first SAS troops, A Squadron, arrived in Aden the following April to counter an uprising of the Qotaibi tribe in the mountainous Radfan area, straddling the road from Lahej to Dhala, near the Yemeni border.

Both the Sultan of Lahej and the Ameer of Dhala were taking tolls from the users of the road but the Qotaibi tribe was forbidden to do so by the Ameer of Dhala who had proclaimed himself their ruler with the agreement of the resident British political officers.

The result of this perceived injustice was an insurrection in the Radfan. The SAS were despatched to put it down, along with other British troops including a battalion of paras, a regiment of tanks, artillery and engineers, about a brigade in total strength, with RAF transport and fighter ground-attack support. It was by no means the first or the last time that British troops had been used to support a despotic ruler.

The deployment was not a knee-jerk response to the deteriorating military situation, however; it had been planned for some time. Arabic courses at Hereford had been heavily stepped up over a year earlier and we had returned to the region on exercise several times since the Jebel Akhdar campaign. We had also carried out a number of desert exercises in Libya and had actually done a training operation in Aden in 1963, the year before we were formally committed to the conflict.

It was preparation for the series of battles we were convinced we would be fighting all the way up the Gulf to Kuwait as the dominoes tumbled one after another.

Those training operations could not fully prepare us for Aden's savage climate and terrain. The precipitous mountains of the interior were formed of black volcanic rock, which soaked up the sun's heat, producing furnace temperatures. Long after dark the rock remained burning hot to the touch. The drenching humidity and the swarms of flies added to the discomfort, leaving us sighing nostalgically for the leech-infested jungles of Borneo.

The road from Lahej to Dhala remained a prime target for the insurgents, romantically titled the Red Wolves in press reports. A punitive expedition by Aden's British-officered Federal Regular Army had temporarily pushed the rebels back, but as soon as the troops withdrew they resumed their positions on the heights commanding the road. From there they constantly mined and ambushed it, and attacked the British forces camped along it to protect the engineers repairing the road.

Under this pressure, the British garrison developed a siege mentality. Before they would move a yard out of camp the whole road had to be swept for mines, and even then they only patrolled in the very near vicinity of their bases. While they stayed in their bunkers, the enemy had the run of the place outside, free to bring in more weapons as they pleased over the Radfan mountains.

A Squadron established a forward base at Habilayn, at the foot of the mountains around sixty miles north of Aden, and immediately discovered that every time new troops moved into a camp the insurgents would attack it that night.

From then on our normal system on each move to a new location was to arrive, sort out our kit and then disappear on to the nearest hill to watch the subsequent attack. It was like a free firework display; we could see the enemy rounds going in and the British army firing back.

General Sir Peter de la Billiere, as he now is – known to us all as DLB – was A Squadron's new commander. He already had experience of Aden, for he'd been attached to the Federal Army the previous year as an intelligence officer.

He had first proved himself in Malaya and was an excellent, fearless soldier. Denied personal involvement in field operations by his advanced rank, however, he slaked his own thirst for action by volunteering his men for any mission going. His enthusiasm for daring operations sometimes led him to overstretch the squadron he commanded.

A Squadron was already scheduled to carry out a training

exercise in Aden in May and June, but DLB had gone to the commander-in-chief and pleaded for the deployment to be brought forward so that his men could take part in a planned attack on the rebel strongholds in the Radfan.

He volunteered to send a patrol to mark a dropping zone for 3 Para at the head of the Wadi Taym, from where they were to mount an attack on the Danaba basin, while 45 Commando launched a simultaneous assault from high ground on the other side of the basin.

The nine-man SAS troop was sent out at last light on 29 April, moving up the Wadi Rabwa and then beginning the climb of the 4,000-foot Jebel Ashqab. They were hampered by one of the troop becoming ill, forcing them to slow their pace, but the distance they were required to cover was almost certainly too great in any case. By two in the morning it was obvious that they could not reach the target area before daybreak.

They established themselves in some old dry-stone sangars on top of a small hill, intending to press on to the target the following night, but around eleven in the morning they were spotted by a local tribesman from a nearby village.

He was immediately shot and killed, a questionable decision from both a moral and a tactical point of view. The shot alerted the enemy and the SAS troop immediately came under attack from rebels advancing from Danaba.

Beyond the range of artillery support, they were in a desperate situation. They remained pinned down throughout the day as the enemy closed to within as little as fifty yards. At one point two of them rushed one of the sangars but Trooper Geordie Tasker killed them both with bursts from his Bren gun at point-blank range.

Two SAS men were wounded and only a fighter ground-attack by RAF Hunters dropping bombs and strafing within feet of their forward positions saved the others from a worse fate. They were firing so close to the heads of the SAS that several troopers were injured by the empty brass cartridge cases ejected from the Hunters' .30-inch cannon.

Nightfall ended the air support, but it also gave the troop the chance to break out under cover of darkness. At last light, as they prepared to do so, the signaller, Trooper Nick Warburton, was hit in the head and killed instantly. The shots that killed him also destroyed the patrol radio. From now on, the troop were completely on their own.

Four men led the break-out while the other four gave covering fire. Corporal Paddy Baker led the group, hobbling as fast as his wounded leg would allow. Three of them reached the relative safety of a wadi, but the fourth, the troop officer, Captain Robin Edwards, was cut down by gunfire and killed.

The other four men crept out of the sangar without being spotted and the survivors began the long march back to safety. They kept to a faint goat track across the steep upper slopes of the side of the wadi, avoiding the path along its floor, which was certain to be ambushed.

Twice during the night they heard the faint sounds of pursuit. The rest of the troop kept moving down the track, while two of them lay in ambush on their back-track. Each time they killed their pursuers.

Despite their exhaustion and dehydration they had managed to struggle back to within a mile of their base by a couple of hours before dawn. Without a radio, they were then forced to lie up and wait for daybreak to avoid being shot by the sentries as they approached.

Half an hour after they again began moving down the wadi towards the base, they heard the rumble of an armoured car sent to search for signs of them. The seven survivors of the patrol were safe.

Instead of the planned brief, surgical strike by special forces and elite troops, it took a massive force of regular troops five weeks to subdue the Radfan, fighting their way slowly from one mountain peak to another.

The two bodies the SAS troop had left behind were later recovered by another patrol, but they had been decapitated by the rebels as proof that they had killed British soldiers. The heads were taken across the border to North Yemen and paraded on stakes through the city of Taiz.

Major-General John Cubbon, the commander of Middle East Land Forces, immediately called a press conference. He disclosed that the SAS was operating in Aden and denounced the atrocity. 'We have reliable information on their decapitation and the exhibition of their heads on stakes.'[4]

It was a thoughtless move, for it resulted in the next of kin receiving the first news of the men's deaths from accounts in the newspapers. The wives and families did not even know the men had been serving overseas, for when away on operations our next of kin were only sent a spare and very occasional multiple-choice letter:

Dear Sir/Madam,
Your husband/son/father/brother is well, but cannot write to you at the moment. Please keep writing to him.

The cover story for the deployment to the Radfan had been that the SAS was involved in an exercise on Salisbury Plain. Further distress was then caused to the grieving relatives when the US State Department issued a denial of the story, later withdrawn.

Controversy raged for several weeks. The Yemeni government also issued denials and Defence Secretary Denis Healey was even persuaded to criticise General Cubbon in the House of Commons for relying on inadequate evidence for his claim. The evidence was all too real, however, and was confirmed in the triumphalist broadcasts made on Yemeni radio at the time of the incident, before its government adopted a more prudent line.

The one modest benefit from the incident was that it led to a revision in SAS policy towards wives and families. As the Regiment's commanding officer, John Woodhouse, pointed

out, 'It is no use telling wives that a squadron is on training
if it is on operations ... Someone will be killed and you
cannot delay the news of this in any overt military operations.
As SAS were in uniform in Aden, it was pointless not to tell
the wives this. This is the lesson – not that Cubbon told the
press.'[5]

The disastrous outcome of that first SAS operation also
determined how the Regiment operated in up-country Aden
for the rest of the campaign. Instead of dropping down to
the usual four-man patrols after the initial troop operation,
the smallest group allowed in any circumstances remained a
troop, which should have been sixteen strong but in most
cases, like the one involved in the abortive patrol, was down
to nine or ten men.

Our operational effectiveness was also hampered by the
inadequate mapping of the region. We could control artillery,
but the maps were so poor that fire could not be directed
with sufficient accuracy.

The Radfan uprising was only a prologue to the campaign
in Aden. The Qotaibi tribe were subdued for the moment,
but the flow of arms and guerrillas from North Yemen continued. We quickly realised that the key to any success up-
country was intelligence. We put Arabic-speaking troopers
on to the North Yemeni infiltration routes and because of a
shortage of suitable SIS men, SAS men also operated as political officers in the most sensitive and threatened areas.

Any intelligence gathered had to be passed to the SIS,
however, who would then decide how much other SAS men
would be allowed to know. It was a flawed policy, for the
SIS were effectively making military decisions without any
military background.

The SAS men working as political officers were allocated a
monthly budget of money and rifles to give away to the local
population. The budget was usually 'thirty-thirty-thirty' –
thirty thousand ryals, thirty Lee Enfield Number 4 rifles and
thirty boxes of .303 ammunition. In return the locals pro-

vided intelligence on enemy movements which led to a number of very successful operations.

On their first up-country operation, B Squadron captured a local. They weren't sure at first if he was an enemy, or just a local who happened to be in the wrong place, so they took him back to Habilayn and sent for an interrogator from the detention centre in Steamer Point.

After a few hours, an overweight, half-caste Arabic speaker turned up by helicopter. He said he was Maltese, but might equally have been Egyptian or Libyan. He was carrying an officer's swagger stick, and when he was taken to the prisoner the interrogator proceeded to beat him with his swagger stick all over the body, including the soles of his feet.

Every SAS man had been through interrogation training and was aware that the last thing you do is to start abusing prisoners. It's not only morally wrong, it's also counter-productive: prisoners won't tell you anything out of fear that they'll be killed once you've got the information you need.

Some members of B Squadron were only restrained with the greatest difficulty from shooting the interrogator. He beat up the prisoner for ten or fifteen minutes, then said, 'He knows nothing,' got in the helicopter and went back to Steamer Point

The episode made a lasting impression on B Squadron. After that, no one that they lifted was ever interrogated by the intelligence side because the people in the squadron didn't trust them.

Aggressive cross-border operations were also used against North Yemen, but unlike the Borneo campaign there was no SAS involvement – allegedly. Instead, Colonel David Stirling, who had been out of the army for many years, ran a covert operation inside North Yemen. A former CO of 21 SAS, Jim Johnston, ran the London end and the commander on the ground was another SAS veteran, Major Johnny Cooper. DLB also played an active role in the early stages while on detachment to the Federal Army as a political officer.[6]

The operation was British-run, but bankrolled by the Saudis, whose previous hostility to British involvement in the region was now far outweighed by their fears that Yemen's pan-Arab socialism might be exported north as well as south. Covert support was also provided by a further assortment of strange bedfellows: Israel, Iran and France.

Stirling's forces carried out ambushes of Yemeni and Egyptian troops in the early stages, but later confined themselves mainly to receiving arms-drops by RAF aircraft and training the royalist troops in the use of the weapons.

There were some successes and it tied up a large number of Egyptian troops, but the whole escapade was doomed to failure, mainly because the royalist rulers of North Yemen were too despotic to be sustained in power.

Several of Stirling's force were killed by Yemeni tribesmen and security was repeatedly breached. As well as embarrassing newspaper revelations of British involvement, compromised security also resulted in a chemical attack by Egyptian aircraft that blinded a mercenary and dozens of royalist tribesmen.[7]

Stirling's recruits were a mixture of mercenaries, former SAS men, and officers and troopers still serving with the Regiment. They were discharged and ostensibly became mercenaries themselves, with a money belt of gold sovereigns to bribe their way out of North Yemen if they were captured.

When the conflict was over most of the mercenaries promptly rejoined the Regiment, many with their gold sovereigns safely banked. Although it can only be a matter for conjecture, there remains a strong suspicion that, had they lived, the ex-SAS men who died in the fighting would also have returned to the Regiment.

Those who did come back suffered no penalty in either financial or career terms from their involvement with the mercenaries. It sparked a small controversy at the time, but it was generally accepted that it had been necessary.

It proved a litmus test for the future and, because of the number of people killed in action, it was not repeated. Other

ways were found to use SAS men in support of covert operations, usually by giving them a permanent discharge from
the army. They would then be rehired by a suitably deniable
third party.

Inside Aden itself, we were running several campaigns in one.
Up-country we were fighting a classical small colonial war,
like the battle for the North-West Frontier in the previous
century. There were pickets on the mountains guarding the
road and long-range attacks to which the British responded
with artillery, armoured cars and aircraft.

Down in Aden Town, particularly in the Crater district,
Sheik Othman, Al Mansoura and the port area of Ma'alla, it
was an urban guerrilla conflict, as hostile and dangerous as
Northern Ireland at its worst.

Crater was the bowl of an extinct volcano at the foot of the
mountains. Beyond it was the port area and Steamer Point,
where the great ships paused to take on supplies and allow
their passengers a brief look at the dusty, fly-blown city. There
were few people seeing the sights by the mid-1960s, as the
urban conflict degenerated into a murderous campaign targeting troops, their families and other civilians. People were
shot in the street and grenades were thrown into crowds.
One was even lobbed into a children's party, killing one child
and injuring four others.[8]

We trained ourselves to operate in the urban area,
conducting covert operations under the code-name
Operation Nina. We called them 'Keeni-Meeni jobs', from
the Swahili phrase for the unseen movement of a snake in
the grass. It was the Regiment's first experience of urban
guerrilla warfare, an invaluable precursor to service in
Northern Ireland.

We drafted in all the Fijian members of the Regiment and
most of the British Arabists with a suitably Arab cast to our
features. With the aid of stage make-up we could pass as
Africans or Arabs in the polyglot warren of streets and alleys

in the Crater district. We went undercover, seeking targets of opportunity.

We developed a mutually supportive method of moving around the streets, one moving while the other covers him, which is still used by troops in Northern Ireland. We also made use of the pistol-shooting methods and techniques for the covert carrying of weapons originally devised for bodyguard training.

Despite the dangers and difficulties involved in passing ourselves off as Arabs, we were highly effective. On one occasion an undercover SAS man was arrested by regular British troops. He maintained his cover and when they eventually let him go, they congratulated him on his excellent English.

We also used an SAS man disguised as a Western woman, who would wander the teeming, jostling streets of Crater offering terrorists an apparently easy target.

Disguised as Arabs, the other members of the patrol tracked him, ready to take out any attackers. It took a great deal of courage to offer yourself as the sacrificial lamb, because this was in the days before body armour. The only protection you had in any terrorist attack was the quick reactions of your colleagues. It was real quick-draw, Wild West shoot-out stuff.

The dangers were not restricted to attacks from terrorists, for other British regiments in Aden also began sending undercover squads on to the streets. The SAS had tried to ensure an adequate two-way flow of information to eliminate the risk of 'friendly fire' contacts, but the inevitable occurred when a patrol opened fire on a group of armed Arabs, who turned out to be members of the Royal Anglian Regiment's newly formed undercover squad.

It was amazing to us that people in the regular army felt that, without any experience whatsoever, they could train men and send them out on covert operations. It was a further indication of how dangerously close to the edge the army was operating in Aden, though the practice of regular troops being set irregular tasks was not confined to there. It has continued to the present day and still goes on in Northern Ireland.

Despite such incidents, Operation Nina continued. We also used vehicles as decoys, sending a Land-Rover full of troops in uniform into danger areas in the hope that someone would shoot at it or try to put a bomb in it.

On one occasion we sent the Land-Rover into Sheik Othman, where you could practically guarantee an attack. A mini-bus full of SAS men disguised as Arabs followed it in and we had half a dozen other men staking out the route.

An Arab ran out of an alley and threw a grenade. The shrapnel from the blast wounded one of the decoys in the arm, but we shot and killed both the grenade-thrower and his handler, whose job was to smuggle weapons away after a shooting.

There was an immediate court of inquiry because two Arabs had been killed. It did not pass without notice in the Regiment that there was no court of inquiry when SAS men were shot.

As in Malaya, the SAS also responded in kind to terrorist attacks. After a bomb targeting SAS officer John Slim had exploded, injuring several people, an explosives expert arrived at our base, a block of flats in downtown Aden. He spent his time making booby-traps and bombs using tiny micro-circuits and camera batteries.

His most successful constructions were a series of elaborately framed portraits of Egypt's President Nasser – a potent symbol to all Arab nationalists. They were delivered to terrorist factions and political leaders whose beliefs did not accord with those of the political officers in Aden. When unwrapped, the portraits exploded.

In this bloody, vicious urban campaign, a hearts and minds operation – one of the most vital parts of SAS strategy in any conflict – would have been difficult, if not impossible, but in any event it had already been ruled out by political interventions.

In July 1964, just as the Regiment was deploying to Aden, the Conservative government made a commitment to grant independence by the end of 1968, though it intended to retain the Aden base. The incoming Labour administration was even less patient.

Intent of disentangling us quickly from our remaining colonial commitments, Harold Wilson's government set a deadline of January 1968, which was later brought forward again to 30 November 1967 for a final withdrawal from Aden. There was no constitution and no provision for elections; Aden was simply to be left to its fate.

There were no hospitals and very few schools in the Aden Protectorate, and the whole infrastructure was in a parlous state. It was perfect ground for a hearts and minds campaign. The Regiment had already been operating in Borneo for three years and knew at first hand the great success you could have with hearts and minds, but as soon as a strict timetable for British withdrawal was put in place there was no hope of winning over any part of the indigenous population.

Collaborating with the British was a sure way of guaranteeing a bullet in the head immediately after independence. The soldiers of the Federal Army lost little time in appreciating the new realities and many defected to the rebels or became informants for them.

There was no meaningful contact at any level between the British and the Arabs, and in the resultant atmosphere of mutual mistrust the local population became fair game for the troops. Their assumption that all Arabs were bad led to a number of civilians being killed, a fact exploited to the full by the various political factions.

The Wilson government's disastrous appointment of a pro-Yemeni Chief Minister, Abdul Makawee, was hastily reversed and the protectorate brought back under direct rule, but that did not alter the fact that Britain was committed to abandon Aden in less than three years. After the 1966 general election, Wilson also scrapped the plan to retain the base in Aden.

We continued our undercover operations in the city and the intermittent patrols up-country, even though any military value they might have had became increasingly irrelevant as the clock ticked down towards the final withdrawal.

The Regiment was already thinking ahead to the next likely area of conflict, however. One of the final SAS up-country operations of the campaign presaged another war we would soon be fighting in the region.

B Squadron was sent to attack Hauf, a coastal village in a remote sultanate bordering the Omani province of Dhofar, to kill or capture Dhofari rebels who were using it as a base for attacks into Oman.

Two troops infiltrated by night to get behind the village and the other two came ashore in Geminis from HMS *Fearless*, lying just offshore. Delays to the operation meant the seaborne troops were still on the water when day broke, but though the Dhofaris were alerted and a few escaped, a large number were killed or rounded up and a huge pile of weapons was captured.

The remainder of the Aden campaign did rather less to boost our morale. We were deployed on patrols of five to ten days, relying heavily on the skill of the helicopter pilots of the RAF and, particularly, the Army Air Corps to insert us and resupply us.

At one point the RAF instituted a policy of only landing at landing zones (LZs) that had already been secured, resulting in a near-farcical charade where an army Scout helicopter would drop off a handful of SAS men a couple of minutes before the RAF helicopter arrived with the rest of the troop, so that we could claim the LZ was defended.[9]

One of the Army Air Corps pilots, Major Greville Edgecombe, became something of a legend for his skill and bravery. Nicknamed 'Low-Level Greville', he flew many missions, usually at night, landing SAS patrols, resupplying us with water and ammunition and evacuating the wounded.

Whereas the RAF remained reluctant to risk its assets to

rescue wounded troops or collect the bodies of the dead, Greville, like his army colleagues, flew many such missions, once rescuing a seriously wounded soldier from a path on the cliffs of the Jebel Shamsan above the Crater district, despite coming under fire from a machine-gun in a burned-out church.

He also retrieved the bodies of four Irish Guards killed in an ambush, using the light of his four-inch flares to locate the bodies high on a bleak mountainside and find a landing spot. He then left the helicopter with its rotors turning and dragged each body in turn back to it. To retrieve the last one, he had to climb down to the village where the ambush had taken place and carry the body back up the mountainside.[10]

The savage heat made our routine on the up-country patrols particularly gruelling. We lay up under camouflage nets by day, observing for rebel movements and calling in air- or artillery-strikes. At night we patrolled or set ambushes on likely routes. Dehydration and exhaustion were constant problems. In theory, two men kept watch by day while the others slept, but the heat was so fierce that sleep was almost impossible. At night there was no opportunity; we needed to be at maximum alertness, whether patrolling or lying in ambush.

Even though the terrain could not have been more different, our techniques on night patrols owed much to our jungle experience. The lead scout operated much further ahead of the patrol, but we still relied on 'very fast reactions and the trained ability to shoot by instinct rather than aim'.[11]

In a rebel ambush, the lead scout's life depended on the ability of the rest of the patrol to lay down a torrent of fast, accurate fire. As usual it was risky work, but we had only a moderate respect for the enemy. They were brave and many were good long-range shots even with antique rifles, but we were fully confident of dealing with them in contacts, had we been allowed to close with them more frequently.

Yet again, however, the caution of our masters – reflecting both the political constraints under which we were operating and their own excessive regard for the capabilities of the rebels – led many opportunities to close with the rebels to be spurned. That only increased the frustration we felt at being asked to do half a job, risking our lives but being denied the chance to strike back with maximum effect.

I went on several patrols led by Lofty Large, who at six foot six inches towered head and shoulders above everyone else. On an operation following a night attack on the Habilayn camp, we were observing during the day when we saw a group of rebel troops moving along a wadi.

We had them bang to rights, but to our barely contained fury we were forced to wait until the political officers from Habilayn flew in to give permission to open fire. By then all the rebels had disappeared into nooks and crannies in the rocks, and we had to spend the great part of the day winkling them out again one by one.

A number of rebel troops always carried sniper rifles. They fired phosphorus-tipped bullets, which caused a puff of smoke when they struck the ground. From that, they knew the range and bearing to the target. It was very frustrating for us because we were constantly under sniper attack and couldn't close up to them.

Lofty Large's recipe for success was to spread us around him and tell us to observe, while he stood up and walked around, offering the snipers a prominent target. At the first shot he would hit the dirt, leaving us to spot where the fire had come from and bring our own fire to bear.

Lofty was scathing about the rebel troops' accuracy, and in any event had calculated that, without a ranging shot, even the best of snipers was highly unlikely to score a first-time hit on a moving target at long range, but it was a gamble that only a supremely brave man would have been willing to take.

It caused a great deal of consternation among the rest of us and as Lofty was about to stand up, one of the troopers said, 'For Christ's sake, Lofty, get down. If they're such bad shots, they might miss you and hit me.'

The contact went on all day, using air support from four Scout helicopters, one of them piloted by Low-Level Greville. During the course of the day, all the Scouts were riddled with bullets and were unserviceable for months afterwards. It was noticeable that none of Greville's superiors was remotely keen on him getting involved in air support for the SAS again, but with his help we had killed nineteen enemy out of twenty and badly wounded the other one. The operation gave Habilayn a great deal of peace, because it was a long time before the rebels risked another attack on it.

By early 1967, even while the guerrilla war was still continuing, different factions had begun fighting each other as they struggled for control after independence. There was even conflict between different battalions of the Federal Army, now renamed the South Arabian Army (SAA).

The approach of the deadline for withdrawal was a relief to us all. In June responsibility for the Radfan and the rest of the interior was handed over to the South Arabian Army and British troops pulled back to a defensive perimeter just outside Aden itself. Travellers were stopped and searched at checkpoints there in a vain attempt to reduce the flow of arms into the city.

Last-minute attempts to ensure some semblance of stable government during and after the transition to independence varied from the ineffectual to the farcical. A UN delegation had arrived in May to 'find an internationally acceptable political solution to the problems of South Arabia'.

It was doomed to failure before it even arrived. 'What three diplomats ... could do in five days that British diplomats and ministers had failed to do in seven hectic years was not immediately apparent.'[12]

The UN delegates refused to meet the Federal government because it did not have UN recognition, and each of the two main nationalist parties would only meet the delegation if it recognised their claim, ahead of their rival, to be the official representative of the South Arabian people.

When the UN delegation tried to broadcast an appeal to the people over the heads of their leaders, the Federal government not unnaturally refused to give them air-time. Riots broke out in the streets and the delegates spent their remaining time in Aden hiding in their hotel.

The defeat inflicted on Arab armies in the Six Day War of June 1967 further inflamed the situation in Aden. Many Arabs suspected Western connivance in Israel's crushing victory.

South Arabian Army troops mutinied on 20 June, firing at the British camp in Khormaksar. The unrest spread to the Armed Police barracks in Crater and in the ensuing fighting more than twenty British soldiers were killed.

In the worst incident, seven Northumberland Fusiliers were ambushed and massacred by the Armed Police. They could have been saved if the commander of an armoured car had opened fire. His main 75mm gun was actually loaded, but he followed to the letter the rules of engagement laid down by the governor: you had to have permission from a higher authority before opening fire in urban Aden.

However well intentioned, such rules were a luxury that soldiers battling a vicious urban guerrilla war could not afford. In truth the commander of the armoured car really should have had the balls to intervene anyway; by the time he got permission to fire it was too late.

In the wake of that incident the Crater area was cordoned off and snipers from a number of units including the SAS were placed on the hills surrounding it. Popular belief has it that whenever anything or anybody moved it was shot.

The post-independence Arab government in Aden claimed there were over 700 civilian martyrs in Crater. I heard contemporary reports from the SAS squadron that was there – G Squadron – that were in broad agreement with those figures.

When Crater was 'liberated' a week later, the myth was created that Lieutenant-Colonel Colin 'Mad Mitch' Mitchell and his Highlanders marched in with pipes playing and drums beating, causing the locals to flee in terror. The truth was rather different. When they finally marched into Crater they were actually greeted with open arms as the means of stopping the slaughter.

Once some semblance of order had been restored, British forces resumed their steady withdrawal. One of the final operations involving the SAS was also one of the most bizarre. A troop from D Squadron was sent several hundred miles from our base near Crater to a small town in the East Aden Protectorate.

They were given very few instructions and didn't quite know why they were there, so they proceeded to do the Wild West marshal thing and walked up and down the town, making sure there was no crime. Every time they went near the bank, a branch of the British Bank of the Middle East, a few shots flew over their heads. They hit the ground and could never see the sniper who was firing at them.

After several days it dawned on the troop that if they kept away from the bank they wouldn't be fired upon. Unsurprisingly, with a final British withdrawal only weeks away, they opted for the quiet life and didn't go near the bank again.

They related the story while being debriefed back in Aden. A member of the SIS attending the debriefing broke into a smile. 'I could have told you that would happen. There's £2 million in the bank in gold sovereigns.'

The thought that the enemy we had been fighting for four years would soon be wandering into the bank and helping themselves to £2 million in gold was too much for most of the troop. It was a very hard job to dissuade them from loading up again and going straight back to the town.

By 24 September the contracting defensive perimeter was just north of Khormaksar airfield. Sheik Othman and Al Mansoura were now outside the zone of British control, and fighting immediately erupted between the two nationalist factions, the Marxist NLF and the Islamic fundamentalist FLOSY.

One of the last acts of British rule in Aden was also one of the most shabby. Brigadier Jack Dye, commander of the SAA, conferred legitimacy on one of the rebel groupings, the NLF, after 'locking [his senior officers] in a room and telling them not to come out until they had chosen who to support ... The colony [was] handed over to an organisation that had earned the right to rule by a campaign of intimidation and murder, waged mostly against their fellow countrymen and political opponents. The British troops in Aden ... were rightly disgusted.'[13]

The troops' outrage was increased when they were ordered to hand over most of their stores and equipment to the SAA. They complied with the letter, if not the spirit, of the request; most of the equipment handed over was 'accidentally' damaged and the engines of virtually every vehicle left behind seized as they were being driven away by their new owners.

Like the final American withdrawal from Saigon a few years later, the British departure from Aden was a hasty and undignified scramble for safety to a soundtrack of screams and pleading voices from collaborators with the departing imperial power, who knew only too well what their fate would be if left behind.

Commandos held the contracting perimeter as British forces withdrew from the city to the harbour and airfield, and transport planes shuttled to and from Cyprus, airlifting the last British civilians to safety.

The Union Jack was lowered for the last time and the High Commissioner was flown out by helicopter to HMS *Eagle*, one of two aircraft carriers waiting offshore. The remaining military personnel were then ferried out to the ships, 42 Commando the last to leave.

Just as in Saigon, the clatter of helicopter rotors was like the drumbeat signalling the final retreat and the last stages of the withdrawal were punctuated by the sounds of gunfire from the city as old scores were settled.

As the British ships sailed away from Steamer Point, never to return, the victorious rebels were already looting the barracks and Government House. The Southern Yemen People's Democratic Republic was declared the next day.

The SAS was not defeated on the battlefield in Aden, but, not for the first or last time, political decisions had made its task impossible. It could be argued that the Regiment had been sent there merely to delay the inevitable until an orderly withdrawal could be achieved, but the campaign was far more significant than that.

The main reason the SAS was originally sent to Aden at all had less to do with the fate of the Aden Protectorate or even the Middle East than with the continent on the other side of the Gulf of Aden.

At the time few people outside the SAS and SIS believed that there was any way to prevent the Middle Eastern states from falling one by one; the most that could be done was to slow the Communist advance.

There was more optimism about influencing events in Africa, which was seen as the major battleground of the conflicting ideologies of East and West. The Russians and Chinese were very active in Africa, while the American pre-occupation with South-East Asia meant that their influence was negligible.

The SAS was sent to Aden primarily as a base from which to work in Africa, but once there, the military command was quick to seize the chance to deploy us. The skills of the SAS far exceeded those of any other unit of the army at the time: individual troopers could control mortars, artillery and ground-attack aircraft, we had the ability to speak languages, could operate outside the normal army rules and had a pro-found positive psychological impact on the troops around us. Every commander, in every theatre in the world, would have wanted to use the SAS.

If that was flattering, it also greatly increased the already heavy load on us. For three years, from 1963 to the end of 1965, the SAS had been operating beyond full stretch. The campaign within Aden was actually a series of simultaneous campaigns, each requiring very different skills, preparation and equipment.

In addition to the support to the acting government, there were overt, up-country military operations, covert operations in which SAS people passed themselves off as political officers, cross-border operations in support of North Yemeni royalists, and covert Nina operations inside Aden.

There was a simultaneous large-scale campaign in Borneo, and various BG training teams were also operating in Africa. All this was being achieved by four Sabre Squadrons totalling fewer than 200 men.

Under such pressure there was a very fine line between discipline and anarchy. On one Aden tour, six of the eight senior NCOs in one squadron were recommended for court martial, but it was an empty threat. There was no way that anyone below the rank of officer could be effectively disciplined because nothing the army could do to you was worse than what was already happening.

We were all losing money by being in the SAS, we were operating in some of the most harsh and unforgiving regions on earth, our living conditions were appalling and our health was at constant risk because of poor nutrition and tropical disease. On top of all that, people were actually shooting at us.

Yet despite all the pressures and problems, virtually no one left the Regiment. We stayed because we wanted to get the job done. The lowest ranks were as involved in the planning and execution of operations as the officers – often more so; morale was high and things were being done. Despite everything, everyone was happy; the Regiment was the place to be.

If the end result of the Aden campaign was a foregone conclusion, the Regiment learned many valuable lessons. It gave us priceless experience of operating in desert conditions and enabled us to rehearse strategies and tactics for the other, more vital Gulf battles to come.

It also had a major side-benefit for the Israelis. The British pressure on the Yemen ensured that 60,000 Egyptian troops were still tied up there when the Six Day War broke out.

The Aden campaign also demonstrated that the SAS could operate outside normal military boundaries, in a way that had previously been the province of eccentric officers with private influence such as Lawrence of Arabia and Colonel David Stirling himself. That now became the domain of the normal SAS trooper.

It proved to be a very significant period in the transition of the SAS from a better-trained and better-motivated but still recognisable part of the regular army to a totally separate and covert instrument of government policy.

Many senior officers drew different conclusions from the Aden campaign, however. By the end of it they no longer saw the SAS working in small groups in the jungle, gathering our own intelligence through local resources. Our approach to small-scale operations remained unaffected, but in any future large-scale campaign, we were now to be the shock troops of the rest of the British army, being drip-fed intelligence by outside sources.

It was not the reason that the SAS was formed and had undergone such super-sensitive and very expensive training, but the die was cast. The Regiment was to be used in that way in all subsequent major campaigns.

The growing demand for SAS teams to train the forces of friendly nations, coupled with simultaneous campaigns in Borneo and Aden, had severely overstretched the SAS. It forced the decision to expand the Regiment by forming two more Sabre Squadrons. There was also a rapid expansion of the Signal Squadron which became a domain all of its own.

The first new Sabre Squadron – Bravo – was the re-formation of a squadron that had been disbanded at the end of the Malayan Emergency, but G Squadron – G for Guards – was brand-new. Its formation caused an angry reaction within the Regiment, ripples of which are still felt today. For many SAS men it was the ultimate betrayal of the ethos of the Regiment, deliberately pushed through when the existing Sabre Squadrons were at full stretch on active service operations.

To the fury of serving SAS men, all the officers and NCOs of the Guards Independent Parachute Squadron were simply ushered into the Regiment without doing Selection or losing their rank. This put many of them in senior positions, without having the faintest knowledge of special forces operations or a single day's service with the SAS.

In some cases, NCOs who had gone through the rigours of Selection, given up their rank to revert to SAS trooper and then served for ten or a dozen years with the Regiment found themselves outranked by complete newcomers. All the years of sacrifice and dedication had been repaid with a swift kick in the balls.

At least one former Guardsman serving as a trooper in one of the other SAS squadrons lost no time in getting a transfer to G Squadron. He was immediately promoted to his old rank of sergeant. It sent a clear message to the other squadrons: a trooper in A, B or D Squadron was worth a sergeant in G.

There was no doubt that extra men were needed, but the SAS hierarchy avoided the easiest option, which was to form a new squadron from the Parachute Regiment. Shock troops like the paras tended to have levels of fitness and skill that made SAS Selection a less daunting ordeal for them than other recruits.

The proof of that was that roughly 90 per cent of SAS men at the time were, like me, former paras. The fear that the SAS would be even more vulnerable to absorption by the

Parachute Regiment if more men were recruited from it undoubtedly influenced the decision to look to the Brigade of Guards for the new SAS squadron, but it was only part of the reason.

At the time, no one in the lower echelons of the SAS could understand why the Regiment's ideals had been ditched in this way. We were a new Regiment without the long and glorious histories of others. Our main tradition was that we had no traditions. The one thing that bound us together was the wearing of the winged dagger beret and badge. Once that vital *esprit de corps* was lost, it could never be recovered.

All of us felt that the senior officers were simply taking their revenge for the irreverence and insubordination they had had to put up with from men who knew the job better than they. Guardsmen in G Squadron would be more malleable, less likely to question their decisions.

In the context of the continuing post-colonial contraction of Britain's armed forces, however, the key reason for the change became obvious. The greatest fear within the SAS, which was never completely banished no matter what its successes in the field, was that the Regiment would be disbanded.

A regiment of opinionated, self-motivated and often rebellious trogs with no permanent officers was always likely to be vulnerable when career officers, under pressure from the politicians, were looking for cuts. To survive, the Regiment needed defenders in the elite circles where its future would be decided. G Squadron gave the establishment – in the shape of the Guards – a stake in the future of the SAS.

One effect of the change was quickly apparent. For the first time in the Regiment's existence, regular deputations of senior officers and officials from the Ministry of Defence began to arrive in Hereford. They came not to visit the Regiment as a whole, but to call on G Squadron.

If the political decision made the future of the SAS a little more secure, however, it damaged morale badly and caused ill-feeling between the squadrons which still continues today. All members of G Squadron now do Selection like any other SAS recruit, but there is continuing preferential treatment for Guardsmen in other ways. The Brigade of Guards could never supply enough men to fill G Squadron and the majority of troops serving with the squadron then and now were non-Guardsmen.

No matter how able, however, the non-Guards officers and other ranks were barred from reaching their respective pinnacles within their squadron, since the posts of Officer Commanding and Squadron Sergeant-Major in G Squadron are permanently reserved for Guardsmen.

This preferential treatment irritated SAS officers from other regiments as much as it did the other ranks, for it affected their future prospects. It has led to a continuing imbalance, and the disproportionately large number of Guardsmen among the senior NCOs and senior officers in the Regiment as a whole remains a source of friction.

The circumstances surrounding the formation of G Squadron were the cause of much of the anti-officer sentiment which exists within the Regiment to this day. Open displays of hostility to the decision or its beneficiaries were not tolerated, but it was amazing how many of us, though lacking the benefits of a classical education, came to know almost by heart the contents of a letter sent by Marcus Flavinius, a centurion in the Second Cohort of the Augusta Legion, to his cousin Tertullus in Rome.

> We had been told, on leaving our native soil, that we were going to defend the sacred rights conferred on us by so many of our citizens settled overseas, so many years of our presence, so many benefits brought by us to populations in need of our assistance and our civilisation.
>
> We were able to verify that all this was true, and,

because it was true, we did not hesitate to shed our quota of blood, to sacrifice our youth and our hopes. We regretted nothing, but whereas we over here are inspired by this frame of mind, I am told that in Rome factions and conspiracies are rife, that treachery flourishes and that many people in their uncertainty and confusion lend a ready ear to the dire temptations of relinquishment and vilify our action.

I cannot believe that all this is true and yet recent wars have shown how pernicious such a state of mind could be and to where it could lead.

Make haste to reassure me, I beg you, and tell me that our fellow citizens understand us, support us and protect us as we ourselves are protecting the glory of the empire.

If it should be otherwise, if we should have to leave our bleached bones on these desert sands in vain, then beware of the anger of the Legions.

The letter was photocopied and fixed to lockers and noticeboards in the SAS bases in Borneo, Aden and Hereford. As fast as they were torn down, new copies would appear.

We soon had three more controversial changes to assimilate which also had significant consequences for the SAS. Administration was taken out of the hands of the individual squadrons and a rapid expansion of the administrative side of the Regiment took place. In the past, if you needed equipment, you got it. Under the new system, your request was subject to interpretation by the administration, who decided how much of it you needed, if you needed it at all.

The repercussions from this apparently anodyne decision were still being keenly felt during the Gulf War twenty years later, when equipment described by one very experienced Sabre Squadron member as 'war-winning kit' was not issued to most SAS men because a staff officer manning a desk several thousand miles from the fighting zone did not see the need for it.

Senior officers also decided that men attached to the Regiment in administrative capacities would in future be rewarded for their long and good service by being allowed to wear the insignia of SAS men. The right to wear the winged dagger and beige beret had previously been the exclusive right of combat troops; now even a stores clerk could be an SAS man.

This was tantamount to giving those people a licence to lie. Outside the closed society of the Regiment there was now no way for the rest of the army, and indeed the rest of the world, to differentiate between a real SAS soldier and a desk-bound pen-pusher.

The third change established a formal connection for the first time between 22 SAS and the second Territorial Regiment, 23 SAS. The question of how it was possible to train a civilian to SAS standards at weekends and on a one-month training camp every year when it took three years to make an SAS trooper out of a full-time regular soldier has never been answered.

The expansion of the TAs entailed a corresponding increase in the support and administrative sides of the Regiment. Coupled with the earlier 'badging' of administrative workers, it led to a degree of bitterness within the regular SAS and to a dilution of the understanding of the SAS within the regular army. It was becoming less and less easy for an outsider to distinguish between an SAS trooper and a 'Chindit warrior' who was a civilian five days a week and an SAS killer on Saturdays and Sundays.

Every existing NCO and trooper was up in arms about the changes, but the senior officers had a powerful reason to support them. It was a classic case of empire-building: the bigger the empire, the greater the highest rank must be.

A scarcity of junior officers had been a problem for the Regiment ever since it was re-formed. It was often assumed that the severe physical barrier set by Selection had much to do with that, but in truth the problem with those who did apply lay more often in a lack of intelligence, creative and lateral thought and the self-reliance that one chronicler of the SAS described as 'moral courage'.

Men in whom the hierarchical structures of other army units were too deeply ingrained found it hard to function in the distinctive atmosphere of the SAS.

> A man without much moral courage will be more afraid of unpopularity than physical pain and, if left to his own, will perform much less efficiently than when surrounded by others. Survival may depend more on moral courage than physical endurance ... When a man has been kept in solitary confinement, with nothing in prospect but torture and death, courage may enable him to bear pain with dignity but it is moral courage which will preserve him intact to the end.[14]

Moral courage requires not only the bravery to go where the firing is fiercest, but also the wisdom to hold back when others, afraid of being thought cowards, might jump in, guns blazing. In this sense, the SAS patrol leader during the Gulf War who assessed that his troop's chances of success were minimal and immediately pulled them out showed more moral courage than those who carried on despite the flaws in intelligence reports, maps and equipment that doomed their mission to failure.

There was no suggestion that junior officers with the right qualities did not exist; simply that for a variety of reasons they did not apply for SAS Selection in sufficient numbers. Whereas the Regiment tended to attract the cream of other ranks, good young officers were often reluctant to join the SAS, fearing that it was not a wise career move. Those who did try to volunteer were often hindered by their own regiments, which had no wish to see promising officers disappear to the special forces for three years.

The shortage of officers in 1965 was such that all four troops of D Squadron were led by sergeants, giving formal recognition to the de facto rule of the NCOs that had existed for years. Even if more junior officers could be persuaded to join the SAS on three-year tours, however, there was no recognised career ladder beyond the Regiment and certainly no jobs within the military establishment for senior SAS officers.

Some of them had no alternative but to leave the army altogether. An SAS commanding officer, John Woodhouse, in many ways the father of the modern Regiment, had found that his path to further promotion was barred. He was forced to take his outstanding qualities as a man and his knowledge of counter-insurgency into premature retirement in the mid-1960s.

In SAS terms, the old army saying that the best generals leave the army as captains was not quite correct: the best generals left the SAS as lieutenant-colonels.

The lack of career prospects encouraged the senior officers to develop the Regiment to further their own ambitions. The larger they could make it, the higher their own career ladder would reach.

The ranking structure of the army is based entirely on numbers and in a very short space of time the expansion of the Regiment ensured that beyond the lieutenant-colonel commanding 22 SAS, we now had a Director, Special Air Service and Special Air Service Group, with the rank of brigadier. The first holder of the title, Fergus Semple, had not even served with the Regiment in the past.

The senior officers had succeeded admirably from their own narrow point of view. There was jam today and also jam tomorrow. The most senior officer in the SAS had been a lieutenant-colonel with no promotion prospects. Now he was a brigadier with accelerated promotion to general. No fewer than ten current generals, including the present Chief of the Defence Staff, have previously served with the SAS. In the process of developing their own career structure, however, they dealt a severe blow to the morale of the regular Regiment.

If you impose the most rigorous demands on those wishing to join the SAS, you maintain the highest standards within it. Once you start making exceptions – like G Squadron, like administrative personnel, like those on attachment – you cannot maintain or regain those former standards.

Prior to the changes, people joined the SAS solely to be fighting soldiers, members of an active service Sabre Squadron. Afterwards, some people were joining with the sole intention of using the SAS for their own ends. The long, gradual decline of the Regiment, so slow as to be almost imperceptible at first, dates from this time.

The doubling in size of the SAS was in marked contrast to what was happening in the rest of the army, where virtually every other unit was being cut back.

Harold Wilson had come into power in 1964, promising the 'white heat of a technological revolution'. Service chiefs quailing at the thought of what a socialist government might do to them were reassured by a rather more old-fashioned pronouncement from the new Prime Minister: 'We are a world power and a world influence or we are nothing.'[15]

His assumption of the need for a world military role to match Britain's world trading status was refuted by the evidence from two far stronger trading nations, however. The US and USSR might have matched their economic power with a comparable flexing of military muscle, but the experience of Japan and Germany suggested that a lack of military forces had been a boon, not an obstacle, to their post-war economic success.

Wilson's pledge to continue Britain's east of Suez role arose partly from his fear of the effect withdrawal would have on relations with the US. But neither the 'special relationship' nor the continuing military presence in the Far East gave

Britain the faintest influence on American policy in Vietnam, and, in any event, the attempts to keep forces east of Suez were soon undermined by harsh financial realities.

The first major financial crisis of the Labour administration in 1965–66 forced a series of cuts, including the withdrawal of one-third of the remaining British forces overseas, a reduction in the Territorial Army, the end of construction of aircraft-carriers and the cancellation of a fifth Polaris submarine. The TSR-2 aircraft was also cancelled though Defence Secretary Denis Healey did sugar the pill by pledging to purchase fifty American FB-111A fighter bombers as replacement.

The run on sterling in 1967 completed the job, resulting in devaluation of the pound and a further round of savage cuts. Denis Healey had assured the Australian parliament in February 1966 that 'We have no intention of ratting on any of our commitments.'[16]

Inside two years he was forced to rat on most of them. The supplementary Defence White Paper of 18 July 1967 imposed a package of cuts including a timetable for the complete withdrawal of forces from east of Suez over the next ten years, to the considerable annoyance of the Americans, the Australians and Britain's other Far Eastern allies.

The Middle Eastern allies were no more reassured, for as recently as November 1966 Foreign Office Minister Goronwy Roberts had been reassuring the Gulf states that Britain had no intention of pulling its forces out of the region.[17]

With the exception of token garrisons in Hong Kong, Gibraltar, Belize, Cyprus and the Falkland Islands, all British forces outside Europe would be withdrawn. A swathe of pink that had once extended from Suez to the International Dateline, 150 degrees of longitude to the east, would now be reduced to one tiny colony – Hong Kong – and one small protectorate – Brunei.

A further crisis in November led to the devaluation of sterling and another round of forced cuts announced in January 1968, in which the timetable for withdrawal was accelerated, the order for the FB-111A aircraft was cancelled and all aircraft-carriers were to be scrapped by the end of 1971.

The withdrawal from east of Suez was a belated acknow-ledgement that 'defence must be the servant of foreign policy, not its master'.[18] Governments of both political colours had taken twenty years to recognise the truth that John Maynard Keynes had expressed in 1946: 'Britain cannot police half the world while we are in debt to the other half.'

When the Commonwealth Office was abolished in 1968 – it merged with the Foreign Office – a symbolic curtain was brought down on the last vestiges of empire. The new realities were acknowledged in a speech by Denis Healey in February 1969, announcing Britain's 'transformation from a world power to a European power', and confirmed by Britain's admission to the EEC in January 1973.

A few die-hard Conservative right-wingers huffed and puffed, but from then on the arguments about defence were only ever to be about the level of spending required, not the strategy to be followed.

The Defence Review of December 1974 imposed yet more cuts and confirmed the

Clear strategic priority areas:
1 Nato Central Front in West Germany
2 Defence of the Eastern Atlantic and English Channel
3 Defence of the United Kingdom and its approaches
4 Maintenance of the strategic nuclear deterrent ... Tactical nuclear capability also to be retained. [The Labour government's further pledge that the nuclear deterrent would not be renewed when it became obsolete was quickly abandoned.]

The defence of Europe and Britain's commitments to NATO were now the sole preoccupations of 99 per cent of the armed forces. The one per cent exception was the SAS.

8

OPERATION STORM
DHOFAR 1970–77

We travelled away from the coast through the wind-scoured sand-dunes and began to climb higher across classical desert. Sparse scrub and thorn bushes speckled the sand and bare rock. Then we left the coastal plain behind, travelling on across the rock-strewn foothills of the Oman Mountains. Boulders of coal-black lava littered the area as far as the eye could see.

The black rocks were baked by the sun but the air temperature was noticeably cooler and the humidity almost zero, a relief after the sticky heat of the coast.

Suddenly in the distance we saw the sun glinting from the tin-sheet roofs of the huts at Manama, the headquarters of the Trucial Oman Scouts. It was a British-trained, British-officered and British-administered unit, drawn from the Trucial States and Oman to police the area now known as the United Arab Emirates.

Flags were flying above the camp. Land-Rovers were parked in neat rows and a line of white-painted stones marked out the parade square, as if this were a Guards depot rather than a base in the middle of the Arabian peninsula.

I was part of a small SAS team sent there to train a thirty-strong cadre of non-commissioned officers. We ran a very intense, high-information training programme on the capabilities and uses of modern heavy weapons –

mortars, artillery and machine-guns – in war situations, and how to direct and control them by radio.

The soldiers we were training were small, wiry and much darker-skinned than Arabs. I was fluent in Arabic, but the troops used an entirely different language among themselves. I couldn't understand a word of it. Then it dawned on me. The entire cadre were jebalis – troops drawn from the Omani province of Dhofar.

They were some of the best and most attentive students we had trained. Whenever we called a halt because we were tired, they just wanted to carry on. The older men in the group could only read and write with difficulty and their Arabic was patchy, but the younger ones were literate and fluent in Arabic. The one officer on the course, who'd been trained at the British army language school in Beaconsfield, was also fluent in English.

The course ran for six weeks and we were pleased and impressed with the results they achieved. The final test was a huge live-firing exercise using all the weapons we'd been training with. I shared the observation post with the officer as he controlled the fire that the senior and junior NCOs were putting down. It was a textbook display which could not have been bettered at the School of Infantry at Warminster.

We returned to the UK delighted with the results of our work. Within a couple of years the same officer and NCOs were using their knowledge to attack my squadron in Dhofar at the start of Operation Storm. I crouched in my sangar as the first incomers started to explode around us, thinking, The man controlling that's well trained.

Several weeks later, the same officer was forced to surrender to us. We sat down with him to discuss how he'd applied the training we'd done in Manama to such good effect. Having defected to the rebels, he was now seeking to save his skin by changing sides once more.

We had no problems with that. Part of our job was to

turn captured rebels and send them back into action against their former comrades. He clearly wasn't a man you could trust any further than you could spit, but we weren't planning to trust him, just to make use of the skills we'd taught him.

He settled happily into his new role. His fluent English allowed him to bypass the Arabic linguists on the squadron and speak directly to the senior officers, but it was not the most diplomatic of moves. The other jebalis were agitated by his use of a language they did not understand, fearing that he was making secret deals with the officers.

They described him as 'siaseet', a word they also used about every intelligence operator. The literal translation from the Arabic was 'political' but in colloquial use it meant 'not a straight dealer'.

Shortly afterwards, we mounted an operation using intelligence that the officer had supplied. A joint group of jebalis and SAS men climbed the jebel at night to lay a series of ambushes in areas where the officer's former friends were operating.

We left the base just before dusk and spent several hours making the arduous climb through the foothills of the jebel and up a very steep path to the top of the escarpment. Just before we reached the summit the jebalis stopped, apparently suspecting an enemy ambush on the ridge. They told us to stay where we were while they went ahead to clear the route, then disappeared silently into the night.

Not long afterwards there was a burst of firing which lasted for several minutes. We took up our defensive positions, but couldn't see what was happening above us because the contact was taking place in dead ground just over the edge of the escarpment.

After the shooting stopped there was a long silence and then the jebalis reappeared. They said that they'd been ambushed as they reached the top of the ridge but, strangely enough, the only casualty that either side had taken was the recently surrendered Dhofari officer.

Although nothing was ever said, by either the jebalis or ourselves, it was tacitly understood that, not trusting the officer, they'd solved the problem in their own way.

The author, Wadi Darbat, Dhofar, 1971

Britain's withdrawal from east of Suez did not signal an end to the Regiment's overseas role, but it coincided with the second short period since the SAS had re-formed when we were not an overt active service overseas.

Under the leadership of Lieutenant-Colonel John Slim, now promoted to commanding officer of the Regiment and one of the most forward-thinking men in the forces, the SAS put the rare period of calm – 1968 was 'the only year in the fifty years since the Second World War in which a British soldier did not die in action somewhere in the world'[1] – to good use. The whole emphasis was now to improve skills and lay down strategic guidelines for the next ten to twenty years.

New standards of excellence were set in the Regiment's own training, and cross-training was also stepped up so that each individual in a troop could take on the duties of any other. Beyond the range of purely military skills – infiltration through any climatic zone or terrain, navigation, endurance, combat survival, close-quarter combat, jungle warfare, counter-interrogation, sabotage and demolition, familiarity with enemy weapons, signals and paramedicine – SAS commanders could also call on men with a host of specialist abilities.

Different SAS men were fluent in Arabic, Russian, German, Swahili, Malay, Thai, French, Spanish and many other languages. We were also well versed in the techniques of espionage, like covert entry, surveillance and electronic eavesdropping, which had once been the sole province of the SIS.

BG teams passed on their bodyguarding skills to the forces

protecting rulers of friendly states, but they could also use the same skills to penetrate the security of hostile rulers.

SAS snipers were trained to infiltrate within 800 yards of a closely guarded target, changing camouflage up to half a dozen times as they crossed different areas of ground, and then hit the target with their first shot.

Saboteurs and demolitionists could destroy military targets, communication links or industrial plant with equal efficiency, using explosives, arson or a range of other anonymous techniques as the occasion demanded.

Alongside the refinement of old skills and the development of new ones, the concept of SAS men routinely operating in civilian clothes was also introduced. Before 1967 SAS men in the beige beret and winged dagger badge had been a familiar sight around Hereford, and operations were primarily carried out in uniform. The only departures from the norm were the groups in civilian clothes working undercover in Aden and the BG teams training bodyguard groups abroad.

Almost overnight the whole emphasis changed. Although we remained ready and able to fight in any of the three forms of potential conflict – counter-insurgency; limited, conventional war; or total, nuclear war – SAS men were now trained to operate in total anonymity, whether in the UK or overseas.

The policy also had one side-benefit. It would no longer be possible for armed robbers dressed in army uniforms with SAS badges to pretend they were special forces on exercise, as the 1963 Great Train Robbers had planned to do had they been caught in the act.[2]

The SAS beige berets now disappeared completely from public view. Sometimes we wore the uniforms of other military units, but in the majority of cases we operated in civilian clothes. It was another highly significant development for the Regiment, giving us the ability to operate as both a military force and a covert civilian force.

The most important factor in making that possible was the shooting method developed for bodyguard and close-quarter battle work, which made it possible to put SAS men into extremely hazardous situations. Under threat, we had the ability to draw concealed weapons in split seconds and actively engage targets.

One of the proving grounds of the system was Northern Ireland where, after a period of relative calm, sectarian tensions were building towards a fresh outbreak of the Troubles. SAS men were sent in simply to wander around nationalist areas, where every stranger was immediately suspect. The aim was to condition us, developing the mental toughness we would need to operate undercover both in Northern Ireland and in other trouble spots around the globe.

Once again, the drive to perfect SAS skills came from the bottom up, not the top down, but John Slim was astute enough to see the opportunities that a unique force like the SAS offered Britain.

He shared a vision with the SIS section of the Foreign Office. Both saw America's continuing obsession and entanglement with Vietnam as a further opportunity to extend British influence. Even after President Nixon finally began to wind down US involvement, American forces were so demoralised by Vietnam that it took them at least a decade to recover. They were also perceived as losers by other armies, and no one wants to be trained by losers.

While they contemplated their navels, Britain – through the SAS, who were definitely not perceived as losers – strengthened old alliances and cultivated new ones. Large-scale military adventures were unacceptable on both cost and political grounds. The covert use of the SAS was the best – and often the only – possible alternative in an era when there was the distinct feeling in Britain of a 'sudden and total revulsion against anything that reminds us of past advantages and past glories, a sudden shift into an isolationist little-Englandism with unhealthy overtones of xenophobia and even racialism accompanying it'.[3]

In consultation with the Foreign Office, John Slim chose

to concentrate SAS training on two areas, the Gulf and Africa, though jungle training continued, as it does to this day. That also allowed us to deal with any fresh outbreaks of insurgency in Malaya before they could develop. In 1969 an SAS squadron was deployed in northern Malaya after the government requested help in dealing with insurgents infiltrating across the border with Thailand.

Superficially it appeared that Britain, the dominant power in the Middle East for so long, had lost all its former influence. It was not even invited to participate in either the US–Soviet summit on the Middle East in New Jersey following the Six Day War of 1967, or the broader Geneva conference after the 1973 Arab–Israeli conflict.

Yet despite the surface impression, Britain still exerted a considerable influence in the Middle East. John Slim capitalised on the residue of goodwill from our campaigns in Aden and Jebel Akhdar and organised training tasks in virtually every Gulf country. They were major, prestigious jobs that had to be approved by the heads of state.

Most of the Gulf States only had embryonic armies at that time. As well as training the bodyguards charged with protecting the heads of state, the SAS provided much of the training necessary to convert their armies into effective fighting units, ready for the wars we felt sure would come as the Soviets and their Egyptian and Yemeni clients tried to set the Gulf dominoes falling.

Contingency plans were also drawn up at 'the Kremlin' – the Intelligence and Planning Cell in Hereford – enabling us to react rapidly to any crisis anywhere in the Middle East.

All our training visits were covert and SAS men travelling abroad always used pseudonyms. The host country was usually just as keen to keep our involvement clandestine, but there was one jarring incident when an SAS squadron was sent to Iran.

A list of pseudonyms was presented to the immigration official, but he then demanded to see everybody's passport. The squadron commander refused and threatened to take his men straight back to England, but after an assurance from the British Embassy that the dissemination of names could be controlled and restricted, he reluctantly complied.

We were subsequently told that the immigration official had been put in jail and the key thrown away, but that did not address our real worry. Somewhere in Iran was a list of the real names and personal details of an entire SAS squadron. Those worries were multiplied a thousandfold after the Shah of Iran was deposed in the revolution that swept Ayatollah Khomeini to power.

It was a rare own goal, however, and the political and financial dividends to Britain from our work throughout the Gulf were enormous. Alliances were forged that still hold today and through the SAS, Britain ensured that there was no power vacuum in the Gulf. There was an orderly transition from protectorate status to self-rule, which allowed the economic development of the Gulf to continue unchecked.

The benefits to Britain were shown most clearly during the oil crisis that followed the Arab–Israeli War of October 1973. Britain and every other West European state except the Netherlands had refused US planes airlifting supplies to Israel permission to land or overfly its territory.

That was not enough to prevent cuts in oil supplies to Europe, but although there was a lot of cosmetic screaming and shouting about the shortage of oil, supplies to Britain were not reduced at all, though Britain's close friendship with the Gulf States was not enough to protect it from the 70 per cent price rises pushed through by OPEC (Organisation of Petroleum-Exporting Countries).

The kingdom of Jordan had been created by the British in 1946 out of the former Emirate of Transjordan. Those parts of Palestine not under Israeli occupation after the Arab–Israeli War of 1948 were also added to the new state, which was heavily subsidised by Britain in its early years. King Hussein's father received annual payments rising from £2 million to £12 million.[4]

Despite the largesse, there had been times of real tension between the two countries, not least the sacking of Glubb Pasha by the young King Hussein and the subsequent unconfirmed rumour, circulated by John Foster Dulles, that Britain had offered Israel a slice of Jordan in the event of a successful outcome to the Suez affair.[5]

They were isolated storms in a generally close relationship, however, and Jordan remained one of Britain's strongest allies. It didn't appear to have too many other friends in 1970.

The sprawling refugee camps crammed with Palestinians enduring their long exile from their own homeland had been a constant ticking time-bomb ever since they had fled Israel. It had exploded in a violent uprising that threatened the survival of the state.

The trigger was 'Skyjack Sunday', 6 September 1970, when terrorists from the Popular Front for the Liberation of Palestine – an umbrella sheltering various terrorist groups acting on behalf of the Palestine Liberation Organisation – carried out a series of attempted hijackings. A TWA jet and a Swissair DC8 were seized and flown to Dawson's Field, a disused RAF base outside Amman, which the terrorists immediately rechristened Revolution Airfield.

The hijacked jets were then surrounded by more armed guerrillas, who filled them with explosives and threatened to blow the planes and their passengers sky-high unless terrorist prisoners held in Britain, Germany and Switzerland were released.

A PanAm 747 was also hijacked, taken to Cairo and blown up, but the attempted seizure of a fourth jet, an El Al flight to New York, was thwarted by security guards who shot one terrorist dead and overpowered the other, Leila Khaled.

The plane was diverted to London, where Khaled was arrested, but the hijackers merely added her name to the list of terrorists they wanted released. They reinforced the message by hijacking yet another plane, a BOAC VC-10, during a refuelling stop in Bahrain a couple of days later. It was also flown to Jordan.

Negotiations through the Red Cross over the next week led to the PFLP demands being met. All the terrorist prisoners held in Europe, including Leila Khaled, were released in exchange for the freeing of 375 hostages.

The hijackers still held a further fifty-five hostages, but fearing an assault by Israeli commandos, they staged a television spectacular for the world's media on 15 September by blowing up the hijacked planes on the tarmac. They then disappeared into the teeming Palestinian camps surrounding Amman, taking their hostages with them.

The terrorists' actions had laid down a direct challenge to the authority of King Hussein, but he soon faced two even greater threats. Almost half of the Jordanian army were Palestinian at the time and the loyalty of some of them was less to the state of Jordan than to their dreams of a Palestinian homeland.

One Palestinian officer gave Syria the codes used by a Jordanian tank brigade guarding the northern border. A Syrian tank division used the codes to move unchallenged through the Jordanian brigade's lines at night and then turned and attacked from the rear. It was the worst-case military scenario for the Jordanians but somehow they executed the very complicated manoeuvre of redeploying at night and under fire to face the threat from the rear.

The outnumbered Syrians had failed to achieve the surprise victory they sought and now found themselves cut off from retreat and were destroyed. On a flight over the region we counted over 300 wrecked Soviet-made tanks.

The external threat had been repelled, but the internal one was very much active. The final challenge to King Hussein came when PLO-supporting members of his forces began setting up roadblocks and exacting taxes from travellers. Even members of the Jordanian armed forces going on leave were forced to pay.

When King Hussein still hesitated to confront the PLO, a furious tank commander ordered his regiment to drive into Amman, flying women's underwear from the aerials of their tanks, saying, 'If we're going to be women, let's be women.'

He succeeded in shaming King Hussein into ordering his troops into action to crush the Palestinians. His previous hesitation was understandable, for the PLO were heavily armed and though Hussein's armed forces were at least as capable as any in the region, they suffered acutely from shortages of finance and equipment.

In the brief but savage civil war, all the remaining hostages from the hijackings were either released by the Palestinians or freed by Jordanian commandos. But during the vicious fighting as King Hussein's troops fought their way through the refugee camps, over 7,000 Palestinians died. Thousands more were then expelled from the country.

The Jordanian army had won the civil war, but the events of 'Black September' were to lead to the rise of another extremist Palestinian faction, which was to claim its own infamous place in history two years later.

In relation to a similar area of tension in the Middle East Britain had helped to ease its ally's equipment problems by persuading the US to set up a covert supply operation, routeing several flights a day to that country through Turkey. Britain sent only a thousandth, perhaps even a millionth of the military aid secretly supplied by America, but while the US were sending supplies, Britain sent men – the SAS.

I led an SAS team that spent several weeks cross-training with the nation's special forces in a number of skills and teaching them how to control and direct fighter ground-attacks. One of their officers sought me out at the end of the demonstration. 'Now I understand how the enemy beat the shit out of us in the last war.'

We also patrolled through villages with the special forces,

showing the flag, and put on several live fire demonstrations for other parts of the armed forces. Some of them were filmed and whenever the cameras were around we drifted into the background.

It was a propaganda exercise for both domestic and international consumption. Man for man, the country's forces were the equal of any in the region but they were at a great disadvantage in terms of equipment and technology compared to the Israelis or even the Iraqis. Television film of their firepower and effectiveness was a warning and a deterrent both to the rebels inside the country and to the neighbouring countries, including Israel.

The country in question was a pariah state at the time, friendless even among other Arab nations. Although the United States continued to supply military equipment, it was openly censorious of the country's expulsion of dissident factions after the civil war. Britain was virtually the only country in the world not to join the chorus of condemnation, and the SAS visit was designed to give concrete – and visible – form to British expressions of support. We even wore the beige beret and winged dagger badge of the Regiment.

As I stood outside the country's near-deserted main airport one morning, I heard a distant rumble and saw the sun flashing on the aluminium fuselage of an enormous jet transporter. The unmarked aircraft touched down and taxied to the far side of the airport where it was immediately surrounded by army trucks. It was unloaded in haste and minutes later it took off again, the thunder of its engines shaking the ground as it lumbered into the air.

An Arab wearing the distinctive black and white headdress of the country's Bedou had stopped to watch the jet disappear into the haze.

He turned to look at me. 'The Americans send us several aircraft a day full of arms and ammunition, but the aircraft carry no national flag and always unload and depart in a hurry, as if they are ashamed to be here. You British come here in uniform and everyone can see you. We now know that even when everyone else is against us, our true friends the British are here to support us.'

It is impossible to overstate the military and psychological value of that commitment of flesh and blood instead of money. Once more, the involvement was absolutely clandestine – no one in Britain, not even SAS wives, knew the SAS was there – but, once more, the Foreign Office ensured that every friendly head of state in the Gulf was made aware of it.

Relations were also very friendly with Oman, despite the feudal eccentricities of its ageing ruler. We continued regular desert exercises there and also trained the new sultan's bodyguards and elements of the armed forces, but there was one mission we lived to regret. Having trained the Trucial Oman Scouts, we found ourselves fighting against many of them when an insurrection erupted in Dhofar.

Operation Storm began in 1970. Certain of its hold over its own territory, the government of the People's Democratic Republic of Yemen – the former British colony of Aden – was now ready to start the Gulf dominoes falling.

Yemen shared a common border with the province of Dhofar, ruled by the Sultan of Oman, and was fomenting and supplying an insurrection by the jebalis, the tribesmen of the mountainous region. It also had the side-benefit for the Yemenis of diverting attention away from their own domestic difficulties. The Russians had filled the vacuum left by the British departure from Aden, but they soon found themselves facing similar problems; several Soviet helicopters were shot down in the Radfan area.

Intelligence reports of Iraqi-backed guerrillas infiltrating the Musandam peninsula at the opposite end of Oman had already led to one brief SAS intervention the previous year. A narrow spit of land dominating the narrow Straits of Hormuz at the entrance to the Gulf, Musandam was the most strategically vital piece of land in the Middle East.

Three troops of G Squadron with an accompanying force

of the Trucial Oman Scouts made seaborne landings using Gemini inflatables, or were inserted by helicopter. The free-fall troop carried out a simultaneous HALO – high altitude, low opening – insertion from 11,000 feet into the Wadi Rawdah, a high-level valley enclosed by mountain peaks rising to 7,000 feet. The aim was to cut off any insurgents fleeing from the coastal landing force.

One of the free-fallers, Trooper Paul 'Rip' Reddy, died when his parachute failed to open, and the intelligence report on which the operation had been based proved to be as defective as his parachute. The reconnaissance failed to reveal any convincing trace of insurgents. G Squadron remained in Mus-andam for another month, however, carrying out hearts and minds work with the Shihoo tribe who inhabited the area, mapping the peninsula and clearing rough airstrips in case of future problems there.

The uprising in Dhofar was an altogether different matter. A rebellion had been bubbling there throughout the 1960s. Guerrillas were trained by Soviet military advisers at the former British base at Khormaksar in Yemen and then sent back across the border into Dhofar. Cadres were also sent to the Soviet Union and China for training and political indoctrination.

Not all the training was supplied by Communist regimes. Many jebalis joined the Trucial Oman Scouts and were trained by the British. Some of them even took leave from the TOS during the dry season to go home to Dhofar and have a shoot-up with the sultan's armed forces.

It was hard to understand the British position, for the jebalis' motives and intentions were widely known from the start. The only assumption we could make was that the SIS was playing a particularly Byzantine double-game, trying to back both horses in the same race.

During the 1960s the insurrection had remained a classical low-key guerrilla conflict. The forces trying to contain it were a curious hybrid. The sultan's armed forces – universally known as the gaysh, the Arabic word for army – were British-officered mercenaries from Baluchistan, a hangover from the days of empire when Oman was governed from India and policed by troops recruited from the subcontinent. There were also Askaris – actually Omanis from the north of the country – who operated as a gendarmerie, policing the nightly curfew and generally oppressing the people.

The focus of the conflict was the Midway Road, bisecting the jebel. Little more than a rough track, it was the only road connecting the coastal plain with the rest of the country. It passed near the territory of the Bait Ma'ashini, the main tribe on the jebel and the focus of opposition to the sultan. They were fierce fighters and regularly attacked and closed the road.

For several years the insurrection followed a regular annual pattern dictated by the monsoon. Each dry season the gaysh would move up from the coastal plain, clear the road and establish defensive positions. The rebels would harry them, mounting ambushes and small-scale attacks, and then retreat deeper into the mountains. When the monsoon arrived, the gaysh would withdraw and the rebels would reoccupy the area and close the Midway Road again.

Each year the struggle to open the road, the lifeline for the regional capital, Salalah, became more prolonged. The rebels were mounting a classical guerrilla campaign, straight from the pages of Chairman Mao's 'Little Red Book'.

By 1970 they believed themselves strong enough to abandon the War of the Flea and move on to phase two of Chairman Mao's prescription: open, conventional warfare.

When the gaysh tried to make their annual push to open the Midway Road they were defeated and driven back. Salalah and the other coastal towns were now in a stranglehold, completely cut off from the rest of Oman.

Although much smaller in scale, the conflict in Dhofar was almost exactly mirroring the war in Vietnam; it seemed that Communism was in the ascendancy everywhere.

The rebels controlled 90 per cent of the region, a situation that terrified the SIS. If Dhofar fell, the rest of Oman would not be far behind, opening the way to Dubai, Abu Dhabi and the other oil-rich but militarily weak Trucial States.

The deteriorating military situation in Dhofar was made worse by the autocratic policies of the sultan, Sa'id bin Taimur. Neither the medieval remedy of hanging the beheaded bodies of captured rebels in the centre of Salalah and torching their villages in reprisal, nor ringing the city with barbed wire to stop food supplies getting out or armed rebels getting in had any effect.

The sultan's rule was sustained by fear alone and only those on his payroll had any reason to feel loyalty to him. There was no hope of winning the hearts and minds of any of his population while he remained in power and he was finally toppled in a British-backed coup on 23 July 1970.

The timing of the coup was significant. It was early in the dry season, allowing maximum time for military operations before the onset of the next monsoon. It also came within a month of the Conservative Edward Heath taking office, after his surprise victory over Harold Wilson in the June British general election.

The Heath government did not feel itself irrevocably bound by Wilson's plan for a total withdrawal from east of Suez by 1971. It was also more willing than its predecessor to contemplate low-key military interventions overseas, particularly in areas crucial to the defence of our oil supplies.

The coup in Oman went ahead, with the Wali of Dhofar having the thankless task of explaining to the sultan that it was time to go. It was a practical choice, for the wali faced death anyway if the rebels took Salalah, as seemed almost inevitable.

The sultan responded to the invitation to abdicate by pulling a pistol out of his desk drawer and loosing off a few rounds. When the smoke cleared, a palace servant lay dead and both the sultan and the wali had been wounded – all by shots fired by the sultan, whose aim proved to be little better than the bodyguards who had tried to assassinate him four years before. The wali, the sultan and his servant were the only casualties in an otherwise bloodless coup.

When it became clear to the sultan that his British protectors had also turned against him, he bowed to the inevitable and agreed to abdicate. He was flown out of Oman that night, sharing the plane with the wounded wali, who was also on his way to hospital.

After treatment for his self-inflicted gunshot wound, the old sultan went into permanent exile, living out the last two years of his life in a suite at the Dorchester Hotel in London.

His Western-educated and infinitely more liberal son, Sultan Qaboos, who had been a virtual prisoner in the royal palace in Salalah, began the task of dragging Oman into the twentieth century. In his first public address, he told his people: 'Oman in the past was in darkness, but ... a new dawn will rise.'[6]

Decades of poverty and grievances could not be rectified overnight, however, and meanwhile the rebellion in Dhofar threatened the survival of the whole state. The sultan had some credibility in the region, since his mother was a Dhofari, but his only real hope was to use military force to stem further rebel advances, buying time for a programme of civil development to begin winning over his dissident population.

The Omani army was not equal to the task and the Sandhurst-trained sultan needed little persuasion from the Political Resident to call in British troops.

The first SAS troops in Oman were a five-man BG team, there to protect the new sultan while an Omani team was trained to take over the role. The use of the SAS suited Sultan Qaboos very well; while at Sandhurst he had shared a room with an officer who was now serving with the Regiment.

In order to avoid arousing anti-Western sentiment, the SAS team carried out surveillance from behind a two-way mirror as the sultan received sheiks arriving to declare their allegiance, and petitioners seeking settlement of grievances.

Regimental legend has it that one sheik was lucky not

to be shot by the unseen bodyguards. In the course of his extravagant hand gestures as he made his obeisances, he appeared to be reaching into his robes for a gun.

While the SAS BG team watched over the sultan, a fifteen-man SAS troop began the first phase of Operation Storm – a plan that had been drawn up the previous spring, four months before the coup.

Like every other deployment throughout the six-year duration of the war, the SAS men were notionally posted to the British base at Sharjah. They stepped off the RAF plane in Sharjah in September 1970 and the second leg of the journey never happened. They arrived in Oman as the euphemistically titled British Army Training Team – BATT for short.

The secrecy caused its own problems, however. Resupply was continually hampered in the early stages of the campaign as requests for equipment were denied with the unanswerable question, 'Why do you need that in Sharjah?'

We finally solved the problem by routeing supplies through the RAF in Salalah who provided whatever we wanted with no questions asked.

Seasoned by the campaigns in the Jebel Akhdar and Aden, the SAS was the obvious force to take the fight to the rebels in the mountains of Dhofar. Just as in Aden, however, when we arrived the war was already as good as lost. The rebels controlled virtually the whole of Dhofar apart from the city of Salalah and part of the coastal plain, but, crucially, unlike Aden, this time there was no British wish to withdraw and leave the region to its fate.

With a commitment to stay in Dhofar rather than a looming deadline to leave, a hearts and minds policy became possible. In mounting it we had two straws at which we could clutch. Unlike every other force involved in the conflict, we were untarnished by any previous record of atrocities. Most of the previous outrages had been committed by the Baluchs and Askaris, but one group of rebels had also given their cause a savage, self-inflicted wound, which we hoped to turn to our advantage.

Buoyed by the victory over the gaysh in conventional battle, the political commissars of the rebels had advanced to the next stage of the grand plan. They began a programme of political indoctrination, attempting to convert the tribes from Islam to the secular religion of Communism.

Eighty to one hundred children of the Bait Ma'ashini tribe were being taken to Hauf in Yemen for indoctrination when a group of them tried to run away and return to their homes. In retaliation, the rebels in charge of them massacred them all.

From the rebel point of view it was a catastrophic mistake. A group of the Bait Ma'ashini broke with them and came down off the jebel. They were still too mistrustful of the sultan to switch sides at once, but they were now at worst neutral and were open to persuasion – and the SAS could be very persuasive.

The boss of D Squadron, Major Tony Jeapes, had developed his own blueprint for success in Operation Storm, involving what was known as the 'Five Fronts':

1 Intelligence operations aiming to isolate and demoralise the rebels as well as directing the military campaign.
2 Psychological operations to counter rebel propaganda and persuade rebel soldiers to defect.
3 A civil aid programme, with particular emphasis on providing water, funded to a level far in excess of anything the rebels could support.
4 Medical help to improve the health of the population.
5 Veterinary help to improve farm stock and offer advice on improved animal husbandry.

The concept was fine in theory, and though it was an

expensive programme there was no shortage of funds. Other Middle Eastern rulers casting an anxious eye over the progress of the rebellion in Oman were more than willing to help underwrite the cost of suppressing it.

There was a certain wry amusement among the SAS men as Tony Jeapes unveiled his grand design. He was more interested in the academic approach to a conflict than in the blood and guts business of trying to win a war. We regarded him as a romantic, building castles in the air before he had even put in the foundations.

Most of us preferred the more hard-bitten, pragmatic approach of his superior, the commanding officer, Lieutenant-Colonel Johnny Watts. He knew that to defeat an insurrection you had to fire bullets as well as drop leaflets. The conflict between their contrasting approaches was a continuing feature of Operation Storm. Even when Tony Jeapes was promoted to lieutenant-colonel and made CO later in the campaign, Johnny Watts remained his superior, for he was also promoted, to brigadier, and became Director, SAS Group.

The friction between the two men reached a climax over the disciplinary action Jeapes tried to impose on one troop officer in Dhofar. Having lost confidence in the officer's ability to run his troop, Jeapes relieved him of command and sent him back to HQ, ready to be returned to England and RTU'd.

Johnny Watts then arrived at HQ on a tour of inspection, however, and immediately countermanded the order. The unfortunate officer unpacked and repacked his bags several times as each man stuck to his guns, but, in the end, a face-saving compromise was reached. The officer was moved sideways to another squadron, allowing both Jeapes and Watts to claim that they had achieved their objective.

The final victory undoubtedly went to Watts, however. The junior officer went on to win a DSO in the Falklands campaign and later became commanding officer of the Regiment and then Director, SAS Group.

The first SAS troop in Dhofar, based initially at Mirbat and Taqa, had to assess ways of ensuring the security of the coastal plain before beginning any assault on the jebel. It began aggressive patrols and made an immediate start on hearts and minds work, setting up the first medical clinics the inhabitants had ever seen.

It also carried out a few simple construction projects to improve water supplies and repair irrigation channels destroyed on the orders of the old sultan. A vet from the Royal Army Veterinary Corps – which none of us even knew existed until then – also set up animal husbandry clinics.

Preliminary psychological warfare operations, innocently entitled Information Services, were run by an SAS corporal, Johnny Ward, under the enthusiastic patronage of Tony Jeapes. They included the air-drop of leaflets offering incentives to rebels to defect but were treated by the rest of us as little more than a joke.

Meanwhile Johnny Watts returned to Hereford to make final plans for the main deployment and to organise the necessary equipment. The initial requisitions caused some head-scratching among the Regiment's quartermasters.

In addition to the customary weapons and ammunition, and the now familiar hearts and minds kit of medical equipment and trinkets like transistor radios, were requests for a drilling rig – needed not to search for oil, but to sink boreholes for water – and a range of pedigree livestock. Most of it was bought around Hereford, another significant boost to the hearts and minds operations on our own doorstep.

The arrival of a full SAS squadron in Dhofar signalled the start of operations on the jebel. The campaign to win over the population there depended on convincing them that the sultan and his forces were there to stay and were determined to win. The SAS was sent in as a last throw of the dice, a short, sharp shock, to give a psychological boost.

Like the Jebel Akhdar, the terrain held by the rebels was horrendously difficult to attack, a 200-mile range of mountains rising 3,000 to 5,000 feet above the narrow coastal plain. Never more than ten miles wide, the coastal strip narrowed in places to as little as a few hundred yards.

The mountain plateau was cut with scores of wadis. Some were broad valleys, others narrow, precipitous ravines. Almost the only source of fresh water in the mountains lay in the streams among the dense scrub at the bottom of the wadis. Beyond the mountains was an arid, gravel plateau stretching away to the Rub al Khali – the Empty Quarter of Saudi Arabia.

The climate was as unforgiving as the terrain, with day temperatures well into the forties centigrade, stifling humidity and a monsoon season in which a month of torrential rain was followed by weeks of persistent low cloud and drizzle. Those conditions grounded aircraft, but offered perfect cover for the infiltration of insurgents and camel- or donkey-trains loaded with arms.

Despite the dismal living conditions we only received a basic overseas allowance, with none of the 'discomfort allowance' paid to men serving in Northern Ireland. We should have received the same money on active service in Dhofar, but when I asked, 'Why don't we get the allowance?' I was told, 'Because you're all officially posted to Sharjah. Anyway, you people actually like these conditions.'

It was no belt and braces rebellion that we had been tasked to suppress, for the Russians and their Yemeni clients were supporting it on a massive scale. The 2,000 rebels were well equipped and heavily armed; at the peak of the insurrection we were getting several hundred incomers a day, all from heavy weapons – mortars and artillery.

The adoo – Arabic for enemy – more formally known as the People's Front for the Liberation of the Occupied Arabian Gulf, were also ferocious fighters. Unlike their counterparts in the Jebel Akhdar, they had been well trained – either in China, Russia or the Trucial Oman Scouts – and their Communist beliefs and profound fatalism made them almost indifferent to injury or death.

The conventional military wisdom is that an attacking force needs to outnumber the defenders by at least five to one; the build-up to the Gulf War was so prolonged for that reason; none of the generals would move until they had overwhelming superiority of numbers and equipment.

We did not look at the conflict in Dhofar in that light. We simply felt we could get the job done, despite our shortage of numbers. We still had our doubts about the ultimate outcome, however, particularly in view of our limited confidence in the forces aligned alongside us.

We felt that the gaysh were ground-holders and nothing more. Once we had taken a piece of territory we could hand it over to them and they would defend it while we moved on, but we had very little confidence in their ability to conduct aggressive operations.

To strengthen our hand, we set about recruiting jebali SEPs – Surrendered Enemy Personnel. Some were volunteers, but our task was also to turn prisoners, train them, give them a weapon and then send them back into battle against their own side. In this we were helped by the split in the rebel side between the Islamic fundamentalists and the Marxists which had been exacerbated by the massacre of the Bait Ma'ashini people.

The Marxists won the argument and the fundamentalists promptly defected in droves – 200 SEP changed sides in the first six months of the campaign. We formed them into groups known as firqat, named after legendary Islamic heroes; the first we recruited was named Firqat al Salahadin. It was led by Said Mubarrak, a devout Muslim, whose previous allegiance to the rebel cause had been replaced by a burning determination to wage a jihad – a holy war – against them.

The members of the different jebali tribes may have been united in their Islamic faith, but that proved to be almost their only common ground. Our initial attempts to mix different tribes in the same firqat troops proved disastrous. They spent more time fighting each other than the enemy and from then on each firqat was based on a single tribe.

The jebalis were good fighters but often volatile, and trust between us was very fragile in the early stages of the campaign. On more than one occasion we found ourselves forced to face down the troops we were training as both sides fingered their weapons.

When Said Mubarrak died of a heart attack in his sleep one night, his men immediately suspected that he'd been poisoned. Only their uncertainty about whether the poisoners were ourselves, the adoo, or agents of the sultan prevented a fire-fight.

Our firqat troops proved to be incredibly brave and quite well trained, but they tended to treat battle like a football match. After fighting ferociously for a while, they would then withdraw and go to sleep for three days. Working alongside the SAS gave them the impetus to keep going, maintaining the pressure on the enemy, instead of knocking off for a rest. The relationship between us and our firqat allies was not a love match – we had virtually nothing in common – but it was founded on a mutual respect.

We also altered the military balance in other ways. The adoo had more and better heavy weapons – recoilless rifles, artillery and mortars – than the gaysh and could knock seven bells out of them in any set-piece battle. SAS men changed that. We could carry phenomenally heavy weights – including some heavy weapons – into battle, and we could also control artillery and aircraft, nullifying the rebels' previous advantage.

Apart from strength on the ground, the other defining factor for operations on the mountain plateau where the rebels had their bases was resupply. The sultan's forces had virtually no air assets; all they had were a couple of ancient helicopters and a couple of Skyvans – like a Ford Transit with wings. As a result, all resupply of the gaysh had to be done by ground, and in the trackless, mountainous terrain that meant on foot. Once the SAS had established a bridgehead in the mountains, however, we could call in air resupply and extend the duration of our operations almost indefinitely.

Our first task was simply to make our presence felt on the plateau. As in the Jebel Akhdar campaign, we carried out extensive reconnaissance patrols, probing the rebel defences and searching for unprotected routes up the mountain.

A small patrol from Mountain Troop with half a dozen men from the Firqat al Salahadin then made a night ascent of the 3,000-foot escarpment. After lying up on a rock ledge throughout the next day, they carried out a recce for the main force, two SAS troops and sixty men from the firqat, who followed them up the mountain on 13 March.

Supplies were helicoptered in on the first morning and we then pushed on to Tawi Atair, where the firqat knew there was water. There we came under mortar fire directed by the Dhofari officer we had trained years before.

We remained on the plateau for twelve days, killing nine enemy and capturing several more without sustaining any casualties. That one operation showed the calibre of the SAS to both the adoo and the firqat. A further operation against an adoo gun emplacement overlooking the town of Taqa also led to a number of enemy casualties. We had made an immediate impact on the conflict, even though those first operations had been little more than shows of strength. As the British government became convinced that it was a winnable war after all, a second Sabre Squadron was also committed. Over the next five and a half years all four SAS squadrons rotated through a succession of four-month tours of duty in Oman.

The euphoria from our initial successes soon evaporated as the next operation, an assault on the Jebel Aram, showed what a long, hard and bloody battle we faced. The whole of D Squadron and half of A Squadron, who had just arrived to begin their tour of duty, were committed, together with two firqat troops – about sixty men – and three companies of gaysh, with artillery support from the plain.

Tony Jeapes took the final briefing, telling us that we were 'going up on the Jebal Aram to teach them a lesson'. We spent three days up there and if anyone was administering a lesson, it was the adoo; they gave us a pounding.

The original plan had been to pull off after dark on the third night, but when I told my firqat at two o'clock that afternoon, their leader said, 'If we go off tonight, we'll be slaughtered. We go off now.'

We managed to persuade the Head Shed – the planning group of officers and senior NCOs including Tony Jeapes – that it made sense to get out while the adoo were sleeping through the heat of the day, and made a hasty and undignified retreat.

As we reached the foot of the jebel and began to cross the arid plain towards Taqa, plumes of dust rising from our boots at each step, a dour Scots sergeant, Mac Maclean, shook his fist at the jebel and shouted, 'And let that be a lesson to you.'

We had recced the jebel from both the north and south and knew what had to be done to succeed. We had also studied Mao's 'Little Red Book' ourselves and our first aim was to defeat the adoo in conventional warfare and knock them back to phase one – hit-and-run guerrilla attacks.

We settled in to the long, hard grind of winning the war and made moves to establish a permanent foothold on the plateau as soon as the monsoon had passed. Operation Jaguar, involving two full SAS squadrons and all the available firqat, was launched on 2 October 1971.

The plan was to clear an area of adoo, set up a defensive perimeter, bring in an immediate air-drop resupply and then construct an airstrip to enable permanent air resupply to be carried out.

One party of SAS with two firqat troops climbed one of the mountains to make a diversionary attack on a point nicknamed Eagle's Nest, while the main force attacked and seized an area of the plateau at Lympne, east of Jibjat. All these targets were on the north side of the jebel, where our recces had shown that the approaches were less precipitous than on the seaward side.

Just the same, the steep climb to the plateau over boulder fields and screes of sharp rock on a night of fierce heat and humidity took its toll. Barely half the force were still together as we reached the undefended target just after 4.30 in the morning and began constructing rough sangars.

We were so exhausted and dehydrated from the climb that we would have been hard pressed to repel an immediate counter-attack, but the rebels held back and resupply air-drops of water and equipment helped us to consolidate our position.

The most telling contribution Johnny Watts made to the whole conflict in Dhofar had been to gear up those resupply arrangements. He insisted that the SOAF (Sultan of Oman's Air Force) rules of aircraft safety – which had previously forbidden landings within six miles of a fire-fight – be torn up.

More groups of firqat joined us on the plateau and the next night we advanced on Jibjat. The march over rock-strewn ground in suffocating heat was almost as gruelling as the ascent of the mountain, but by 4 October the force was in control of Jibjat and aggressive patrols began pushing deeper into the plateau.

Two SAS troops, each with firqat support, then advanced down either flank of the Wadi Darbat, the heartland of the Bait Ma'ashini, and the focus of resistance for the whole of the eastern jebel. We drove the rebels back in a series of fierce contacts in which we suffered our first casualties of the campaign. Three men were wounded by enemy fire and one of them, Sergeant Steve Moores, later died of his wounds.

Casualties were treated at the tented Army Field Surgical Unit set up at our base camp. There was no other surgical facility in the whole of Oman. The men working there did a great job, but the unit proved to be inadequate to cope with the type of injuries that were sustained in the fighting.

As we advanced across the plateau, we created a series of rough airstrips, allowing the British pilots with the SOAF to fly in supplies, but landing aircraft in the rough and boulder-strewn terrain was a job for the brave only.

Air support was to prove crucial in the Dhofar campaign, but the pivotal role was not that provided by the jet-jockey Strikemaster pilots flying ground-attack missions, but the humble 'truckies' bringing in supplies in Skyvans and Caribous.

Well supplied, we continued to advance and by 9 October the adoo had been driven into hiding in the dense scrub of the deep wadis that pierced the plateau. Attempts to flush them from those sanctuaries were hampered by the firqat's insistence on observing Ramadan, despite dispensations from their religious leaders allowing them to continue the jihad against the godless Communists.

We SAS, who did not normally stop fighting for religious festivals, weekends or bank holidays, had to grind our teeth and withdraw from some of the more exposed positions we had just taken.

After threats to pull out altogether and leave the firqat to fend for themselves, normal service was resumed. Bases were established at Jibjat and Medinat al Haq, the City of Truth. Less poetically, the SAS men christened it White City, not for its fine architecture but because the place had gone to the dogs.

A defensive line, the Leopard Line, was also established to control the flow of arms and the movement of the rebels. It was fortified with barbed wire and Claymore mines, and watched over by a series of guardposts along its length. When secure, responsibility for the Leopard Line was handed to the sultan's armed forces, while the SAS, Baluch and firqat continued to push forward into rebel territory.

By the end of Operation Jaguar the eastern jebel up to and including the Midway Road was largely under our control. It had been the defining operation of the conflict. At the end of it, we knew that we were going to win, the only question was how long it would take.

As each area was pacified, a well-rehearsed hearts and minds operation swung into gear. The firqat local to that area would choose a suitable site for a permanent base. The perimeter was fortified and bulldozers would then rumble over the plateau, constructing a graded road. The first traffic along it would be the arrival of a drilling rig.

The only natural water on the jebel was found in the wadis, the last refuges of the adoo. To break the link between them and the local population we sank boreholes on the plateau, removing the need for villagers to go down into the wadis for water for themselves and their livestock.

After the road and the borehole, the next arrival was invariably a consignment of televisions. The programming was a monotonous diet of government propaganda but there were only two choices for the villagers, on or off. The TV sets were supplied by Johnny Ward's Psy-Ops Team and could not be tuned to any other channel.

Solid, permanent buildings were also constructed, housing a health clinic, a school, a mosque and a shop. At first free rations were issued, later they were sold at heavily subsidised prices.

In a region without doctors, where a common treatment for aches and pains was to brand the area with a red-hot iron,[7] SAS medics were soon overwhelmed with patients.

Hearts and minds operations took some unconventional forms on the jebel, including one on 28 November 1971 that 'must surely be unique in military history, a Texan-style cattle drive supported by jet-fighter cover and 5.5-inch artillery'.

It had been organised to guarantee a safe trip to market for the livestock of the firqat's families and friends in the villages scattered across the plateau. Goats could be airlifted out, but cattle were too heavy and 'amidst scenes like shots from a Marx Brothers' comedy mixed with a John Wayne western, fire-fights between pickets and adoo on the high ground, whoops of delight from the firqat and expressions of amused disbelief by the SAF and SAS, 500 head of cattle were driven across the plateau and down the jebel'.[8]

In fact, we were less than impressed with the operation. There was more than a suspicion that the cattle had actually been rustled from their rightful owners and we felt that it was a high-risk operation for a very modest reward. Although trivial in itself, however, the cattle drive did help to reinforce the message that after decades of neglect interspersed with bouts of medieval violence against them, the new sultan was dedicated to improving the life of his subjects.

As in other hearts and minds schemes, the local population attending our clinics or collecting food and water provided intelligence on enemy movements in return, but despite our good relations with them, only the local firqat patrolled inside the villages on the plateau. They spoke the Dhofari language and knew the people. We'd occasionally send in a medic if someone was too ill to come to the clinics set up at our camps, but even then he would only go in if accompanied by the firqat.

Early in the campaign some atrocities had been committed by both sides – the Baluch and the adoo. The Baluch, who did not share our enthusiasm for hearts and minds, were forbidden to go near the villages at all and we also kept out of them ourselves, ensuring there was no risk of an incident that could turn the population against us.

If an old man came out of a hut with a rifle during a search of a village, he could easily have been shot as a suspected rebel. If it then transpired that he was just a goatherd carrying his gun to work, we would have lost the support of an entire village in one easily avoidable incident.

The hearts and minds charm offensive was combined with continuing military operations against the adoo. We drove them further and further back into the jebel until they were restricted to small bands hiding in the more inaccessible wadis.

Our successes stung the adoo into a full-scale retaliation in a contact that entered SAS legend as the Battle of Mirbat. The eastern jebel was now largely pacified and the attack by the rebels was a last desperate throw of the dice, an attempt to relieve the pressure further west. It came perilously close to success.

The coastal town of Mirbat, forty miles east of Salalah, was a cluster of mud houses, protected by an ancient fort. It was manned by thirty members of the Omani gendarmerie, armed with ancient Lee Enfield rifles. Within the same compound, though separated from the fort by about a quarter of a mile, was the BATT house, with an SAS troop numbering nine men, and forty firqat based nearby, and the wali's fort, with a troop of thirty Askari.

Before dawn on the morning of 19 July 1972 it came under attack from a force of some 250 rebels, backed by artillery, mortars, rocket-launchers and machine-guns. The defenders had only a single twenty-five-pounder, one mortar, a heavy machine-gun and a few GPMGs – general purpose machine-guns – with which to hold them off.

The enemy had waited for the monsoon to launch their attack. The low cloud and rain that accompanied the monsoon prevented detection of their build-up of troops and heavy weapons. The low cloud ceiling also stopped fighter ground-attack aircraft being called in. Even helicopters had difficulty in getting airborne.

A gendarmerie outpost on Jebel Ali, a small hill beyond the perimeter fence, was overwhelmed in the first minutes of the battle. After a sustained barrage from artillery and mortars, the adoo then made a frontal attack on the fort.

'The whole corner of the fort erupted with the sound of machine-guns and rifles mixed with the explosion of shells. All the enemy's fire seemed to be directed at the fort and the SAS men looked on in disbelief as it disappeared from sight. A cloud of brown smoke and dust, lit up in spasms by the bright flashes of shell-bursts against the walls, hid the fort entirely.'[9]

As soon as the firing started, a Fijian SAS man, Corporal 'Lab' Labalaba, had sprinted to the gun-pit at the fort to help the Omani gunner. When he was injured Lab took over and, despite a serious wound to his face, he kept firing the twenty-five-pounder at point-blank range against the enemy advancing through the perimeter wire. Another Fijian SAS man, 'Tak' Takavesi, went to his aid.

After a brief lull in the fighting, possibly to bring up more ammunition, the enemy pressed home the attack. Tak was now also seriously wounded and Captain Mike Kealy and Trooper Tommy Tobin made the perilous run to the gun-pit using fire and movement to avoid the hail of fire directed at them. Corporal Roger Chapman also poured machine-gun fire into the enemy.

Lab was killed, still firing the twenty-five-pounder, as the rebels all but overwhelmed the gun position. Seconds later Tobin was also hit. He died later of his wounds. The adoo were tossing grenades at the gun-pit and one landed between Mike and the badly injured Tak, but failed to explode. In frenzied hand-to-hand fighting, they held out as the remaining SAS men in the BATT house fired mortar shells and machine-gun bullets within inches of their own men.

The mortar could not be elevated far enough to fire at such close range and Corporal Bob Bradshaw had to tilt it back against his chest and grip it with his thighs, while another man dropped the mortar shells down the barrel.[10]

An attempt to evacuate the casualties by helicopter was abandoned when it came under heavy fire. The position for the SAS men seemed hopeless. All communication had been lost with the fort and only two of the men in the gun-pit – Mike and Tak – were still capable of firing their weapons.

They were saved only by two chance events. A fractional lifting of the overcast allowed the Omani air force's Strikemaster jets to get airborne. Flying conditions were still extremely hazardous, with the cloud ceiling down almost to ground level, but the pilots used the clearer conditions out to sea to descend to low level and then made repeated strafing runs which drove the rebels back a little.

The message then came through on the radio that reinforcements were airborne. By the purest good fortune, twenty-three men of G Squadron, who had just arrived in

Dhofar to relieve B Squadron, were at Salalah airfield at eight that morning, on their way to a firing range. Two helicopters flew them in at low level and after landing just south-east of Mirbat, they began advancing on the fort.

Under the combined assault of the fresh SAS troops and the continuing strafing runs by the Strikemasters, the rebels turned and ran. They left thirty-eight of their dead behind and the battlefield was strewn with their Chinese- and Russian-made weapons. The SAS lost two men, Lab and Tommy Tobin, and two seriously wounded.

Lab's courage and coolness under fire, even when wounded, should have earned him far more than a posthumous Mention in Despatches, but few knew just how much courage it had taken even for him to go to Mirbat, where he already knew that he would die.

Before leaving Hereford for Dhofar, Lab had told several of us that he would not be coming back. On the approach to Salalah, the Hercules flew over Mirbat. Lab had never even been to Dhofar before, let alone Mirbat, but he pointed out of the window and told his Fijian colleague Jim, 'That's where I'm going to die.'

When they arrived at base they discovered that while Jim had been posted to Mirbat, Lab was being sent somewhere else. 'Looks like you got it wrong,' Jim said.

The next morning, just as they were deploying, the OC made a last-minute change and switched Lab's posting. Despite his premonition, Lab went to Mirbat without protest, still with a smile on his face.

The Battle of Mirbat had been a knife-edge from a famous victory for the rebels. They had bypassed several other outposts to strike at it, and had they chosen any other outpost, on any other day, they would have succeeded.

The day before, G Squadron were not even in Oman. The day after, they would have been dispersed. There would have been no reinforcements and the fort would have been overrun. Had the rebels attacked any other outpost, the

Strikemasters and helicopters would have been powerless to intervene.

Mirbat was right on the coast, at zero feet above sea level, and the Strikemasters were able to fly out to sea beyond the cloudbank covering the land, then descend to wave-top height and fly back in on a bearing that took them straight over the fort. The helicopters made their approach the same way.

All the other outposts were well above sea level and much closer to the sheer wall of the jebel. Neither the jets nor the helicopters could have reached them until the cloud had lifted, by which time it would have been too late.

As it was, the arrival of the Strikemasters and the SAS reinforcements turned a certain defeat into a victory. There were to be no more frontal assaults by the rebels on strongholds of the sultan's forces, either on the coastal strip or even high in the jebel. Like us, the rebels now knew that we were going to win, but it was to be four more years before the conflict was finally over.

During the remainder of the dry season we dominated more and more of the plateau, but the monsoon made air resupply impossible and drove us back to the coast. Even the Leopard Line had to be abandoned. The adoo lost no time in taking advantage of our withdrawal. Fresh supplies of arms and ammunition were soon moving across the jebel and the adoo also began hit-and-run attacks, even rocketing the outskirts of Salalah.

As soon as the monsoon eased, we returned to the plateau. We re-established control over the old areas and then began pushing out into new ones. The rebels were driven further on to the back foot as more and more troops flooded into the area and new defensive lines were constructed to interdict adoo and arms convoys closer and closer to the Yemeni border.

The sultan's armed forces had doubled in size by the end of 1973 and fresh foreign troops had also arrived. The Shah of Iran had supported Sultan Qaboos from the start and C130s flew regular shuttles from Tehran, bringing in arms and ammunition. The military supplies were later followed by combat troops and eventually a complete Iranian Imperial Battle Group was serving in Dhofar. Jordan also sent equipment and a contingent of special forces.

We had re-established the Leopard Line and the Iranians set up another defensive line, the Damavand Line. They also built their own airstrip at Manston. Despite their numbers, the Iranians were poorly led and poorly trained. They took fearsome casualties; guesstimates range up to thousands of dead.

Not knowing where they were or what they were doing, they constructed big round sangars – like sheepfolds in the Yorkshire Dales – and remained inside them, not even daring to put their heads above the parapet.

SEPs recounted stories to us of massacres of scores of Iranians at a time. A group of adoo would open fire on a sangar and while the Iranians kept their heads down, a couple of rebels would sneak up, toss grenades inside or jump on the wall and wipe them out. There were tents full of coffins at Manston, but there was no publicity about the Iranian deaths at all.

Had we suffered even a hundredth of their losses, the UK government would have pulled us out, but our casualties – both official and unofficial – were sufficiently light for us to stay and complete the job.

By the following summer we were well enough established on the jebel to maintain our positions right through the monsoon period. The conditions restricted our ability to carry out aggressive patrols and we came under frequent hit-and-run attacks from mortars and rocket-launchers, but our continuing presence sent a clear signal to the adoo. There would be no further withdrawals from the plateau until they had been defeated.

The constant attrition from rebel casualties in contacts with SAS patrols was exacerbated by the flow of defections to the sultan's side, swelling to a flood as more and more of the jebel came under our control.

As usual, the campaign inside Dhofar was not the whole

story of SAS involvement, however. Even though the whole of Operation Storm was covert, there was a deeper level of secrecy. The Saudis also had a powerful interest in pacifying the region, for oil was reputed to have been found in that part of the Empty Quarter. The rumours turned out to be true. A massive oilfield now straddles the border areas, generating substantial revenue for Oman, Saudi Arabia and the Yemen.

SAS-sponsored patrols operated in the area and trained local forces. The effect was to tie down at least a brigade of troops, who were compelled to protect vulnerable areas and patrol to deter further attacks. Without their protection, parties of insurgents infiltrating Oman and the camel-trains carrying food, weapons and ammunition were much more open to interception and ambush.

One of the destinations of the camel-trains, the Shershitti Caves, a rebel bastion and arms store, had defied the best attempts of the Iranians and the sultan's armed forces to take it. An Iranian assault had been beaten off and a subsequent combined assault by a battalion of SAF troops backed by SAS and firqat was also fruitless.

The firqat in that area were nowhere near the calibre of those in the eastern jebel, but the Bait Ma'ashini considered that they had done their job by clearing their own areas and it was time for the other tribes to play their part in the fighting.

The firqat commanders involved in the attack on the Shershitti Caves insisted on an artillery barrage at the start of the assault. Having robbed themselves of the element of surprise, they came under heavy attack. An infantry company led by an inexperienced officer was advancing over open ground when it was ambushed and sustained 40 per cent casualties.

The SAS squadron was in a similar position, being led by an officer who had been posted in as OC without ever having served in the Regiment or been on active service in Dhofar. The OCs of both the SAS squadron and the infantry unit were acting against the advice of their men.

The only reason the SAS did not suffer similar casualties is that, knowing what to expect, instead of waiting while their OC assessed the situation, they legged it across the open ground. They then led the rescue of the surviving infantry, laying down a barrage of fire to pin down the enemy as the wounded were extracted.

A second SAS squadron also had to contend with an OC who had never served with the Regiment as the repercussions from the chronic shortage of officers in the 1960s continued to be felt. The obvious solution – to promote more men from the ranks – was not adopted for some considerable time.

People often had to return to their former units to win a commission. Some then came back to the SAS as officers, causing friction with the men, who could not understand why the Head Shed would accept a former lance-corporal as an officer if some other unit commissioned him, but wouldn't consider commissioning their own other ranks.

Even when the principle of promoting from the ranks was finally accepted, a bizarre restriction was imposed: the new officers were prohibited from serving with a Sabre Squadron, tossing away the years of combat experience they had accumulated.

What the Regiment was missing by their blinkered policy was demonstrated by the failed attempts to take the Shershitti Caves. After the combined brainpower of the officers of the SAS, SAF and Iranian forces had failed to find a solution to the problem, an SAS trooper produced the answer.

Instead of frontal assaults on the caves, his proposal was simply to shell the rebels out of them. Recoilless guns borrowed from the Iranians were used at first, but a rough track was then bulldozed to a nearby vantage point, bringing the caves within range of Saracen armoured cars. Fire from their 75mm guns proved sufficient to deny the enemy the use of the caves and the surrounding network of tracks for the rest of the conflict.

The crews of the Saracens – Omani soldiers with British officers and NCOs – did a magnificent job throughout the conflict, providing mobile heavy weapon support wherever it was needed, without question. If it was possible for a vehicle to reach an area, they would be there.

We kept up the unrelenting pressure on the adoo, continuing to push them back towards the Yemeni border, and steadily flushing them out of their last refuges among the dense scrub of the wadi floors. Even the direct intervention of Yemeni forces failed to stem the tide. The last of my squadron's seven four-month tours of duty in Dhofar saw a huge contact in October 1975 with Yemeni forces who had infiltrated fifty miles inside Dhofar.

The attack was launched almost by accident. A diversionary attack was mounted from a position held by SAF forces on a mountain-top near Sarfait. It was completely surrounded by rebel territory at that time and resupplied by air. The only other way out was down narrow steps cut into the near-vertical cliffs.

Correctly confident that any attack from that quarter would be a diversion, the rebels left it undefended. When our vanguard forces reached the first plateau without firing a shot, however, the whole battle plan was tossed aside. The rapidly reinforced diversionary attack became the main thrust and within twenty-four hours we had driven a wedge from the mountain to the sea, severing the rebels' last supply lines.

That part of the jebel was very rugged and precipitous, and therefore sparsely populated. With no local firqat available, the SAS became the point section for the attack – the shock troops. Just one troop – a dozen SAS men – inflicted enemy losses of between 100 and 200. Our own losses were one dead and one very seriously wounded, though everybody was damaged to some degree. The Yemenis retreated and never came back.

A follow-up operation captured the last rebel bases, including the Shershitti Caves, and swept most of the remaining adoo back over the border. The enemy stores we found in the caves included 50,000 heavy weapon rounds and 250,000 light weapon rounds.

It was a vivid demonstration of the worth of the intelligence provided by the group from Intelligence Corps, christened 'the Green Slime' after the colour of their berets. Throughout the conflict they had been assuring us that the adoo were desperately short of supplies, 'down to their last tea-bag and five rounds'. The evidence from the Shershitti Caves proved how wildly wide of the mark they had been.

The capture of the caves was the final blow for the insurrection. A few small bands of rebels battled on, but most of the survivors had only the option of surrender or a dangerous retreat across the border to Yemen, harried by SAS, firqat and SAF patrols.

The sultan's announcement in December 1975 that the war was over proved a little premature, but by the following spring, guerrilla activity had completely ceased. The last SAS Sabre Squadron was withdrawn in September 1976. Operation Storm had lasted six years.

To a greater or lesser extent, each of Tony Jeapes's beloved Five Fronts had had some impact on the Dhofar campaign, but the most important factor was the one in which he showed least interest. All the psy-ops and civil aid in the world won't make any difference if the enemy forces sweep you into the sea; the first thing you have to do is win the battles.

The only one of the Five Fronts with relevance to that was the first – intelligence gathering – which had originally been placed under the control of the Green Slime. They were to establish a permanent section at Hereford after the campaign, but they were largely ineffectual in Oman.

The jebali SEPs were the only reliable sources of intelligence. Initially they were sent to the Green Slime for debriefing, but the jebalis saw them as devious, 'siaseet' types and wouldn't talk to them. We put a stop to that procedure and had them debriefed by other jebalis from the firqat troops. In most cases we did an immediate op based on their information and we always got kills.

After fighting alongside the rebels for as much as ten years, a jebali would go back with a firqat troop the day after defecting and kill his former friends and allies. We were very wary of the instant converts at first because their attitude was so alien to anything we had experienced, but in the end we came to accept it as just another part of the jebali character.

Psy-ops, the second of Tony Jeapes's fronts, had minimal impact. A disparate group from different regiments under the command of a lieutenant – which shows the importance attached to the programme – spent most of their time dropping leaflets or organising film shows. The jebalis loved cowboy films, but they inevitably ended in disappointment; they always cheered for the Indians and in hundreds of celluloid battles they never once got a result.

Veterinary advice was also of minor importance in hearts and minds work, but medical help was crucial, the vital first step in building trust with the jebalis. The SAS medics were excellent – they had to be to look after their own men in the field – but that also gave them the skills to treat the jebalis. They became trusted, even occasionally revered; Dhofar was the only place in the whole of the Middle East where male medics were allowed to treat women patients.

The civil aid programme – another part of hearts and minds under another name – was also fundamental to the success of Operation Storm, but, vital though it was, it always went one pace behind the military effort.

Our message to the jebalis was straightforward: Life will be better for your people from now on. Help us to fight this battle and clear this area of adoo and things will get better. They had to; after decades under the old sultan's blighted rule, the people had nothing at all. If I'd been a jebali, I'd have joined the rebels.

As well as carrying out hearts and minds operations, the prime task of the Regiment had been to recruit and train the firqat. The use of the firqat was not only dictated by their value as fighters and their knowledge of the terrain. The training and front-line use of indigenous forces also minimised the risk of politically unacceptable levels of British casualties.

The policy was in part an echo of President Nixon's 'Vietnamisation' policy in Vietnam, which reduced US casualty rates in the cynical – and correct – belief that the American public would be indifferent to continuing huge numbers of Vietnamese casualties, as long as US servicemen were no longer being killed.

Yet whatever UK politicians might have preferred, there was no question of the Regiment merely training the firqat in Dhofar and then leaving them to do the dirty work unaided. SAS men fought ferociously alongside the firqat and on our own account.

The claim made by Tony Jeapes in a book published not long after the Oman conflict – the first ever breach of the SAS wall of secrecy by an insider – that the war 'was won in the end by civil development, with military action merely a means to that end'[11] was a grotesque distortion.

SAS casualty figures told a truer story and even they did not give the full picture, for many casualties went unreported. Throughout Operation Storm the Head Shed remained terrified that the UK government would pull the plug if heavy casualties were sustained, but SAS men helped to conceal the true extent of casualties by opting to stay on the jebel for treatment of wounds that would normally have required evacuation to the field unit. The casualties went unreported but the resulting crude 'bush surgery' left many men with permanent scars.

Seriously wounded men who could not be treated on the jebel were patched up enough to travel, then sent back through Sharjah to military hospitals in Cyprus and Britain, where casualties were reported to have suffered their injuries in road accidents. When I called in at the military hospital at

Akrotiri in Cyprus, a doctor told me, 'They must have the worst drivers in the world in Sharjah.'

Tony Jeapes had lost much of his remaining credibility within the Regiment after saying that if there were to be casualties he would rather lose an SAS man than a member of a firqat. He later denied making the remark, but I was there when he said it. His rationale was that we could stand a loss, whereas the firqat might just melt back into the mountains, but it was an inappropriate and unfortunate message to give to his own troops.

We took heavy casualties in Oman, in purely human terms, the politicians regarded them as entirely acceptable. Twelve SAS men were killed and many others were wounded. The numbers were small, but they represented almost 10 per cent of the actual fighting strength of the Regiment's Sabre Squadrons.

The scale of the conflict we had fought may be judged not from Tony Jeapes's self-justifying observations, but from one simple statistic: we used the British army's entire front-line reserve of ammunition during Operation Storm.

Our reward was to have inflicted only the second significant defeat ever on a Communist insurrection. Malaya was the other, and the SAS had played a vital role in both. Our success was in marked contrast to the American defeat in Vietnam and was a very significant factor in the decision of the US to form a near-replica of the SAS, Delta Force.

Many decorations and Mentions in Despatches were awarded to SAS men for Operation Storm, though none was gazetted until the campaign was over. We weren't even given the General Service Medal – the campaign medal – until well into the conflict. The award was then devalued when RAF base personnel were given the same medal, even though their orders forbade them ever to go beyond the perimeter of their camps.

Decorations were the only tangible rewards for the SAS, for rates of pay in the Regiment remained abysmal throughout the 1970s. The campaign in Dhofar inadvertently helped to change that, however, for the well-financed civil-aid operations proved a magnet for SAS men. Many left the Regiment to take up jobs in Oman at five and six times their previous pay and such large-scale defections had a serious impact on the Regiment's morale and efficiency.

Our experience in Dhofar gave the Regiment the ammunition for a sustained lobbying campaign within the MoD, which finally bore fruit in 1980 with the introduction of Special Forces Pay. After that, the SAS was not only the best place to soldier, for the first time it was also the best paid. The influx of eager would-be recruits swelled to a flood after the orgy of publicity surrounding the siege of the Iranian Embassy twelve months later.

Operation Storm remained so secret that long after the conflict had ended, even those who had heard of it had no idea where it had taken place. By contrast, our next deployment was carried out in the full glare of publicity and media attention.

It was rare for the British government to confirm SAS involvement in any conflict, even after it had finished. Now, for the first and only time in the Regiment's history, the government made a public announcement of an SAS operation before it had even begun.

9

NORTHERN IRELAND
1968–97

Six of us lay in a hedge bottom a few yards from the Three Steps Inn in Camlough, deep in the bandit country of South Armagh. We were wearing combat fatigues and our faces were smeared with black camouflage paint.

Each of us carried an automatic pistol, a Heckler-Koch submachine-gun, a few flash-bang grenades, a jemmy to break windows and a car jack to spread door jambs – all the equipment we needed to break into a building, rescue hostages and get them out alive.

It had taken us a long time to get into position, crawling over the sodden ground, pausing several times to change camouflage. We had used up the remains of the daylight; it was now almost dusk.

There was a glow of warm yellow light from the pub. We could hear the sounds of people talking and laughing, and music playing. It was a normal Saturday night scene; we could have been anywhere in the British Isles.

Then I saw two giants of men striding down the street. Both were well over six feet tall and very powerfully built. They were unarmed, but wearing camouflage uniforms and beige berets badged with a winged dagger. Lawrence and Rover were SAS men and were advertising the fact to anyone who cared to look.

Without breaking stride, they walked straight up the steps and through the door of the pub. The music came to an abrupt stop, as if the bad guys had just walked into a saloon.

Voices were raised for a few seconds and then everything went quiet. A couple of minutes later the music restarted.

The tension grew as we waited for the signal to tell us everything was all right. Lawrence and Rover were to contact us every five minutes. If the signal did not come we would be breaking down the pub door to rescue them.

Our tension was understandable. A few weeks previously Captain Robert Nairac had been abducted from the Three Steps, and tortured and murdered by the IRA. He was operating in plain clothes and was co-located with us, but was not a member of the SAS and had never served with the Regiment. He was a Guards officer, serving with the Fourteenth Intelligence Company – 14 Int.

Had he been an SAS member, he would not have been allowed to operate in the way he did. Before his death we had been very concerned at the lack of checks on his activities. No one seemed to know who his boss was, and he appeared to have been allowed to get out of control, deciding himself what tasks he would do.

His death reinforced the lessons of Northern Ireland. It was virtually impossible for an outsider to simulate not only the nuances of accent and dialect, but the shared assumptions and attitudes which made the republican communities so hard to infiltrate.

Nairac may well have been overconfident of his ability to pass unrecognised. He also committed the cardinal errors of operating without back-up, leaving his weapon in his car and not adhering strictly to standard operational drills. There was evidence that he had become lax about checking in with his base; as a result thirty-five minutes were allowed to elapse after his scheduled check-in time before the alarm was raised. By then he was dead.[1]

We were determined not to make the same mistakes. The signaller was lying next to me and I heard the faint double-click in his headphones, the signal we had been waiting for, tapped out on the radio concealed in Rover's sleeve.

It meant 'Everything's okay,' and we all relaxed a little.

The minutes ticked slowly by between the signals. Rain had begun to fall again and the cold and damp seemed to seep into my bones. Six weeks ago we had been in the Middle East finishing off Operation Storm. It was only eight weeks since Rover had led his troop in the clearing of the Shershitti Caves, for which he had been awarded the Distinguished Conduct Medal.

Now we had been sent to South Armagh to confront the IRA on the express – and very public – orders of Prime Minister Harold Wilson.

It was a very different campaign. Nationalist sympathies were naturally strong in that predominantly Catholic area, and the IRA had successfully turned much of the local population against the army. Those not won over by the force of the IRA's arguments were encouraged to see the light by punishment beatings with hurley bats and iron bars, and by knee-cappings.

As soon as we arrived in South Armagh we were told by the battalion sharing our camp that the Three Steps pub was a no-go area for British troops. That was not a term we used in our vocabulary. In order to demonstrate the fact to the local population and the IRA, we decided to send Rover and Lawrence – the biggest and most imposing members of the squadron – into the Three Steps for a drink.

They were unarmed but relatively safe. An IRA active service unit would be most unlikely to repeat the mistake they had made with Robert Nairac of murdering men they suspected to be special forces without first interrogating them.

If they tried to take Rover and Lawrence from the pub we would ambush them; if the two were held inside the pub a rescue team would batter their way in when the five-minute signal was missed and deal with any IRA men in there.

The operation had been carefully planned and there was no reason why it should not succeed, but things could go wrong with even the best-laid plans, and the approach of each five-minute deadline saw the tension among us rise again.

Instead of staying inside for the planned fifteen to twenty minutes, Rover kept sending the signal that they were staying in a bit longer and a bit longer. In the meantime we were lying under the hedge, cold, damp and miserable.

Suddenly the signaller clicked his fingers and whispered that Rover had missed the check-in time. We could hear nothing above the music from the pub which was now even louder.

We tooled up, ready to go in at a word. Everyone was now very tense and I could feel my heart thumping as the adrenalin started to pump. I checked my watch, keeping track of the seconds towards the next five-minute check.

It passed without a signal from Rover. The Boss gave the nod and we burst out of the hedge in our prearranged formation. Half the patrol covered the rear of the pub in case Rover and Lawrence were abducted that way, the rest of us smashed down the door and burst in, weapons drawn, looking for trouble.

Blinking in the bright lights from the stage, I saw a three-piece folk band banging out a rebel tune. Then I spotted Rover standing in front of the microphone, leading the singing. Lawrence was sitting at a table nearby, nursing a pint of Guinness and chatting to a couple of the Camlough boys as if they'd been friends for life.

We grabbed Rover and Lawrence and dragged them outside. The Boss was incandescent with rage. 'What the fuck is going on?'

Lawrence gave a sheepish smile. 'When we went in, the

landlord told us he didn't serve British soldiers. So I said, "Fine, I'll serve myself." I pulled us a couple of pints and everything deteriorated from there. He wouldn't take our money anyway, so I kept pulling us another couple of pints and we forgot to keep sending the signals and' – he checked the Boss's expression – 'sorry about the trouble.'

After we'd finished laughing, we wandered back into the pub and helped ourselves to a pint each. We left enough money on the bar to pay for the beer and some new hinges for the door, then wished the landlord and the locals good night and went back to our base at Bessbrook. The foundations for another SAS legend were already firmly laid.

The author, Camlough, South Armagh, 1976

When the Troubles erupted in Northern Ireland in 1968–69, the first British troops deployed there had been welcomed by the nationalist population as their protectors from the Protestant mobs and the hated B-Specials.

The initial welcome cooled rapidly. There was certainly no general prejudice against the Catholic population; the number of Catholics in the armed forces is a great deal larger than in the population as a whole. Around 10 per cent of the population of the UK is Catholic; the proportion in the army is closer to 30 per cent. That also holds true for the SAS.

Politicians at Westminster and soldiers serving in Ulster shared the general British ignorance about the realities of Northern Ireland, however. They were vulnerable to the machinations of the loyalists and the newly formed Provisional IRA, who were both eager to drive a wedge between the army and the nationalists.

The IRA's aim was to usurp the role of defender of the nationalists from the army and, by attacking British troops, provoke reactions that would further alienate the population and swell the flow of recruits to the Provisionals.

The Regiment had been covertly committed to Northern Ireland as early as 1966, the first time we had ever been deployed in plain clothes inside the UK. David Stirling would have viewed both developments with equal horror.

Northern Ireland was used as a proving ground for SAS men to practise carrying concealed weapons on the streets, but with the start of the Troubles we took a more active role.

D Squadron were sent to Northern Ireland in August 1969 on a training exercise. We were staking out Belfast Lough and checking the radio transmissions from ships coming into the port to unload. Signals intercepted a message from an Argentinian freighter arriving to unload '1,500 *pistolas*'. We roared across the Lough in half a dozen Gemini inflatables, stormed the ship, seized the crew and began interrogating the captain.

It turned out that *pistolas* was an Argentinian trade name for half a cow. We had intercepted 1,500 sides of beef. Red-faced, we made our excuses and left. It was one daring SAS raid that would not be finding its way into the annals of the Regiment.

As the security situation in Northern Ireland deteriorated, so the Regiment's interest increased. It was seen as an ideal place to test the new counter-terrorist techniques we were evolving. The original intention was never that the Regiment would be used aggressively against the IRA, however, and our initial role was limited to intelligence-gathering. A small group, passing themselves off as regular army signallers or engineers on our way into the province, then changed into civilian clothes and took on specialist tasks, but we found that we could not operate on the streets of the province without better cover.

We went to HQ Northern Ireland and spoke to the chief of staff, who agreed to lend us women soldiers from the WRAC to help our cover. We took them along on what were often very hairy operations, even though they were completely unarmed.

The SAS teams continued to work from Hereford and spent only short periods in the province. When the conflict erupted in Dhofar, the demands on SAS manpower made it impossible to sustain our involvement in Northern Ireland at anything like the same level. The SIS saw the Middle East, not Ulster, as the top priority, and from 1971 to 1977 we were effectively committed full time to Dhofar.

Small groups continued to visit Northern Ireland, however, maintaining a watching brief on intelligence operations. We soon discovered that some aspects of intelligence-gathering were staggeringly inefficient. The whole of the army was involved in bringing the photographs of IRA suspects up to date. Hundreds of thousands of man-hours were being invested, yet a bit of common sense would have eliminated 90 per cent of the effort. The IRA now discourages its volunteers from claiming state benefits, but at the time we could find any IRA suspect we wanted, any Thursday, signing on at the dole office.

Intelligence-gathering was then conducted mainly through two organisations. A group of ten IRA terrorists had been turned and were being run by the Parachute Regiment from Holywood Barracks in Belfast as agents of the Special Detachment of the Military Reconnaissance Force – also known as Freds.

They provided some intelligence and were also a useful conduit for disinformation, but the potential for double-crossing and betrayal was high, and in the end two of them blew the cover of a far more important intelligence operation, the Four Square Laundry.

While ostensibly carrying out a normal laundry business in republican areas, it had been sending out vans fitted with false roofs, concealing intelligence operatives. They used cameras and electronic surveillance gear to document the movements and contacts of IRA suspects.

Information extracted from the two men led the IRA to attack one of the vans on the Twinbrook Estate, killing the driver. On the same day, 2 October 1972, a massage parlour being run as another cover for intelligence-gathering was also attacked.

I was one of a three-man IRA assessment team sent to Northern Ireland to evaluate the Military Reconnaissance Force and the Four Square Laundry organisation in the aftermath of those IRA attacks. It soon became apparent that its cover was blown and the group of people running it were so out of control that it had to be disbanded at once.

Without reference to each other, we all produced the same recommendation: it's been a useful tool, but it's well past its sell-by date. Get rid of it, acquire the needed skills, then reform it in a different guise.

The result was 14 Int – the Fourteenth Intelligence Company. The SAS developed a selection procedure, ran the induction course and training and staffed the upper echelons of the company with SAS officers.

That gave the Regiment a means of maintaining its influence over an area that should technically have been controlled by the Intelligence Corps. The SAS could have its cake and eat it too, maintaining an involvement in Northern Ireland without using manpower that was needed in the Middle East.

Fourteen Int was organised into three detachments, each about the size of an SAS troop, and given areas of responsibility broadly corresponding to the boundaries of the IRA's three Northern Ireland brigades. Sub-units concentrated on tasks like planting bugs and tracking devices into IRA weapons dumps, arms and explosives.

Until the formation of 14 Int the only surveillance unit in the whole of the British army was a section of the Intelligence Corps used to track members of the Soviet Military Mission in West Germany. I'd been to see this unit in operation, but found them much less professional than they could have been. It was the main reason why the Intelligence Corps – the obvious choice – was not given the task of forming 14 Int.

Fourteen Int proved an immediate success. In the first three months of its deployment, intelligence acquired by its agents led to the whole of the Belfast Brigade's active service units being locked up in jail. As 14 Int developed, its techniques grew steadily more sophisticated, but the response of the Provisional IRA also became far more subtle.

After the end of Operation Storm, the SAS again became available for full-scale duty in Northern Ireland, but in a dangerous break with the tradition of total secrecy that had surrounded the Regiment's activities over the previous decade, Harold Wilson publicly committed the SAS to South Armagh. On 7 January 1976 Downing Street announced the deployment, for 'patrolling and surveillance tasks'. It was a disastrous mistake.

SAS men had been active in covert intelligence-gathering in Northern Ireland for nine years. Now Wilson had publicly committed an SAS Sabre Squadron on a political whim.

The announcement, a knee-jerk reaction by Downing Street to a particularly bad period of sectarian violence, was as much news to us as it was to the rest of the world. Just back from Oman, D Squadron had fewer than a dozen fighting men available and had done no work-up training. The commitment was in the wrong strength, in the wrong place, at the wrong time, and achieved very little other than the short-term disruption of the IRA in the area.

We had some initial successes. Using intelligence supplied by 14 Int we set up covert OPs – observation posts – in likely areas. In rural areas the OP might be in a hedge or a patch of brambles. In urban areas it would be in the attic of a disused or even an occupied house. A part of a brick or roof-slate would be removed to allow observation and photography of suspects.

They were manned for as much as ten days before a patrol was relieved and everything needed – food, water, surveillance and communications equipment, weapons and ammunition – had to be carried in with us. The hide was often close to a road or occupied building and had to be well enough camouflaged to be invisible even to a man standing almost on top of it.

Noise and smell were certain giveaways, so cooking and smoking were out and all waste including excrement and urine had to be bagged or stored in plastic containers. We might risk a brew of tea at first light – coffee had too strong an aroma – but otherwise we lived on cold food and drink for ten days at a time.

Dogs were a real problem, a constant threat to the security of the hide, but rats were even worse. No matter how carefully our food and waste was sealed, rats would find it. At some OPs we had to bring in bags of rat poison and then ship out the bodies of the dead rats.

We spoke only in whispers and even then only when necessary. Communications with base were also difficult, for VHF signals caused interference on TV sets and alerted the local IRA. Much of our intelligence was left for collection in prearranged RVs or dead-letter boxes. The lucky recipient of the intelligence first had to sort the tapes and rolls of films from the bags of empty food tins, excrement, containers of urine and rat corpses shoved in the same bergen for disposal.

Our initial operations in South Armagh greatly reduced IRA activity in the area, but we were under few illusions. We had arrested or killed a few terrorists but most of the main players had simply melted away across the border and would return at the first opportunity.

Just as in Aden, we were hamstrung by political constraints. There was no deadline to leave Northern Ireland, but there was no possibility of operating a hearts and minds policy in a province divided into two mutually uncomprehending armed camps. The tribal loyalties of the Iban in Borneo or the jebalis in Dhofar were as nothing to those of the loyalists and republicans of Northern Ireland.

Unable to win hearts and minds, the SAS was prevented from even winning the battle. Taking on the terrorists was impossible without the ability to confront them on their own terms in the North and track them to their sanctuaries in the Republic.

Our freedom of action inside Northern Ireland was circumscribed by political restraints; there were to be no exploding portraits of Irish revolutionary heroes in this conflict. The IRA could also flee across the border with relative impunity. In earlier campaigns in Borneo, Aden or Oman, we would simply have pursued them across the border, but the political realities in Ireland made that a very dubious proposition.

Far from co-operating in the suppression of the terrorists, the Fianna Fail government in Dublin gave the Provisionals covert support, including money and weapons, in return for their agreement to refrain from operations against the institutions and security forces of the Republic.

The arrangement was of incalculable value to the Provisionals, so much so that all IRA volunteers doing weapons training in the Republic were ordered on pain of court martial to surrender their weapons immediately if challenged by Gardai or Irish soldiers and to state that the weapons were only for use against the North.[2]

Despite the political difficulties, discreet SAS cross-border operations were still mounted, using a suitable cover story. On 12 March 1976, for example, it was announced that IRA terrorist Sean McKenna had been found, dead drunk, wandering around north of the border. The IRA's counterclaim that he had been kidnapped from his home in the Republic, brought back to the North and handed over to the army may or may not have been closer to the truth, but in the absence of hard evidence the governments in London and Dublin could afford to turn a blind eye.

Many of our planned operations were vetoed by our squad-

In the aftermath of the Suez disaster, the Foreign Office turned to diplomacy, backed by covert use of the SAS to rebuild Britain's lost power and influence in key strategic areas.

A young paratrooper on SAS selection in the Brecon Beacons. His posture and the way he is carrying – almost dragging – his rifle suggest that he will not complete the course. In most cases the crucial factor in failing is the feeling of utter isolation and alienation.

DLB and Johnny Watts on active service in the Jebel Akhdar campaign, two of ten SAS officers who have gone on to reach the rank of General. There are three classic tests of a good General – intelligence, ruthlessness and luck. Only one of the ten had all three qualities.

A patrol recovering after a contact near the Sarawak/Sabah borders with Kalimantan, in which a patrol member was killed. The signaller is reloading his magazines. In a contact, he would normally be protected by the other members of the patrol. For the signaller to have been firing too shows the intensity of the contact.

Alfie Tasker – 'The Ancient Brit' – just after returning from an operation in Aden in which two comrades were killed and beheaded. He later took his revenge by killing two enemy in an ambush.

ABOVE 17 Troop, D Squadron, on operations in Aden. Second from the left is a US Special Forces Master-Sergeant, on detachment to the SAS. He went on active service with the Regiment despite specific orders from the Pentagon forbidding it.

LEFT An Indonesian senior NCO in a camp in Kalimantan. The man was responsible for killing a captured member of an SAS patrol. At the instigation of the SAS the photograph was obtained by tribesmen of the Kelabit Highlands, which straddled the border. A price was put on the man's head, which was later claimed and paid.

Insertion methods practised in the mid to late 1960s. Helmeted free-fallers stand in the foreground, behind them are men in scuba suits, wet suits and mountain kit. The bars across the small portion of the free-fallers' faces not already obscured by their helmets shows the curious obsession with protecting individual identities while revealing information – such as clues to SAS techniques for water-borne insertion – that a hostile military analyst would find very valuable.

ABOVE Troopers using
the Grant-Taylor
method of shooting in
the First Close Quarter
Battle House on the
slopes of Mount Kenya
in the early 1960s.

RIGHT The lateral think-
ing of 'The Master' led
to the instinctive SAS
method of shooting
used by the assault team
training in the Killing
House in Hereford.

RIGHT Men from two different patrols immediately after a four month operation in Borneo. The man on the left had been patrolling the kampongs and still looks reasonably well-fed. The other two had been patrolling a section of the border deep in the jungle. They are as thin as gypsy dogs, their ribs showing.

BELOW Part of the author's troop in Dhofar, using a Swift Scope and map to check their position after a long night march from White City to Qatn Ridge. Shortly afterwards they were involved in a firefight in which three adoo, including a political commissar, were killed.

The author in a sangar in Dhofar, after an exhausting patrol

A mortar being fired during Operation Storm. The unusually bright muzzle-flash is significant. Despite fighting the British Army's biggest war since Korea, we were technically not on Active Service and the Army refused to issue us with the most powerful charges. Instead we improvised our own, using petrol as the propellant.

FOLLOWING PAGES
The author and 17 Troop,
D Squadron, training in
Iran in 1970, just before
the beginning of
Operation Storm.

The results of the attack on the airfield on Pebble Island during the Falklands War. Using standard Special Forces procedures, the explosive charges were placed on the same part of each aircraft to prevent 'cannibalization' of them for spares.

A Soviet barracks in East Germany. By noting the side-numbers and vehicle registration plates of Soviet vehicles, Brixmis operations could calculate the routes and training areas they were using, and even the tactics likely to be employed.

One of the SAS's prime targets in the event of the Cold War turning hot. A Soviet invasion of Western Europe relied on traffic regulators to direct their tanks and transport along pre-designated routes. So poor were the Soviet forces' navigation skills that, without the regulators, the Soviet troops would not have been able to find Western Europe, let alone invade it.

An East German border guard in an armoured car. The man was photographed by another Brixmis tour while the author was elsewhere in East Germany. The man's striking resemblance to the author led to another SAS myth that Ken Connor had disguised himself as a border guard and stolen one of their armoured cars.

A new Soviet artillery piece photographed on a training area south of Karl Marx Stadt (now Chemnitz). To get close enough to take such photographs was risky; the Soviet sentries were armed and would shoot. The risk was worth it, however. From photographs like this, Western analysts could calculate the capabilities of the gun, its cost, how it would be resupplied in battle and its probable impact in a war.

A 'Pink Panther'. The Land Rovers used since the early 1960s remain in service today, but the original concept has gradually been lost. In the Gulf War, they were used as attack vehicles, even though they could neither outrun nor outgun the Iraqi BMPs.

ron OC, however, an inexperienced officer who lacked the stomach for the darker end of special forces operations. There were rumours that some cross-border ops continued despite his reservations and that other Army units also staged clandestine operations in the Republic. If their activities were exposed they had the perfect alibi – they could blame the SAS.

A major political row blew up in May 1976 when two SAS troopers in plain clothes and driving a car registered in the Republic were stopped at a Gardai checkpoint half a mile over the border from crossing point 'Hotel One' near Newry. The excuse that they had made a map-reading error was not believed. In any event two more car-loads of SAS men, searching for their missing comrades, were then stopped at the same checkpoint.

To the considerable political embarrassment of both the British and Irish governments, a total of eight SAS men were arrested and taken to Dublin for interrogation. They were then charged with possession of firearms with intent to endanger life.

The OC of the squadron involved had originally left the Regiment as a corporal and gone back to his own regiment where he had been commissioned. On his return to the SAS he had spent several years as an adjutant – laying down rules and regulations – and then become OC of a Sabre Squadron without having any sympathy for how the squadron operated.

He effectively washed his hands of the men who had been caught. After twenty-four hours' interrogation in Dublin they were bailed and helicoptered back to Bessbrook, but instead of allowing the exhausted men to get a night's sleep, the OC sent them straight on to Aldergrove to be interrogated by the Army Investigations Branch.

Despite furious protests from myself and the other senior men in the squadron he refused to rescind his order, provoking a near-mutiny. The commanding officer of the Regiment and the Director, SAS, both flew out to pacify us and both stated categorically that they would resign if the men were returned to Dublin to face charges.

They were duly sent back for trial in Dublin, but neither officer offered his resignation. When the case came to court the eight men were acquitted on the main charge of possession of firearms with intent to endanger life, but were fined £100 for possession of unlicensed weapons.

The subsequent restrictions placed on our close-to-border activities to avoid further political embarrassments severely hampered our counter-terrorist operations. Even within Northern Ireland operations were restricted by political considerations, and further damaged by the incessant rivalries and jealousies between the competing arms of the security forces. There may have been a war raging between the IRA and the security forces, but at times it seemed to pale beside the turf wars between the various different military and police intelligence agencies competing for a slice of the Northern Ireland action.

We operated in the province under a national policy of 'police primacy', giving the RUC Chief Constable the ultimate sanction on where and how we were deployed. That authority was delegated to three Tasking and Co-ordination Groups jointly manned by Military Intelligence and RUC Special Branch operatives.

Despite the overall police control the RUC bitterly resented the presence of the SAS on their territory, regarding it as a slight on their own abilities. They were less worried by the presence of 14 Int because it was an entirely passive organisation, gathering intelligence for dissemination to others, though they eventually set up their own agency, A4A, to try and give them tighter control over the flow of intelligence.

The RUC remained implacably opposed to the SAS and there was a strong suspicion that the arrests of our men over the border had been a set-up engineered by the RUC Special

Branch and their colleagues in the Gardai, neither of whom had any love for the Regiment.

We found ourselves marginalised in the conflict, as the RUC Special Branch, Army Intelligence and MI5 all jealously guarded their own territory. Even MI6, theoretically restricted by its charter to gathering intelligence outside the British Isles, used its previous operations and connections in the Republic to muscle in on the action north of the border.

The intelligence-gathering role of 14 Int was also being compromised, but this was less the result of inter-service rivalries than of 14 Int's reliance on men-only operations. It became obvious that the use of women operatives would be tremendously advantageous in certain situations.

As we had found on our initial operations in Northern Ireland, outsiders were always suspect in the IRA strongholds, but two women laden with supermarket shopping bags or a man and woman kissing passionately in a doorway attracted far less attention than two men driving through in a car or loitering in the street.

No operative could be sent unarmed into the republican ghettos, but training women to carry and use weapons was a significant departure not just for the special forces but for the British army as a whole.

British servicewomen had never been allowed to carry weapons in war situations and the sceptics – not all of them male chauvinists – had to be convinced that women had the mental toughness to cope with situations where they had to kill an armed enemy. I myself had no doubts, for I remembered the bravery of the unarmed WRAC soldiers who had accompanied our undercover patrols.

Early in 1978 I was called to a meeting in the SAS headquarters. It was attended by a number of senior generals, the Director, SAS, and the Director, WRAC, a woman brigadier. She asked me whether I could train a female soldier to carry arms on active service.

My reply was less than wholly diplomatic: 'Given enough time, I could train a monkey.'

I was speedily ushered out of the meeting, but soon afterwards I was given *carte blanche* to devise a selection procedure, visit establishments where female soldiers were posted and select a group of potential recruits, the first women ever to bear arms for the British army.

The aim was to have women working on active service in Northern Ireland, on equal terms with the men, as soon as possible. The difficulty was never going to be the qualities and suitability of the women; it was always going to be their acceptability to the men of 14 Int. To ensure acceptance, I knew that the women would have to go through the same selection course as the men, under the same terms and conditions.

I started off by taking groups of potential recruits on to the firing range; those who flinched while firing weapons were automatically discarded. I then ran a simultaneous selection course for the remaining women and a group of male applicants.

I had no worries about the women's ability to meet the physical demands of the course. The role of the SAS often requires the sheer physical strength and stamina to carry heavy weights and cope with very arduous conditions but 14 Int's role is purely intelligence-gathering and its selection procedure is nothing like as rigorous or demanding as SAS Selection.

One of the motivational tools I used was to arrange for the women to observe covertly the male students as they postured, preened and generally derided the women. Their derision was misplaced. As the selection progressed it was obvious that the calibre of the women was at least as high, if not higher, than most of the men.

We started with eight women and at the end of the selection and training course we were down to four. Before the final decision was taken to allow them to go on active service in

Northern Ireland, a group of very senior officers, including the WRAC brigadier, insisted on seeing the women using weapons on the range.

We set up a very complex test exercise at Sennybridge in Wales and put the men through it several times. Then we put the women through it individually and in pairs. The results they achieved were far superior to most of the men.

The only remaining obstacle to be overcome was the acceptability of women to the men already serving with 14 Int. The ones who felt confident in their own ability accepted the women as they were. The ones who felt slightly defensive retreated behind barriers of male chauvinism and continued to pretend that the women were not up to the job.

One or two male dinosaurs had to be moved on, but women soon became accepted in 14 Int and in a short while they were stating the terms of the working relationships.

Women are now a valued part of the special forces and in certain situations they work on an equal basis with SAS troops. Their involvement has given a new dimension to some of the Regiment's operations and has led to a new realisation of women's potential within the armed forces as a whole.

Where women are physically able to do the work, they are more than able to contribute on equal terms with the men, but they will never be able to play an active part in pure SAS operations. That is not because of any residual male chauvinism in the Regiment, nor any lack of the necessary mental disciplines in the women. It simply reflects the fact that they do not have the physical attributes to carry out the pure, aggressive, long-range infiltrations often required in the SAS. Scaling a mountain such as the Jebel Akhdar or crossing miles of desert or rough terrain with a 120-pound bergen on your back is a task that taxes even the strongest man.

The new women operatives gave 14 Int an extra edge in intelligence-gathering, but the very success of our offshoot caused us problems. It contributed to a mindset among staff officers dealing with the conflict in Northern Ireland who saw the battle against the IRA more in terms of intelligence-gathering and compromise than military defeat.

Meanwhile the friction between the other intelligence agencies continued. MI5 and MI6 had diametrically opposed agendas for the conflict. While MI6 pursued a political solution through secret contacts with the Dublin government and the Provisional leadership, MI5 sabotaged their efforts.

The judicious spin put by MI5 upon a Provisional IRA document discovered during a raid on their Belfast HQ convinced Harold Wilson's government that the IRA were about to launch terror attacks on whole Protestant communities.

In fact it was a contingency plan, only to be put into effect in the event of another wave of Protestant attacks such as the ones that had ushered in the new era of the Troubles in 1969. As MI5 intended, however, their misleading information both discredited the political overtures engineered by MI6 and stampeded the government into a rapid expansion of undercover army operations.

Such operations were often clouded by the use of touts – informers. Army Intelligence, MI5, MI6, the RUC Special Branch and even the intelligence sections of infantry battalions were all running their own touts, usually unknown to each other. We remarked, only half-jokingly, that some IRA cells were composed of nothing but touts.

The rivalry between different agencies also cost us valuable intelligence after the introduction of internment. Around 350 suspects were rounded up in one night, far exceeding the number that could be handled and processed. There were nowhere near enough trained interrogators available and the use of unskilled interrogators resulted in the loss of information and caused allegations of ill-treatment that left lasting problems.

When good intelligence was obtained it was often poorly collated and evaluated, and inadequately distributed. MI5 and MI6 had only one thing in common: a shared contempt for the RUC Special Branch, which they regarded as staffed by bungling incompetents. They hoarded the intelligence they gained and the Special Branch in turn kept to itself much information from its touts in the North and its contacts in the Gardai Special Branch in the Republic.

Were it not so dangerous and sometimes tragic, the potential for chaos and lapses of security engendered by the multiplicity of different intelligence operations would have been comic.

On one occasion two undercover teams fired on each other, each believing that the other group was an IRA active service unit. On another, ten informants were betrayed and executed by the IRA after a leak.

The SAS, reliant on the fullest intelligence for success in any operation, did its best to encourage liaison between the other groups, but in such an atmosphere of mutual suspicion and mistrust much intelligence was never passed beyond the organisation that had obtained it.

The need for absolute precision in intelligence-gathering was never more cruelly demonstrated than in the operation that resulted in the Regiment's first fatality from enemy fire in Northern Ireland.

An eight-man team investigating intelligence reports of an IRA arms dump at 369 Antrim Road made a fruitless search of the house. The arms cache and a group of IRA men were actually in the next-door property and the SAS came under fire from an upstairs window. All the terrorists were eventually arrested, but not before Captain Herbert Westmacott, a Guards officer serving with G Squadron, had been shot and killed.

Only when a centralised agent-handling system was imposed on the warring factions at the insistence of the SAS was some form of order restored from the anarchy. Even so, we were often forced to stand by while a terrorist operation was carried out, purely to protect the cover of somebody's tout. Areas were devastated and innocent people probably killed as a result. SAS patrols would be sent to the area where the incident was to take place and put on heightened alert, but the squaddies still had to patrol the streets and were never told the nature of the threat in any detail. If it all went wrong, they were invariably left holding the shitty end of the stick.

The real heroes of Northern Ireland were neither the SAS, nor 14 Int, nor the RUC Special Branch, nor any of the high-profile figures involved, but the poor bloody infantry, trapped between the IRA on one side and politicians, senior officers playing politics and the intelligence community protecting their touts by playing the Northern Ireland variant of the great game on the other.

The recent furore over the revelations of an ex-MI5 agent who confirmed that the agency had prior intelligence of the bombing of the Israeli Embassy in London, which was then allowed to go ahead, confirms that the practice of protecting informants at almost any price continues.

It was a curious double standard, a morality that allowed known terrorist operations to go ahead, risking military and civilian casualties, but which drew the line at 'black' actions by our own side. Had the aim been the elimination of IRA terrorism by any means it could have been done, but our suggestions of 'Mossad-type' operations against the IRA around the globe were rejected.

The SAS squadron in Northern Ireland had been redeployed in 1977, with one troop remaining at Bessbrook in South Armagh, while others were sent to Londonderry and Belfast, and the fourth was held as a rapid-response reserve under the orders of the Commander, Land Forces.

We were still being used aggressively, in stake-outs of known arms dumps and in ambushes of suspected IRA oper-ations, but the RUC's always strong opposition to the use of the SAS on its turf was hardened by a series of incidents.

In June 1978 four IRA terrorists were ambushed on their way to fire-bomb a Belfast post office. Three were killed but a passer-by strayed into the line of fire and was also shot dead.

In September of the same year a Protestant carrying a shotgun on a rough shoot with some friends was killed in disputed circumstances, and even the shooting of a known IRA man, Patrick Duffy, at an arms dump in Londonderry was clouded by controversy.

In March 1979 the *Daily Telegraph* made an extraordinary claim against the SAS. It reported that a police surgeon who had made allegations of ill-treatment of IRA prisoners at the Castlereagh Interrogation Centre was motivated by hostility towards the authorities because an SAS NCO had raped his wife three years earlier.[3]

There was no shred of truth in the story, but in the feverish atmosphere of claim, counter-claim and disinformation, DLB – Brigadier Peter de la Billiere – was panicked into persuading the Colonel Commandant of the SAS, Colonel Brian Franks, to issue a public denial of the allegations in a letter to the *Telegraph*.[4]

He went on to complain about: 'The ever-growing, ill-informed comment in the press and elsewhere about my Regiment ... I am disturbed at the increasing tendency to report on the SAS as if it were some secret undercover organisation. In fact it is a corps of the British army, subject to both military and civil law in exactly the same way as any other corps.'[5]

Not everyone was convinced and, under heavy pressure from the RUC, SAS aggressive operations were scaled down and the deployment of the Regiment was altered. Instead of full squadrons serving four-month tours in Northern Ireland, a single expanded troop of around twenty men – Ulster Troop – was based in the province for a year at a time. At the same time, the SAS and 14 Int were given an even closer formal link under the umbrella code-name of the Group – the Intelligence and Security Group.

For the next five years our role was largely confined to intelligence-gathering while the RUC Special Branch took a much more active role in aggressive undercover operations.

The government's aim may have been in part a 'Vietnamisation' of the conflict, but there is no doubt that politicians had also been unsettled by the series of accidental killings and the allegations made against the Regiment.

The pressure was increased by the activities of ambulance-chasing lawyers. In the immediate aftermath of every incident, one lot would be chasing the IRA side while the others were chasing the soldiers.

The civilian lawyers in Northern Ireland appeared to be much better than their army equivalents, leaving soldiers with the feeling that the scales were already loaded against them. If they got something wrong, they were going to swing for it and no one else, for no senior officer in Northern Ireland has ever stepped forward after a controversial incident to take public responsibility for the actions of the men carrying out his orders.

For the first time, we were also operating under a media spotlight, with our actions subject to relentless scrutiny by the press. Every killing of a terrorist provoked an outcry and a blizzard of competing versions of events.

The IRA fought the public-relations war every bit as resourcefully as they waged their terrorist campaign. Every terrorist killed was either unarmed, or his gun was not loaded, or he was shot in the back without a verbal warning being issued, or executed after he had been wounded or surrendered.

Their attempts to blur the issues were often successful and in this they were helped by the occasionally inept handling of the army's responses to such claims. Questions about whether a gun was loaded at the time of a shooting, for example, are purely academic. The only way to be certain that a gun pointed at you is loaded is to wait until the firer pulls the trigger. By then it's too late to shoot back.

Anyone of normal intelligence could grasp that point, and the army's information officers would certainly have been expected to be aware of it. Yet in the aftermath of one fatal shooting, when a sixteen-year-old boy was killed after taking a rifle from an IRA arms cache, the army rushed out a press statement that the gun had been loaded. The statement was later proved to have been a lie.

The boy, John Boyle, had stumbled on the arms cache in a cemetery in Dunloy, County Antrim. He went home and told his father, who tipped off the RUC. As a result an SAS patrol staked out the site.

An RUC call to warn the Boyles to stay away from the graveyard came too late to save the boy. He had returned to look at the arms cache again and when he stooped and picked up an Armalite, he was shot dead.

The army information officers' claim that the gun was loaded infuriated the RUC, who made it clear that they disagreed with the army's version of events. Two SAS men were subsequently charged with murder, but though the judge described one of them as an unreliable witness, they were acquitted.

The incident left a bad taste in the mouths of many and continuing attempts to justify it – except as a tragic accident – do both the victim and the SAS a disservice. Yet in his autobiography, written several years later, DLB still maintained a version of events that bore small relation to the reality.

> Our soldiers had found a weapons cache in a grave and had staked the site out for several days and nights hidden in a wet ditch at the edge of the churchyard. One night a man appeared, lifted the top of the grave and took out a semi-automatic weapon, which he pointed in the direction of the watchers ... Clearly the dead man knew how to access the arms dump, though he was only sixteen and probably a low-grade operator.[6]

Those eighty words contain four serious factual errors: the

arms dump had been found and reported by the boy, not the SAS patrol; they had been staking it out for less than one day, not several; the incident occurred at ten in the morning, not at night; the victim had never been an IRA member.

To maintain such fictions in the face of the evidence merely weakens genuine denials in other circumstances and lends credence to wilder IRA claims of SAS murders and cover-ups. It would be reprehensible from a lowly trooper and is inexcusable from someone drawing on the full authority of a senior army rank.

The claims by the army information officers that the gun was loaded had been made in an attempt to deflect criticism of the SAS for shooting someone who turned out not to have been an IRA member, just a boy curious about the guns he had found. Yet when the gun was loaded was irrelevant. The proper defence of the SAS patrol's actions was that an unidentified figure had picked up a rifle and pointed it in their direction.

By issuing a statement that they knew to be false, the army information officers not only missed the point, they also greatly damaged the SAS men's case in that particular incident and the image of the Regiment as a whole.

If they could display such woeful ignorance of the realities of armed combat, there was no reason to expect the journalists they briefed to be any better informed. There was a frequent, perhaps predictable complaint among SAS men that those journalists who criticised their actions had never known what it was like to look into the mouth of a gun. Yet to suggest that the press as a whole was biased against the Regiment is a nonsense.

If some left-wing journalists were perhaps too ready to believe the propaganda of the IRA, the right-wing press and particularly the tabloids showed no such qualms and exulted in the death of IRA terrorists almost as much as hardline Ulster loyalists.

There is no doubt that innocent people were accidentally

shot by the SAS in Northern Ireland or that on occasions some SAS men did not fulfil the letter of the rules of engagement, but those cases were a tiny minority and though each was a needless tragedy for the families involved, the circumstances of the conflict in Northern Ireland made such incidents almost inevitable.

If you are confronted by an armed terrorist it is impossible to follow the step-by-step rules of engagement laid down in the 'Yellow Card' and stay alive. There have been a number of incidents in Northern Ireland where armed soldiers have been killed because they were frightened to draw their weapons and defend themselves for fear of breaching the rules. The SAS took a different view of the Yellow Card. As Andy McNab remarked, he would rather be judged by twelve good men and true than carried by six of them.

The Yellow Card was only one of a series of cards that a soldier was expected to carry and obey at all times. The rules bore little relevance to the actual situations a soldier would face but they allowed more senior officers and politicians to insulate themselves from any unpleasant consequences. They had laid down the rules and if the soldier had not followed them exactly, the soldier, not the system, was to blame.

The multicoloured cards were far from the only problem soldiers had to face. The rules of evidence also required that terrorists be caught red-handed, in the act of perpetrating their outrages. Even if we knew from advance intelligence that an IRA attack was planned, there was no point in trying to arrest the terrorists when all they were carrying was an air of injured innocence.

We had to wait until they had collected their weapons and sometimes until they had rendezvoused with their colleagues at the scene of their planned crime. Even then, the aim would still be to arrest them if possible, not through any British sense of decency and fair play, but because of the hard-nosed calculation that every captured terrorist is a potential source of information on others.

In situations where we faced heavily armed and ruthless men, however, the line between observing the legal niceties to make arrests and saving your own life by firing first was a very narrow one.

One specific account of an operation helps to illustrate the almost insuperable difficulties the Regiment faced. In May 1987 intelligence was obtained that two active service units of the IRA's East Tyrone Brigade were combining forces for a joint operation to blow up the police station at Loughgall.

It was to be a mirror image of a successful attack they had made the previous year, when a huge bomb placed in the bucket of a stolen JCB was rammed through the perimeter fence of the Beeches police station and then detonated, causing massive damage and loss of life.

The SAS troop already based in Ulster was strengthened by reinforcements sent from Hereford and an intensive surveillance operation was mounted.

In the late afternoon of Friday, 8 May, the IRA began to put their plan into action. A blue Toyota Hiace van was hijacked in Dungannon and a JCB stolen from a farm. The farmer and his family were held hostage by two IRA men to prevent them from alerting the security forces.

The SAS waited in hiding as the IRA men converged on Loughgall. One group of SAS was actually inside the police station, at some considerable risk to themselves; the others were lying in wait in a thin belt of trees and bushes at the edge of a football field, facing the building. Other smaller groups were in OPs overlooking the approach roads.

At 7.15 that evening the Toyota van containing five IRA men drove slowly past the police station. It moved on, but returned a few minutes later, followed by the JCB, carrying another three men. One of them lit the short fuse of the 200-pound bomb as it rumbled on towards the gates. The van had stopped just past the police station, the back doors were thrown open and three men jumped out and began raking the building with fire as the JCB smashed into the gates. As it came to rest against the building, the three men jumped off and ran towards the van.

The SAS men lying in ambush opened fire, riddling the van and the surrounding area with bullets, but the massive bomb detonated, destroying the police station. Six of the eight IRA men were cut down and killed in the murderous crossfire, the other two were killed by SAS cut-off groups.

IRA men were not the only dead, however. Just before the blast, two brothers had driven into the village. Like the IRA men, they were wearing blue overalls. As they stopped and began to reverse, they were shot by the SAS. One man was killed, the other wounded. It later transpired that they were not terrorists but mechanics who had been repairing a broken-down lorry.

The shooting of two men who had innocently strayed into the line of fire marred what would otherwise have been a textbook operation and created an inevitable furore. There were complaints that none of the inhabitants of the village had been informed of the operation and no cordon had been thrown around it. Had that happened, the innocent men would not have been shot, but the terrorists would have escaped. The government paid financial compensation but refused a public inquiry into the shooting of the two brothers.

Despite the lurid publicity surrounding such incidents, most SAS operations ended in arrests, not deaths. In the eight years after Harold Wilson's very public deployment of the Regiment only nine IRA men had been shot by the SAS, and in the five years from December 1978 to December 1983 not a single IRA man was killed in SAS operations.[7]

In the next nine years the figure rose to thirty-five. The rising kill-rate coincided with a change in terminology which, while a long way short of orders to kill, did give SAS men more leeway of interpretation on operations. The previous instructions to carry out 'surveillance and hard arrests' were replaced by orders to man what were described as 'Aggressive OPs' or 'OP/Reactives'.[8] The commendations and decorations that followed clean kills of IRA players showed that arrests were only one of the acceptable results of such operations.

None the less, a clear majority of SAS operations still ended in arrests not deaths, and the increasing kill-rate in the mid-1980s was less a function of a determination by the government to take the gloves off after the Brighton bombing in which Margaret Thatcher and the rest of her Cabinet almost lost their lives than of the increased scope and scale of IRA operations.

An organisation once starved of weapons and ammunition was now awash with Armalites, Semtex and even some heavy weapons, courtesy of its fund-raising operations in the USA and its links to other terrorist groups such as the PLO and maverick states such as Libya.

As the IRA undertook more and bigger operations, so it became more vulnerable to ambush and counter-attack. The SAS Ulster Troop was the first call of commanders when ambushes were to be deployed, and in five years during the mid-1980s the twenty-man troop accounted for eighteen IRA dead.

The remainder of the army – some 12,000 troops – shot only two IRA men during the same period,[9] but the explanation of the high kill-rate lay in the regular use of the Regiment at the cutting edge, not in the freeing of the SAS to ignore the rules of engagement and start a shoot-to-kill policy.

None the less, hostility to our role in Northern Ireland was behind the view circulating in certain quarters that the SAS – the most highly trained and disciplined military unit in the world – could not be trusted to operate freely there, in case it 'went out of control'.

Virtually every other unit operating in Northern Ireland used squaddies in plain clothes, travelling in civilian cars. They were trying to do a very strenuous, specialist job with men who had no training for it whatsoever. The ludicrous thing was that senior officers preferred that highly dangerous scenario to the alternative of trusting the SAS.

The absurd suggestion that the SAS might go out of control has never been challenged by SAS Group Headquarters, where there has been a subtle policy shift. The SAS are now seen primarily as foreign service troops, even though that view has held them back from a significant role in the most important conflict the UK has faced during the last quarter-century.

The SAS has never been more than tangentially involved in the battle against the IRA, but it played the leading role in one of the conflict's most controversial incidents. An operation involving no civilian casualties but culminating in the deaths of three IRA personnel created an uproar that reverberated around the world and revived allegations of a shoot-to-kill policy.

Intelligence obtained in the autumn of 1987 indicated that two notorious IRA men, Daniel McCann and Sean Savage, were about to fly to Malaga, where it was known that another IRA team had already cached a supply of weapons and explosives.

Malaga's close proximity to Gibraltar left little room for doubt about their intended target area and the presence of Savage was particularly alarming. He was a known bomb-maker and we had intelligence that the IRA had recently perfected a remotely operated, push-button detonator. They were put under surveillance by Spanish police and an MI5 team flew out to Gibraltar.

McCann and Savage returned to Ireland soon afterwards, but early the following year an IRA man and woman team based themselves in Malaga and began regular day visits to Gibraltar. On 23 February and 1 March the woman was observed taking a close interest in the route followed during the weekly Changing of the Guard ceremony outside the governor's residence.

Anticipating an imminent IRA attack, an SAS Special Projects Team was deployed to Gibraltar on 3 March under the code-name Operation Flavius. The following day McCann and Savage flew back to Malaga, where they were joined by a third terrorist, Mairead Farrell. Despite her diminutive stature and angelic features, she was a hardened IRA operative who had already served ten years' imprisonment for terrorist offences.

The briefing given to the SAS men was crucial to what followed. Three salient points emerged from the evidence presented at the subsequent inquest. The SAS men were told that the IRA personnel were almost certainly armed and that any or all of them could be carrying a remote button to detonate the bomb. There was recent evidence of the likelihood of this: an IRA car-bomb discovered and disarmed in Brussels on 21 January 1988 had included a remotely activated detonator.[10]

Even more important, intelligence also suggested that there would be no blocking car, the normal IRA tactic where one car is used to keep a parking space which is then occupied by the one carrying the bomb shortly before the scheduled blast. On this occasion, the SAS were told, the car carrying the bomb would be brought straight in to the chosen site, ready to be detonated.

The SAS were then issued with the rules of engagement for the operation. They contained the standard mixture of admonishments to use restraint, hedged around with vague authorisations to shoot first in certain circumstances. They were familiar to all soldiers from the Yellow Card rules of engagement in Northern Ireland, requiring the use of 'minimum force' and prohibiting a soldier from firing first unless he has first issued a verbal warning and is sure beyond a reasonable doubt that lives are at immediate risk.

Your objective will be to assist the civil power to arrest members of the IRA, but subject to the overriding requirement to do all in your power to protect the lives and safety of members of the public and of the security

forces ... [You] may only open fire against a person if
you or they have reasonable grounds for believing that
he/she is currently committing, or is about to commit,
an action which is likely to endanger you or their lives,
or the life of any person, and if there is no other way
to prevent this ... [You] may fire without a warning if
the giving of a warning or any delay in firing could lead
to death or injury to you or them or any other person,
or if the giving of a warning is clearly impracticable ...

What occurred next is a matter of dispute between the
Spanish and British governments. The British claimed
that the Spanish police surveillance team unaccountably
lost the IRA active service unit as they left the airport,
the Spanish say that they tracked them all the way to the
border.

Whatever the reality, early in the afternoon of Sunday, 6
March, there were reported sightings of McCann and Farrell
approaching the frontier from Spain, La Linea Gate, on foot.
Savage was also spotted, already inside Gibraltar. He was
standing near a white Renault 5, parked by the assembly area
for the military band from the First Battalion of the Royal
Anglian Regiment, due to play in the Changing of the Guard
ceremony.

Shortly afterwards, surveillance teams confirmed that
Savage had parked the car there a couple of hours earlier and
had leaned inside it for a few moments, doing something
that the watchers could not see. Despite police surveillance
of the border crossing he had managed to pass through
undetected. One of the SAS men later made the barbed
comment that they were not responsible for the siting of the
surveillance teams at the border.

Two pairs of SAS men were immediately deployed on the
streets. They were in plain clothes and armed with Browning
9mm pistols. They tracked the three terrorists as they rendezvoused and walked around the centre of the town for

some time. They returned to the band assembly area at 3.25, exchanged a few words and a joke, then began heading back towards the border.

The Gibraltar police had already handed over control to the army twice and then rescinded their decision. At their insistence, an explosives expert now made a swift external check of the Renault. The suspension showed no sign of the heavy loading that would be associated with a massive bomb, but fifty or sixty pounds of Semtex – enough to devastate a huge area – would have had little or no visible effect on a car's springs. In any event, the brand-new car had been fitted with a rusty aerial which made him very suspicious.

He reported that the car could contain a remote-controlled device and at 3.40 the police once more handed over responsibility to the SAS. In less than two minutes all three terrorists were shot dead.

While McCann and Farrell continued north towards the border, Savage turned and headed back towards the centre of town, brushing past two of the SAS men. They continued to track McCann and Farrell, while the other two followed Savage.

At the same time, a local police inspector was recalled to his base, by a wicked irony, so that his car would be available to transport the terrorists after their capture. He had no knowledge of the operation being carried out and, as his way was blocked by traffic, he switched on his siren.

The noise alarmed McCann, who swung around and made eye contact with one of the SAS men tracking him. The SAS trooper described seeing the smile wiped from McCann's face and feared that he had been recognised as a threat. As the IRA man moved his hand 'aggressively across the front of his body',[11] the SAS man drew his pistol and shot him with a single round in the back from a range of around three yards.

Seeing Farrell also make a hand movement towards her handbag, he fired another round into her back, then put three more rounds into McCann, one to the body, two to the head. By now his partner was also firing, putting another seven shots into Farrell and McCann, including one into Farrell as she lay on the ground because he 'could not see her hands'.[12]

Savage was 100 yards away when the first shot was fired. He whipped round, and as his right hand moved towards his pocket, both SAS men tracking him opened fire. 'Soldier C' shot him four times in the chest and twice in the head, 'Soldier D' moved a female passer-by to one side with one hand and fired another nine shots, seven into his body and two at his head. 'I kept firing until he was on the ground and his hands were away from his body because at any time he could press a button and detonate the bomb.'[13]

All three terrorists lay dead. The SAS men were spirited away from the scene in police cars and after an unexplained twenty-minute delay the SAS officer in charge returned control to the police at six minutes past four. The entire party of SAS and MI5 'watchers' checked out of the Rock Hotel that evening and were back in Britain before midnight.

Two official press releases were issued on the day of the killing, once more demonstrating the information officers' penchant for pointless mendacity. The first, a terse statement an hour after the killings, stated, 'A suspected bomb has been found in Gibraltar and three suspects have been shot by civilian police.' By nine that evening the 'civilian police' had become 'security forces' who had dealt with 'a suspect bomb'.[14]

The Armed Forces Minister then claimed in a radio interview the next morning that a large bomb had been found and defused in Gibraltar. The first doubts about that straightforward version of events, in which three terrorists had been killed in the act of planting a bomb, were raised by a statement in the House of Commons that afternoon from the Foreign Secretary, Geoffrey Howe.

After expressing the gratitude of the House to both the SAS team and the Spanish authorities for their co-operation in the surveillance operation, Howe went on to admit that though the terrorists had made suspicious hand movements, 'those killed were subsequently found not to have been carrying arms'[15] or remote controls for a bomb. He also admitted that the white Renault did not contain any explosive device.

Despite the alleged intelligence to the contrary, the car was in fact being used in the standard terrorist technique, simply to block a parking space for the vehicle containing the bomb. That was found the next day in a Marbella car park, a red Ford Fiesta, loaded with sixty-four pounds of Semtex.

The Spanish police then stirred the pot further by issuing a public denial that they had lost the terrorists at Malaga and insisting that they had tracked them right to the Gibraltar border. When eye-witnesses then came forward claiming that the shootings appeared more like executions, with the IRA people trying to surrender and the final shots fired by the SAS men as they stood directly over the prone bodies of the terrorists, the stage was set for a worldwide press sensation.

Government officials who only hours before had been basking in the glow of a successful strike against terrorism now embarked on a delaying action and damage-limitation exercise that raised as many fresh questions as it answered.

The findings of Professor Alan Watson, the government-appointed pathologist who examined the corpses, also fuelled the fires of speculation. He found that in 'a frenzied attack', Savage had been hit by at least sixteen bullets. Four of them, according to Watson, had been fired into his head from above. Farrell was shot three times in the back and four times in the face; McCann was hit four times, twice in the back, twice in the head.

The Conservative government maintained its public support for the actions of the SAS men – Margaret Thatcher herself warned in a speech that those who 'live by the bomb and the gun ... cannot in all circumstances be accorded exactly the same rights as everyone else' – but it also discreetly distanced itself from the men. Any decision on whether they should attend the inquiry into the deaths was left to the individual soldiers, who were to make up their own minds after consulting their lawyers.

It was a situation as old as the hills, the military Catch 22: soldiers acting under orders were held to be individually responsible for the consequences of those orders. Yet in the SAS, as in any other branch of the armed forces, refusal to follow orders is an offence punishable by anything from RTU to death by firing squad if it occurs in the face of the enemy. But following orders does not, according to the courts, absolve individual soldiers of responsibility for their actions. The buck stops at a convenient point on the chain of command.

Yet hard though senior officers and governments of all political colours have tried to distance themselves from the consequences of the chains of events they set in motion, the buck should stop with them. If they wish to carry out counter-terrorist operations entirely within the rule of law, then those operations should be entrusted to police forces. If they wish to utilise the cutting edge of military special forces, they must accept the consequences.

Evaluating a threat in the hair-trigger, split-second business of a contact is something SAS men do almost by instinct. It is not a process that lends itself easily to analysis in the arid calm of a courtroom, well away from the heat and tension of the moment.

In the event, all the SAS men involved in the Gibraltar operation voluntarily returned to give evidence at the inquiry. All testified that they believed the lives of themselves and others were threatened by the sudden hand-movements of the victims and fired in response.

There is no doubt that the SAS men were giving a genuine explanation of their actions. There is also little doubt that they had been coached by lawyers from the Army Legal Service in the best defence to adopt, just as any civilian would be coached before a trial by his counsel.

Previous trials following accidental shootings of civilians or the deaths of terrorists had shown that a soldier believing that his life or the lives of others were in danger was justified in opening fire with or without a warning. Soldiers professing to have fired in response to sudden, threatening movements by their target were likely to be acquitted, even if the target was later shown to have been unarmed or even an innocent bystander.

The Gibraltar coroner's jury did not deviate from this precedent. They eventually delivered a nine to two verdict of lawful killing, but it did little to stop the tide of rumour and speculation surrounding the deaths on the Rock.

There was friction between the army and MI5, with MI5 operatives blaming the SAS men's near-identical casual 'uniform' of bomber jackets, jeans and trainers for alerting McCann. Co-operation between MI5 and the Regiment was noticeably stepped down after Gibraltar and subsequent MI5 'hard-arrest' operations often involved armed police rather than SAS men.

There were also hints that the deaths of the three terrorists in such controversial circumstances had handed the IRA a propaganda victory out of the jaws of a crushing defeat. If that was so, it was hardly the fault of the SAS. There is an almost complete lack of understanding of PR in the army and MI5. The Army Information Office is largely staffed by career soldiers with minimal experience of the press and media who are suspicious – if not terrified – of journalists.

It appeared from their reaction that they would almost have preferred the SAS to have allowed the IRA to detonate a bomb than to have to defend their actions in killing three notorious terrorists. If they had prepared a proactive story on the Gibraltar operation they might have won the propaganda battle. Instead they kept their heads down, reacting only when the story was already three times around the world.

The definitive story of Gibraltar may never be known, but enough of the facts and motivation of the men involved can be adduced. There were powerful reasons for stopping the terrorists inside Gibraltar. If arrested in Spain there was no guarantee that the Spanish authorities would be willing to extradite them to Britain or prosecute them through their own courts. The Spanish had their own internal terrorist problem – the Basque separatist group ETA, who themselves have informal links to the IRA – and were not noted for their firmness in dealing with terrorism.

If the IRA team were allowed back to Spain, they might have detonated a bomb remotely without returning to Gibraltar. If arrested too soon, the other members of the IRA working with the active service unit might still have been in a position to detonate the bomb.

The simple justification for the SAS men's actions remained the same: when combating known terrorists, presumed to be armed and carrying a remote-control device, the priority of SAS men was to protect both themselves and the innocent civilians thronging the square where the white Renault was parked. There was no lack of recent evidence of the IRA's indifference to civilian casualties; eleven had died in the Enniskillen Remembrance Day outrage only six months before.

Counter-terrorist operations are not duels where the honourable participant gives his foe the opportunity to shoot first. There are no Queensberry Rules and no benefit of the doubt is given. If you face an opponent you suspect may be armed, either with a weapon or an explosive device, your job is to disarm or disable him.

In a situation where a hesitation of even a second can mean death, SAS men must act with lightning speed, interpreting a target's body language as they draw their own weapons and prepare to fire. Any movement of the target's hands up and away from the body is an indication of a willingness to surrender. Any movement down and in towards the clothes or pockets can only be interpreted as an attempt to reach a weapon or detonate an explosive device.

Once an SAS man has made the decision to fire, there can only be one result. Deliberately shooting a target in the arm or leg is something that only happens in Hollywood Westerns. The reality is that to stop a target and prevent him returning fire you must take the percentage shot, aiming at the centre of the body mass or the head. There is no such thing as shooting to wound. When a trooper fires his pistol he shoots to kill. Given the skill and training of the SAS, the inevitable consequence for the target will be death.

Instead of basing a robust defence of the SAS men's actions on that simple principle, government officials once more muddied the waters by a string of more or less dubious tactics which included delaying the inquest into the killings for several months and using disinformation to try and discredit the testimony of witnesses.

Several newspapers given off-the-record briefings on the character of one of the key witnesses, Mrs Carmen Proetta, whose flat overlooked the scene of the killings, published untrue allegations about her that resulted in libel actions and the award of substantial damages, but by then the inquiry into the shootings was over.

The impression created by the inaccurate press statements in the wake of the shootings and the subsequent shabby manoeuvres to delay or influence the inquiry was that the government and the SAS had something to hide.

Perhaps they did. I played no part in the planning or execution of Operation Flavius, for I had left the Regiment two years earlier, but if I had been debriefing the operation, I would have wanted an answer to one outstanding question.

SAS marksmanship is legendary; the fact that not one of the rounds fired by the four SAS men in Gibraltar missed its target tells its own story. Why, therefore, was it necessary for an SAS team trained to take out any target, in any circumstances, with two shots – the famous double-tap – to pump no fewer than twenty-seven bullets into the bodies of the three terrorists and sixteen into one man alone?

I would also have wanted to examine the magazines of the pistols used in the shootings. The evidence presented to the court of inquiry suggested that all four SAS men had fired their guns, five, six, seven and nine times. That is an unusual pattern, for in most similar incidents it is not uncommon for one or more members of a team not to fire their weapons at all.

The Browning 9mm pistol is equipped to fire thirteen shots. In practice SAS men count their shots and change magazines after twelve shots – six double taps – leaving a round in the breach as they reload. If an examination of their weapons had shown that any of them had changed magazines and then fired again, despite the enforced two-second pause for reflection, it would paint a very different picture of events on that spring afternoon.

Gibraltar was the extreme example of the contradictions inherent in the deployment of SAS Sabre Squadrons against the IRA. If the Regiment was to be confined to a policing role, then Northern Ireland should have been left to the police. If the SAS was to use its full armoury of counter-terrorist techniques to eliminate the IRA threat, the inevitable corollary was that some terrorists would be denied the full benefits of due process and the rule of law. In the confusion of ambush and fire-fight, minimum force becomes an academic concept.

Successive British governments wanted it both ways, however. They wanted to claim the moral high ground, but they also wanted the domestic political returns from striking back at the IRA. Yet they could not accept the wider political consequences of allowing the Regiment to operate in Northern Ireland as it did in other conflicts. Working completely outside the law was acceptable in Aden, Malaya or Borneo, but Northern Ireland was too close to home.

There has never been a clear statement of British political aims in Northern Ireland, no expression of the desire to unify

Ireland, or grant full independence to Ulster, or even set a deadline for withdrawal. That is not entirely the fault of government, for despite the current climate of optimism, in the face of the intransigence of both communities it may be that there is no long-term solution to the problem of Ulster.

Too many parties have a vested interest in prolonging the Troubles. Terrorism is an industry from which many people – on all sides – prosper. Heavy government subsidies give the population of Northern Ireland one of the highest standards of living in the UK, despite its modest GNP.

Others gain even more from the conflict. To see the situation at first hand was a sickening experience. The paramilitaries have divided up the province between them and grown fat on rackets and extortion from their semi-captive populations. Extremist politicians on both sides can also only benefit from continuing violence, instability and sectarian hatred. Even the upholders of the law, the RUC, know that their huge budget and establishment would be under immediate threat if ever a lasting peace were achieved.

Plenty of soldiers serving in Northern Ireland in the 1970s saw the money made available for policing the province and voted with their feet, leaving the army to join the RUC or the Northern Ireland prison service. The rates of pay were so high in comparison to the army that they paid more in tax than the gross earnings of squaddies on the street.

Even the injured and wounded had a financial stake in the conflict. Whether military or civilian, any person injured in an incident could claim substantial compensation from the government. I can still remember one soldier laughing after being hit in the face by a house brick because he knew he would now be getting a cash lump sum in compensation.

We began active service in Northern Ireland immediately after Operation Storm, an infinitely more severe conflict. Many of our comrades had been wounded there, but did not receive a penny in compensation. The difference in treatment stuck in the craw more than a little, just another of the frustrations of our involvement in Northern Ireland.

Another was the number of medals issued there, so many that it has devalued the honours system. A Military Cross or a Military Medal was routinely issued in Northern Ireland for incidents in which rounds were fired. There was one spectacular incident in the SAS where an officer was awarded an MC for being in charge of an operation, even though he was actually on leave in England when the shooting incident took place.

Many veterans of Operation Storm, the Falklands War and the Gulf War are disgusted by the way medals have been doled out like Smarties in Northern Ireland. The fact that SAS men were among the beneficiaries is irrelevant; medals won in Northern Ireland are seen as less valuable than those gained in other conflicts. My own belief is that it has been done to head off internal dissent in the army over the prolonged and largely futile deployment of troops there.

There was a time in the early 1970s when the Provisional IRA could have been defeated militarily. That opportunity was allowed to pass and when the army began to rotate the British Army of the Rhine regiments through Northern Ireland the battle became unwinnable. They had never served anywhere but peacetime West Germany and the only thing they understood was army bullshit: spit, polish, forms, indents, parades and unproductive training. They brought in the Yellow Cards and buried the fighting soldiers under a blizzard of paperwork, rules and regulations.

The SAS could have dealt with the IRA if the British government had been willing to take the political consequences, but that was never likely to happen so close to home and under such intense media scrutiny. Committed to action by a government eager to be seen doing something, the Regiment was then fenced around with constraints, prevented from doing the tasks for which it was trained and used instead in a role that was more properly the province of the RUC.

We were heading into the gutters and backstreets, bowed under the weight of bergens loaded to over- flowing with Whitehall edicts and the ten com- mandment rules of engagement ... to face an opposition unfettered by constitutional laws and diplo- matic niceties ... We were completely pinioned, like men buried to the neck in sand, watching the rising tide of political confusion, intelligence confusion, military confusion and legal confusion.[16]

Despite the doubts surrounding some SAS operations against the IRA, the 'shoot-to-kill policy' remained IRA propaganda, not fact. Had it really been the policy, there would have been a bloodbath, for we knew all the main IRA players and where they were to be found.

The IRA was fighting a war; the British government pre- ferred to regard it as a policing operation, which begs the inevitable question. If it was a police operation not a war, why send the SAS?

While the Troubles in Ulster dragged on and on, the Regi- ment was also deployed on operations in a number of other theatres where the political constraints were far less rigid. The results demonstrated what the SAS could achieve against terrorists when the gloves really were off. A series of daring operations culminated in the incident that remains the high point in the Regiment's public reputation, but which also changed the SAS for ever.

10

TERRORISM
1968–98

The formation of an SAS counter-terrorism team was a closely guarded secret, but as news slowly began to filter through the other security services, anyone who felt they had a contribution to make in the fight against terrorism rang and offered their help.

Among the calls was one from the Hard Dog Section of the Metropolitan Police who felt that their dogs would be able to assist in siege situations. They laid on a demonstration at Biggin Hill in Kent to prove the point.

When we arrived at the airfield we saw a row of small police vans parked close to the aircraft. My colleague Moon, a bit of a joker, stuck his face against the window of each van. There was a frenzy of ferocious barking. The vans were bouncing so hard on their springs as the dogs tried to get at Moon that they were almost lifting clear of the ground.

When its handler went to get one of the Alsatians, it was immediately clear that he was as frightened of the dog as we were. It was still barking furiously and began trying to bite the handler.

'Christ,' Moon said. 'That's an alligator-cross.'

I could see what he meant, the dog's jaws were about half as long as its body.

'Let's call it Singer,' Moon said. 'If it gets hold of you, it'll have you in stitches.'

The other dogs were equally wild and the relationship with their handlers was pure mutual hatred. There was no question of them responding to verbal commands; the only way the police could control them was by laying into them with batons to try and make them more frightened of the handlers than the handlers were of the dogs.

The task for the chosen police Alsatian was to clear an aircraft that had been hijacked by a man with a pistol. The aircraft was the fuselage of an old RAF transport plane, precariously propped on forty-gallon oil drums. The invited audience of civil servants, staff officers, police and SAS men clambered aboard and sat down on rows of canvas seats as if we were about to watch an in-flight movie.

Moon took one look at the assembled multitude and muttered, 'Let's get right to the back and hang on to the side of the plane, because if anyone moves suddenly, it's going to topple over; and when one of those dogs is let loose, everyone is going to be moving suddenly.'

We both took a firm grip on the fuselage at the rear of the plane. When everyone was in position, the gunman entered and stood at the front of the aircraft with a pistol. He fired a couple of blank shots and then the Alsatian came hurtling through the door.

It proceeded to ignore the man with the pistol but bit everyone else it could reach. In the panic to get away from the dog there was a stampede for the front of the aircraft, which duly toppled on to its nose. After a pregnant pause, the Alsatian slid down the floor as if in slow motion, and disappeared into the pile of terrified dignitaries.

We remained dangling from the back of the aircraft enjoying a vision to gladden the heart of any soldier: twenty quite senior officers in a heap with a ravening canine Jaws in the middle biting lumps out of all of them. The end result was that most of them were treated for dog bites and three people were hospitalised, though the mock-terrorist escaped without a scratch.

In spite – or because – of these teething troubles, we still felt that dogs might have their uses in counter-terrorist operations, and we invited the whole Metropolitan Police Hard Dog Section down to Hereford for further trials.

We were particularly curious about whether dogs would be affected by CS or CR gas. The dog-handlers had no idea so we constructed another exercise involving a supposed terrorist with a pistol, a hostage and a dog, but this time we took the precaution of involving the dog's handler as well. All the humans were equipped with gas masks, then the area was filled with clouds of gas and the dog was released.

Several things soon became apparent. The dog would work very effectively on commands from his handler, but if there was no audible command it went on to automatic pilot. Since the gas mask muffled the handler's commands, the dog was left to its own devices. After the by now traditional round of dog bites, the handler pulled off his gas mask to call off the dog.

Before he could speak, he collapsed to the ground coughing and retching from the effects of the gas. The dog was not feeling too happy about the gas either and it vented its displeasure on the handler who, like three senior officers before him, was hospitalised for dog bites. Once more the mock-terrorist escaped unscathed. The tears we wiped from our eyes had more to do with laughter than CS gas.

The police and their dogs remained with us for a week. The training was intensive and progressive but although the dogs were potentially a great weapon, they were not sufficiently controllable; three more people went to hospital with dog bites.

Some good did come out of the exercise, however. It taught me and the rest of the team that in any terrorist situation what counts most is the greatest terror. If someone is holding a pistol to your head and telling you not to move while a dog is simultaneously chewing your bollocks off, the chances are that you are going to ignore the pistol. It was still only a theory but after our previous experiences with the police dogs, there were no volunteers to test it in practice.

The author, Biggin Hill, Kent, 1972

The birth of modern terrorism could be dated to 1964, when the Palestine Liberation Organisation was formed, but it was the tumultuous events of May 1968 in Paris, pushing France to the brink of civil war, that seemed to herald a worldwide explosion of revolutionary violence.

Almost every country had its own terrorists: the Angry Brigade in Britain, the IRA in Ireland, the Red Army Faction in Germany, Action Directe in France, the Red Brigade in Italy, ETA in Spain, the Red Army in Japan, the Tupamaros in Uruguay, the Grey Wolves in Turkey, the Tamils in Sri Lanka and the various Palestinian factions scattered around the Middle East.

A rising tide of terrorist attacks threatened the nationals of almost every state. As one anonymous member of the Red Brigade warned in the aftermath of a bombing that killed eighty-four civilians and left 200 injured, 'There are no innocents.'[1]

According to the US State Department, there were over 300 terrorist acts worldwide in 1970 alone[2] and the pace accelerated still more over the rest of the decade. Between 1970 and 1985 terrorism was estimated to have claimed over 40,000 lives.[3]

The terrorist organisations operated in isolation but also combined forces in high-profile bombings, kidnappings and hijackings. In 1975, one team of terrorists infiltrated the Vienna headquarters of OPEC – the Organisation of Petroleum-Exporting Countries – murdered three security guards and kidnapped the assembled Arab oil ministers, holding them hostage as they tried to exact a pan-Arab commitment to destroy the state of Israel.

Among the multinational team of terrorists was a West German woman, Gabrielle Krocher-Tiedemann, and a Venezuelan man, Ilich Ramirez Sanchez, who became notorious under his pseudonym of Carlos the Jackal.[4]

For a while, the terrorist problem appeared to lack a solution. Several incidents had ended inconclusively. Instead of being killed, the terrorists survived to commit further outrages, for even though they failed to achieve their goals, they were given safe passage to sympathetic countries in return for releasing their hostages.

The concept of training and establishing a UK counter-terrorist team was first discussed in Hereford in the late 1960s. There had been no active service operations since the end of the Aden conflict and the Regiment was scratching around for gainful employment.

Terrorism was very much in the ascendancy at the time. Every government was terrified of it and everything the terrorists attempted seemed to come off, but there appeared to be no reason why the techniques originating in Keeni-Meeni operations in Aden and practised on the streets of Northern Ireland should not be developed for use against international terrorism.

The CRW – Counter-Revolutionary Warfare – Wing originated partly in ideas thrown up in a brainstorming session among SAS men and partly as the result of one individual's zeal.

On the face of it the ex-Goon Michael Bentine was just about the least likely person to have useful ideas on combating terrorism, but the zany front concealed a very intelligent and far-sighted man. He had been a member of the Peruvian Secret Service before coming to Britain and was a crack shot with a pistol. He had even devised his own shooting method, a variant on the Grant Taylor system.

The Master and I were invited to a shooting demonstration by him at Paddington Green police station in the autumn of 1968. The shooting system the Master had devised was now in wide use in BG work and training, but we were looking for other uses for it and went along as much to sell our own system as to see what was on offer.

The assembled throng in the firing range beneath the police station was the usual mixture of senior civil servants, police and army officers, a couple of SBS, the Master and myself. None was in uniform and no one was introduced but within a couple of minutes Michael Bentine had worked out who we all were.

He reached us last. 'And you must be the SAS,' he said, extending his hand. He then put on a Goonish voice and shouted, 'I vill now show you all my enormous weapon.'

He reached down into his trouser waistband, did a quick draw with a ·44 Magnum revolver with a twelve-inch barrel and began rapid fire. Flames were leaping a couple of inches out of the end of the barrel and the concussions were almost shaking the range apart. When the smoke cleared, every single target had been blasted apart.

Having got our attention, he went on to lay out his thesis. He was absolutely convinced that within a very short time the UK police would have to carry arms to combat the threat from international terrorism and the growing menace of the narcotics trade.

He spoke with passion and authority but he was faced with a roomful of mainly blank looks and shuffling feet, because few people in the room had any concept of the threat he was outlining; terrorists and drug gangs were problems for other countries, not Britain. We felt almost embarrassed at the reception he was getting, but we were very eager to talk more with him.

At the end of Michael's presentation the Master walked up to him and they began discussing the merits of teaching the various methods of pistol-shooting. It was as if two lost souls had found each other. Everyone else in the room was forgotten as the two men embarked on a lengthy exploration of the finer points of each shooting method and what their potential future uses might be.

In the end the Master said, 'Right, come to Hereford, come to the Killing House, and we'll show you what we can do.'

Michael was in Hereford two days later. The camp was closed to all outsiders at that time, and in inviting him the Master had greatly exceeded his authority, but quite apart from their shared obsession with pistol-shooting, what Michael had said about terrorism had struck a chord. He was duly admitted to the camp and became the first non-SAS person ever to fire a gun inside the Killing House.

He felt an immediate affinity with the people in the Regiment and described Hereford as 'like coming home'. The respect and affection was reciprocated. He was a great believer in fairness and he hated the thought of terrorism and its brutal indifference to the lives of innocent people.

As much as anyone, he deserves the credit for promoting the idea of a counter-terrorist force within the SAS several years before the Munich Olympics massacre triggered the actual formation of the CT team. His death in 1997 was a sad loss not only to his family but to his friends in the Regiment.

Although we had no authorisation to set up an active counter-terrorist team, we were given permission to acquire the necessary equipment and begin to develop the techniques that were to become world famous. The early work was carried out by the Bodyguard Cell, but once the viability of the counter-terrorist techniques had been proved, a permanent Counter-Revolutionary Warfare Wing was established.

We deliberately kept things simple, realising that the secret to success in this field was training and not equipment. Even so, the development of the CRW concept led directly to a number of innovations.

The new close-quarter shooting techniques required the expenditure of a vast amount of ammunition. We had decided to stick to the tried and trusted 9mm Browning automatic, both because it was a reliable weapon and because the ammunition was British army issue and readily available.

We also acquired Remington repeater shotguns, used to blast door locks and hinges, and plastic explosives to blow in doors and windows. We then did a trawl to find the most suitable submachine-gun for the job. At the time the American M10/11, which could be suppressed, was not quite the best submachine-gun around, but it was the best available to us.

The Heckler-Koch later replaced it, mainly because it was the only submachine-gun that fired from a closed bolt position. You could drop it and it would not discharge accidentally, which was important when you were climbing over buildings and aircraft.

The velocity of the rounds that we were using caused us some concern. At close range, the standard rounds could easily pass through the body of the terrorist you were targeting and do secondary damage to the hostages behind him.

This realisation led us into a series of tests at the research establishment at Porton Down. In due course they developed a round which would expand and lose all its energy on entering the body. It was fatal for the target, but greatly reduced the risk of hostages being wounded or killed by friendly fire.

We also spent some time trying to improvise a safe stun grenade. We experimented with various mixtures of fireworks and CS gas without success, and then again approached Porton Down. In a matter of weeks they produced a prototype flash-bang grenade. It was about six inches long by three inches wide and filled with magnesium particles and fulminate of mercury.

It could be used safely near hostages because it did not incapacitate anybody, but the blinding flashes – equivalent to 50,000 watts – and thunderous detonations severely disorientated people who were unused to them. Flash-bang grenades became an essential part of the team's armoury and were later used to good effect in the Iranian Embassy siege. The early models made just one loud bang, while later ones exploded half a dozen times in rapid succession.

Anti-personnel gas also played a vital part in operations. We initially trained wearing gas masks in gas-filled environments, but one of the team decided he could operate without a gas mask and this led to us all working without masks in a very heavy CS and CR gas environment. The scientists had told us it was impossible, but we found that if we took it slowly and built up our tolerances over a period of time, we could operate effectively in a gas-filled environment that would bring anyone else to their knees.

We had a vivid demonstration of our newly acquired tolerance one day when we had been working on the shooting range in a very heavy concentration of gas. We decided to wander down to the club for a cup of tea and incapacitated half the Regiment because of the gas globules still sticking to our clothing.

Some of the enthusiasm for realistic testing went far beyond the call of duty. The live test of a new flak jacket proposed by one of my colleagues involved firing a Browning 9mm pistol at the jacket – while he was wearing it. For obvious reasons I was very reluctant but he was even more insistent.

In the end I allowed myself to be persuaded. I took the most careful aim I have ever done in my life and fired. The impact hurled him back several feet and as he lay on the ground, for a moment I thought I had killed him. Then there was a fearsome burst of swearing. The ceramic plate inside the jacket had absorbed the impact, but without any padding to soften the blow my friend had an enormous bruise right across his chest. His sacrifice was not in vain; the flak jackets are now fitted with shock pads.

Undeterred by his experience, he next proposed a similar test on a new helmet, but I told him he'd have to shoot himself in the head, because neither I nor anyone else in the

Regiment was going to. The test was eventually conducted using a dummy.

When not testing our own equipment or honing our CRW skills in a series of demanding exercises, we also hired ourselves out as poachers-turned-gamekeepers to test security equipment for the Home Office.

Brigadier M. S. K. Maunsell, the Inspector-General of Prisons, was one of the first to ask for our help to test the security of a new 'escape-proof' prison. We were over the fence and away inside two minutes.

A new security door that the Home Office asked us to evaluate took even less time to defeat. It was claimed to be immune to explosives, lock picks, thermic lances and a host of other devices. There was something about it, however ... One of the lads picked up a sledgehammer, gave it a couple of sharp blows, and the wonder door toppled and fell.

The next test of the Regiment's skills was rather more demanding. On 18 May 1972 a telephone call to Cunard claimed that bombs had been planted on the *QE2* – then in mid-Atlantic – and would be detonated if a ransom of £100,000 was not paid. A mixed SAS and SBS team was hastily assembled and flown out.

They parachuted into the sea near the *QE2*, climbed aboard and carried out a thorough search of the huge liner without finding any trace of explosives. It had been a hoax, but it had provoked a useful training exercise.

We had been working hard on the CRW concept for a couple of years and the techniques and skills were largely in place. All that was now needed was the political will to form a dedicated and fully equipped counter-terrorist team. The catalyst came later the same year. The terrorist attack by Black September guerrillas at the Munich Olympic Games pushed counter-terrorism to the top of everyone's political agenda.

Black September already had a formidable track record that included the hijacking and destruction of four passenger jets at Dawson's Field in Amman in 1970 and the assassination of the Jordanian Prime Minister.

Before dawn on 5 September 1972, eight members of Black September broke into the Olympic Village and occupied the Israeli athletes' dormitory. Two people – wrestling coach Moshe Weinberger and weightlifter Yossef Romano – were shot immediately, the other nine were taken hostage.

The terrorists demanded the release of over 200 Palestinians held in Israeli jails and a number of members of the Red Army Faction held in West Germany, but while the Germans were ready to accede to the demands the Israeli government refused to consider a deal.

After day-long negotiations, the West German authorities offered the terrorists safe conduct out of the country for themselves and their hostages, while laying plans to ambush them at the airport. Two helicopters transferred the terrorists and hostages to the military airfield at Furstenfeldbruk, where a Boeing 727 was allegedly waiting to transport them to Cairo.

As the terrorists emerged from the helicopters, police snipers opened fire from the roof of the terminal building. They were poorly positioned, too far from their targets, but in the first burst of fire two of the terrorists were killed and three others wounded. Two of the helicopter crew were also hit.

Two other police snipers had terrorists in their sights but failed to fire, afraid of hitting the wrong targets at such long range. The surviving terrorists reboarded the helicopters and when German troops in armoured cars began a frontal assault the terrorists in the first helicopter killed their five hostages and blew it up. Shortly afterwards the remaining hostages also perished as the second helicopter exploded.

The rescue attempt had been a disaster. Five terrorists were killed and the other three taken prisoner, but every single one of the nine hostages lay dead. A policeman was also killed and the humiliation of the German security forces was witnessed by a worldwide television audience.

The errors of Munich were later compounded when the three captured terrorists were released in a deal with another group who had hijacked a plane. It was another disastrous mistake, merely encouraging those terrorists – and others – to commit fresh outrages.

Immediately after the Munich incident we received formal approval from the highest ministerial levels of Edward Heath's government to form a counter-terrorist team. In a phrase unheard of in recent British military history, we were told that 'money was no object'.

For some reason, the first group charged with forming the counter-terrorist team ignored virtually all the work that had already been done, went off at a tangent and did not develop the concept in the way we all wanted.

I was then drafted in and given a composite troop of extremely experienced and very dedicated people. From our point of view the hard work had already been done. We knew exactly how we were going to do it and almost overnight the team was put together: a sixteen-man group with some communications and command and control elements.

Most of the government's largesse was spent on communications and surveillance equipment and a fleet of Range Rovers, each fitted with a strengthened chassis and anti-roll bars.

We trained day and night for months until we could operate in any conditions and circumstances and were ready to face every conceivable terrorist scenario. The training with live ammunition took place in the Killing House.

Most members of the royal family have been in a hostage situation inside the Killing House, sitting on a chair in a darkened room while bullets flew all around them. The point was not to entertain them or scare them witless but to give them confidence if the nightmare scenario ever occurred. If we had to stage a genuine rescue of a member of the royal family, we did not want them jumping up in fright and running into the line of fire.

The Queen was probably the most imperturbable VIP we ever treated to a demonstration. An SAS officer acted as hostage and provided a running commentary for Her Majesty during a three-part demonstration. He laconically set the scene, describing 'the three vital factors in the exercise, which have the same initials as the Regiment: Speed, Aggression, Surprise'. On the word 'surprise' there was an explosion and the assault team burst into the room, sprinting, diving and rolling across the floor, while pouring a stream of live rounds into the targets.

'As I engaged my target, I was firing straight down the line of observers, sending a torrent of bullets within inches of the Queen's nose. Amongst the normal blinks, twitches and uncontrolled movements of her retinue, the Queen remained absolutely unperturbed as the hostage was removed and we backed out of the room.'[5]

The second demonstration was conducted in total darkness. The SAS men had the benefit of night-vision goggles, but the VIPs were completely shrouded in darkness and could see nothing but the flashes of the guns. As well as enabling them to identify their targets, the goggles also allowed the assault team to observe the reactions of the VIPs, who were normally less inhibited about squirming and taking cover in the dark.

Once again the explosions and shots had Her Majesty's retinue twitching and looking nervously for the exits, but her own stiff upper lip never quivered. She was as serene as if she was watching the Trooping of the Colour rather than an armed assault.

The final demonstration involved the rescue and extraction by helicopter of a hostage, suitably clothed and wearing a Margaret Thatcher mask. As we rose into the sky, dangling beneath the heli with our imitation Maggie, I thought I detected a slight change in the

Queen's expression. For a moment I could have sworn
that there was a twinkle in her eye.[6]

Princess Diana brought in Prince William and Prince Harry
for their first taste of the Killing House on 21 October 1995.
All three of them seemed to enjoy it. Princess Diana could
relax, knowing that there could scarcely be a more paparazzi-
free zone than Stirling Lines, while there was more equipment
for the boys to play on than the most lavishly equipped
adventure playground.

Apart from putting on demonstrations for VIPs, a major
CRW exercise was staged every month, with the assault group
attacking the target – an aircraft, a train, a bus, a building,
even an ocean liner – and freeing the hostages. Two-man
teams moved from room to room or area to area, clearing
each in seconds, instantly identifying and killing terrorists,
while safeguarding the hostages. At the same time a perimeter containment group armed with sniper rifles threw
a cordon around the area and ensured that no terrorist
escaped.

DLB, promoted to CO of the Regiment in January 1972,
was keen to ensure that vigilance against terrorism extended
throughout the SAS. He authorised a series of raids in which
one group of SAS men launched a surprise attack on another
and to show that he was not above the need for vigilance
himself, he issued a challenge to us to kidnap him.

We watched him carrying out counter-surveillance drills
and jumping at shadows every time he emerged from his
office for the next few days, but we bided our time until he
had begun to relax again. Then we pounced. He had fallen
into the classic trap of establishing a routine.

One morning as he was coming down the lane from his
home, on his way to the camp at his usual time, he found
himself grabbed, bound and gagged, and tossed into the back
of a van. We drove him round some of the roughest, bumpiest
roads in Hereford for an hour or two, then hauled him out,

stripped him to his underpants, sealed him inside a wooden crate and drove off. Once safely back in camp and going about our innocent business, an anonymous telephone call to the Officers' Mess revealed where the Regiment's rather dishevelled CO could be found.

DLB soon had ample compensation for his rough treatment, for once the SAS CT team was established, it became a growth industry. It had such high ministerial approval that budgets were ignored and money was spent like water. Counter-terrorism was the area to be involved in for recognition and promotion, and the handful of SAS men actually at the cutting edge soon became a tiny part of the three-ring circus going on around them.

Senior officers in the forces saw it as the tool that would keep them in the ministerial eye and give them access to places they could not reach in any other way. As a result it was used ruthlessly by a number of people to promote their own careers.

When the team was set up, the Director, SAS, was co-opted on to the Cabinet Office Committee. The most senior officer, the Chief of the General Staff, had previously represented the armed forces. In the event of any terrorist incident, he would now be replaced by a relatively junior officer. The Director, SAS, would go to 10 Downing Street and sit at the same table as the Home Secretary and often the Prime Minister.

Edward Heath's decision to authorise an SAS counter-terrorist unit was far from popular with everyone. There were plenty of critics of SAS primacy in counter-terrorism within the military and, in an echo of our problems in Northern Ireland with the RUC, senior policemen were also annoyed that the SAS was going to be used on mainland UK to do a job which by law and by police preference they felt they should be doing.

Unsurprisingly, we disagreed. Our levels of skill and training were way ahead of anything the police could offer. That remained true even years later, as a training exercise for a regional police force amply demonstrated. To spare their blushes, I will not identify which region.

An ex-member of the Regiment and I constructed an exercise in which the elite armed police team had to storm a building and rescue a group of hostages. My colleague and I were playing the terrorists. He had brought his wife along as well and though she had never fired a pistol before, she joined us as we lay in wait in the darkened building, taking up a position halfway up the stairs.

The police team duly burst in, but in the paint-ball firefight that followed they took massive casualties without hitting any of us. My colleague's wife personally accounted for three of them before retreating unscathed to the upstairs landing. The police were forced into an ignominious retreat without rescuing a single hostage. A rapid re-evaluation of police tactics and procedures ensued.

The aim of the CT team differed from most functions of the SAS in one very significant respect. As a general rule, it was not there to carry out intelligence-gathering. Its primary aim was, is and always will be to secure the safe release of the hostages. No one would lose any great amount of sleep if killing the terrorists was a by-product of saving the hostages, but despite terrorist propaganda it was never the principal aim of the counter-terrorist team.

At the same time that we were setting up the team in Hereford, the French and Germans also began training elite counter-terrorist teams: GIGN in France and GSG-9 in Germany. The German force was developed in close consultation with the SAS, and we provided much of their training.

The main difference lay in the origin of the recruits. The members of GSG-9 were recruited from the German border police, and GIGN was an offshoot of the French gendarmerie.

In the late 1960s and early 1970s most hijackings and hostage incidents ended in the terrorists' favour, but now the tide began to turn. Our first operational deployment came in

January 1975 when an aircraft was hijacked at Manchester by an Iranian armed with a pistol, demanding to be flown to Paris.

The plane took off, flew south for a couple of hours and was then talked down by a French air traffic controller. A group of gendarmes surrounded the plane after landing and kept the terrorist distracted as the assault team stormed the aircraft, overpowered him and released the hostages. His pistol turned out to be a replica gun and the only casualty was a trooper bitten by an excitable police dog as he left the aircraft.

The terrorist was a little puzzled at being seized by British troops in the French capital but the CT team had actually arranged for the aircraft to be diverted to Stansted. A French-speaking air traffic controller, a few borrowed gendarmes' uniforms and a hastily painted sign saying 'Orly' were enough to convince him that he'd arrived at his chosen destination.

A second hijack, of a Tanzanian Airlines Boeing 737, was also diverted to Stansted. We were well rehearsed, having carried out an anti-hijacking exercise at the USAF base at Weathersfield just down the road a couple of weeks before. The only flaw was that the Chief Constable of Essex had not participated in the exercise, preferring to delegate it to his deputy.

When a real emergency occurred, the chief constable insisted on assuming control. His first action was to authorise the refuelling of the aircraft, in breach of every previously agreed practice.

Fortunately the error was not fatal, though that did not lessen the foolishness of his action. Had we been able to countermand his order we would have done so, but at that stage the police had not relinquished control and no one, not even the Home Secretary or the Prime Minister, had the authority to overrule a chief constable on his own turf.

While the jet remained on the tarmac, we were studying the passenger manifest to identify the terrorists. It is important to know exactly how many terrorists you are dealing with, because the worry is not the men waving guns in the cockpit or standing guard over the hostages, but the sleepers, apparently hostages themselves, who may blow up the aircraft or shoot hostages or members of the assault team as they storm it.

In a normal hijacking suspicious individuals, usually travelling alone, will be identified from the manifest. Enquiries may be made by the police in the individuals' countries of origin, both with the booking agency issuing the tickets and at the workplaces and homes of the suspects.

In a very short time the potential terrorists will be identified and the plan to storm the aircraft can be laid. In this case there was not a single individual booked on the plane.

We then began to examine the 'completes' – the family groups. Within a few minutes the tension had largely evaporated and we were running a book on when the hijackers would surrender. Our study of the manifest and enquiries in Tanzania showed a couple of large extended families travelling without visas. It was immediately clear that the hijackers were not politically motivated terrorists, but economic migrants.

The heads of the families who had carried out the hijacking surrendered to us soon afterwards. They were imprisoned, but their families were fed and housed at taxpayers' expense while they served their sentences. They remain UK residents and one of the group is now a successful lawyer here, his family having achieved their aims by a lawless act. Some admired their resourcefulness, but I could only detest those who achieved their ends by subjecting innocent people to a terrifying ordeal that could have ended in their deaths.

It was our second bloodless counter-terrorist victory, for in December 1975, after bomb outrages in London, Guildford and Birmingham over the previous twelve months, the police cornered a four-man Provisional IRA team in a flat in Balcombe Street, Marylebone. The owners of the flat, a man and wife, were taken hostage.

The terrorists had been holding out for some sort of deal or a chance to escape, but from our surveillance we knew that they were listening to the radio. We persuaded the BBC to report that the SAS had arrived on the scene and the police were about to hand over control of the incident to us. Knowing what the consequences of further resistance would be, the IRA men immediately surrendered.

As well as carrying out operations in our own right, we were also interested observers – and on one occasion participants – in a series of operations by the counter-terrorist forces of other countries. Some were models of intelligent planning and bold, ruthless execution, others were catastrophic failures. We drew valuable lessons from them all.

The most successful, which set a benchmark for all future counter-terrorist operations, was mounted by the Israelis. On 27 June 1976, two Palestinian terrorists from the Popular Front for the Liberation of Palestine and two German members of the Baader-Meinhof gang – Wilfried Boese and the ubiquitous Gabrielle Krocher-Tiedemann – hijacked Air France Flight 139 *en route* from Tel Aviv to Paris, after a stop in Athens.

They forced the pilot to fly to Benghazi in Libya and, after refuelling, they flew on to Entebbe in Uganda, where they rendezvoused with five other waiting terrorists.

The Ugandan dictator Idi Amin was also there to welcome them and offer them support. His soldiers manned the airfield perimeter and helped to guard the hostages – 258 passengers and crew – who were herded into a disused terminal building.

The terrorists' demands were a familiar litany, including the release of imprisoned comrades in Germany, Israel and elsewhere. Whatever the attitude of the other nations, however, Israel made it clear that it would not co-operate and Unit 269 of the Israeli paratroops was immediately placed on stand-by.

Over the next few days 152 hostages were released, but 106, most of them Jewish, were detained. By their decision to let the others go, the terrorists had unwittingly lifted the pressure from other countries on Israel to protect their nationals at all costs and made it easier for an assault to be staged.

The Israelis had one other lucky break. The disused terminal had originally been constructed by an Israeli firm, which made it easy for plans of the building to be obtained. Released hostages were also debriefed, though the accuracy of their descriptions of the disposition of the terrorists and Ugandan troops could not be relied on.

The Israeli paratroops assessed and rejected plans for an amphibious assault from Lake Victoria or a land attack from Kenya. Instead, an airborne assault would be mounted.

It was at extreme range for the Hercules transports they would be using – the nearest Israeli base at Ophira in Sinai was over 3,000 miles from Entebbe – and the Israelis had to ensure the co-operation of the Kenyan government so that the aircraft could refuel at Nairobi after the hostage rescue.

Four Hercs took off from Ophira at dawn on 2 July and flew at wave-top height down the Red Sea and then across the potentially hostile territory of Ethiopia at extreme low level towards Entebbe. A Boeing 707 flew ahead of the assault teams as a mobile command and communication post. It also had the ability to jam electronically Ugandan radar and would act as an emergency hospital for any casualties.

The Israeli plan involved an audacious deception. As they approached Entebbe, the pilot of the Boeing radioed the tower, told them that President Amin was coming in to visit the hijackers and asked for the runway lights to be switched on.

The Boeing remained airborne as the Hercs landed at one minute past eleven and taxied to a halt. The cargo doors of the first Hercules swung open and a black Mercedes identical to that owned by President Amin was driven down the ramp. Two jeeps full of 'Presidential Guards' followed it across the airfield. The convoy had got within fifty yards of the old terminal before they were challenged by two Ugandan soldiers.

One was shot dead immediately, the other managed to shout a warning before he too was killed. The Israeli paratroops burst in through the glass doors, shouted to the hostages to lie flat on the floor and began shooting the terrorists.

At the same time, troops from the other aircraft took the new terminal building and the control tower, secured the airfield perimeter and destroyed a squadron of Ugandan MiG fighters on the ground to prevent any pursuit of the Hercs.

The terrorists all lay dead within three minutes of the assault beginning. The Israelis' only casualties were a wounded soldier and their commander, Lieutenant-Colonel Jonathan Netanyahu, who was shot and killed.

Fifty minutes after landing the Hercs were airborne again, bearing the assault team and all but one of the hostages. The last one, Mrs Dora Bloch, had fallen ill before the raid and been taken to a hospital. The Ugandans vented their rage on her; she was murdered and her body dumped in a ditch.

The Israeli forces were rightly praised and admired around the world. The SAS too took full note of their achievement. The assault combined the classic virtues of such operations: simplicity of planning, a brilliant deception to disguise the true intention, and great skill and daring coupled with absolute ruthlessness of execution.

The Israelis had led the fight against the terrorists in the late 1960s and early 1970s. The skill and courage of their forces was backed by the political will to fight and not to give in to terrorism. A few countries, including the UK, had the capability to carry out an Entebbe-style raid, but their politicians did not have the balls to back them.

Terrorism was rampant; at one stage hijacked aircraft were flying into Cuba almost every day. Yet most states – again including the UK, which gave in to terrorist blackmail by releasing the Palestinian hijacker Leila Khaled from gaol – were scared witless by terrorism. Only the mounting evidence that giving in to one terrorist act merely invited a repetition persuaded the politicians to stiffen their spines.

West German politicians had been particularly guilty of dithering and hesitating from one terrorist crisis to another, but the year after Entebbe another hostage crisis offered the West German government a chance to lay the ghost of the disaster at the Munich Olympics and half a dozen craven retreats before terrorism.

On 13 October 1977, four terrorists – two men and two women – hijacked a Lufthansa 737 with eighty-six passengers on a flight from Palma, Majorca, to Frankfurt.

They were armed with automatic pistols and grenades that had probably been smuggled in by airport workers and passed to the terrorists after they had passed through the security checks.

The terrorists demanded the freeing of ten imprisoned members of the Red Army Faction in Germany, two Palestinians held in Turkey and a ransom of $15 million. Similar demands had been made six weeks earlier after the kidnapping of a West German industrialist, Hans-Martin Schleyer.

The hijacking was to be the first serious test of the West Germans' own counter-terrorist team, GSG-9. Two SAS men, Major Alastair Morrison and Sergeant Barry Davies, were also attached to GSG-9 for the operation, for the Germans had neither supplies of flash-bang grenades nor expertise in using them.

SIS diplomacy and SAS expertise had combined to produce the first trans-national response to a terrorist incident, pointing the way forward for counter-terrorist operations. Just as organisations like the Red Army Faction, the Red Brigade and the Popular Front for the Liberation of Palestine were combining on terrorist operations, so the counter-terrorist forces of Western countries would combine to defeat them.

Over the next five days the aircraft made a series of flights from country to country, landing successively at Rome, Cyprus, Bahrain and Dubai, where the governments granted fuel but no other concessions. At each stage of the journey the hijacked jet was tracked by the combined GSG-9 and SAS team.

When it came to rest in Dubai the team prepared to storm it, but the aircraft took off again before the plan could be put into effect, landing at Aden, where the Marxist government refused the aircraft carrying the GSG-9 and SAS men permission to land.

While in Aden, the terrorist leader, styling himself 'Captain Mahmoud', murdered the Lufthansa pilot, Jurgen Schumann, accusing him of passing information over the radio to the tower. The co-pilot then flew the jet on to Mogadishu in Somalia with the captain's body still lying on the cabin floor.

The terrorists then dumped Schumann's body out on to the runway. The action sealed their fate. The converted 707 carrying the GSG-9 team also held a steel box containing the ransom and until Schumann's body hit the tarmac the West German government had still been hoping to negotiate its way out of the crisis.

Now the decision was taken to storm the plane. The 707 carrying the twenty-six-man GSG-9 team landed at Mogadishu at 5.30 p.m. on 17 October 1977 and stopped at the far end of the runway, about a mile from the hijacked jet.

At eight minutes to midnight that night Somali soldiers lit a bonfire a hundred yards in front of the plane. The diversion succeeded: two terrorists were spotted in the cockpit of the jet a few moments later, peering towards the blaze.

The assault team had placed rubber-coated ladders against the sides of the jet and climbed on to the wings. As the emergency doors over the wings were blown in, the SAS men hurled in flash-bang grenades.

The Germans stormed the aircraft, firing over the heads of the hostages, who were still strapped in their seats. One of the women terrorists was shot and killed as she fired at the assault team from the first-class area; the other, Suhaila Sayeh, was captured alive.

The two male terrorists trapped in the cockpit threw grenades but they exploded beneath empty seats, which absorbed most of the blast. The men, including the murderous Captain Mahmoud, were killed before they could detonate the other grenades that they had rigged up around the plane.

The interior of the aircraft had also been liberally doused with aviation fuel and duty-free alcohol by the terrorists, but aviation fuel is hard to ignite – you can drop a lighted cigarette into it without it catching fire – and fortunately no blaze broke out.

At the end of the eight-minute fire-fight, three terrorists had been killed and the other one captured. One member of the assault team and four of the hostages were slightly wounded. The rest were released unharmed.

When they heard that their would-be rescuers had failed, three German terrorists – the Baader-Meinhof leaders, Andreas Baader, Gudrun Ensslin and Jan-Carl Raspe – committed suicide in their cells in Stammheim prison. The body of the German industrialist Hans-Martin Schleyer was found a week later. He had been shot and dumped in the boot of a car.

The successful collaboration of British and German counter-terrorist forces at Mogadishu put a seal on Western co-operation against terrorism. Intelligence on terrorist organisations was freely shared and observers from friendly nations attended the debriefs of all subsequent major incidents, including the siege of the Iranian Embassy.

Some damaging blows had been struck against terrorism but there was no room for complacency whatsoever. The counter-terrorist forces were not the only ones to draw lessons from successes such as Entebbe and Mogadishu. Terrorists also learned from the mistakes of their dead comrades. Hijackings continued, albeit at a much reduced level, and the newer breed of hijackers were even more formidable: more vigilant, more ruthless and more indifferent to their own survival.

As an immediate consequence of Mogadishu, the SAS CT team was expanded to full squadron strength. The four SAS squadrons – A, B, D and G – began a permanent rotation through periods of CT training, tours in Northern Ireland and training abroad. An overlap of a few weeks allowed the outgoing CT team to brief the incoming one on all recent developments.

New equipment was also purchased, including body armour, flame-retardant suits, respirators and helmets with integral microphones, allowing constant communication between members of the assault team.

As well as carrying out CT training and operations in our own right, we also trained the special forces of close allies in the new techniques we had developed, for when the US and other Western states wanted to set up their own elite troops, only one organisation in the world had the skills and experience to train them.

Such training continues to this day. A typical example was that the SAS worked with the German force, the KSK – Kommando Spetziale Krafte – that was designed to give the German army a special forces capacity. It may well ultimately replace the police-based anti-terrorist force, GSG-9.

Our closest and most fruitful relationship was with the American special forces. Senior US government and military figures fell on the SAS concept of counter-revolutionary warfare like starving men.

The Vietnam War had so traumatised the US that the acceptable level of American casualties in an overseas conflict had fallen close to zero. Even one dead soldier was enough to erode Congressional support. The use of clandestine forces like the SAS offered a way to intervene and achieve the desired results without the downside of visible casualties and negative public reaction back home.

The Americans had originally re-formed their special forces to fight the Korean War in the early 1950s. At first they were similar to the SAS – small, select and very professional – but the Kennedy government organised a dramatic expansion of the special forces at the beginning of the Vietnam War, and the ethos instilled by their founders was thrown away. Their former methods of selection were disregarded and as their numbers mushroomed their quality declined. One statistic says it all: the number of rejected recruits fell from 90 per cent in 1962 to 30 per cent in 1964.[7]

At the same time, special forces commanders dropped their previous insistence on accepting only recruits who had previously been trained by the airborne forces and started taking volunteers straight from Civvy Street.

The inevitable result was that in a short time the only thing that was special about the US special forces was their name. The American military came to realise that the only way to restore standards was to revert to rigorous selection and training. Scrapping the existing special forces was politically impossible; the only solution was to create a new force alongside them.

Two American special forces soldiers – one officer and one warrant officer – had been permanently attached to the British SAS since the beginning of the 1960s. Among the Hereford alumni was Major Nathan 'Charlie' Beckwith.

At first stupefied by the way the SAS went about its business: 'Everything I'd been taught about soldiering, been trained to believe, was turned upside down,'[8] he came to be so impressed by what he learned in Hereford that he subsequently tried to instil the same SAS ethos and doctrine into his own command.

Charlie Beckwith's initial attempts to form an American SAS-style special forces group were rejected. Even the commander of the Special Warfare Centre, General William P. Yarborough, who had been made an honorary SAS member for his help in providing training facilities for us at Fort Bragg, refused to countenance the idea of an American SAS.

Beckwith shelved the idea while he served in the existing US special forces in Vietnam, carrying out operations in Thailand and Cambodia as well as Vietnam itself, but when he returned to the US in 1974 he raised the subject of an SAS-type force once more. By then there was a new commander of the Special Warfare Centre, General Bob Kingston, who was an enthusiastic supporter of the SAS approach.

A plan was drawn up, but even with Bob Kingston's support it took over two years of argument and hard bargaining before permission was obtained to form the First Special Forces Operations Detachment Delta – Delta Force.

One of the most difficult problems they had to overcome was the Affirmative Action programme. Designed to end discrimination on grounds of sex, race, creed or colour, it compelled any US government organisation – including the armed forces – to include a representative cross-section of the population as a whole. For a force dedicated to selecting an elite on merit alone, Affirmative Action was a nightmare. After intensive lobbying, Delta Force finally secured an exemption from the programme.

Although it was now up and running, Delta Force was still bitterly resented by many senior officers who had an implacable suspicion of special forces, and it still had no formal approval from the President, Jimmy Carter.

That was hastily granted in the wake of the Mogadishu rescue. Having prevaricated for the best part of three years, military advisers had Jimmy Carter's signature on a document the very same day as the Mogadishu operation, 19 November 1977.

Under US law it is illegal for American armed forces to be used inside the continental United States and Delta's charter restricted it to overseas operations. That created an anomaly: Delta Force had responsibility for counter-terrorist operations abroad, but the FBI had responsibility within the United States. The duplication of resources and the strong possibility of failures to pool intelligence made it a risky way to proceed.

Even after Delta Force had received its charter, its opponents continued to try and hamper it. A rival force, Blue Light, was even set up by disgruntled officers in the existing US special forces.

For a year the two organisations existed side by side and we were put in the bizarre position of receiving visits from both Delta Force and Blue Light within a few weeks of each other. Finally the army chief of staff, General Bernard Rogers, discovered the farcical situation. He informed President Carter and Blue Light was abruptly cancelled.

There was still one cloud on Delta's horizon. The SAS and GSG-9 had direct links to the highest political levels. The SAS had access to the Cabinet Office and the Prime Minister in Britain, GSG-9 reported directly to the Chancellor in Bonn. Delta Force had no such link to the White House and was burdened with an endless chain of command. Even when it was simplified after vociferous protests from Charlie Beckwith, Delta's access reached no higher than the Department of the Army.

The bureaucratic command structure and the still-simmering resentment of other branches of the US armed forces were to cause Delta Force massive operational difficulties when it was finally deployed in earnest.

In every other respect it grew to equal the SAS. Training was as rigorous and demanding as that for the Regiment, but America's well-endowed military could also support Delta Force with assets that, despite our priority funding, the British Regiment could only dream of.

Given Bob Kingston and Charlie Beckwith's admiration for the SAS, it was natural that they should turn to us for help in setting up Delta Force. They sent a number of highly experienced officers to do the SAS Selection course. Not all were successful by any means but the ones who did pass took that knowledge home with them.

They then borrowed a number of SAS instructors, who went to the US special forces headquarters in Fort Bragg, North Carolina, to advise them on constructing a similar selection process.

Based in the Stockade, a disused jail in Fort Bragg, Beckwith recruited a force on the SAS model: four squadrons composed of sixteen-man troops, which broke down into four- or two-man patrols.

The only major difference of opinion was over the American wish to include a number of psychological tests which the SAS felt were of dubious value. In every other respect, US Special Operations Forces paid its British counterpart the ultimate compliment: it became a clone of its role model. Over the next two years it recruited its men, and trained them in the skills of special forces operations. On one occasion, we were in an exercise involving the Americans. It took place in the grounds of a disused military hospital in the south of England. It had been cordoned off, sealed from the outside world. Figures moved purposefully to and fro around the buildings and the hum of generators was counterpointed by bursts of Morse traffic.

Helicopters clattered overhead, and troops dressed in the familiar black fireproof coveralls of the SAS counter-terrorist team began abseiling to the ground. Their coveralls bristled with flash-bang grenades and all the other complex equipment needed by the CT team. Gas masks were locked on to their arms, there were automatic pistols in holsters on their leather belts and the Heckler-Koch submachine-guns made famous in the assault on the Iranian Embassy hung around their necks.

They secured their initial objectives with brisk, ruthless efficiency. Only when they began to speak did a few American accents reveal that members of the SOF were operating alongside the SAS.

There were some differences in support – the Americans used different types of vehicle and different helicopters – but the personal equipment, training, tactics and philosophy were essentially identical.

I was controlling the enemy side. We had spent several months planning and putting all the assets together to ensure that the troops got the maximum possible value from the exercise.

The Americans had arrived in conditions of the utmost secrecy. The plan was for both the exercise and the fact that the Americans were even over here to be kept under wraps.

Suddenly there was a commotion from the other side of the building. The main door was being manned by a soldier with strict instructions to allow no entrance to anyone up to and including the second coming of Jesus Christ.

As the commotion grew louder, I walked through the building to see what the excitement was about. The guard was arguing with a man in a suit. He identified himself as a senior reporter on an aviation magazine.

He had been driving along the motorway past the exercise area when he spotted a Blackhawk helicopter overhead. At the time the Blackhawk was still on the American Secret List. He had hot-footed it to the place where he had seen it land.

We checked his credentials, which were genuine. I was now faced with a major predicament. I could not just throw him out; he could blow the whole story of the exercise and leave us with not one, but a hundred journalists on our doorstep. Nor could I buy him off easily: the scoop of a lifetime was staring him in the face.

I thought about it for a few minutes, then made him an offer I was pretty sure he could not refuse. If he promised to sit on the story for three weeks – long enough for the SOF to complete the exercise and return to their base – I would arrange for him to have a flight in the Blackhawk.

I could tell from his expression that we had a deal. Not only was he going to see a top-secret aircraft, he was going to be the first British civilian to have a ride in it.

I then took him to the senior US officer present who agreed the terms, and we sent the reporter off for his flight. He arrived back an hour later as breathless and excited as a schoolboy. I shook hands and reminded him of our agreement. I was still far from convinced that he would keep his word but, to my surprise, the article did not appear during the agreed three weeks nor the weeks and months that followed.

We never discovered whether he had been scared off by fears of SAS retaliation, or had had his scoop dismissed as a hallucination by his hard-boiled editor, or had simply decided to keep his big story as a private highpoint of his career. Whatever the reason, the story was never published.

My only reservation about the close ties between the SOF and the SAS was that the American unit contained a number of born-again Christians. This even led to a number of the more impressionable members of the SAS returning from the US having been born again.

I would not dispute the right of anyone to adhere to their own religious convictions, but many of the fundamentalist Christians in the SOF seemed unwilling to show a similar tolerance to others.

I do not believe it is possible to follow an effective hearts and minds policy while despising the religion, culture and beliefs of the people one is operating among, but my reservations about the SOF's hard-core Christians went deeper than that.

They had a dangerous tendency to see the SOF's role as part of a holy war as intense as any Muslim jihad. They appeared to view the large part of the world that did not subscribe to their beliefs as uniformly hostile territory. If its peoples could not be persuaded to see the one true path, they were to be subjugated or destroyed.

While deploring that attitude, it also offered the SAS opportunities to strengthen British ties with regimes alienated by this implacable American approach. Just as in bodyguard training, CT teams were used by the SIS to extend British influence.

The CRW Wing only comprises a small group of people who define doctrine in counter-revolutionary warfare. When they get a request to send a training team to a foreign country they call in a group from one of the four SAS squadrons and train them. The team then go to the host country and pass on that expertise. On their return they are assimilated back into their squadron.

The system is one of the great strengths of the SAS approach to counter-terrorism. The continual throughput of different SAS men prevents the CT teams from becoming stale and promotes a constant flow of fresh ideas.

The huge SAS commitment to the Dhofar war had acted as a brake on the number of available CT training teams for a while, but as the Dhofar war wound down, the number began to expand again. Between 1977 and 1980 alone, we trained the fledgling counter-terrorist forces of well over thirty different countries.

That number increased even more dramatically after 1980, when two special forces operations were mounted in the full glare of worldwide media attention. The first, in April of that year, destroyed Jimmy Carter's hopes of re-election and dealt a blow to the reputation of Delta Force from which it took a decade to recover. The second, just a month later, cemented the reputation of the SAS as the most efficient, ruthless and deadly special forces in the world.

In the early hours of 3 November 1979 Delta Force's A and B Squadrons completed an exercise requiring a simultaneous assault on an aircraft and a building, clearing them of terrorists and rescuing hostages from both. The planning and execution of the operation were immaculate.

Within twenty-four hours, Charlie Beckwith's men were ordered to begin preparations for a real-life hostage rescue in Iran. Its outcome was to be very different from that exercise.

The toppling of the Shah of Iran seemed to take the US by surprise. Only a week before his fall the American Secretary of State had been describing the shah as one of America's most stable and dependable allies. Within a week he had been deposed in the revolution that swept Ayatollah Khomeini to power.

The Americans appeared to have had few contingency

plans for such a situation, but it was less of an overnight sensation in Britain where a prearranged evacuation plan we had formulated for British expatriates in Iran was immediately activated. All of them made their way south to Bandar Abbas, where they were picked up by plane and flown to safety in a friendly Gulf state.

The ailing shah took refuge in America, still hoping that another American-backed coup might yet restore him to the peacock throne, but the US government appeared to believe that Khomeini's regime was less extreme than its blood-curdling rhetoric. The US Embassy in Tehran was kept open in the hope of maintaining a dialogue with 'moderates' in the ayatollah's regime.

There was none in evidence when a mob stormed the embassy compound, took sixty-three Americans hostage and collected a mountain of hastily shredded confidential documents. When pieced back together, they not only provided the Iranians with a thousand different ways to embarrass the Americans through the leaking of selected documents, they also blew secret US operations and led to the deaths of several American agents.

American public opinion demanded that President Carter do something to retrieve the situation and in an election year it was not a pressure he could resist. Delta Force, the counter-terrorist team whose formation he had authorised, was handed its first major operation, the rescue of the US hostages in Tehran.

Operation Eagle Claw was fatally flawed from the outset. The unwieldy chain of command instituted when Delta Force was set up posed massive problems to the operation. These were compounded by political interference from a more than usually indecisive Jimmy Carter and by absurd inter-service rivalries that saw every arm of the American forces squabbling with each other for a share of the action.

The list of things that went wrong with Eagle Claw is endless. The first problem was the complexity of the target.

The embassy compound covered twenty-seven acres and contained fourteen different buildings. Three US hostages were also being held at the Foreign Ministry, which would have to be attacked as well.

Intelligence was minimal. The members of the shah's secret police, Savak, once the primary US source of intelligence on the region, were dead, under arrest or in hiding, and the few CIA operatives remaining in Iran not blown by the documents seized at the embassy were among the hostages.

The rescue plan that was eventually developed breached one of the SAS's most basic tenets: KISS – Keep It Simple, Stupid. The less complex a plan, the less can go wrong with it and the greater the chance of success. The plan for Eagle Claw could scarcely have been more complex, involving 'twenty-one different agencies or units ... using fifty-one different radio frequencies, with more than 150 code words and call-signs and ... seventeen different landing zones and airfields'.[9]

The assault team would be carried in C130s flying at minimum low level to a rough landing strip in the Iranian desert 200 miles from Tehran. There they would rendezvous with eight Sea Stallion helicopters flown by navy pilots – later replaced by marines. After refuelling the helicopters – giant air-dropped rubber fuel bladders were initially proposed, then rejected in favour of more C130 aircraft – they would fly on to a second site closer to Tehran, and be hidden under camouflage nets. Teams of US Rangers would also be flown in to guard the different sites.

The Delta team would lie up at yet another site throughout the next day while Beckwith and a few members of the team, together with Farsi-speaking Iranian exiles, drove into Tehran, carried out a reconnaissance and brought out six Mercedes trucks purchased earlier by an undercover team.

Delta Force would then travel back into Tehran the following night to carry out the assault on the embassy. Meanwhile a separate group of men from the Tenth Special Forces

Group would rescue the three hostages held at the Foreign Ministry.

The helicopters would then fly into Tehran, collect the assault teams and hostages from a dozen different pick-up points and transfer them to Manzariyeh, a disused airfield twenty miles outside Tehran. That would have been captured by another force of US Rangers flown in that night. AC130 Spectre gunships would deal with any counter-attack by Iranian ground troops while jets from two US aircraft-carriers in the Gulf would engage any Iranian fighters.

As four months of fruitless negotiations continued with the Iranian regime, the constituent parts of the assault force all trained for the mission in different places. While Delta Force practised at Fort Stewart in Georgia, the Tenth Special Forces Group trained at their base in Germany, the helicopter pilots were practising at a marine base in Arizona, the US Rangers were training in Savannah, Georgia, and the C130 pilots trained at a USAF base in Florida. The different elements in the operation only finally came together three days before the operation began. It was another ingredient in the recipe for disaster.

On Thursday, 24 April, President Carter finally gave permission for the operation to proceed – as far as the first stage. Each subsequent part of the plan had to be confirmed by Tac-sat communications with Washington. In an already unwieldy operation it was yet another unnecessary complexity.

The assault force flew from Qena outside Cairo, refuelling at Masirah in Oman before entering Iranian airspace. The cock-ups started soon after they landed at the first site, Desert One, a rough strip alongside a road. A bus full of Iranians was intercepted soon after the landing and then an excitable US Ranger fired an anti-tank rocket at a petrol tanker. The resulting explosion lit up the night sky for miles.

The helicopters arrived an hour and a half late, having hit dust storms en route. Two of the eight Sea Stallions had already aborted the mission and returned to the carriers in the Gulf. Any further problems would leave insufficient helicopters to carry out the mission.

The scene at Desert One was now utter chaos. All the C130s were sitting with their engines running to minimise the risk of engine failure and the helicopters were moving around the site as they took turns to refuel. The rotors and jet wash stirred up such a fog of dust and sand that face-to-face recognition, let alone communication, was practically impossible.

The four commanders on the ground – one each for Delta Force, the US Rangers, the marine helicopter pilots and the air force C130s – were all on different nets and the only way that Charlie Beckwith could communicate with any of the other commanders within a hundred yards of him was via headquarters thousands of miles away.

Charlie was then told – via headquarters – that one of the helicopters had developed a problem and was unfit to fly further. It would have to return to the aircraft-carriers in the Gulf. How an unfit helicopter could fly several hundred miles back to the Gulf but could not manage the 100-mile journey north to Tehran has never been explained.

There were now insufficient choppers to extract all the assault force and hostages. If it went ahead, a score of Delta Force soldiers would be left behind in Tehran. After the obligatory communication with the White House, the operation was called off on President Carter's orders.

Later suggestions that Charlie made the decision himself because he would not countenance leaving so many men behind are wide of the mark. Beckwith cared for his men but he also had the ruthless streak needed by any effective officer. He would not have liked leaving his men to face an escape and evasion run to the Turkish border, but if it had been necessary to the success of the operation he would have done it.

Delta also shares the same brief as the SAS in such operations. The absolute priority is the safe rescue of the hostages. If it is necessary for the rescue team to take hits – casualties –

in order to extricate the hostages, that is entirely acceptable in military terms. When we take the Queen's shilling or the President's dollar bill, that is the risk we are accepting.

At this stage there was still nothing to stop the assault force returning with fresh helicopters the following night for another attempt but now the operation went even more disastrously wrong.

As a helicopter manoeuvred to complete its refuelling from a C130 already containing part of the disappointed and disillusioned Delta Force team, its rotor hit the cockpit of the aircraft. In a moment both aircraft were engulfed in flames.

As the fire spread towards the 3,000-gallon fuel bladder in the tail of the C130, the Delta Force men ran for their lives, fighting and scrambling to escape as tracer and exploding Redeye rockets sent shrapnel screaming around them. They all survived, some wounded or badly burned, but three helicopter crew and all five of the C130 crew died.

Against their orders, the other marine helicopter pilots then joined the scramble for the remaining C130s, leaving their Sea Stallions intact with the rotors still turning. The force returned unscathed to Masirah, but the aborted mission had left a rich prize for the Iranians: five undamaged Sea Stallions full of the latest communications equipment, code books, the plans of Operation Eagle Claw and even details of the few remaining US undercover agents operating inside Iran.

President Carter announced the disaster the next day, 25 April 1980, and took full responsibility for it, but the search for scapegoats was well and truly on. The American public was treated to the unedifying spectacle of senior officers taking it in turns to blame other branches of the armed forces for the débâcle. In the end Charlie Beckwith – who had little control of the planning of the operation – was pushed in front of the media and forced to take the rap for a failure that had little to do with any shortcomings of himself or the force that he commanded.

Charlie was transferred to a staff job producing training

manuals – the US forces equivalent of a spell in the Siberian salt mines. Soon afterwards he resigned from the army and set up Security Assistance Services. The acronym of his company was his final homage to the Regiment.

The whole sorry episode was analysed in great detail at Hereford so that we could learn the lessons from it. Two points emerged most strongly. We felt that despite its complexities, the operation was feasible, but it would have taken a superhuman effort to persuade the RAF to allow its pilots to fly such a perilous mission. If they had agreed, however, they would have completed it, not bottled out halfway.

We would also never have had imposed – or accepted – the ramshackle system of command and control under which Delta was forced to operate. President Carter insisted on being consulted at every stage of the operation. Only after the fiasco of Eagle Claw was Delta allowed to introduce a system of delegated command and control on the SAS model.

The new British Prime Minister, Margaret Thatcher, would have authorised the original plan and then left us to get on with it. We had only ten days to wait after the failure of Eagle Claw to prove the truth of that analysis.

Over the years the SAS has been a lucky regiment. There was a calculated risk in much of what we set out to achieve, but generally you make your own luck. DLB, appointed Director, SAS, at the end of 1978 and promoted to brigadier, shared the same lucky thread and his meetings with Margaret Thatcher in the COBRA Committee – the Cabinet Office Briefing Room – that oversaw responses to terrorism were his biggest lucky breaks of all.

Mrs Thatcher took a liking to DLB's direct, no-frills approach, and her trust in him and the service he headed was to lead to the biggest spectacular in the modern history of the British army: the siege of the Iranian Embassy.

11

IRANIAN EMBASSY
1980

'This is the BBC News. There has been a loud explosion at the scene of the siege of the Iranian Embassy in Prince's Gate, London. It has been revealed that the Special Air Service are involved. In the event of any further developments—'

I switched off the radio. Chris leaned forward from the back seat. 'Do you think that's true, Ken?'

I nodded. 'I've known about it ever since it started.'

The driver, Jock, glanced across at me. 'But aren't you worried?'

'No. There's only going to be one winner and it isn't going to be the terrorists.'

We sat in silence for a few moments. 'Do you want to cut short the patrol?' Chris asked in his cultured Guards officer tones. 'We've still got thirty-six hours to go.'

'No. Let's go on.'

Jock hesitated, then swung the wheel of the Opel, turning off on to a side road leading even deeper into East Germany.

We were in the Lueben Triangle, 100 miles south-east of Berlin, one of the Soviets' favourite areas for the movement of armoured columns.

I had been stationed with the Brixmis Mission in Berlin for almost two years. In that time I had had very little contact with the Regiment, except through official channels. I had helped to train the men and shape the techniques of the counter-terrorist team and I knew that the SAS would be involved in an attempt to rescue the hostages, but I had no inside knowledge of how they would storm the embassy or how their most difficult and public assignment would turn out.

For the next thirty-six hours we went about our normal business, playing hide and seek with the Soviet military police and the Stasi as we monitored the movements of Soviet and East German troops. There was enough going on to require my full concentration but occasionally I had a stab of anxiety at the thought of what might be happening in London.

Whenever we were able to spare the time we tried to catch the news on the BBC World Service, but bad reception prevented us hearing any further bulletins.

At the end of our tour of duty we headed west, passing through Potsdam and crossing into West Berlin through the border checkpoint on the Glienicke Bridge. We drove through the Grunewald Forest to the British Army Headquarters in the Berlin Olympic Stadium.

As we pulled up by the sweeping flight of steps at the front of the London Block, shared jointly by the Military Headquarters and the British Military Government, I caught a few curious glances from people, but thought no more about it. My mind was on the debrief, passing our film and observation reports to the intelligence analysts.

As I carried my bags of maps and cameras into the building, I passed somebody on the stairs. He called after me, 'Well done. You must be very proud.'

I stopped, puzzled – this had probably been my 150th tour and it had been no different from normal – but he had already disappeared into an office.

I went through the double-locked, iron-barred gates into the mission headquarters, a maximum security area, separated from the rest of the building. The chief of mission's secretary, Maureen, popped her head out of her office. 'Well done, Ken, you made us proud.'

I gave her a puzzled smile, beginning to wonder if the whole army HQ had gone insane. I walked along the corridor towards my own office but the deputy head of mission, a group captain, spotted me and called me into his office. He shook my hand and congratulated me.

After forty-eight hours without sleep, I was in no mood for riddles or guessing games. I almost screamed at him, 'What are you talking about? What's happened?'

He sat me down and we shared a couple of cigarettes as he told me what had happened at the Iranian Embassy the previous day. I was so elated that I was laughing as I walked along to the office I shared with the other NCOs attached to the mission.

As soon as we'd completed the debrief, I rang my wife. Her first question was, 'Have you heard? Well, go and have a pint, because I think you need one. I'll see you when I see you.'

I walked across to the Brigade Mess. The embassy siege had been over for twenty-four hours, but the mess was still bulging with people celebrating. Most of them were seriously drunk. As I walked in, the lads began cheering and slapping me on the back.

'Look,' I said, very embarrassed, 'I wasn't at the embassy, I was in East Germany.'

My protests were ignored. Because I was in the SAS, I was a hero.

I tried to catch the eye of the civilian barman, Alec. He saw me over the heads of the people crowding the bar and shouted, 'Make way for a real soldier.'

They parted like the Red Sea and I walked up and asked for a pint. About fifteen people offered to pay for it, but in his inimitable style, Alec shook his head. 'I'll buy the first one. You bastards can buy the rest.'

The feeling in the mess was euphoric. A warrant officer

grinned at me. 'You know what? Now everyone knows that the army can actually do things and not just grind pebbles into dust on parade squares.'

I shared his pride in the achievement, but my only personal claim to fame in this world-famous episode is that I am one of the few people, military or civilian, who has not claimed to have been on the Iranian Embassy balcony when the siege started.

It forms one of the largest clubs in the world. At the last count, the balcony was holding at least 15,000 people.

The author, Lueben Triangle, East Germany, 1980

The siege of the Iranian Embassy began at 11.15 on the morning of 30 April 1980. Six terrorists – members of the minority Arab population of Iran – occupied the embassy. They took twenty-six hostages, including a two-man BBC sound crew, six other visitors and a policeman from the Diplomatic Protection Squad, Trevor Lock, who was on guard duty outside.

The self-proclaimed Democratic Revolutionary Front for the Liberation of Arabistan – their name for the oil-rich Iranian province of Khuzestan – were armed with grenades, submachine-guns and pistols. Their demands included autonomy for Khuzestan and the release of ninety-two Arabs held in Iranian jails.

Their previously unknown organisation was a cover for the involvement of Iraq, which had trained, paid and weaponed the terrorists, and flown them to London on Iraqi passports. Once the siege began they were on their own; their Iraqi handler returned to Baghdad the same day.

The first news of the incident to reach the SAS came through unofficial channels. A man who had been part of the very first counter-terrorist team that I had put together had left the Regiment and was serving with the Metropolitan

Police as a dog-handler. He phoned Hereford to say that the police were responding to a terrorist incident.

At 11.48 the bleepers of the duty Special Projects Team – 6 Troop of B Squadron – began to sound and they were called together for a briefing. Even before any official notification or a request for assistance had been received, the team was on its way to London.

They paused briefly at the Army Language School in Beaconsfield, waiting for the formal police request for assistance. By then, the commanding officer of the SAS, Mike Rose, had already turned up in plain clothes at the police cordon around the embassy and made a preliminary reconnaissance of the outside of the building.

Six Troop then deployed to a building close to the embassy, ready to put a hastily improvised rescue plan into effect if the terrorists began killing the hostages.

As soon as reinforcements arrived to take over that role, the original team – Red Team – moved to Regent's Park Barracks and began detailed planning for an assault, using plans of the embassy and a plywood and hessian replica of part of the building constructed in record time.

Surveillance equipment was also inserted into the embassy walls by tactical support teams, as aircraft coming in to land at Heathrow were diverted to a lower-level approach over Hyde Park to drown the noise of drilling. The prime targets of most previous terrorist incidents had been aircraft and once the pilots flying over Hyde Park realised what was happening at Prince's Gate, they were exceeding the requested level of co-operation by gunning their engines against the flaps to make even more noise.

Their help was invaluable in disguising the noise of drilling, but the embassy walls were thicker than shown on the plans and the listening devices and fibre-optic cameras yielded little useful information. The British caretaker of the embassy building and a hostage released by the terrorists because of illness proved more useful sources of intelligence.

Having formulated a plan, the team then transferred to a forward holding area – the Royal College of General Practitioners next door to the embassy – and a recce was made across the rooftops on the night of 2 May, when the team checked that a skylight could be opened. Then they sat back to wait.

The terrorists' ultimate demands were aimed at the ayatollah in Tehran, over whom the British government exercised minimal influence. Negotiations began on their intermediate demands for a plane to fly them and their hostages out of London, even though the Prime Minister had already decided that the incident was going to end as it began, in Prince's Gate.

Trained police negotiators continued a patient dialogue with the terrorists by telephone over the next six days, first raising their hopes by telling them that their demands would be met within a day or two at most, then stalling them.

Psychologists believe that endless negotiations punctuated by small concessions – usually food, drink and media access – is the safest way to deal with a siege involving hostages. The terrorists' morale is sapped and they grow progressively more exhausted by the stresses of the siege, making them more suggestible and more vulnerable if an assault has to be called.

The Stockholm Syndrome – named after an earlier terrorist incident – also suggests that prolonged contact between captors and captives reduces the likelihood of a massacre of the hostages. It has two downsides. Hostages also begin to feel a bond for their captors and will even try to protect them if the siege ends in an assault by security forces.

The syndrome also operates only where there is some common ground – a shared language or culture – between the terrorists and their prisoners. Israelis held by Islamic Jihad or Ian Paisley in a room full of IRA terrorists would have to spend an awful long time together before any meaningful dialogue would ensue.

Sophisticated terrorists are well aware of the existence of the syndrome and of the delaying tactics of police negotiators. They will take steps to curtail negotiations, impose tight deadlines and isolate the hostages to prevent bonds being formed.

The Blue and Red SAS teams endured days of stand-tos and stand-downs as each terrorist deadline approached, but all passed without incident until 5 May. At 12.40 that lunchtime the terrorist spokesman, Oan Ali Mohammed, given the code-name Salim by police, warned that he would begin killing hostages in two hours' time. In fact, the first gunfire was heard just fifteen minutes later, two single shots separated by about three seconds.

The death of a hostage is the standard trigger to activate an assault; once the terrorists have killed one of their captives they have nothing to lose by killing again and again.

The SAS were ready to go in immediately, but were restrained by the bizarre formula arrived at by the advisers to the Home Secretary, Willie Whitelaw: only when two hostages had been killed could armed intervention begin. The farcical justification for this procrastination was that one killing could conceivably have been accidental.

Permission to put the assault force on 'notice to move' – the final stage before the authorisation of the actual attack – was eventually given at 3.50 and by 5.00 they were in position in the building next door to the embassy, ready to respond instantly to the order to go.

The police had brought a Muslim imam from the Regent's Park mosque to talk to the terrorists. During his conversation with them, three further shots were heard. Salim then announced that another hostage had been shot. 'Another in half an hour. All the hostages together.'[1] Just before 6.30 the front door of the embassy was opened wide enough for a body to be dumped on the steps.

The body was retrieved by the police and a swift post-mortem showed that the man, the embassy press officer, had been dead for several hours. This indicated that a second person might also be dead and under the 'two deaths rule' the SAS requested permission to make the attack.

The Home Secretary felt unable to make that decision on his own initiative but when it was referred to the Prime Minister, Mrs Thatcher gave her immediate consent. The senior police officer at the incident, Assistant Commissioner John Dellow, handed over control to Mike Rose at 7.07 that evening.

As the Aid to the Civil Power Act required, he put the handover in writing and signed and dated it, using the only piece of paper he could lay his hands on at that moment, a dog-eared scrap. The precious souvenir was saved and framed and now hangs on the wall of a bar in Stirling Lines in Hereford.

Police negotiators continued to talk to Salim, soothing him by promising that his demands would now be met immediately and assuring him that a coach was already on its way to transport the terrorists and the hostages to Heathrow.

While that conversation was going on, Red Team were abseiling into position from the embassy roof while members of Blue Team fixed frame charges to blow out the first-floor windows.

Salim was in a first-floor room with PC Lock and another hostage. The remaining hostages were held in two rooms on the second floor, each guarded by a terrorist. Two more were patrolling the second-floor corridor, while the sixth was in the ground-floor hallway, but the failure of the attempted surveillance meant that those precise locations of terrorists and hostages were unknown to the SAS at the time.

The last words on the police tape of the negotiations came from Salim as he heard suspicious noises. 'There is suspicion ... Okay, just a minute ... I'll come back again ... I'm going to check.'

As the assault team abseiled down the rear of the building, one of them had become stuck. Additional nylon rope purchased in London proved defective, partly melting with the friction of the descent and jamming the abseil mechanism. He was left dangling helplessly above the balcony. As one of his men struggled to free him, his boot broke a window.

The noise had alerted Salim and the order to launch the assault was immediately given. It was 7.23. The next noise on the tape was a huge blast. A large charge designed to disorientate the terrorists had been lowered through the glass skylight to detonate in the stairwell. The sound of it was heard several miles away. A few seconds later frame charges blew out the windows. SAS men poured into the building, hurling stun grenades and CS gas ahead of them.

The frame charges had set fire to the curtains, however, and the dangling SAS man trapped in his abseil harness received serious burns before being cut down. Meanwhile the rest of the assault team swept through the building, clearing each room in seconds.

Seizing his chance when Salim was distracted by the noise and confusion, Trevor Lock wrestled him to the ground just before SAS men burst into the room. One ordered Lock to roll away, then despatched Salim with a burst from his submachine-gun. The terrorist in the ground-floor hallway was also shot before he could use his weapon.

One hostage was killed and others were wounded by two terrorists firing wildly at them. As they heard the SAS men approaching, they threw down their weapons and tried to conceal themselves among the hostages lying on the floor. The SAS men shouted at the hostages to identify the terrorists and shot them both dead.

Two terrorists were still unaccounted for. The hostages were rough-handled down the stairs, passed from hand to hand along a human chain of SAS men searching for any clue that a terrorist was hiding among them.

Suddenly a trooper spotted a fragmentation grenade in a man's hand. The trooper could not fire without risking hitting others in the line of fire. Instead, he smashed the stock of his weapon into the back of the terrorist's neck. He tumbled to the bottom of the flight of stairs, where two SAS men riddled him with fire.

The rest of the hostages were shoved and pushed along the chain and out into the street, where they were spread-eagled, face down, while their identity was checked. A further terrorist was found among them and taken prisoner. He was the only one to survive; the other five all lay dead in the burning building.

The hostage shot in the first moments of the assault was the only one to die, apart from the press officer whose dumped body had precipitated the assault. The second shooting by Salim that had precipitated the storming of the building proved to have been a bluff.

The team handed control back to the police, turned in their weapons for forensic examination and were then whisked back to the Regent's Park Barracks. The celebrations there were fuelled by large amounts of complimentary beer and whisky supplied by London breweries and distilleries.

Mrs Thatcher also arrived at the barracks with Denis, her ministers and her new best friend, DLB. They brought with them the video footage of the siege. As a television was hastily set up, Mrs Thatcher stood near the front of the room with a broad smile on her face. Although surrounded by the team, still dressed in their black assault gear, she looked as much at home there as she was in the Cabinet Office.

When the film appeared on the television screen, a voice at the back, fortified by a few complimentary drinks, shouted, 'You in the front, get your arse out of the way.'

Mrs Thatcher turned round. smiled and immediately sat down. It was the one and only time that her officials could ever remember her taking orders from anyone.

The party went on well into the evening, but by five the next morning everyone was back in Hereford, including the NCO severely burned in the initial assault. He was rescued from hospital by his mates, still with a drip in his arm, and flown back to Hereford to be looked after by his wife – a trained nurse.

From start to finish the siege of the embassy had followed the exact scenario we'd been using in training exercises for years. Terrorists occupy a building, aircraft, ship or train, and take hostages. They then issue demands against a government over which Britain has little influence or control. Police start negotiations, rewarding the terrorists with food, water and access to media coverage instead of meeting their demands.

As negotiations stall, the terrorists threaten to execute a hostage and later carry out their threat, dumping the body of their victim as proof. They then set a timetable of further executions if their demands are not met. As a result, police hand over control of operations to the SAS and an assault begins. Immediately after the successful conclusion of the assault, control is returned to the police.

The line between success and failure in any military operation is a very fine one. That is nowhere more true than in a hostage rescue, but dedication, training, skill and daring had ensured that the SAS finished on the right side of the line at Prince's Gate.

The hostage crisis was solved by a team of people who had developed systems and trained to deal with such an eventuality for a decade; the man in charge of the team during the Iranian Embassy siege was the officer who had set up the original team with me.

They were in a position to train every day, had unlimited support and were fighting a battle on a piece of ground they knew very well. They were not going to lose. They had a measure of luck, but we tend to believe that you make your own luck; by a strange coincidence, the people who do the most training also turn out to be the luckiest ones.

The assault on the embassy was made much easier by our intimate knowledge of the building. In addition to acquiring full plans of the building, an SAS officer and NCO had actually carried out a precautionary survey of its security several years before, when the shah was still ruler of Iran.

One of the recommendations made at the time was to reinforce the windows with bullet-proof glass. Nobody could establish whether the Iranians had actually done so and when the plans for the assault were drawn up, the SAS played on the side of caution and prepared explosive charges powerful enough to blow in bullet-proof windows. It turned out that the windows had never been modified, so there was an over-use of explosives which caused the fire, but that was the lesser risk.

Like the nemesis of Delta Force, Eagle Claw, there were some glitches in the SAS operation: the lack of prior intelligence on the location of terrorists and hostages, the NCO trapped in his abseil harness, the building catching fire, the SAS team on the second floor entering through the windows of a locked room.

The years of training for every contingency and the SAS men's basic skill, self-reliance and freedom of action allowed them to adapt and improvise on the move, sustaining their momentum to complete a classic counter-terrorist operation. What made the operation such a success was not that the terrorists were killed, however, but that almost all of the hostages were released unharmed.

In counter-terrorist operations where hostages are not involved, the primary aim is to prevent the terrorists from firing their weapons or detonating their bombs. There is no more effective way to achieve that aim than by killing them, but terrorists known to be unarmed will not be murdered in cold blood, and even armed terrorists will be detained rather than killed in circumstances where it is safe to do so.

The capture of terrorists can lead to more terrorist incidents, as the repeated attempts by the Red Army Faction and their Palestinian allies to free terrorists imprisoned in West Germany and Israel demonstrated, but it is the lesser of two evils.

Allegations that the SAS were officially instructed to kill all the terrorists in the Iranian Embassy are false. All briefings of SAS counter-terrorist operations are carried out in the presence of a lawyer from the army's Legal Service, and video- and audio-taped. As soon as the briefing ends, the tapes are sealed and handed to the lawyer, who retains them for use in evidence if required.

Apart from the legal safeguards, there are other, self-imposed restraints. The policy of killing as a last resort, not a first priority, is not followed through altruism, nor a deeply held belief in the sanctity of all human life, but through cold, hard pragmatism.

Interrogation of captured terrorists can yield priceless intelligence, but it is even more important that other terrorists are not given the message that surrender is pointless because they will be killed anyway. A terrorist who believes his only option is martyrdom will not hesitate to push the button that will blow up a car bomb, a hijacked plane – or an Iranian Embassy.

The siege of the Iranian Embassy has passed into folk history; an example to the rest of the world of British expertise, courage and daring. It was the best – and the worst – thing that ever happened to the Regiment.

As the dust settled, several things became clear. For the first time ever, the future of the Regiment was secure. No one would now be able to disband it. We had won over some of our most persistent critics, but the prime significance of the assault on the Iranian Embassy was not its influence on securing the pre-eminent role in British counter-terrorism for the SAS, but the fact that it was played out in front of the world's press and television.

The coverage of the assault itself was unplanned. The team had deliberately chosen to make the main assault from the rear, out of sight of the army of media camped in the area reserved for them 100 yards from the front door of the embassy.

Substantial media coverage of the siege was regarded as essential to convince the British public that the event was of a scale and seriousness to merit armed intervention by the SAS. The downside of the media presence was that it was known that there were three television sets inside the embassy. The last thing we wanted was for the terrorists to watch the preparations for the assault on television, but ITN had managed to get a camera crew into a flat overlooking the embassy. We were very fortunate that their pictures did not alert the terrorists.

The pictures transmitted live as the events unfolded sent a powerful warning to every terrorist organisation around the world, but the same message was also received loud and clear by every foreign government and head of state.

The contrast between the fortunes of Delta Force at Desert One and the SAS at the Iranian Embassy could not have been more marked. Once more, while publicly sympathetic about the American misfortune, the SIS were privately ecstatic.

The Kennedy assassination had been the catalyst for the spread of British influence through SAS bodyguard training. The abortive hostage rescue attempt by Delta Force followed within weeks by the successful storming of the Iranian Embassy by the SAS had ensured another bull market for SAS counter-terrorist training and another massive boost to British influence overseas.

The SAS was already a substantial indirect contributor to Britain's balance of payments through its role in securing allies and influence. After the Iranian Embassy siege, SAS expertise became one of Britain's more successful exports in its own right. SAS troops would be hired out to friendly governments for training purposes or even covert operations at a rate that covered the actual costs many times over.

Prime Minister Margaret Thatcher was no doubt heartily impressed by this introduction of the rigours of the market-place to yet another part of the public sector. She exploited to the full the influence with foreign governments that the SAS had won for her.

It was particularly important in equalising the relationship between Britain and the United States. The 'Special Relationship' is both a recent invention and in large part a convenient fiction to disguise Britain's increasing military dependence on the United States. Even though nominally allies, the US spent much of the period from 1939 to 1960 seeking to weaken Britain's trading position and undermine its hold on its colonies and client states.

Since 1960 the relationship has been generally amicable, but more that between a client and bank manager than two equals. Only for a brief period under Margaret Thatcher has it been remotely equal. Her personal relationship with Ronald Reagan and their similar political ideologies played a part, but with the American military still in crisis after Vietnam and further humiliated by the shambles of Eagle Claw, the right of the British Prime Minister to sit at the top table with the American President – which Margaret Thatcher exploited to the hilt – had largely been earned by the efforts of the SAS.

The successful storming of the Iranian Embassy also had a downside for the Regiment. Everyone and his dog now knew about the SAS. From then on every fact, every rumour about the Regiment would be seized on by the media.

The publicity also began to attract a different kind of recruit. Enough were drawn by the glamorous, macho image to alter the nature of the Regiment and its men.

The change was not even evident at first, but over the course of the next decade it became progressively more dramatic. The concept of absolute secrecy became a dead letter and the Regiment reached the point where it is now publicly celebrated for its heroic failures rather than privately congratulated for its covert successes.

12

THE FALKLANDS
1982

The noise inside the helicopter was deafening. The insulation that normally reduced the din from the engine and gearboxes had, like the seats, been stripped out to reduce weight. The SAS patrol were sitting on the floor, surrounded by their bergens and equipment.

The only thing visible in the dim glow of the tiny cockpit light was the outline of the pilot's passive night goggles, giving him green-flecked vision into the darkness ahead. Outside, the SAS men could just glimpse the faint luminescence of the white-topped waves of the South Atlantic a few feet below them.

Two of the men, Gibbo and Taff, kept a note of their speed and heading. Previous experience on other helicopter insertions had taught them to use their own navigation to check that of the pilot. If they were dropped in the wrong place the mission could be aborted before it had begun.

They had left the relative safety of the aircraft-carrier an hour before. Immediately after take-off they had dropped down to wave-top height and headed due west towards the mainland of Argentina.

The biggest threats to the entire Falklands invasion plan were the Exocet-carrying Super Etendards of the Argentinian air force. Air photography and other intelligence had showed that they were regularly based at the airfields at

Rio Grande in the Argentine half of the island of Tierra del Fuego, and at Rio Gallegos, on the mainland, the closest airfield, at the same latitude as the Falklands and little more than 300 miles to the west – the distance from London to Newcastle.

The eight-man SAS team were to land close to Rio Grande, infiltrate covertly and take out the Etendards using explosive charges. Once clear of the airfield, they would head to the pick-up point.

If they were unable to infiltrate the airfield, the fall-back plan was to lie up in a position aligned on the centre of the runway and try to bring down some of the aircraft using surface-to-air missiles. They all hoped it would not have to come to that; their chances of a successful escape and evasion in those circumstances were much, much slimmer.

Once the helicopter had dropped them off, its three-man Fleet Air Arm crew would use the little fuel left to try and reach Chile, where they would ditch it and set it on fire. They would then follow their own escape and evasion plan overland.

Everyone in the team was aware of how vitally important the mission was to the rest of the task-force. Time restrictions had made it impossible to train with their normal thoroughness, but the amount of experience within the patrol made them confident that they would be successful.

Suddenly the cockpit radar warning system started to shriek. The din was audible even above the roar of the engines, and set everyone's heart thumping.

The pilot squeezed the cyclic stick, taking the Sea King closer to the waves. The sound faded, but a few seconds later the alarm squealed again. The pilot eased the helicopter even lower, until spray was hitting the cockpit windows and streaming along the sides of the fuselage.

The sound of the alarm died. They were no longer being painted by the Argentinian radar, but the tension in the cabin grew. Individual members of the patrol were studying their maps, trying to anticipate their landfall. It was now possible to see the land mass of the Argentinian mainland ahead, a blacker shape against the dark night sky.

The co-pilot turned around and pointed to his map, indicating where he thought they were. Gibbo and Taff nodded in agreement and the tension relaxed slightly. At least they were not lost.

The surf line skimmed below them in a flash of phosphorescence. The Sea King scudded over the beach and headed inland, still staying as low as possible, flying at the extreme limits of the capabilities of the pilots and the aircraft.

They had flown SAS patrols on operations and training missions before, but the passive night goggles were brand-new equipment. They had only been issued as the task-force sailed and they had had no more than a handful of hours' flying time since then to familiarise themselves with them.

Gibbo stared out of the side door of the Sea King, checking navigation points as they flew on. He was certain that the pilot was taking them where they needed to be.

There was a crackle in his headset and he heard the pilot's voice. 'Five minutes to touchdown.'

There was a stir of movement as everyone began collecting their equipment ready for the drop-off.

The pilot chose a relatively flat piece of ground for the landing. The engine noise appeared to grow even louder as the helicopter slowed. The tension in the back was almost unbearable. This was always the worst time, the point of no return, the last few moments before you were out of the helicopter and ready to hit the ground running.

As the wheels touched the ground Gibbo and Taff jumped out. Andy, the Boss, was still checking his map. He shouted to them and shook his head.

Gibbo shouted back. 'No, we're right.' The wind whipping across the flatlands near the tip of South America carried his words away. An argument developed and Gibbo tried to pull the Boss out of the helicopter but he resisted, again pointing at his map.

Gibbo climbed back in to try and sort out this ridiculous problem at the most critical time of the insertion. The other members of the patrol looked from one to the other, waiting for a decision.

After waiting a few more moments, Taff also climbed back in. Without any warning Andy spoke into his microphone. 'Move further west, we're in the wrong place.'

Gibbo tried to stop him but the pilot was already responding to the order. The helicopter again rose into the air and continued west at very low level. The co-pilot kept looking back at Andy, puzzled at being told to move from what he was sure was the right place, but Andy had the ultimate authority.

Several minutes later Andy pointed towards the ground. The Sea King again touched down and the patrol clambered out. Within seconds the helicopter was disappearing westwards. Its crew torched and abandoned it on the beach at Agua Fresca, ten miles south of the Chilean airbase at Punta Arenas.

Gibbo crouched down, scanning the surrounding area and trying to orient himself. There were no definite landmarks in sight, just the endless plain stretching away into unbroken blackness. The only sounds were the rapidly diminishing noise of the Sea King's engines and the wind blowing in from the west.

Gibbo and Taff began to remonstrate with Andy, asking why they had moved from what all the others thought was the correct position, but Andy insisted that he was right.

The argument was set aside for the moment; the important thing was the mission. Everyone knuckled down to the task of finding exactly where they were in relation to the airfield target. It very quickly became apparent that they were nowhere near their chosen landing zone.

They split up into groups of two and spent the rest of the night trying to find a landscape feature that would tell them where they were. At first light they regrouped. None of them had found anything conclusive.

They opened up the satellite communications and explained their problems to the headquarters in Hereford, but the only advice that could be given from 9,000 miles away was to continue to look for a feature to orientate themselves and then carry out their mission.

For the next couple of days the patrol lay up and hid by day and searched for a navigational feature at night. Eventually they managed to establish their position. They were over fifty miles west of their target.

They went through an options exercise, working out time and distance, food available and how they could still achieve their goal. They were forced to accept that they could not reach the target and then escape with the remaining food that they had.

The information was relayed to Hereford and they were then told to exfiltrate to the border to rendezvous with a reception committee and be returned to the UK.

Seventy-two hours later the band of brothers arrived back in Hereford. A grim-faced planning committee, which had spent several weeks putting all the parts of the equation together, was waiting for them. The importance of the mission could not be overstressed; the reason for its failure had to be found. They began an immediate investigation.

The air crew remained convinced – as did most of the patrol – that they had originally landed in the right place, but the one person with the authority to overrule them did so.

The investigating group's diplomatic conclusion was

that at a time of stress, performing at the ultimate level, Andy had made a minor navigational error.

That minor error was to have catastrophic consequences for the task-force in the South Atlantic. What could and should have been another spectacular chapter in the annals of the SAS had the covers closed on it with almost indecent haste.

B Squadron corporal, Tierra del Fuego, Argentina, 1982

The Falklands War was an accident waiting to happen. Every decade since the Second World War had seen at least one savage round of cuts to the armed forces.

There was no end to the process. As Britain shed more and more overseas possessions and commitments, the temptation to make further cuts increased as the ever-rising cost of new technology continued to put pressure on the defence budget; the next economic crisis and the next round of cuts were always just around the corner. Margaret Thatcher's new Conservative administration had given the forces an immediate 33 per cent pay rise, but the need to make economies as part of its wider commitment to cut public expenditure forced it to make correspondingly large cuts in other areas of the defence budget.

The navy bore the brunt of Defence Secretary John Nott's 1981 defence review, *The Way Forward*. Despite a furious campaign to get the decision reversed, many ships, including the aircraft-carriers *Hermes* and *Invincible*, and the ice-patrol ship HMS *Endurance*, were scheduled to be scrapped or sold. After all, what was the need for so many ships?

The once mighty British Empire was now reduced to a dwindling handful of tiny, scattered possessions such as Tristan da Cunha, Ascension Island and the Falklands. Acquired as 'part of a larger pattern of commercial penetration and naval ascendancy, they had been pieces in a jigsaw and made sense [only] in relation to the pieces around them'.[1]

Now the larger pieces were gone, but the remaining 'strategic outposts, scattered island territories, too small to be self-governing, too British in their origin or outlook to be readily associated with neighbouring territories ... might yet impose on Britain obligations carried over from another age which she was no longer well-equipped to meet'.[2]

The signal sent to Argentina by the scrapping of the *Endurance* only reinforced a message that the Foreign Office had been privately conveying for years. Britain had no interest in retaining the Falklands in the long term and had no objection in principle to a transfer of sovereignty, with a period of lease-back to allow Britain time to persuade the islanders of the inevitability of ultimate Argentine rule. Far from being paramount, the wishes of the Falklanders themselves were regarded as nothing more than a nuisance, an obstacle to be overcome.

Argentina's mistake was to rush into a take-over by force before the *Hermes*, *Invincible*, *Endurance* and several other ships on John Nott's chopping list had been decommissioned and scrapped or sold.

In fact there is some evidence that the timing of the invasion of the Falklands was largely accidental. The scrap men raising the Argentine flag on South Georgia on 19 March 1982 may even have been acting from simple patriotism rather than Machiavellian intention, but the end result was the same.

The British Antarctic Survey station on South Georgia reported the raising of the Argentine flag to the Falklands' governor, Rex Hunt, and told him that shooting had been heard. It could easily have been the scrap men shooting seabirds for food, but either innocently or with Machiavellian intentions of his own, the governor's report to London suggested that Argentine soldiers, not scrap men, had come ashore.

Britain's protest to Argentina and the despatch of the *Endurance* from Port Stanley with a party of marines led Argentina's ruler, General Leopoldo Galtieri, to put into effect a contingency plan that had been drawn up the previous winter. A full-scale invasion was mounted, at 'twenty-four hours' notice',[3] to unite Las Malvinas with the motherland.

To Mrs Thatcher's unconcealed fury, the SIS had failed to give any advance warning of the invasion, ignoring their own intelligence reports and dismissing as a bluff or negotiating tactic the authoritative Argentine newspaper stories trailing the intention to invade. During a review of contingency plans the SIS had assured SAS headquarters that 'no scenario could be conceived where it would be necessary to deploy the SAS to the Falkland Islands'.[4] Two months later Argentina invaded.

There is also evidence to suggest that the Foreign Office may have given the Argentine government at the very least a nod and a wink that if they invaded the Falklands Britain would indulge in some public hand-wringing and then accept the situation. The theory would certainly help to explain Mrs Thatcher's savaging of the Foreign Office after the Falklands War.

By the end of March 1982 the warnings were at last being taken seriously. The reprieved HMS *Endurance* was sent to South Georgia and the nuclear submarine *Conqueror* was despatched to the South Atlantic, but by then the Argentine invasion fleet was already at sea. The invasion of the Falklands took place on Friday, 2 April 1982.

Any doubts about the British response were ended by an angry special debate in the House of Commons the next day. Attacked from both sides of the House for failing to anticipate the crisis, Mrs Thatcher pledged that Britain would take 'all necessary steps' to restore the Falklands to British rule.

The doomed British ships were hastily recalled from the journey to the scrapyard and pressed into service as part of the task-force to retake the Falklands. The first ships, *Hermes*,

Invincible and the assault ship *Fearless*, sailed from Portsmouth on 5 April, beginning the seven-week journey to the Falklands. With another assault ship, *Intrepid*, they formed the heart of the task-force fleet. All four had been scheduled for sale or scrapping.

The CO of the Regiment, Lieutenant-Colonel Mike Rose, having sold at least some of the task-force commanders on the roles the Regiment could fulfil in the conflict, embarked on *Fearless* with a team from headquarters. He also took with him 200 tons of supplies, catering for every conceivable contingency. Later in the campaign, when other units were clamouring for equipment jammed in the Ascension Islands bottle-neck on the supply line, the lavishly equipped SAS men had good reason to be grateful for Mike's prescience.

The *Fearless* was also the HQ of the Task-Force Commander, Land Forces, Brigadier Julian Thomson. He needed no convincing of the value of the SAS, but his superior, Major-General Jeremy Moore, the overall commander of the task-force, had very different views. His intense scepticism about the role of the SAS – and his basic misunderstanding of what that role properly constituted – led to conflict during the campaign and a bitter war of words in its aftermath.

Mike Rose's insistence on being close to the action instead of remaining in Hereford was also controversial, and created further problems with the Director, SAS, Brigadier Peter de la Billiere.

Occasional friction between the two men was almost inevitable, for both were strong-willed individuals with very firm ideas on how the Regiment should be run. Like DLB, Mike Rose went on to become a general, further evidence that both men of action could also play the political game when necessary.

Of the ten SAS generals whom I knew well enough to form a judgement of their qualities, DLB and Mike were among the most impressive. There are three classic tests of a good general: is he intelligent, is he ruthless and is he lucky? Only one of the ten had all three qualities, in my opinion. All the others were lacking in at least one.

The SAS troops Mike Rose commanded were soon in action. Sixty-six men of D Squadron were flown out to Ascension Island on 4 April. With them went fourteen signallers and another twenty-five tons of equipment permanently stored on pallets at Hereford as part of a rapid-deployment plan.

D Squadron sailed for South Georgia five days later. The island had no strategic value in the conflict, but it offered the possibility of a quick and cheap victory to ease the embarrassment of the politicians back home.

The SAS men received their first useful intelligence on South Georgia from the crew of HMS *Endeavour*. The existing mapping of the Falkland Islands was poor enough; there were no maps at all of South Georgia, but the crew of *Endeavour* supplied sketch plans of Grytviken, Leith, Stromness, Husvik, and the British Antarctic Survey out-station at King Edward Point. They also gave useful information about the coastline and topography of the island.

Apart from the BAS team and a wildlife film crew who happened to be there, South Georgia had been uninhabited when the Argentinians took the island. The disposition of their forces and the scrap merchants who had precipitated the invasion was not known, but it was expected that they would be concentrated at the disused whaling station at Leith, and at Grytviken where the BAS team had their headquarters.

After two attempts at insertion were aborted because of blizzards, 19 Troop, dressed in Arctic gear, were helicoptered on to the Fortuna Glacier on 23 April to carry out reconnaissance.

Weather conditions were appalling, with fierce katabatic winds, blizzards and white-outs. Struggling over crevasses and through deep snowfields, the troop made just 500 yards in five hours. They found what shelter they could, but their supposedly arctic-quality tents were ripped apart in the wind and the tent poles snapped like toothpicks. After a night in which many of the troop slept in the open with only a bivi-bag for protection, they requested extraction before hypothermia and frostbite set in.

One of the three Wessex helicopters sent to extract them crashed in a white-out immediately after picking up the men. Fortunately there were only minor injuries. The two other helicopters then landed again, jettisoned some fuel and equipment and divided the remaining troops between them.

Overloaded, they took off again, but the second helicopter pilot also lost his horizons in a white-out and crashed, again without serious injury. The sole surviving helicopter managed to deliver its part of the SAS troop safely, then returned some time later for the other men. When the pilot took off again, he had seventeen men on board, twelve more than the permitted maximum. He reached the mother ship safely, but the helicopter was so overloaded that it was unable to hover and he had to fly straight on to the deck of the ship like an aircraft approaching a carrier.

17 – Boat – Troop made the next attempt. Five Geminis were launched but their notoriously unreliable engines lived up to their reputation: three of them failed. One Gemini was carried away on the tide and its crew was rescued after several perilous hours. Another crew was also swept away. Their Gemini hit a rock off the very southernmost tip of the island. It saved their lives. Had it not done so they would have been swept into the wilds of the Antarctic. They managed to get ashore where they remained huddled in a survival shelter in radio silence for several days, fearing that any radio signal to summon help would jeopardise the operation.

The other three Geminis made shore safely, one under paddle power. Securing a foothold on South Georgia proved to be the hardest part of the operation, for resistance from the Argentinians was minimal.

Plans for the traditional stealthy approach were abandoned after an Argentinian submarine, the *Santa Fe*, was spotted on the surface and attacked by navy Wasp anti-submarine helicopters. The badly damaged sub limped into Grytviken, where its crew raised the alarm.

A barrage of naval gunfire from the frigates HMS *Plymouth* and *Antrim* had a damaging impact on Argentinian morale. When a follow-up attack was mounted by Squadron HQ and one troop of D Squadron, white sheets appeared on every building in Grytviken. After further softening up by naval gunfire, the remaining Argentinian forces surrendered on 26 April.

Most of the casualties in the action were sustained by a group of elephant seals. In the half-light they were mistaken for Argentinian soldiers crawling along a ridgeline, and were engaged with a Milan missile.

The operation had succeeded and was greeted with delight at home. Much of the nation accepted Mrs Thatcher's invitation to 'Rejoice, rejoice,' but the near-bloodless victory cost the task-force two vitally needed helicopters.

As the unwitting agents of that loss, the SAS came in for some heavy criticism after the conflict. It was correctly stated that they had been warned that weather conditions on the glacier were impossible but had ignored those warnings.

On the face of it, that was a damning indictment, but it ignored the fact that the SAS is continually attempting and achieving what others regard as impossible tasks. Living for a month in the Malayan swamps, scaling the Jebel Akhdar under a 100-pound bergen, storming the Iranian Embassy: all are impossible to most military units but they do not have the training, endurance, character, intelligence and self-belief that set the SAS apart.

The sceptics were proved right about the conditions on the Fortuna Glacier, but the Regimental motto, 'Who dares wins', was not earned by taking the line of least risk. Conditions were equally impossible for the Boat Troop making a seaborne landing, but some of them got ashore and the bridgehead they formed and the intelligence they supplied enabled South

Georgia to be retaken without a serious casualty being suffered.

A more serious criticism of the SAS was entirely justified, however. The captain of the *Endeavour* had insisted from the start that he could sail his ship straight into the harbour at Grytviken and put the SAS ashore but, eager to put their particular troop skills to use, the SAS troop officers ignored his offer.

After the helicopter losses on the Fortuna Glacier and the Gemini losses in the sea, the main landing on South Georgia by Squadron HQ and the troop from D Squadron was made in exactly the way the captain of the *Endeavour* had wanted. Had the troop commanders been more experienced, they would have used the best option first, not last.

It was a minor irritation compared to the massive boost to task-force morale that the SAS had achieved. Several thousand men who had never been in action before were cooped up on ships steaming towards the Falklands, worrying and wondering about what might happen. The decisive early blow against the enemy was crucial to their morale. They now knew that the enemy could be fought and beaten.

South Georgia was now back in British hands but the way in which Argentinian resistance had crumbled led some SAS men to underestimate the fighting ability of the forces holding the Falkland Islands. The battle there was yet to begin.

Mike Rose decided to use G Squadron to gather intelligence and D Squadron to act on it. D Squadron was commanded by Cedric Delves, a quiet and introverted officer. G Squadron's OC was 'Fablon' Houston, who earned his nickname by his very envied ability to mould his body to any surface when under enemy fire.

Patrols from G Squadron were inserted into East Falkland – the major and far more densely populated of the two main Falkland Islands – on 1 May. They were dropped by helicopter at last light up to twenty miles from their designated lying-up positions and with their bergens loaded down with equipment. They had to trek over rock, tussock grass and glutinous peat to reach their LUPs and construct their hides before daybreak. They then established covert OPs close to the enemy lines, one patrol even setting up an OP in a rotting hulk in the middle of Stanley harbour.

Our experience of operations in rural Northern Ireland had been ideal preparation for this kind of prolonged surveillance, but conditions were infinitely worse in the Falklands. There were virtually no trees and no cover; even the gorse bushes were beaten flat by the incessant wind. Most of the hides were little more than rough scrapes in the peat. They were cold, wet and miserable.

The men of G Squadron remained in position in abysmal conditions for six weeks, often without shelter and living on cold food, but relaying priceless intelligence on enemy deployments of troops, aircraft and equipment. To obtain detailed intelligence they not only had to observe from a distance, but also sometimes penetrate the enemy positions to report on the exact location of guns, aircraft, troops, radar and command and control positions.

Communicating the intelligence gained also carried the risk of discovery. The Argentinians had excellent direction-finding equipment and were reported to be able to locate any transmission in a very short time, but such reports were inaccurate. In reality, direction-finding is a very imprecise science. It requires the target radio to remain still and keep transmitting while the DF stations move around until they have located it.

Two SAS men were to die and one was captured as a result of their OPs being compromised during the conflict but they were compromised by patrols not DF equipment. The Argentinians did not succeed in locating a single transmission.

The signals plan set up by the Signals Squadron in Hereford before the conflict was to use a set called the 320 with a burst-transmission capability. Signals were to be sent from the patrol on the Falklands back to Ascension, then to the UK and then back to the task-force, a round-the-world journey to cover a distance of a few miles.

Perhaps unsurprisingly, the system didn't work. The patrols then switched to a VHF voice set, the 351, working directly to the fleet. The Argentinians' fabled DF capability couldn't even locate voice-to-voice transmissions.

Far from revealing Argentinian success, G Squadron's modest compromise and casualty rate shows how successful their OPs had been. Had the positions been reversed, we would have expected to compromise every single enemy OP in an area as small as the Falklands.

Some of the most important work done by the G Squadron OPs was in tracking the movement of enemy aircraft and helicopters. The Argentinian defensive strategy rested on a large mobile reserve held in Port Stanley, which could be deployed by helicopters, including the massive Chinooks, to meet any invasion force at any site.

Each night these helicopters were dispersed to different sites around Port Stanley to make attacks on them less likely. The dispersal sites were changed every day. One G Squadron patrol tracked the helicopters night after night, travelling on foot for miles over the bleak hills to the west of Port Stanley as they searched for the helicopters' hiding-places. Twice they located them and called in air-attacks, but both times they were frustrated because the helicopters were again moved before the air-strikes came in.

The third time they found them the air-attack was successful. Four helicopters, including two Chinooks, were destroyed on the ground, blowing a giant hole in the Argentinian defensive plan. They were no longer able to deploy their mobile reserve to counter an invasion. Had the helicopters survived, the eventual landings from San Carlos Water might have turned out differently.

The Argentinian ground-attack aircraft based in the

Falklands were also widely dispersed in anticipation of attacks. As well as the main airfield at Port Stanley there were a number of minor ones scattered around the islands, most little more than grass strips.

A patrol from Boat Troop of D Squadron had set up an OP near an airstrip on Pebble Island, where a number of Pucara ground-attack aircraft were based. The Pucaras were out of their depth in air combat against a sophisticated aircraft like the Harrier, but armed with bombs, rockets, napalm, two 20mm cannon and four 7·62mm machine-guns, they were deadly against ground troops.

A raid by D Squadron was authorised the same night the Pucaras were spotted: 14 May. From the moment the OP made its report, the planning and organisation of the raid took well under one hour. Mike Rose, Cedric Delves and the Hereford Head Shed held a round-table discussion in which the plan was thrashed out and Mike then organised the necessary naval support. The aim was to destroy the aircraft and wipe out the aircrew and the entire Argentinian garrison, even though it outnumbered the raiding party by over two to one.

The navy commanders were reluctant to risk their ships too close to the Falklands, however – a problem throughout the conflict, exacerbated after HMS *Sheffield* was sunk on 4 May – and the helicopters inserting the SAS had to operate at close to maximum range, increasing the risks to the crews and their passengers.

Navy officers also underestimated the time required to bring HMS *Hermes* and *Glamorgan* within range. The resultant top-speed approach made it impossible to prepare the helicopters on the steeply pitching decks, and the start time for the raid was missed by ninety minutes. That brought the time dangerously close to daybreak. The plan was therefore modified, restricting the aim of the raid to the destruction of the aircraft. The Argentinian garrison never knew what a lucky escape they'd had.

The helicopter pilots making the minimum low-level insertion of the raiding party were using the new passive night-vision goggles, which allowed them to fly in the dark, but they had a very restricted field of vision and could induce feelings of vertigo in those unused to them. With no Terrain-Following Radar to aid them, the pilots worked wonders to bring their helicopters in safely.

The assault force were dropped five miles from the target. They linked up with the Boat Troop, who led them to the pre-recced site for an 81mm mortar, which laid down illumination and stood ready to give covering fire as the attack went in.

Under fire-control from the SAS, the guns of HMS *Glamorgan* lying off the coast also put down a barrage of fire. One troop systematically began destroying the aircraft on the ground with explosive charges and 66mm rockets. The remainder of the assault force gave covering fire, though very few defenders showed themselves.

After a few minutes the glow from burning aircraft comfortably outshone the illumination from the shells. All eleven aircraft at the strip – one third of the Argentinians' total ground-attack force in the Falklands – and an ammunition dump were destroyed. There were no SAS fatalities and only two casualties: one man hit in the leg by shrapnel and the other wounded after a command-detonated land-mine exploded close to him.

Two other SAS men suffered facial cuts and bruising but their wounds were very minor and entirely self-inflicted. As the attack went in and the first Starshell rounds from the *Glamorgan* illuminated the area, an SAS man was astonished to see two senior NCOs from different troops setting about each other in the eerie glow.

They had a feud going back many years and in the cramped confines of the ships it had been further exacerbated, with no chance to settle it. This was the first opportunity to clear the air and neither man was going to allow the fact that they were supposed to be fighting the enemy to get in the way of settling scores.

In every other way, the raid on Pebble Island had been a classical SAS attack, like those carried out by David Stirling's originals in the Western Desert forty years before. It was executed with clinical efficiency and significantly reduced the risk to task-force ground troops.

With only twenty-six Sea Harriers to provide air cover, further protection of the assault force from aircraft attack was an absolute priority. Without it the invasion could not take place. The raid on Pebble Island had reduced the risk to ground troops, but not eliminated it altogether. There was also a separate but related problem to solve: the protection of the task-force fleet from Argentine aircraft – Mirages, Skyhawks and, most dangerous of all, Super Etendards carrying Exocet missiles, against which the Royal Navy ships had little defence.

The first attempt to solve that problem had been the insertion by helicopter of the force to attack the Argentinian Mirages and Super Etendards at Rio Grande. The urgency of the operation was heightened by the knowledge that, even though the European Community was ostensibly supporting Britain in the Falklands dispute, the French were still supplying Exocet missiles to the Argentinians.

Mrs Thatcher's ferocious hostility to the EC may date from that time, for in addition to the French arms sales, the Spanish and Italians were also actively supporting Argentina in the United Nations.

The attack on Rio Grande was such a politically sensitive operation – if it had been compromised, the revelation that Britain was attacking mainland Argentina might easily have unravelled the already fragile EC and UN support for Britain – that it had to be cleared at the very highest political level.

Briefed by DLB, Mrs Thatcher gave the plan her blessing, despite a personal intervention from Ronald Reagan. His warning to her to avoid any military action against the Argentinian mainland fell on deaf ears.

After the failure of the mission, the news that the burned-out wreck of a British military helicopter had been found in Chile created widespread media speculation that special forces were operating in Argentina. The MoD's explanation that it 'had got into difficulties and was trying to make an emergency landing' in the nearest neutral country stretched credulity to its limits.

Undeterred, military planners cast about for another means of achieving the same ends. The solution they came up with was to lead to the celebrated 'mutiny' by B Squadron.

As part of a NATO exercise, the planning committee had previously staged an airborne assault on an airfield using SAS troops flown in by two Hercules. They advocated it as a possible blueprint for another attempt to attack the airfield at Rio Grande.

The attack force would be landed on the airfield after a minimum low-level approach. Three troops would destroy all the Argentinian aircraft on the ground, while the fourth located the Officers' Mess and killed all the personnel inside, depriving Argentina of its pilots as well as its planes. The assault force would then exfiltrate overland to safety in Chile.

B Squadron was being held in reserve in Hereford, and was ordered to carry out a series of mock attacks on airfields in the UK and Germany to evaluate techniques and see if it was a viable option.

In the meantime a series of liaison officers at the task-force headquarters in Northwood gave daily reports to DLB, the Director, SAS, who relayed them to the directing staff of the campaign.

By the nature of such reports and their intended audience, the temptation for those compiling them is to accentuate the positive and eliminate the negative altogether. Often the only thing the eager staff officers could find to report was how the mock attacks on the airfields were going, how well the techniques were developing and how keen the men were to get on and do something positive by carrying out the attack for real.

This did not wholly accord with the view from B Squadron, who had realised while carrying out the training that the viability of the Hercules option was almost zero. The mapping of the target was virtually non-existent; the assault was being planned with the help of a pre-Second World War map, a commercial atlas and a handful of less than perfect aerial photographs supplied by the Americans.

The assault team had no intelligence on where the Super Etendards and Exocets were stored on the airfield, and no idea which of the many buildings scattered around the site was the Officers' Mess.

The news from the RAF was even more worrying. On each mock attack, the RAF simulated Argentina's air-defence system and reported the time that the approaching Hercs were first spotted. Even at rock-bottom low level, the chances of reaching the airfield undetected by Argentinian radar appeared to be minimal.

Argentine forces were likely to have at least six minutes' warning of the impending attack and two lumbering Hercs would make easy targets for the anti-aircraft defences encircling the airfield. In the unlikely event that the Hercs managed to evade the missiles and anti-aircraft fire, the Argentinian defenders could still defeat the entire raid by the simple expedient of blocking the runway.

The element of surprise might have given the attack some slim chance of success, but the certain penalty was very, very high casualties. The odds were also stacked against anyone successfully exfiltrating afterwards.

Over and above all these reservations was one other factor which alone should have been enough to cause the cancellation of the operation: there was no way of knowing if the Super Etendards would even be at Rio Grande when the attack went in. As prudent commanders do, the Argentinians kept moving their aircraft around to reduce their vulnerability to surprise attack.

It was entirely possible that the Super Etendards would be at Rio Grande, but they might equally have been at the base at Rio Gallegos on the Argentine mainland, or at one of the other bases further north.

The SAS always make a prior estimate of the chances of success of any mission. The percentage chance given to this operation was in the very low double figures.

Long odds do not of themselves deter SAS men from attempting operations but we do like to feel that our destiny is in our own hands. On this mission B Squadron might well have been wiped out without getting in a shot, either blown out of the skies by missiles, shot to pieces by ground defences or dying in a crash-landing after the one runway they had fuel to reach was blocked to them.

Even if B Squadron's scepticism had not been justified, the plan was another instance of the SAS being used in a way that ran counter to the whole philosophy and doctrine of the Regiment. The SAS are not shock troops. If the assault on Rio Grande airfield really was a valid option, it would have been much better carried out by a unit of the Parachute Regiment.

B Squadron kept practising the planned assault only in the belief, bordering on a hope, that if they did it long enough something useful might emerge from it. The elements of a farce were all in place.

DLB could not entirely be blamed for what followed. He had merely been repeating to the planning staff what he had been told by his staff officers, but the result was a disaster. His attempts to persuade the task-force commanders to allow B Squadron to carry out this vital but extremely hazardous mission were ultimately successful.

DLB arrived in Hereford to bring the glad tidings to B Squadron in person and found that his announcement was met with total disbelief. The B Squadron OC could not believe that the directing staff at Northwood actually wanted them to attempt such a stupid mission. When he tried to argue the point with DLB, an altercation developed.

Briefed by his staff officers, DLB had assumed that the squadron commander had been clamouring for permission to do the operation for the past several weeks and couldn't understand his apparent change of mind.

'I was dismayed to find the attitude of this unit seemed lukewarm. I was also puzzled, because I had never known such a lack of enthusiasm: throughout my career the SAS had invariably reacted like hounds to a fox the moment they scented conflict. The trouble, I found, lay in the squadron commander, who himself did not believe in the proposed operation. To my mind there was only one thing to be done.'[5]

The argument ended with the squadron commander being summarily dismissed. The second-in-command of the Regiment, Ian Crooke, was placed in charge of B Squadron, who were ordered to pack their kit and were then flown to Ascension Island ready for the assault on the Argentinian mainland. It says much for Ian Crooke's qualities that he was able to lift his men and take them *en bloc* to carry out a task they knew to be close to impossible.

DLB was wrong to attribute B Squadron's lack of enthusiasm for the plan to its OC; his reservations were shared by many experienced NCOs and troopers on the squadron, men of unimpeachable record and courage. The extent of their bravery was shown by the fact that when B Squadron embarked for the flight to Ascension only two men were missing, the sacked OC and the senior staff-sergeant, who had left the squadron voluntarily.

Even though they knew it was a mission that would probably cost most, if not all of them their lives, the SAS men were still willing to go. They checked their wills and made sure that their families were well cared for, then they got on the plane.

DLB's actions in sending them on such a hazardous and possibly pointless mission were hardly in line with the philosophy of special forces operations espoused by one very senior British officer: 'When sending people in behind enemy lines, one essential principle is that a commander must not commit them to operations from which there is no hope of recovery. In Western military terms, it is simply not acceptable, either morally from the point of view of senior officers, or in terms of the morale and welfare of the units in the field.'

The author of that commendable piece of wisdom was Sir Peter de la Billiere.[6]

Only at the eleventh hour, when B Squadron was already on Ascension Island, did common sense finally prevail. The crews of the two Hercules revealed that they could not guarantee to get the squadron on to the airfield they were supposed to be attacking, and one of the pilots had a nervous breakdown. The mission was then cancelled at the insistence of the RAF.

The problem of defending the ships of the task-force and our ground troops against air-attack remained. The solution to both problems lay not in the Falklands but several thousand miles to the north.

I was at the Gerbil Cage – the FBI headquarters in Quantico – when Argentina invaded the Falklands. Three of us, Trevor, Paddy and myself, were training with FBI men in counter-terrorist team techniques, ready for the Los Angeles Olympics.

We monitored the situation on the radio and were already looking outwards, wondering how and where we might be used in any conflict. With our country on the brink of war, training the FBI did not seem the most valuable way to be spending our time.

Eventually we could stand the suspense no longer. We contacted Hereford for instructions and were told to make our way to a military airfield near Washington DC where we would be picked up and taken to Fort Bragg, the headquarters of Delta Force. We were to evaluate hand-held Stinger ground-to-air missiles and seek Delta's help in obtaining a supply.

They were new and super-secret – I'd never even heard of them – but they were known to our intelligence people and regarded as vital to the invasion plan for the Falklands.

Not long afterwards, we found ourselves standing at the side of the runway, as if we were waiting at a bus-stop. A small, six-seater aircraft landed a few moments later and taxied to a stop alongside us.

On the flight to Fort Bragg, the crewman sharing the passenger compartment began asking us how we were finding America and how the political system in the UK compared to the system in the USA. This puzzled us greatly, but we kept our replies non-committal.

We landed at Hope air force base at Fort Bragg and as we taxied round to the terminal we could see two colleagues in Delta Force, one of them an old friend of mine, standing near the main door of the terminal. A red carpet stretched out across the tarmac in front of them. The aircraft stopped, the doors opened and we got out to be greeted by a reception committee of several senior American air force officers, who saluted us and thanked us for flying air force. We ignored the salutes and marched along the red carpet towards the two Delta Force men.

'Don't laugh,' one of them whispered. 'You'll give the game away.'

We strode through the terminal to a waiting car. As we drove away, they were convulsed with laughter. The aircraft, red carpet and welcoming committee had been laid on because they had told everybody that we were a visiting delegation of British Members of Parliament.

We drove swiftly to the Delta Force headquarters and were taken straight to the ops room. The Americans were analysing the Argentinian and British options. Their interpretation appeared to be that the British would invade the Falklands.

That was also our own view but it was heartening to see the Americans were thinking along the same lines because at the time the Secretary of State, Alexander Haig, was still carrying out his diplomatic shuttle between Argentina, Washington and London.

We took just two men at Fort Bragg into our confidence: the colonel of Delta Force and my friend. They were the only ones involved in what followed. The Stinger was so secret that even its existence was classified information, but next day it was arranged for us to do some training with the missile. We worked with it for several days and were very impressed; it appeared to be an almost foolproof weapon.

I remarked to my Delta Force friend, 'Some of these would definitely come in handy in the Falklands.'

He immediately arranged for a quantity to be delivered to Delta Force and handed them over to us. When Hereford also asked us to see if we could get our hands on some communications equipment, he again obliged. Such equipment was just as secret, virtually unknown outside the States. The only other examples were on nuclear submarines and they were only allowed access to the channel for a few minutes a day. We were given blanket, total access.

No paperwork was involved and no questions asked; it was a private arrangement between Delta Force and the SAS. With a nod and a wink from the commander of Delta Force, communications equipment and Stinger missiles, two of the United States' most closely guarded military secrets, were simply loaded on to a Hertz rent-a-truck. It was parked in Delta's ultra-secure compound while we awaited the outcome of General Haig's diplomatic shuttle.

Hereford had arranged for a VC10 to be stationed at Washington DC airport to transport the equipment back home and the minute Haig announced that he could not do any more to avoid the disagreement developing into a conflict, the commander released the Hertz rent-a-truck.

The rented truck was soon on its way to Washington airport. We followed it in Buckie's car, loaded the boxes on to the VC10 and took off for Brize Norton in Oxfordshire.

The crew of the VC10 were intrigued to know what they

were carrying. They had been held there for several days and were now going back three-quarters empty, and carrying only three passengers. In the absence of any information from us they managed to convince themselves that they were carrying tactical nuclear weapons.

I called Hereford from Brize Norton and was told to transfer the kit to a C130 for an immediate flight to Ascension. I would be going with it and both I and the equipment would be parachuted down to the ship carrying D Squadron towards the Falklands.

To my relief, the order had been rescinded before I broke the connection and I was told to go back to Hereford instead and prepare to leave in a couple of days. I was packing my kit when the order was again rescinded. The Head Shed admitted that there had been a mix-up of names; the man they wanted to take the equipment down to the fleet was not Ken Connor, but Paddy O'Connor, my companion in America.

I tried hard to sound frustrated and disappointed, but twenty years in the SAS had not noticeably increased my enthusiasm for parachuting anywhere, least of all into the icy waters of the South Atlantic, and I was mightily relieved.

Paddy and the precious equipment both made safe landings and the value of those Stingers and communications equipment to the invasion force cannot be overstated. The SAS were the most battle-hardened troops in the Western world but even the SAS couldn't invade the Falklands if the Argentinians had air superiority. Stingers enabled ground troops to hold off and shoot down ground-attack aircraft.

The communications equipment had an even greater value, playing a vital part in defeating an even greater danger to the whole Falklands invasion plan. British Harrier jump-jets carried very limited fuel. If they were airborne too early or too late they would be in no position to defend the fleet, leaving it at the mercy of the Argentine strike aircraft. A way had to be found to get the Harriers airborne at the right time.

The solution involved another SAS secret within a secret. Rumours circulated after the conflict that American intelligence from spy satellites had been made available to Britain but the truth was more complex.

After the abortive attempt by the SAS patrol to attack Rio Grande airfield and the ditching of the Sea King helicopter inside Chile, the problem still remained of the British forces needing to know about military aircraft taking off from Argentina.

To meet this problem a small SAS team was infiltrated into Chile with communications equipment to monitor every take-off by an Argentinian military jet and to pass this information on to the fleet. Even with that vital advance warning the invasion fleet was still losing ships; without it we would have lost many more and the invasion could never have happened. The SAS team was able to avoid capture in Chile.

The equipment revolutionised our communications on long-range ops, enabling the CO in the Falklands to talk to Hereford in real time. I was the first man in the UK to hear that *Sheffield* and *Antelope* had been hit, for example. The Regiment's access to top-quality, high-speed communications went down like a lead balloon in some quarters, however. The only communications link between the task-force and the UK was a single Mari-Sat – maritime satellite. It was soon swamped by the volume of signals traffic, causing delays running into hours to get a signal through.

To the fury of assorted civil servants in Whitehall and senior officers in Fleet HQ in Northwood, Middlesex, SAS men both in the Falklands and in Hereford were always immediately aware of events that took hours to reach other, higher-ranking pairs of ears.

In the rigid hierarchies of the armed forces, there was nothing to stop the most senior officers with the fleet – the task-force commanders – ordering the SAS to hand over their sat-coms equipment. Whether the war would have been prosecuted as vigorously if that had been the case can only be a matter for conjecture.

As the senior officers, they had every right to expect priority access to the fastest and most efficient communications. The fact that they were unable to get it shows the political clout that the Regiment wielded in the wake of the Iranian Embassy siege – and no one outranked the supreme commander of the task-force, the Prime Minister, Margaret Thatcher.

The communications equipment had tactical as well as strategic implications and enabled SAS men from Mike Rose right down to patrol leaders to discuss tactical problems in operations as they happened. The discussions and consultations could also encompass the Head Shed in Hereford and DLB in London.

The speed of communication with Hereford was not always an advantage, however. Prior to the Falklands, the Regiment relied on extensive planning and training to prepare patrols for mission. Once committed, the execution of the mission was left to the judgement and determination of the patrol. Over the next few years, sat-coms transformed the conduct of operations.

The Head Shed in Hereford could now control the execution of a mission literally anywhere in the world, with limitless potential for damaging interference in the conduct of operations. Sat-coms were an unmixed blessing in the Falklands, however, though the next news they carried to Hereford was of a terrible tragedy.

On 20 May men from D and G Squadrons were cross-decking by helicopter from *Hermes* to *Intrepid* in final preparations for the diversionary attacks the SAS would launch to conceal the real focus of the invasion. Thirty people, including the three crew, were in a Sea King as it lifted off for the half-mile journey. Another helicopter was on the flight deck of the *Intrepid* and the Sea King had to circle until it was moved.

As it did so there was a sudden violent impact. A large

seabird – an albatross or giant petrel – had flown into the engine intake. The Sea King crashed into the sea immediately and within seconds it had disappeared beneath the waves. Most of the men went down with it, but a few fought their way back to the surface and clung to the only support, a one-man aircrew life-raft.

The survivors remained in the icy waters for half an hour and most were close to unconsciousness from hypothermia when a rescue helicopter and a dinghy finally appeared. Twenty men, including eighteen members of the Regiment, had drowned. Among the dead was Paddy O'Connor.

I could not avoid a sense of guilt that I had survived while Paddy had died. Had the mix-up of our names remained undetected for a few more hours, I would now be lying at the bottom of the South Atlantic and Paddy would still be alive.

The crash was the worst loss of life the modern Regiment had ever endured. It was made worse by the seniority of the men involved. Two squadron sergeant-majors and six sergeants had died; the average age of the victims was thirty-four. It would take the Regiment a decade and more to replace their accumulated knowledge and priceless experience.

The tragedy stunned everyone; we had all lost good friends and comrades-in-arms in a needless accident, but there was still a war to be fought. Our grief at the loss of so many men had to be suppressed until the job was done.

The very next day the remaining men of D Squadron launched diversionary attacks against Argentinian forces around Darwin and Goose Green. The aim was to convince the Argentinians that a very large force was confronting them, so the plan was to attack from long range using as many heavy weapons as the squadron could carry.

The low-level helicopter insertion was made in the last hours of daylight. As their helicopter flew along the floor of one valley, the SAS men found themselves looking up at an Argentine gun position on the hillside above them.

After an endless, gruelling night march into position, carrying the heavy weapons and maximum ammunition in addition to their usual bergen loads, the squadron fanned out along a broad front and began their attacks. They moved constantly, so that every piece of cover seemed to conceal a firing position and so ferocious was the SAS onslaught that intercepted communications from the Argentinian commander revealed that he thought he was facing a whole battalion.

As the main invasion began, the SAS patrols broke off their assault to rendezvous with the Squadron HQ group on Mount Osborne before daylight. It had the only air-defence, including Stingers. As the reunited squadron was moving off from the RV, an Argentine Pucara ground-attack aircraft appeared around the shoulder of the hill less than 100 yards from them.

It was immediately engaged by a trooper carrying a Stinger. The missile flew straight through the aircraft and out the other side, and for a moment the SAS men thought it had somehow escaped damage. Then the pilot ejected and the aircraft smashed into the hillside.

Two more Pucaras appeared and adopted an attack profile. They flew into a blizzard of ground fire, some men lying flat on their backs and firing directly above them as the Pucaras made attack runs overhead. They were driven off by the ground fire, one so badly damaged that it took no further part in the conflict.[7] The Stingers had already proved their worth. The ground troops drew enormous confidence from them and, after a few more losses, the Argentine Pucaras virtually disappeared from the conflict.

With a beachhead secured, conflict developed between the marines, who wanted to hold their ground and consolidate, and the other units who wanted to take a more aggressive role and push out rapidly.

The difference of opinion was settled by orders from London demanding a quick victory somewhere to counter the gloom generated by the heavy losses of task-force ships. The flurry of communications – by sat-coms – between Mike

Rose, Hereford and London preceding the order to break out further soured Mike's already fractious relationship with Jeremy Moore.

He had the not entirely groundless belief that Mike had used his direct access to the Prime Minister to press for an order to begin an immediate advance beyond the beachhead. If that message was indeed transmitted, it chimed perfectly with Mrs Thatcher's political instinct that only a continuous diet of battlefield success could maintain public support for the war in the face of steady losses of lives, ships and aircraft.

There was also a risk that the UN might seek to impose a ceasefire and open negotiations on sovereignty. That could only favour the Argentinians who had de facto control of 99 per cent of the disputed territory. If full-scale battle was raging, however, any UN calls for a ceasefire could safely be ignored.

Despite protests from the task-force commanders that more ammunition and stores should be landed before an advance began, the order was given direct from Downing Street via Fleet HQ at Northwood to break out immediately and inflict a defeat on the Argentinian forces at the first available opportunity.

The chosen targets were Goose Green and Darwin. They were well off the direct line of march on Port Stanley and the military necessity of taking them at all is open to debate. Deploying some troops to guard the task-force's flank might well have been sufficient insurance had the decision to attack Goose Green been a strategic rather than a political one.

The assault by 2 Para on the Argentinian forces has been mythologised since the event, but even with the layers of myth stripped away it remains a remarkable feat of arms. The paras are arguably the best-trained shock troops in the world, with an inbuilt self-belief that they are better than anyone else in this type of action. It was needed to the full at Goose Green and it is doubtful if any other unit in the task-force could have successfully carried out the assault.

Some accounts have claimed that the intelligence provided by G Squadron greatly underestimated the number of Argentine forces at Goose Green. It was one of the sticks that Jeremy Moore used to beat the Regiment after the conflict, but the claims are incorrect.

Suggestions that the paras were outnumbered by as much as ten to one are also wildly wide of the mark. G Squadron accurately reported that the area was defended by a battalion of Argentine troops: 500 men. The number of Argentine prisoners taken was double that, but it included the air force and support personnel who took no part in the fighting. The number of ground troops was exactly as predicted and the paras' achievement needs no exaggeration of the odds to justify it; an attacking force overcoming an equal number of well-entrenched defenders is remarkable enough in itself.

Having won the requested victory – at the loss of several lives, including that of Colonel H. Jones – the para battalions began the push towards Port Stanley, advancing along either flank of the hilly spine of East Falkland in a classic pincer movement. The marines, still operating under a policy of cautious consolidation, were lagging far behind.

With characteristic decisiveness, Mike Rose found a way to force the pace. A report from a G Squadron OP indicated that, despite being in undisputed possession of the Falklands for several weeks, the Argentinians had made no effort to secure some of the main high-ground features around Port Stanley. They had no outlying bases and were making virtually no patrols.

It was an invitation the SAS could not refuse. Mike Rose deployed D Squadron to take and hold a position on Mount Kent, forty miles in front of the main invasion force. It was a particularly bold move, because the loss of nine more helicopters aboard the *Atlantic Conveyor* meant that reinforcement by chopper could not happen. The SAS would have to hold the position until the slowly advancing marines caught up with them.

A helicopter was found to fly Mike Rose and a journalist, Max Hastings, in to bear witness to the successful occupation of the summit of Mount Kent, however. Like the other journalists covering the campaign, Max Hastings had enthusiastically courted Mike in the hope of getting access to his sat-coms to file his copy.

As well as the seizure of the strategic high ground, Mike Rose's *coup de main* forced Jeremy Moore both to advance artillery to support the SAS and to order the marines forward with considerably more speed than had previously been shown.

D Squadron set up OPs on Mount Kent, Mount Challenger and other nearby high points, and called in artillery strikes on exposed enemy forces. They fought off repeated attempts by the Argentinians to dislodge them and held their ground until reinforced by marines, then led them into position on Mount Challenger ready for the final assault on Port Stanley.

Shortly afterwards there was a tragic incident when an SBS man was killed by 'friendly fire' from an SAS patrol near Estancia House on the slopes of Mount Kent. Such incidents were not infrequent in the confusion of battle, with so many different units operating in front of our lines, but SAS insistence on clearly designated zones of operation was designed to minimise the risk.

Unfortunately for the SBS man, his patrol had strayed well over the boundaries of their own zone into an SAS area of operation. Seeing armed soldiers on the move at night in an area supposedly free of friendly forces, the SAS patrol naturally opened fire.

In the final stages of the war, D Squadron were again redeployed to West Falkland, where they carried out further operations behind enemy lines. One OP set up near Port Howard was compromised by an Argentinian patrol, and Captain John Hamilton was killed while holding off the enemy to allow his radio operator to escape.

Having played a significant part in the waging of the war,

the SAS also made a crucial input into bringing the fighting to a swift end without a massacre of the demoralised Argentinian troops.

A communications landline to the Argentine Joint Services HQ was the first essential. Once that was established, the delicate process began of persuading the Argentines to surrender. Based on intelligence from our OPs on the crumbling morale of the Argentine troops, Mike Rose put forward a plan.

By laying maximum stress during the negotiations on the Argentine forces' 'stubborn and courageous resistance', the stratagem aimed to convince the Argentine commanders that they had put up a sufficiently brave fight and could now surrender with their honour intact. They would earn praise for sparing the forces of both sides from further killings, whereas fighting on would only delay the inevitable end and spill further blood to no useful purpose.

It took eight days of negotiation to persuade the Argentine commanders to swallow the bait and agree a ceasefire. Mike Rose and an SAS signaller flew in to Port Stanley in a helicopter flying a white flag, just in case the news of a ceasefire had not reached all the Argentine troops. The helicopter landed at the wrong RV in Stanley, leaving the SAS group to negotiate a quarter of a mile of Argentinian defensive positions to reach the waiting Argentine officers.

General Menendez led his side in the negotiations. They lasted for two hours, punctuated by his visits to his communications centre to confer with General Galtieri back in Buenos Aires. The initial offer to surrender on behalf of the East Falkland garrison, but not the one on West Falkland, was rejected, but once one or two minor but necessary face-saving adjustments to the surrender terms had been made, General Menendez was ready to sign. Jeremy Moore was then flown in to accept the surrender on behalf of the British government.

The first ground troops into Port Stanley, B Company, 2 Para, a mortar detachment led by a former SAS troop commander, raised the Union Jack over Government House.

It flew there proudly for the next two hours until the arrival of the Royal Marines in Stanley. They pulled it down and then raised it again to give the accompanying photographers and television crews the 'exclusive film of the first British troops raising the flag over Government House'.

The attempt to give the marines the publicity and public credit for the liberation of Stanley was part of the agenda that Jeremy Moore had been following since he was appointed commander of the task-force.

The swingeing cuts imposed on the navy the previous year had been suspended when the Argentinians invaded the Falklands. Both Major-General Moore – a career officer in the Royal Marines – and Rear-Admiral John 'Sandy' Woodward, the task-force naval commander, saw the conflict as the ideal way to re-establish the credibility of a seaborne force. If the marines, supported by naval gunfire and navy Sea Harriers, could recapture the Falklands, the cuts to the navy, which by extension threatened Jeremy Moore's own regiment, could be permanently reversed.

Until the Falklands War, the only active service the members of the task-force had seen were policing actions in Northern Ireland. The SAS were the exceptions, the only troops with any combat experience, and Mike Rose also had the great advantage of being advised by a very experienced Hereford Head Shed.

Despite this, Jeremy Moore opposed the use of any other troops than the marines in the task-force. When compelled to accept the SAS, the paras and the other army units, he was reluctant to use them and displayed a misunderstanding of the proper role of the SAS that bordered on the wilful.

When the war was over he wrote a report that was bitterly critical of Mike Rose and the Regiment, and persistently denigrated the contribution of not only the SAS but of all the other army units as well. In this he was no doubt only fighting the corner of his own sector, but inter-service rivalries and office politics should have been set aside in the interests of the task-force as a whole.

Jeremy Moore's agenda for the conflict also involved pushing forward the claims of the SBS – a subdivision of the marines – at every opportunity. The public tend to make the understandable assumption that the SAS and SBS are similar units of similar qualities. Jeremy Moore was in a position to know that was not the case. In special forces terms the SBS are not very professional. The SAS nickname for them, 'the Shaky Boats', is no reflection on the men themselves, just the way the unit is run.

The SBS are the poor relations even of the marines, who are themselves the poor relations of the navy. The SBS are underfunded, understaffed and dependent on the marines for a slice of their budget. There is also no career structure for either officers or men within the SBS. They serve only a three-year tour before returning to the marines.

Their ranks were also severely depleted in the late 1960s when the North Sea oil industry was clamouring for divers and offering phenomenal rates of pay. Virtually all the SBS men left the service to work in the North Sea.

During the 1970s the SBS did not have a role and were used merely as a recruiting arm of the Royal Marines, but when the SAS counter-terrorist teams were set up we gave the SBS the seaborne role, the only one they had.

They subsequently concentrated on underwater work: diving. There was no place for divers on operations around the Falklands, and when it came to working on the surface using canoes and Geminis, the SBS were not up to it. Their abilities and usefulness ended at the high-water mark.

They were given the option of setting up the OP before the raid on Pebble Island but could not do the task. As a consolation prize they were eventually put on to the Falklands, long after G Squadron, but they were not trained to do the job they had been given. That was the main reason for the loss of one of their men in the friendly fire incident with an SAS patrol.

The amount of in-fighting that goes on between the different branches of the forces, even in the face of a campaign like the Falklands War, would shock the British public. The turf wars between the marines and the army units were only one facet of the bickering and manoeuvring.

After the Argentine invasion of the Falklands, the Royal Green Jackets had been sent to Sennybridge and had completed intensive training ready for the Falklands. At the last minute they were replaced by a Guards battalion. The decision had nothing to do with military considerations – the Guards came straight from public duties and were not remotely trained for the campaign they were about to undertake – and everything to do with the considerable influence the Guards have always been able to exert within the MoD.

Apart from using their own influence to promote the navy and the marines at the expense of the army, both Jeremy Moore and Sandy Woodward were constant proponents of caution during the campaign. The preference of the marines for 'consolidation' rather than a fast break-out from the beachhead at San Carlos caused ill-disguised anger among the SAS and the paras, who favoured the bold, direct approach.

Uppermost in their minds was the knowledge that the Antarctic winter was fast approaching. If the Falklands War was not settled before the onset of winter, it would never be settled in Britain's favour at all.

The rear-admiral's insistence on keeping his fleet out of harm's way, well to the east of the Falklands, also raised hackles, making helicopter insertions much more difficult and dangerous. Sandy Woodward could point to the losses of task-force ships in San Carlos Water once the invasion began as justification, but his cautious approach apparently did not extend to the preparation of any contingency plans if the *Hermes* and/or the *Invincible* were sunk. Had the carriers gone down, the only apparent contingency plan for the rest of the task-force was to turn round and slink home.

Mike Rose's famously blunt approach did little to soothe the inter-service frictions. He expressed his feelings about the value of the naval contribution in a withering aside to Rear-Admiral Woodward: 'All you are is a taxi-driver. Get your taxis to put my men where they can do the work.'

Mike's ability to annoy his peers was reflected in the honours awarded at the end of the conflict. While medals were handed out like sweets to other officers, many of whom had made far smaller contributions to the victory than Mike, he had to be content with a Mention in Despatches.

He did claim one other prize however. A statue presented to General Menendez by General Galtieri as a reward for 'liberating' the Malvinas was subsequently liberated by Mike Rose after the surrender. It found its way to the Officers' Mess in Hereford.

There was much subsequent controversy about trophy-taking during the campaign and Field-Marshal Lord Bramall was at pains to point out during a visit to Hereford how he had been forced to crack down hard to prevent the pernicious practice of looting by British troops.

As he was speaking, an SAS officer detached himself from the party accompanying him and made a rapid trip to the Officers' Mess to remove Mike Rose's trophy from view before the field-marshal arrived for lunch.

The SAS also collected some far more valuable souvenirs from the war: two Argentinian Agusta 109 helicopters. They were better than anything to which we had access in the UK military and were shipped back to Hereford.

Two Americans received a more legitimate, though still discreet, reward for their help to the SAS. The Delta Force ops officer, my old friend, was given the MBE and Caspar Weinberger, the US Secretary of Defence, got a knighthood – which suggests that he at least was in the loop when the

Stingers and communications equipment were being loaded into that Hertz rent-a-truck.

If we could have got my friend a knighthood too we would have done, because he saved a lot of British lives at great cost to his own career. He never said anything about it himself, but he was never promoted after that. He's now retired from Delta Force and writing novels.

General Pinochet's regime in Chile had previously made repeated attempts to obtain Canberra bombers from Britain. On each occasion the sale was vetoed because of the Pinochet junta's lamentable record on human rights.

In the wake of the Falklands conflict, Margaret Thatcher quietly approved the sale of the bombers. The news was leaked to the press and there was much speculation about Mrs Thatcher's motives for allowing the sale, but the real reason remained buried.

There were many medals and commendations – some posthumous – for SAS men as reward for their crucial role in a conflict that had cost us dear: twenty men died and many more were wounded.

The casualty figures could have been even higher as a result of Mike Rose's insistence that the SAS had to be seen to be taking an active part in the latter stages of the Falklands campaign.

It caused great upset to many people in the Regiment. SAS patrols had been operating in the Falklands several weeks before the main body of troops landed. They spent weeks on end in bleak, cold and wet OPs, gathering intelligence on Argentinian troop positions and deployments. SAS men had also been heavily involved in the fighting in South Georgia, Pebble Island and on East and West Falkland.

This was evidently not enough for Mike who, in the last stages of hostilities, wanted D Squadron to do a helicopter-borne assault on to Wireless Ridge, a piece of high ground occupied by an Argentinian battalion.

An assault force of sixty men attacking 500 troops in pre-

pared defensive positions was an extremely high-risk operation at the best of times and certain to result in heavy
casualties. Had it been at a crucial stage of the campaign, the
advantages might well have outweighed those risks, but with
the war as good as over there was no military point to it
whatsoever.

In the end the operation was cancelled, not because of any
change of heart on Mike's part, but because the commander
of the naval helicopter force refused to risk his pilots and his
assets on such a needless task.

Mike's other masterplan was to launch B Squadron, still
cooling their heels on Ascension Island, in an airborne assault
in Hercs straight on to the runway at Port Stanley. By this
time B Squadron had had a bellyful. They had taken to
wearing long rubber false noses and white bands around
their foreheads, inscribed with Japanese characters, and called
themselves the 'long-nose kamikazes'.

Some troopers wondered whether B Squadron was still
being punished for its reluctance to implement the plan to
attack Rio Grande, but that was unfair. Mike showed his own
sympathy for the squadron and its former Officer Commanding by his comment that if he himself had been at
Hereford he could have controlled the errant officer without
the need to dismiss him. 'Maybe,' DLB told him, 'but that's
the whole point. You weren't there when you were needed.'[8]

DLB's comment was a harsh one. Two, and later three,
of the Regiment's four squadrons were committed to the
campaign in the Falklands. Mike was in the right place to
supervise them and that was the top priority for the Regiment.
He played a significant role in helping to ensure a successful
outcome to the conflict and need apologise to no one.

There are reservations about one or two of the tasks Mike
authorised in the closing stages of the campaign, but my own
feeling is simply that he had got a bit carried away with the
fact that he had had a very successful war and was pushing
his luck a little.

One such task was a planned SAS raid on the penultimate day of the war. As 2 Para began the assault on Wireless Ridge – at battalion not squadron strength – a force from D and G Squadrons in Rigid Raider craft crossed Stanley harbour to attack the lower end of Wireless Ridge, described by Mike Rose as 'the soft underbelly' of the Argentinian defences.

The Argentinian hospital ship berthed in the harbour promptly illuminated the craft with its floodlights and they took a pounding from shore defences. The raiding party reached the beach but were then forced to retreat under a hail of fire.

The hospital ship had breached its neutrality by aiding the defenders and the SAS had no compunction about sheltering behind it to protect themselves from enemy fire. They eventually returned to their start point aboard four distinctly unseaworthy Rigid Raiders. They were very fortunate that their only casualties were three men slightly wounded. The soft underbelly of the Argentinian defences had proved to be remarkably hard and scaly.

That minor reverse had no impact on the outcome of the war; the surrender document was signed the next day, 14 June 1982. The successful campaign to liberate the Falklands forced the resignation of General Galtieri and hastened the return of democracy in Argentina.

In the wake of the war, a huge investment in military and civil infrastructure transformed the economy of the Falklands Islands. The population, though still tiny, is growing and revenues from fisheries and oil exploration have made the Falklands self-sufficient in everything except defence.

The effect of the war on Britain was less dramatic but it had an undeniable impact on the morale of the nation. The largest deployment of British troops since Suez had ended in a victory that helped to erase the lingering memory of that massive humiliation and a hundred lesser ones on the long, hard road home from empire.

The Falklands War was fought over one of the last remnants

of the British Empire, but there were no imperial motives behind it. The oil and fisheries revenues that have now given the Falklands an economic importance that sheep-farming never did were barely considered by Margaret Thatcher's Cabinet.

Britain did not fight 'for profit, or for the security of her sea-lanes, or for the material or spiritual good of anyone. She fought ... for a principle [to resist aggression], to restore her government's injured *amour-propre*, and possibly for electoral profit – though that was a less certain advantage at the time than it afterwards turned out to be.'[9]

In one respect only, the cynics questioning Mrs Thatcher's motives for launching the task-force were right, for 'the moral imperative which lay behind the Falklands War did not extend into other areas of foreign policy'.[10]

Yet to describe her decision to go to war over the Falklands as little more than an attempt to secure her re-election by wrapping herself in the Union Jack unjustly denigrates Mrs Thatcher and greatly underplays the very real dangers that the enterprise might have failed.

This was no policing action or skirmish against some Ruritanian army. The Argentine armed forces were well entrenched in the territory – 10,000 men were stationed on the Falklands – outnumbered the invading forces, had theoretical air superiority and were well supplied from a home base only a few hundred miles away.

The British task-force was operating at the end of a long and tenuous supply chain extending 9,000 miles. It had minimal air-cover and barely enough ships and men for the job in hand. That it succeeded was partly due to the professionalism and bravery of the forces involved and partly to the luck that any successful military venture must have.

Had the Argentine bomb-primers done their job better – six ships of the task-force fleet were hit by bombs that failed to explode – had Argentina possessed even a few more Exocet missiles, or had two of their pilots not mistaken the *Atlantic*

Conveyor for an aircraft-carrier, the outcome might have been very different.

The Argentine forces were neither as well equipped nor as well trained as the British, but they were not a rabble; a CIA report before the conflict had described them as the most effective fighting force in South America.

There is always a tendency to overestimate the fighting qualities of the enemy, however, and accepting an estimate of the strength of another country's forces without knowing the agendas of those compiling the report is very unwise.

The SAS had learned the lessons of numerous campaigns including Operation Storm in Dhofar, the biggest conflict in which the British army had been involved since the Korean War. Whatever the apparent strength of the opposition, you must impose your will on them in the early stages of any conflict. By doing so you will explode any myths about their strength and invincibility, damage the enemy morale and significantly lift that of your own troops.

Lacking similar combat experience, Jeremy Moore was very reluctant to commit his forces in the vital early stages of the campaign, but Mike Rose was more than happy to do so.

Mike's bold and decisive leadership won the Regiment some significant battle honours, but he also exposed his men to needless risk in operations that were not strategic and therefore not the proper province of the SAS. His justification was that the Regiment had to be doing something when other units were taking casualties, but the implication that the yardstick for measuring the effectiveness of the Regiment was the number of SAS men being killed beggared belief.

It caused a long-lasting schism within the Regiment, fuelled by the curious decision not to debrief the returning SAS troops at the end of the Falklands campaign. It was the first time in the history of the SAS that there had been no Regimental debrief.

The debrief is a crucial release valve. Once all the problems and frustrations have been aired, you can put them behind you and get on with improving, evolving and changing your training to prevent any repetition of mistakes in the future.

There was considerable controversy over several aspects of the conduct of the Falklands campaign, yet the returning troops had no forum to express their frustration. It had a severe impact on the morale of the Regiment; it has arguably still not recovered from it.

Although the public view was that the SAS had again covered itself in glory in the Falklands, the lack of any proper retrospective analysis of the campaign masked some fundamental flaws in the way the Regiment had operated in the Falklands and would operate again in the future. Many of the mistakes made in the Gulf War could be directly attributed to the failure to debrief after the Falklands.

That problem was exacerbated by an unexpected consequence of the meteoric rise of the Regiment. It was now the ultimate military/political machine, the cutting edge of a strategy that had not only sustained British interests in regions where it had formerly been the imperial power, but had even extended it into areas where Britain had previously had little or no influence at all.

The political impact of the Regiment was matched by the access enjoyed by its senior members. As a result of the storming of the Iranian Embassy, both DLB and Mike Rose were personally known to Margaret Thatcher and had direct access to her.

Mrs Thatcher's influence had also secured for the Regiment a place for an SAS liaison officer at the task-force HQ at Northwood and a direct link with GCHQ in Cheltenham. Whenever an SAS operation was being planned in the Falklands, one of our intelligence officers would make the twenty-minute chopper flight to GCHQ and compare our intelligence from the OPs in the field with the sigint from GCHQ.

It was an unheard-of privilege. Collected by ground stations in the UK, Hong Kong, Cyprus and at several British embassies, by Royal Navy ships and by aircraft of RAF 51 Squadron, which was permanently tasked by GCHQ, signals intelligence from GCHQ was the crown jewels.

Even senior military commanders had to take their place in the queue and accept whatever scraps of intelligence were deemed suitable for them; the SAS was given blanket access.

The vastly experienced Head Shed in Hereford would then institute round-robin discussions with Mike Rose, DLB and the SAS patrol leaders to produce solutions to any problems.

If authorisation for an operation was needed, DLB and Mike Rose could bypass the chain of command and go right to the very top to obtain it, but the link with Margaret Thatcher was also two-way. The Prime Minister got up-to-the-minute information from the front line and could also send characteristically blunt and vigorous messages to the commanders in the field whenever she felt it was warranted. DLB in particular became the bearer of good and bad tidings, and the message: 'The Prime Minister is not very pleased about this,' was enough to guarantee a flurry of action.

This privileged SAS access, to both top-level intelligence and the ear of the Prime Minister, infuriated MoD officials, staff officers and task-force commanders alike. They could only watch as DLB and Mike Rose used their political contacts to great effect and the Regiment received far more publicity than was strictly merited by the part it had played in the campaign.

As long as Mrs Thatcher remained Prime Minister the senior officers and MoD officials had to like it or lump it, but they were to gain their revenge in the Gulf War. With Mrs Thatcher gone and the Prime Ministerial patronage removed, the SAS was starved of intelligence, equipment, access and influence, and largely denied a strategic role in the conflict.

Fresh from the siege of the Iranian Embassy, the SAS emerged from the Falklands War with its prestige even further enhanced. Immediately after the war a number of Middle

East countries put in requests for the SAS to train their forces – but what they wanted was not the by now traditional body-guard or counter-terrorist training.

An SAS officer and I received a message telling us to go to the embassy of a Gulf state to meet a prince, the son of the ruler. With us was a brigadier from the MoD, a counter-insurgency specialist. When the prince discovered the briga-dier's field of expertise he immediately sent him away. He then got straight down to business with us. 'I want my special forces to be trained to carry out long-range attacks like the ones you did in Argentina.'

'But we didn't.'

'Don't pretend to me. I know what happened.'

We shrugged our shoulders. Who were we to argue with a prince?

The result of our conversation that day was the assembly of one of the largest SAS training teams ever sent abroad. Two squadrons of special forces were duly trained to carry out long-range attacks.

The prince told us they were to be used as part of the Gulf Defence Council's forces – or so he said. What his real purpose might have been can only be speculation; if there was an attack plan it was never put into effect.

The Falklands War also led directly to another extension of the Regiment's role, this time at the expense of one of our patrons. The publicly stated founding principle of the SIS was simply 'to support Her Majesty's government'. The unwritten one was to carry out offensive operations in furtherance of that support. For many years the SIS had maintained this supposed capability by employing ex-military officers. Not all of them had relevant experience and ability.

Anyone who thought about the SIS in any depth soon became aware that they were almost totally unaccountable. Their use of a box system and cut-outs precluded outsiders from drawing any useful conclusions about the efficacy of their operations.

Even this system could not protect them from the wrath of Margaret Thatcher after the Falklands War. In her eyes they were guilty of two unforgivable crimes: not only had they failed to predict the Argentinian invasion, they had also showed themselves incapable of carrying out any offensive operations at all.

Working in this area the SAS operated under the tightest of government controls. Every task, no matter how clandestine, was first put through a series of checks. Was it feasible? Was it politically acceptable? Was it secure? Then it went on the Foreign Secretary's desk for authorisation, making the political deniability of operations something of a fig-leaf.

When Geoffrey Howe became Foreign Secretary the already fading entrepreneurial spirit of the Foreign Office completely disappeared. Like all his predecessors, he had visited Hereford, and after talking to the Regiment in general he would then be briefed on specific tasks with the relevant teams.

On several occasions we found that he was terrified of the potential consequences of tasks we were about to undertake. Even before the job was sanctioned, he was constantly asking, 'What if it goes wrong?'

Often the only way to secure permission for the job was to bypass the Foreign Secretary altogether, using the Regiment's direct access to his rather less timid Prime Minister.

Our re-assumption of the worldwide role we had relinquished after the retreat from east of Suez in 1967 did not distract us from domestic counter-terrorist operations, but the sheer impact of the assault on the Iranian Embassy had earned us a breathing space on that front. No sane terrorist now regarded Britain as a suitable site for hijackings or hostage-takings.

We still found gainful employment, for the police began to approach us for help in incidents that had no terrorist dimension, and which extended our field of operations even further into the domestic arena.

We were even called in to quell a prison riot, at Peterhead

near Aberdeen. A group of fifty long-term inmates took a warder hostage and virtually destroyed the prison's D Wing. Many of the prisoners gave themselves up, but a group of half a dozen of the most violent and dangerous men continued to resist.

They barricaded themselves in the roof space above the top floor of the wing, smashed a hole through the slates, and staged rooftop protests which included threatening their captive with a hammer. The man had a serious kidney condition, which intensified the pressure on the authorities to bring the affair to a swift conclusion.

The Grampian police could see no way to bring the siege to an end without a violent confrontation that would almost certainly end in the death of the hostage. After four days of fruitless negotiations with the rioters, they handed over control of the incident to the SAS.

The duty Special Projects Team flew up to Aberdeen, arriving in the early hours of an October morning. By the time they had assembled in the prison gym there were less than two hours of darkness left.

The briefings were terse and very much to the point. Since the prisoners were armed with knives and clubs, 'reasonable force' dictated that the SAS teams should be issued only with wooden staves, stun grenades and CS gas.

The plan involved a four-man team climbing out of a skylight, lowering themselves by rope to the iron gutter of the Victorian building, and then making their way along the edge of the roof, unroped, above a sheer eighty-foot drop to the prison yard.

They would then force an entry through the hole the prisoners had smashed in the roof. At the same time, three back-up squads would detonate charges to blow their way into the three lower floors of the wing, deal with any prisoners there and cut off the escape route of the rest.[11]

The police expressed horror at the plan, but it was the sort of thing we practised regularly in training. The assault began at five o'clock, an hour before dawn. It was a damp, drizzly morning, the worst conditions in which to be moving down a steeply pitched slate roof and along a slimy gutter that had not been cleaned since the prison was built.

The team, wearing gas masks and the familiar black overalls, began inching their way along the gutter, but they were spotted outlined against the night sky by a prisoner in B Wing on the other side of the prison yard, who yelled a warning.

As the leading SAS man reached the hole in the roof he was confronted by one of the rioters. The lead scout tossed a stun grenade between them and as the prisoner recoiled, he followed it with a CS gas canister.

The four-man team swarmed through the hole in the roof and there was a brief scuffle before the gas overcame the prisoners. Within seconds the hostage was being carried back along the roof and helped through the skylight to safety.

From the time of arrival at the prison it had taken the SAS team less than an hour to secure the release of the hostage and the restraint of the hostage-takers. That included all the preparation and planning; the actual operation had lasted less than seven minutes.

After returning control to the police, the SAS team were airborne and on their way back to Hereford less than two hours after landing in Scotland.

Operations against the IRA continued throughout the 1980s, but Peterhead was one of very few other ops mounted by the SAS within the UK. Our overseas workload steadily increased, mostly in BG and CT training, though there was still scope for active intervention in small-scale conflicts. One group of just three SAS men staged one of the most daring examples of the Regiment's ability to do the job whatever the circumstances.

The President of the Gambia, Sir Dawda Jawara, had come to Britain as a guest at the wedding of the Prince of Wales. His reward for ignoring the dictum that the leader of an insecure regime never leaves his country for any but the most pressing of reasons was to be overthrown in his absence by a Marxist coup on 29 July 1981.

There was no standing army in Gambia and no one to offer armed resistance to the 500-strong band of Cuban-backed rebels, who seized the airport and other key installations, and took several hundred hostages.

The SIS alerted the US and France, which also had interests in the Gambia, and contacted Hereford. In the absence of Mike Rose, Major Ian Crooke, the OC of B Squadron, took charge of the incident.

Ian was an anomaly in the system, a long-term serving officer with the SAS and one of the best advertisements for the merits of professional officers in the Regiment. He joined the SAS in the early 1970s as my troop commander and served continuously until he left in the mid-1980s. He understood how his men thought and acted in a way that few other officers did.

He rounded up just two SAS NCOs and they left for Paris at once, then transferred to an Air France flight to Banjul, the capital of the Gambia. Their passage through French airport security with holdalls full of weapons was smoothed by the GIGN.

Yundum airport, briefly held by the rebels, was already back in friendly hands, taken by a force of troops from Senegal, but after their initial disjointed attempt to advance on Banjul had been repulsed, they showed no inclination to try again.

Ian Crooke decided to show some SAS initiative. The three men slipped through the rebel lines and made their way into Banjul, where they discovered from the British ambassador that some of the hostages, including one of the President's two wives, were being held at the hospital.

The SAS men were unarmed because they expected to be searched before being allowed into the hospital, but used their fists to overpower the rebel guards and took their weapons from them. They led the hostages to the safety of the embassy and then returned to the airport to lead the Senegalese troops in a break-out. Within four days Crooke's three-man expeditionary force had ended rebel resistance and captured the leaders.

Attempts by the panic-stricken British Foreign Secretary to find out what was going on and recall the SAS men were hampered by the Head Shed in Hereford, who made the judicious if implausible claim that they had lost contact with Crooke. The end result, if not the means, must have eased the Foreign Secretary's worries. A British ally had been restored to power by three SAS men, at a cost not much more than three return air-tickets to Banjul.

The Americans could only gaze open-mouthed at such audacity – and success. Alarmed by the seemingly irresistible advance of Communism around the world, one of Ronald Reagan's first actions as President of the US had been to authorise a substantial increase in the defence budget. It included a huge rise in expenditure on the special forces, which the Reagan Doctrine put at the forefront of the war against Communism.

Even with such lavish funding, Delta Force had few chances to show its paces, still hedged around with an unwieldy planning and command structure and hampered by an increasingly nervous Congress.

The rest of the American military had refused to shoulder any responsibility for Eagle Claw, and had manifestly learned nothing from it, as the next major deployment involving Delta Force, the invasion of Grenada in October 1983, vividly demonstrated.

It was a pitiful spectacle. The invasion force was bedevilled with exactly the same faults as Eagle Claw: inter-service rivalries, confused command and control, an over-complex plan, bad intelligence and a host of other avoidable problems. A huge force of prodigiously equipped and supported troops from the world's most mighty nation struggled to overcome the spirited resistance of a few lightly armed Grenadans and Cubans.

Had armed intervention been necessary, which was in itself questionable, the former colonial power, Britain, would have been the obvious candidate, using the SAS. The Queen was still the head of state of Grenada and her governor-general, Sir Paul Scoon, was her representative on the island.

The Americans claimed to have received a letter from him prior to the invasion, requesting their military support, yet they only made it public on 27 October 1983, two days after the invasion, at a time when Sir Paul Scoon was in American hands. Few in the Regiment or in intelligence circles regarded the letter as anything other than a hasty attempt at retrospective justification for the US actions.

Coupled with the American disasters in Lebanon that year in which the US Embassy and a marine base were bombed with massive loss of life, the shambles in Grenada sent a message to the rest of the world that the American military was not up to the job. Whether it was entirely justified was irrelevant. The perception was what counted and in the wake of the Iranian Embassy siege, the worldwide perception was that the only truly effective counter-terrorist force was the SAS.

The contrast between the American and British approaches was pointed by the SAS deployment to Botswana in 1985. The South African Defence Force had been spreading their war against black nationalism wider and wider through southern Africa.

The SADF regularly violated the boundaries of their neighbours to carry out raids, bombings and assassinations. They routinely crossed Botswana's southern frontier and also used the Caprivi Strip in the north to infiltrate into Botswana and Zambia, and intervene on behalf of Unita forces in the Angolan civil war.

In June 1985 the SADF again crossed the border into Botswana, but this time their operation was launched inside the capital, Gaborone. The targets were a dozen alleged ANC guerrillas, who were murdered in their homes. Botswana, which did its best to prevent the ANC from operating from its territory, was outraged by this latest breach of its sovereignty and turned to Britain for help.

After Geoffrey Howe's customary pause for procrastination, approval was given and B Squadron was despatched to Botswana. As cover for the operation they were notionally deployed to Kenya, where we often trained. Another SAS squadron was already there, carrying out operations to suppress ivory poaching in the National Parks.

B Squadron then split up and made their way anonymously into Botswana in small groups travelling by different routes. Andy McNab and five colleagues travelled to Botswana via Zaire and Zambia under the implausible cover of a touring seven-a-side rugby team.

B Squadron carried out the training of the Botswana Defence Force in the Okavango, a area of lakes, rivers and marshes adjoining the infiltration corridor of the Caprivi Strip. The brief was to train soldiers of the BDF to resist the cross-border operations by the well-equipped South Africans.

In addition to the general training, the BDF soldiers were also put through a rudimentary form of Selection and the best of them were given specialised training in sabotage and aggressive counter-attack as a further deterrent to the South Africans.

The Americans supported us by supplying $10 million worth of military supplies – mainly helicopters to improve the BDF's mobility – and they trained them in counter-intelligence techniques to help them prevent South African agents from penetrating their ranks.

In theory, B Squadron's role was purely to provide training, safely distanced from any possibility of contact with the SADF. In practice, as the Botswanans began to interdict the South African infiltration routes and ambush their cross-border raiding parties, the SAS were close enough to the action to learn 'the Afrikaans for "Let's get the hell out of here," and the Botswanan for "Look at that Springbok run".'[12]

The SAS suffered one fatality during the operation, Staff Sergeant Joe Ferragher, killed not in action but in a climbing accident in the Tsodilo Hills.

The government of Botswana was delighted with the results of the SAS involvement. The SADF suffered some sharp reverses and from then on they were much more circumspect about violating Botswana's frontiers. Once more a small contingent of SAS had earned Britain a disproportionate increase in influence and trade.

While the SIS and the British government revelled in the influence and affluence that the SAS was bringing to Britain, a combination of bad luck and the increasing sophistication of terrorist hijackers denied Delta Force further opportunities to rehabilitate their reputation.

The kidnapping of the CIA station chief in Beirut, William Buckley, in March 1984 was another savage blow to the US, but it also had ramifications for every nation involved in the fight against terrorism. Under the most terrible and prolonged torture Buckley revealed virtually all the American counter-terrorist procedures and contingency plans.

The hijacking of a TWA flight by two Arabs in June of that year showed that the terrorists had already learned much about Western counter-terrorist tactics. The hijacked plane was kept constantly on the move, shuttling between Beirut and Algiers, the hijackers were swiftly reinforced by more armed terrorists and when the aircraft finally came to rest in Beirut the hostages were immediately dispersed to different locations around the city, making a rescue almost impossible.

An American hostage was shot, but the remainder were released after massive US pressure forced the Israelis to meet the terrorist demands and release 735 Shi'ite Muslims held in their jails. It was another humiliating reverse for the US.

Delta Force had tracked the hijacked jet without ever being able to get in a blow. They were similarly frustrated after the even more high-profile hijacking of the Italian cruise liner *Achille Lauro* in October 1984, though on this occasion the Americans at least had the satisfaction of saving face.

The assault teams, including Delta Force, were on stand-by but were prevented from intervening as the Egyptian government and the PLO brokered a peace deal. One hostage had been murdered, however, and the Americans intercepted the Egyptian jet carrying the terrorists to freedom in Algeria and forced it to land in Rome, where they were arrested and charged with murder.

SAS tactics had been thoroughly revised and refined in the face of the knowledge the terrorists had extracted from William Buckley, but the need for constant vigilance and absolute professionalism in the battle against terrorism was emphasised the following year in one of the most bloody hijackings ever.

On 23 November 1985, three terrorists armed with automatic pistols and grenades hijacked Egyptair flight MS64 out of Athens, taking ninety-eight passengers and crew hostage. The hijackers had evaded security at the airport, possibly by using corrupt ground crew to smuggle in their weapons, though they may just have carried them in themselves. Athens was notorious for its lax security, a hijacker's dream and the preferred gateway into Europe for Palestinian terrorists.

The three hijackers, all in their twenties, were members of Abu Nidal's extremist Palestinian faction. Throughout the course of the hijack they never made any demands. It was an ominous sign.

While still airborne over the Mediterranean, the hijackers began checking passengers' passports and segregating the Jews and Americans. One of the passengers was an undercover airline security guard, however, and he pulled his pistol and shot one of the hijackers dead.

The other two pumped six bullets into the security guard, but miraculously he survived. Four other undercover security guards on the flight showed infinitely less courage. They simply hid their pistols under the seats and continued to pretend to be normal passengers.

The gunfire had punctured the pressurised cabin and the aircraft went into an emergency dive. The pilot radioed Malta that he was in danger of ditching in the sea and the Maltese authorities gave reluctant permission for the jet to land at Luqa.

They refused to supply fuel for the aircraft until the terrorists released the hostages. Two stewardesses and eleven women passengers were released, but the terrorists then began carrying out a threat to kill one hostage every ten minutes until the plane was refuelled.

Two Israeli women were the first to die, shot and dumped out on the runway. An American man then had an incredible escape. A terrorist pushed him to the door of the aircraft and fired a bullet at his head, but it only grazed his skull. The American fell to the tarmac, played dead for a few minutes, then rolled under the fuselage and made his escape by running down to the tail and away across the runway.

An eighty-strong force of Egyptian commandos, including twenty-six men from the counter-terrorist unit Force 777, had already flown in on a C130. After the deaths of the hostages they made the decision to storm the aircraft. Delta Force were eager to get involved as well, but under pressure from the Egyptians the Maltese refused them permission to land.

The Egyptians then committed a catastrophic series of blunders. They did not debrief any of the released hostages or the American who had escaped and carried out no surveillance with listening devices or infra-red viewing equipment to locate the position of the terrorists within the aircraft.

The runway lights had been turned off early in the evening and then turned back on again, convincing the terrorists that an attack was about to be made. When the lights were turned off a second time, they went on to maximum alert.

The assault began at 8.45 that evening. The Egyptians organised no diversion and did not use stun grenades as they forced the emergency doors over the wings, but their greatest folly was to attempt a simultaneous entry at the rear of the aircraft from the baggage compartment beneath the floor.

Even if explosive charges had been used correctly, a soldier struggling up through a hole in the floor would have been a highly vulnerable target, but the Egyptians compounded the mistake by laying a charge that was many times too big for the job.

When it detonated, it blew six rows of seats off their mountings. The passengers in the seats were blasted against the roof of the aircraft and many of them died instantly.

Flames immediately engulfed the rear of the aircraft and as the Egyptian commandos hurled smoke grenades in through the emergency doors further forward, the whole cabin filled with dense smoke.

In near-nil visibility, the Egyptians could not distinguish the hostages from the terrorists, and the hostages could not find the exits to escape. The terrorists threw grenades and fired bursts from their automatic pistols at random into the smoke, killing hostages and Egyptian commandos alike.

Many of the passengers and crew who did manage to escape by groping their way to an exit and jumping from the burning plane were then shot by the Egyptian troops surrounding it.

When the smoke cleared and the firing finally stopped, fifty-seven of the hostages lay dead. Only one terrorist had been killed. It was a terrible warning of the dangers of using poorly trained troops to attempt hostage rescues.

The dangers of giving in to terrorist demands were equally well known, but Ronald Reagan chose to ignore that lesson. His election as President had been guaranteed by Jimmy Carter's failure to secure the release of the US hostages held in Iran. They were then freed within minutes of Reagan's inauguration in 1981 after a shabby and allegedly illegal deal, trading the hostages for the release of billions of dollars in frozen Iranian assets and a bribe of $150 million.[13]

After a series of Americans were taken hostage by Hizbollah in Lebanon during 1984 and 1985, Reagan made attempts to secure their release through another 'arms for hostages' deal with Iran, which was perceived as the direct sponsor of the terrorists.

Margaret Thatcher's approach to the problem of the seized British hostages, John McCarthy, Brian Keenan and Terry Waite, was the opposite of her American ally. She refused to consider any sort of deal and put the Regiment on stand-by to rescue the hostages. An SAS assault force actually practised a helicopter insertion into Beirut, but the operation was ultimately called off.[14]

Hizbollah had learned well the lessons of earlier hijacks and hostage-takings. Their hostages were well hidden and moved to new locations at regular intervals. Even though plans to free the British hostages by force had been abandoned, the Thatcher government still set its face against any negotiations or deals with the terrorists.

The US government was less squeamish, but its attempts to negotiate the release of American hostages descended rapidly into the blackest farce. Reagan's administration was deceived by the Iranians, by the Israelis who supplied many of the weapons to Iran, and by the queue of murky arms dealers lining up for a share of the action. The US was also undermined by the dubious activities of Colonel Oliver North and Richard Secord, who diverted proceeds from the sale of arms to the US-backed Contra rebels in Nicaragua, again in breach of US law.

As the Iran–Contra scandal became public it further tarnished America's image at home and abroad. Millions of missing dollars were never traced and Congressional outrage was further fuelled by Oliver North's admission to the Iran–Contra hearings that part of the earnings from the sale of arms to Iran had also been earmarked to create a 'stand-alone, self-financing' secret agency. Had the plan succeeded, the agency would have had the ability to conduct worldwide clandestine operations without authorisation from, or reporting to, anyone in the US government.[15]

The revelations about the activities of North and Secord were only part of the wave of scandals engulfing the US intelligence agencies. A Special Senate Committee chaired by Frank Church investigating past intelligence operations by the CIA resulted in fresh constraints, including a law signed by President Gerald Ford banning assassination attempts against foreign leaders. There were to be no more exploding cigars for Fidel Castro.

Congress's imposition of a system of greater public scrutiny, including the Freedom of Information Act, was an attempt to ensure that mavericks like North could never again ignore democratic controls and subvert US policy for their own ends. The largely unlooked-for consequence was that it became virtually impossible for the American secret services to run any clandestine operations at all.

Every major CIA station had a lawyer attached to it and every covert operation had to be scrutinised by the lawyer and approved by Congress. So intense was the Congressional scrutiny that even the most seasoned operatives were running scared of any direct involvement in unauthorised covert operations. Funds could still be provided, but the involvement of any American personnel was absolutely out of the question.

If one more scandal erupted, or an American died on such an operation, or its nature was revealed through the Freedom of Information Act, Congress was in the mood to shut the CIA down altogether.

The attitude of Congress made it more difficult for the Americans to carry out clandestine operations. Increasingly they looked towards their allies.

13

AFGHANISTAN
1982–89

The Secret Intelligence Service used to be housed in Century House, a bleak south London skyscraper dating from the 1960s.

Bill and I had made the journey there one autumn morning in 1982. Even though we were expected and had enough ID to satisfy the most sceptical policeman, the security checks were still interminable. At last we were cleared and shown into the office of the head of the Middle East Desk.

His prime area of concern at that time was Afghanistan, where the Soviet army had been fighting the Mujahedeen ever since the Soviet invasion almost three years before, in December 1979. After thanking us for agreeing to help even though we had left the Regiment some time before, he explained to us that 'our American cousins' were interested in attacking the air assets of the Russians and their client Afghan government.

'I've arranged a meeting with them,' he said. 'They have some information and intelligence for you to look at.'

We took a taxi to a building in central London. A group of Americans were waiting for us in the high-ceilinged meeting room. Two of them carried briefcases with elaborate security locks.

We were introduced by first names only and at first the Americans appeared reluctant to speak about anything other than the weather, but eventually our SIS contact called the meeting to order.

The Americans unlocked their briefcases and spread a mass of maps, charts, photographs and satellite imagery on the table in front of us. In the centre of the largest satellite photograph was a pin-sharp image of an airfield. Along the perimeter track, parked in military parade-ground style, were twenty-four Russian-built MiG 21 fighters. The imagery was spectacular, as good as I had ever seen.

We listened and made a few notes as the Americans explained their problem. Although the Mujahedeen were making great strides against the Russians, they were getting edgy. The air-power the Soviets and the Afghan government were deploying against them was causing a huge morale problem.

The Americans' spokesman shrugged his shoulders. 'Our hands are tied. Anything that we are involved in will eventually become public.' He paused and glanced across the table at me.

By now my heart was pounding. Surely they were not going to ask me to go into Afghanistan?

He gave a brief smile, as if he had read my thoughts. 'What we are looking for is an interpretation of the information in the images and a well-constructed plan of attack that the Mujahedeen can carry out them-selves. If you can come up with one, we'll transmit it to our contacts in Afghanistan and the Mujahedeen will attempt it.' He paused. 'Time's obviously a factor in this.'

I nodded. 'We'll look at it and let you have something tomorrow.'

They left us alone for the rest of the day, apart from an occasional phone call from the SIS man to ask how we were progressing.

We found most of the answers we needed in the imagery

and documentation but carried on right through the night and into the next day. After more than twenty-four hours' continuous work, we had what we thought was a viable plan.

The Americans came back with the SIS man in tow and we explained how we thought the job could be done. We had written out in great detail how to approach the target and how to attack the aircraft, using non-commercial explosives to blow off the tail sections. Nothing in the plan was beyond the capabilities of a reasonably well-trained soldier.

The Americans were delighted. Four weeks later we were again summoned to London. The Americans had come over in another great hurry, insisting on a further meeting with us.

We drove up to London, wondering what had gone wrong with our masterplan. We met in the same room in the building. The Americans' faces were wreathed in smiles as they came into the room.

They shook our hands like long-lost friends, then the bag-carrier opened his briefcase with a magician's flourish and laid out a row of satellite images on the table.

They were of the same area of Afghanistan and the picture he placed at the centre of the table was almost identical to the one we had seen on our previous meeting. There was one slight difference. There were still twenty-four MiG 21 fighters parked in a neat row along the perimeter track, but twenty-three of them had had their tail sections blown off.

Ex-SAS soldier, London, 1982

The well-established strategy of using indigenous forces to fight our battles by proxy became the basis of one of the deepest and darkest secrets of the Cold War: the involvement of the government in equipping and training the Afghan Mujahedeen.

The Americans were the paymasters of the operation, but instead of providing direct support to the Mujahedeen, they found it less politically dangerous to fund us to provide what was needed.

The SIS were the original point of contact and they had first attempted to train the Mujahedeen using their own resources. Under the false impression that the SBS and SAS were interchangeable, the SIS chose an ex-SBS officer to head the team. He recruited a couple of his former comrades, two ex-marines and a number of former marine support personnel such as commando engineers. The men had very little active service experience and their nautical background made them a curious choice for a conflict in an entirely land-locked country.

The Mujahedeen faction of choice for the SIS was that led by Ahmed Shah Mahsood in the Panshir Valley, near the border with the Soviet Union. The SIS team began work in 1981, training the Mujahedeen mainly in the use of communications equipment, in safe houses in Pakistan.

By 1982 the team were carrying out the training in-country, infiltrating from Pakistan, using pack-horses to carry supplies and equipment. It would be fair to say that the training was not a great success.

On their way out of the country after a training operation, they were ambushed by Soviet forces. The pack-horses loaded with the team's bergens and personal equipment were killed, and everything was lost, including the men's British passports. They escaped to Pakistan but they had handed the Soviets a propaganda coup. The passports were produced at a press conference as proof that the British were infiltrating agents into Afghanistan.

As a consequence of this public embarrassment, future operations became ever more unofficial. Some of my colleagues who had resigned from the SAS took part in a secret operation, funded by a third party, to provide military training for the Afghan Mujahedeen. In doing so, they were following a well-worn path taken by many of my predecessors in the Regiment. A path that allowed operations to take place which benefitted from the expertise of men trained by the SAS. Having left for personal reasons some of the men later rejoined the Regiment and continued their career.

In an earlier operation a couple of former Senior NCOs from the Regiment were recruited and sent into Afghanistan, where they had an immediate impact on the quality of the training. They could improve the Mujahedeen's communications and command and control skills in-country but it was not possible to teach aggressive tactics there; practising with live weaponry tended to attract unwelcome attention. Hence the plan my colleagues became involved in.

All the junior officers in Ahmed Shah Mahsood's faction – the men on the ground directing the fighting – were brought out of Afghanistan before the snows blocked the mountain passes for the winter and returned to Panshir with the two ex-SAS NCOs the following spring.

At first the training was carried out in Middle Eastern countries but soon the problems caused by running such a sensitive operation in the Middle East made things very tricky and a plan was arrived at to smuggle the Mujahedeen into the UK. Once the Mujahedeen had been brought into the country they were moved on to a house in the Home Counties which had a couple of acres and a barn.

The ex-SAS men provided a large tent which was erected inside the barn, and camp beds and a field kitchen to make the Mujahedeen as comfortable as possible. They were checked and most of them were found to be suffering from some sort of vitamin deficiency and, in some cases, malnutrition. The rest of the time that they were there was spent building them up to make them fit and healthy enough to go back and continue the fight.

Through their contacts in the military my one-time

colleagues had found three viable, remote and little-used training sites, one in the north of England, one just over the border in Scotland, and one further north on the west coast.

Supplies were no problem; the sponsor had very deep pockets and even the amount of equipment required to supply the Mujahedeen raised no eyebrows.

The Mujahedeen who were being trained were mainly junior commanders. They were very dedicated, extremely capable and quick to learn. They were also unshakeable in their belief that with a bit of help and training they could defeat the Soviet army. That belief turned out to be absolutely correct.

They were well armed and ferocious fighters, but they lacked battlefield organisation. Training in the use of communications enabled the junior commanders to deploy their men much more effectively in combat. They were also trained in the planning of operations, the use of explosives and the fire control of heavy weapons – mortars and artillery.

There was a strong empathy between the ex-SAS men and the Mujahedeen. They could discuss specific battlefield problems and provide constructive solutions based on their own combat experience. The Mujahedeen's greatest fear was of being attacked by aircraft, so it was arranged for them to do helicopter flights, just to show them how difficult it is to spot people on the ground when you're a couple of hundred feet in the air.

They were also shown how vulnerable aircraft are against someone who understands their limitations. Mine-tape was used to construct replicas of the installations where the Russian and government aircraft were kept and they rehearsed entry into bases, hangars and hardened aircraft shelters. They were shown how to attack aircraft on the ground and how to lay anti-aircraft ambushes aligned on the centre line of a runway, hitting them as they landed or took off, when they are most vulnerable.

They also learned to stage incidents to lure ground-attack

aircraft into narrow valleys where they could be destroyed by crossfire from the valley walls, and we taught them to mount linear anti-armour ambushes as well. They later showed their tremendous bravery by standing within fifty yards of columns of Soviet tanks to destroy them with rocket-propelled grenades.

As the information sank in, the growing confidence of the Mujahedeen could be seen. They were very grateful for the help and relations between the two groups were very friendly on a personal level but that did not translate into a corresponding warmth between the British government and the leaders of the Mujahedeen. It was strictly an anti-Communist marriage of convenience between two organisations that had nothing else in common.

The training paid swift dividends. Soviet losses of personnel and equipment mounted steadily over the next few years, rising to a peak of 2,343 Soviet troops killed in 1984. The scale of the casualties and the domestic unrest aroused by them forced the Soviets to adopt the strategy pursued by the Americans in the latter stages of the war in Vietnam.

Soviet forces were largely withdrawn from battlefield confrontation with the Mujahedeen. Instead they used air-power and long-range weapons against them and left the ground war to Afghan troops loyal to the Kabul regime. As a result, Soviet casualties dropped sharply, to 1,868 in 1985, and 1,333 in 1986.[1]

The Mujahedeen continued to hold the initiative in the war of attrition, but they could not deliver a knock-out blow. Part of the reason was the factionalism that divided them: there were around a hundred different organisations, split on tribal lines and often at war with each other as well as the regime in Kabul. The other crippling factor was Soviet air-power, particularly the helicopter-gunships that continued to exact a heavy toll.

The American response to the impasse was to step up military supplies to the Mujahedeen. Since the start of the conflict, huge amounts of equipment had been shipped to them, but to disguise its source most of it was Soviet-made, purchased from former Soviet client states such as Egypt, or from Israel, which had a vast armoury of captured equipment from its wars against its Arab neighbours.

By 1986 the US intelligence agencies were willing to fund the direct supply of sophisticated Western equipment, including hand-held surface-to-air missiles. The first shipments were two batches of 300 British Blowpipe missiles.[2] They were heavy and unwieldy, however, and did not have the desired impact. Before the end of the year the Americans had begun shipping their own lighter and more accurate Stingers, the weapon that had been used to such good effect by SAS patrols in the Falklands.

As well as attacking the Soviet helicopter-gunships – their most potent weapons in the conflict – the Mujahedeen frequently chose the much softer targets of passenger aircraft. Several were shot down with heavy loss of life. Newspaper reports linking Britain with the supply of the missiles led to furious Soviet protests, but 'deniability' allowed the British government to maintain an air of injured innocence.

Stingers did tilt the military balance of the war in Afghanistan a little further away from the Soviet forces, but exaggerated claims have been made for the missiles' role in forcing the Soviet withdrawal.

Mikhail Gorbachev came to power in the Soviet Union in 1985 and by February 1986 he had already committed himself to a withdrawal of all Soviet forces from 'the running sore' of Afghanistan within three years.

Soviet helicopter and aircraft losses may have increased his determination but they did not noticeably quicken the pace of withdrawal. As Gorbachev had pledged, the last Soviet troops left Kabul on 14 February 1989, just inside his three-year deadline.

There was one black irony in the American decision to supply Stingers to the Mujahedeen. After the disintegration of the Communist bloc, America found itself with a new public enemy number one: Muslim fundamentalism. The unused American Stingers supplied to shoot down Soviet aircraft in Afghanistan were now available for use elsewhere.

There was – and is – a genuine fear in Washington that the next targets for the Stingers will be American civilian or military aircraft. The initial wave of panic surrounding the mysterious loss of a civilian jumbo jet – TWA Flight 800 – off New York in July 1996 was not unconnected to the fear that a Stinger might have been responsible.

The Americans originally offered a covert $3 million ransom for the return of the Stingers. When they received intelligence reports that Libya was trying to buy them, the ransom was immediately increased to $30 million. It has yet to be paid and the present whereabouts of the missiles remains unknown.

The disappearance of the Stingers was only one of the dangers for the West in the use of the traditional Cold War strategy employed in Afghanistan: 'my enemy's enemy is my friend'. Many of the 15,000 Saudi Arabian volunteers fighting for the Muslim cause in Afghanistan[3] returned home with an undiminished zeal for holy war, not just against godless Communists but against American imperialists too, as the subsequent bomb outrages at US bases in Saudi Arabia were to demonstrate.

Shi'ite Muslims and Iran are the traditional scapegoats for internal troubles in Saudi Arabia, but the men who carried out the attacks on US bases were Sunni Muslims, just like the Mujahedeen and the Taliban regime that has assumed power in Afghanistan.

The role of Pakistan in the Afghan conflict further strengthened the hand of the fundamentalists. Virtually all supplies to the Mujahedeen had to be routed through Pakistan. They were air-freighted into the country and then carried over the border – the celebrated North-West Frontier – into Afghanistan.

The Islamic regime in Pakistan had its own agenda for the conflict and ensured that, whatever the wishes of the American paymasters, most of the equipment and supplies found their way to fundamentalist rather than moderate Mujahedeen groups.

The British and Americans had secured the result they wanted in Afghanistan and there is little doubt that 'Russia's Vietnam' had played no small part in accelerating the decline and fall of the Soviet Empire. It did not cause its collapse, however, despite the claims of some senior figures in the American intelligence community. Western support for the Mujahedeen has also left a dangerous legacy of sophisticated military equipment in hostile hands.

Whether in the long term a pro-Soviet regime in Kabul was more damaging to Western interests than the present fundamentalist rule of the Taliban is an open question, but in the short term there were no such doubts. The dividends for Britain in every sphere of interest were very substantial.

The British Prime Minister's international power and influence was now at its zenith. It was to be further strengthened by an unofficial operation involving ex-SAS men in another unofficial war by proxy, the last conflict of the Cold War era. Despite constant tension between Thailand and Cambodia the Thais' traditional allies, the Americans, were finding it almost impossible to obtain political clearance for clandestine operations. The Freedom of Information Act ensured that the skeletons could no longer be relied on to stay buried. The threat of exposure coupled with the political fall-out if there were any American casualties made US officials very twitchy. They could offer money and intelligence but there would be no other support.

The Thais looked elsewhere and two ex-SAS NCOs were soon on their way to Thailand. They were met in Bangkok by a senior General in the Thai army. He outlined his problem to the two men.

The Khmer Rouge atrocities in the killing fields of Cambodia had driven several million refugees across the border into Thailand, where their sprawling camps were creating massive problems for the Thais. The general saw the refugees as a financial drain on his country and a potent source of domestic unrest. The only way he could see to get the refugees to return to Cambodia was to defeat the Khmer Rouge militarily and replace them with a more democratic regime.

The Thais could have carried out a conventional attack, but that risked a very expensive and open-ended commitment. Any overt aggression could also have provoked a reaction from the Vietnamese or Chinese, who had their own agendas for Cambodia. The Vietnamese had invaded in 1979 and installed their own regime in Phnom Penh, but the Khmer Rouge still controlled most of the rest of the country, including the northern and western areas bordering Thailand.

The general's plan was to achieve his ends by more covert means. He wanted us to set up a camp near the border and train anti-Khmer factions who would return to Cambodia and start a civil war against the Khmer Rouge.

From the point of view of the two experienced ex-SAS men the mechanics of the operation were simple. The camp could be built and kept secret, and the training was relatively straightforward. As long as the quality of the intelligence being fed to the operation was good there would be no problem. Through his interpreter the general assured the two men that it was. The two ex-SAS men began the job of assessing possible sites for the training camp. When they asked for information on conditions in Cambodia they were put in contact with an officer in the Thai Special Forces. It soon transpired that he had spent most of the last three years operating inside Cambodia against the Khmer Rouge. It became obvious to the two Englishmen what the General was really after. He wanted the Cambodians to be trained to support his own Special Forces.

After finishing their reconnaissance the two men made

their report, the camp was set up and over the next few weeks a succession of unofficial teams, all made up of ex-SAS men, went out to Thailand. They trained a very large number of Cambodians who were then sent across the border in the classical way. The operations inside Cambodia were supported by Intelligence supplied by the Thais and the Americans. They were a complete success, leading to the first military defeat of the Khmer Rouge. Once again the expertise of even ex-SAS men had proved its worth and the UK government was able to reap the benefits of improved relations with a foreign state and increased influence in a far-flung region of the world. The Cambodian forces, trained by the men who had themselves received the best military training available, built on their early successes and by September 1989, the military pressure had forced the withdrawal of Vietnamese troops from Cambodia. Following the Soviet pull-out of Afghanistan in February of that year, it effectively signalled the end of the Cold War.

There were to be no more surrogate wars against Soviet client states or Soviet-backed insurgents and all the assumptions that had underlain Western military strategy for over fifty years now had to be re-examined.

The collapse of the rusting Iron Curtain led to the greatest upheaval in the armed forces since the Second World War and the disbandment of many army regiments and air force squadrons and the scrapping of navy ships. Almost unnoticed among those wholesale changes was the disappearance of one of the most curious products of the Cold War.

14

COLD WAR
1945–90

We were travelling north along a narrow road on the outskirts of Neustrelitz in East Germany. It took us past the edge of a field firing range used by the Soviet garrison.

The Range Rover was very conspicuous in a country where the transport consisted of nothing but Russian military vehicles, Trabants and Ladas. It also had a Union Jack painted on the front and back number plates.

My companions were equally conspicuous. Hugh McLeod was tall and red-haired with a broad Scots accent. Our driver, Wayne Fury, had the look and the name of a fading fifties rock star. His rather less macho nickname was Furry. He was from the Royal Corps of Transport and had previously chauffeured a brigadier around. Like Hugh, he was brave to the point of foolhardiness. I had the experience and hopefully the cool head, and together we made quite a formidable team.

As we passed the range, I glanced to my left and saw a group of the defenders of the Russian Soviet, dressed in uniforms best described as functional. They glanced our way, showing no recognition; they were probably unable to differentiate between the Range Rover and their own military vehicles.

We had set out from Potsdam a couple of hours before. We had a roving commission, but we knew that Intelligence was desperate for information on the new

Kalashnikov AK74 rifle, the prime infantry weapon that was just beginning to be issued to Soviet troops.

If we could establish the calibre of the rifle, Intelligence could assess its capabilities, the likely cost and time of manufacture and the likely resupply requirements for a major battle. The Russians were fighting the war in Afghanistan at the time and the West was hungry for any intelligence it could get.

If the group of soldiers we could see were firing AK74s, there was a possibility of a round being left on the ground. I logged this with Hugh and we drove on to check the railway sidings at the northern end of the range.

As we crossed the railway bridge, I could see several flat-bed railway trucks in the sidings. On them were a number of Russian tanks. All were tarpaulined but the outline of the front plate of one of them made me 99 per cent certain that it was the latest Soviet main battle-tank, the T-64.

We continued north, pretending to have no interest, but Hugh managed to blast off a burst of pictures with the Nikon camera on his lap. We drove a few miles along the road and then pulled off into the woods.

We spent several hours drinking tea and eating sandwiches, waiting for darkness. As with every job in the army, most time is spent hanging around, waiting to do something later.

At dusk we drove back towards the range. We were desperately keen not to be seen. The amount of traffic in East Germany was extremely light but there was always a possibility of an accidental meeting with a Stasi or Soviet vehicle.

Furry swung the Range Rover off the road and we bumped across the uneven ground. Peering into the gathering darkness, I spotted a slightly raised bank with firing pits dug into its side. It was obviously the firing point of a small-arms range.

We checked the area to make sure no one was nearby,

then Hugh and I climbed out of the car. It was now almost pitch black but we could not risk showing a light. Hugh got down on his hands and knees and started feeling for any rounds that might have been left.

I began my own search in less orthodox fashion by tripping over something in the dark and falling into the firing pit. I landed at the bottom on my hands and knees. My right hand was resting on something small, smooth and very hard. It was a live round. I knew at once that it was not an AK47 round. I was extremely familiar with them, having used the weapon several times in different campaigns. This one was smaller, very similar to the American ·556 Armalite round.

I whispered to Hugh, 'I've found one.'

'You jammy bastard.'

'Nonsense. The SAS make their own luck.'

As I was scrabbling for purchase to get out of the pit, my left hand closed around another piece of metal. I put a second AK74 round into my pocket.

We were both giggling at our luck. On a British army firing range every single round would be accounted for and any soldier losing one would be placed on a charge. The Soviets obviously did not operate the same system.

We spent a couple more hours searching in vain for another round, but as we left the range Hugh looked at me. 'We might as well ride our luck.'

I knew exactly what he meant. 'Let's do it.'

If we could get a sample of the titanium armour of the Glacis plate of a T-64, the front plate, where the armour was thickest, our intelligence could analyse it and develop counter-measures against the tank.

We parked just short of the bridge and left Furry observing while Hugh and I walked down the road to the siding. We were quite brazen about it. If we sneaked down there and somebody saw us they would be immediately suspicious. Instead we marched openly up to the flat-bed and climbed on to the T-64.

Hugh dug below the tarpaulin covering the Glacis plate, while I stared imperiously around me, like Montgomery surveying his troops before El Alamein.

I looked straight at the signal box about 100 yards to our right and gave a casual wave to the signalmen. They waved back, then turned away, disinterested. We spent several minutes cutting through the toughened paint with a hacksaw to expose the bright metal and then scratched a sample from the Glacis plate with a super-hard, tungsten-tipped tool shaped like a fountain pen. Then we carefully rearranged the tarpaulin, jumped down and marched smartly back to the Range Rover.

'And now?' Hugh said.

'We've been lucky. Let's not push it any further. What we have, we want to keep.'

We abandoned the rest of our patrol and returned to Berlin with our booty. In around twelve hours we had achieved the two things that the entire mission had been trying and failing to do for several months. It was not luck, just experience – or that's what I told Hugh, anyway.

The author, Neustrelitz, East Germany, 1981

During the late 1970s and early 1980s I had been posted to Berlin for a tour of duty with Brixmis – the British Commander-in-Chief's Mission to the Soviet Forces in East Germany.

Based in the Olympic Stadium in Berlin and a forward base in a lakeside mansion in Potsdam, the mission was a form of institutionalised spying, a legacy of the Four-Power Agreement in Berlin, set up following the Second World War. Brixmis snooped on Warsaw Pact forces in East Germany while the Soviet equivalent, Soxmis, spied on NATO troops from its base at Bunde in West Germany. Later, there were also French and US missions.

Since neither side trusted the other, it was the only way of ensuring compliance with the Four-Power Agreement. Manoeuvres and troop deployments could be detected and monitored, and new military equipment threatening the precarious balancing act between the two sides' forces could be analysed and countered.

Over the years the missions also came to play an important part in maintaining peace. There was constant misinterpretation of the other side's intentions and to some extent both camps also believed their own propaganda; both East and West suspected their rivals would make a preemptive strike at the first opportunity.

The Brixmis and Soxmis teams observing military activity and troop deployments on the ground could apply an often necessary douche of cold water to the occasional bursts of Armageddon frenzy. No matter what Soviet propaganda or CIA or SIS analysts might be saying about Soviet intentions, if their troops were still in their barracks, they were not planning a pre-emptive strike.

Humint – intelligence gathered by human operatives – had been relegated to a distant second place by the rise in importance of sigint – signals intelligence – but, just like the SAS, Brixmis provided repeated reminders of the irreplaceable value of having human eyes on the target.

Brixmis had a system grading the likelihood of an outbreak of hostilities from nought to nine. On one occasion, the indicator of hostilities stood at nine. Huge numbers of Soviet bloc forces had deployed from their barracks to the assembly areas from which they would launch an attack on the West.

We knew because our operatives on the ground were telling us so. The reports were initially dismissed in London because GCHQ – the fount of all wisdom and sigint – had no evidence of any deployment whatsoever.

The Soviets had unsportingly moved their forces in total

radio silence, depriving GCHQ of the normal barrage of radio noise that accompanied deployments. Fortunately, it proved to be an exercise rather than the prelude to total war, but it was a timely warning of the importance of gathering intelligence by every available means.

Brixmis had a staff of close to 200 people, but of those only thirty people actually went on operational tours inside East Germany. Apart from the reconnaissance teams in the field, there were photographic technicians to maintain the cameras and audio equipment, and process the film and surveillance tapes. A number of analysts evaluated the intelligence and hardware that we obtained, linguists translated the intercepted or purloined documents from Russian or German into English, and archivists sorted and sifted the mountains of data.

The Brixmis maps of East Germany were extremely good, the product of years of work by the team of mapmakers within the mission from data supplied by the reconnaissance teams. The maps were constantly updated, with particular attention to any new buildings or features over thirty feet high. In the event of a general war, RAF aircraft would have been penetrating East Germany at those extremely low altitudes.

There were even a couple of RAF pilots attached to the mission, flying Chipmunk civilian light aircraft on surveillance operations from RAF Gatow. From time to time they were fired on and returned to base with a few more bullet-holes in the wings.

There were also a number of East German domestic staff at the Mission House in Potsdam. Under the curious protocols of the Four-Power Agreement, they were directly employed by the Soviet government and every single one of them was controlled by the Stasi or the KGB.

They were kept out of secure areas and had no access to secret material, but we would occasionally toss them a bone – a bit of innocuous information that they could feed to their masters to keep them happy. If they never supplied any information they risked losing their jobs.

We operated at all times – even in our domestic lives – under the assumption that anything we said was being over-heard and passed to the Soviets, but, surprisingly, they made few attempts to bait 'honey-traps' by using glamorous domestic staff to entrap members of the mission.

Brixmis training in covert observation, photography and equipment recognition was done at the Military Intelligence Centre at Ashford in Kent. SAS men were excused most of it since our own training covered the same ground, but we all had to pass one test, correctly identifying almost 1,000 different pieces of Warsaw Pact military equipment ranging from bullets and rifles to tanks and aircraft.

Ostensibly I was just another member of Brixmis, accredited to the Soviet army. Excluding certain defined PRAs – Permanent Restricted Areas – around airports and other key installations, we were free to go anywhere in East Germany.

After the stress of constant active service tours in Dhofar, I found the operational tours for the mission almost relaxing, and even the PRAs presented few problems. We became adept at navigating our way into them through mazes of tiny unmarked roads without ever passing a sign warning us that the area was barred to military missions.

Even if we were caught we usually faced few problems. To their constant fury, the Stasi had no jurisdiction over us at all. If they stopped us, it was classed as an illegal detention. The mission reported directly to the Soviet forces in East Germany and only they had the power to detain us. Although they could threaten us with all sorts of dire fates, if we had anything like a plausible alibi they had to let us go in the end.

We carried no radios or other communications equipment, which were forbidden under the terms of the Four-Power Agreement, and once we crossed the Glienicke Bridge into hostile territory we were on our own. If problems occurred, we had to solve them ourselves.

If the Stasi or the military decided we were showing too much interest in something or were operating in an area they did not wish us to see, they would take steps to intercept or delay us, or even ram us. A sergeant-major with the French Mission was killed in one such incident after being rammed by an East German army truck, and one of the British Chiefs of Mission, Brigadier John Learmont, narrowly escaped a similar fate after another ramming. In the early 1980s a US tour officer was shot by a sentry, causing a major international incident.

The normal level of harassment was rather less severe – an interminable interrogation if caught in a restricted area – but even arrest by the Stasi or Soviet forces could yield priceless intelligence. The first sight of the new AK74 rifle by any Westerner came when an excitable Soviet soldier poked it through the open window of a Brixmis car to threaten the occupants. By the time he withdrew it they had taken the serial number, noted its characteristics and covertly photographed it.

Brixmis reconnaissance teams were charged with checking on the movement of Soviet bloc troops and reporting on deployments in times of heightened tension. We also assessed technical developments in Soviet equipment and, if necessary, we would take samples – like the scratching of titanium tank armour and the AK74 rounds that Hugh McLeod and I obtained.

Much of our work was routine 'shit-digging', however, scouring rubbish bins or sifting the detritus of military exercises, including human excrement. Soviet shortages of consumer goods extended to toilet paper and it was by no means unknown for pages from secret documents to be used in an emergency.

The information collected was often trivial in isolation, but in total could be very valuable. And every now and again out of the mountain of shit would come a nugget of pure gold.

On one occasion a colleague, Graham Geary, and I were searching the rubbish of a Soviet barracks at Neustrelitz in northern East Germany. The troops were rotated every few months and those departing simply dumped their rubbish on public land near the back gate. Among the items we found this time was a logbook, compiled in neat cyrillic script and illustrated with technical drawings.

I could tell from the buzz among the mission staff when they began to examine it that we had found something very valuable. A couple of weeks later a senior intelligence officer asked me, 'Do you want to know about the stuff you brought back from Neustrelitz?'

I shook my head. 'It's better if I don't. I might end up in Soviet hands one of these days.'

'Fair enough. But if I told you it was the most important thing we've had from any source for ten years would you be impressed?'

I certainly was. Many years later, long after I had left Brixmis, they finally told me the contents of the logbook. It contained detailed data about the performance, strengths and weaknesses of the latest Soviet battle tanks, the T-64 and even its planned successor the T-80. It also gave details of other Soviet armoured warfare equipment including a plough attached to tanks which rendered anti-tank mines ineffective, digging them up and pushing them aside.

Within weeks of obtaining the information NATO had responded by pushing through a massive increase in anti-tank missiles and weapons as a temporary expedient to counter the threat. In the longer term, that one piece of intelligence influenced the development of reactive armour on the next generation of NATO tanks and anti-tank missiles.

Sometimes the importance of intelligence gathered by Brixmis was less immediately apparent. The fearsome Soviet helicopter-gunship, the Hind, had been thought to be unfly-able in severe winter weather because snow and icing adversely affected the rotors. A reconnaissance team then observed an exercise held in East Germany in appalling winter weather early in 1978 which gave the lie to the theory.

It was filed away as an interesting but not particularly useful piece of intelligence until the following year, when the Soviet invasion of Afghanistan began in the depths of the Afghan winter. Hind helicopters had a devastating impact on the forces resisting the invasion.

Brixmis's impact on the Soviets was less dramatic, but it was not confined to the intelligence we collected, valuable though that was. The expertise shown by the junior officers and senior NCOs also had an undoubted psychological effect on the Russians.

The Brixmis personnel were extremely dedicated and well trained and in the case of the NCOs were specially selected to work there. The level of expertise of a British army sergeant in the mission was at least comparable to that of a senior captain in the Soviet forces.

That was not lost on the Russians and contributed to a feeling of inferiority. As I told one Soviet commanding officer who expressed incredulity that I, a mere NCO, was leading a Brixmis tour, 'In the British army, you'd be working for me.'

Although the British Army of the Rhine was tiny in comparison to the number of Soviet troops in East Germany, the Russians knew that if the Cold War ever turned hot the consequences for themselves would not have been good.

One of the major problems that the Soviet forces faced – and one of the reasons they admired the British army – was that British troops in the field could break down to units as small as one or two men.

The smallest group the Soviets could let loose had to be commanded by a lieutenant and every single Soviet vehicle had an officer of at least the rank of lieutenant sitting alongside the driver to make sure he didn't get lost.

While I worked at Brixmis we had East German or Soviet shadows constantly monitoring our movements and activities behind the Iron Curtain, but when we needed to lose them we did so easily; they were less than wholly professional.

They were also less than well equipped, especially their vehicles, which were a mixture of clapped-out Trabants and Ladas. We could comfortably outrun them. If we wanted to pass unnoticed after dark, our Range Rovers had a switch that changed the front and rear light configurations to resemble those of a Trabant. If that didn't work, we had a further trick up our sleeves once NVGs – night-vision goggles – became available. We could turn off the lights altogether and blast off into the darkness at top speed.

The Soviets caught us on one occasion, however, when the mission car we were driving burst into flames. We were in the early stages of the tour and had a full load of fuel – almost 120 gallons, since the mission cars were fitted with reserve tanks to increase our range.

I was less concerned about the risk of an explosion than about the Soviets getting their hands on our cameras, including the film we had just taken in a forbidden area. We grabbed all the gear and took off across the fields. I ran as far as I could in twenty minutes, buried the stuff and then headed back to the burned-out wreck of the car, which was now surrounded by Stasi and East German civilians.

We were hauled off to the local Soviet headquarters and interrogated at length while troops combed the area, searching for the cameras and surveillance gear they knew we must have had. They did not spread the net wide enough, however, considerably underestimating the distance that an SAS man – even a forty-year-old one – could cover when the adrenalin was pumping.

In the end they had to let us go. Hugh Mcleod picked us up in another car and on our way back, having shaken off our tail, we retrieved the buried cameras.

Soviet forces also had their own clandestine operations on our side of the Wall, of course, many of them carried out by the Soviet special forces, the Spetsnaz.

The one installation in East Germany that was very difficult – though not impossible – to penetrate was the base at Furstenburg where the Spetsnaz carried out much of their training. The base was so secret that even regular Soviet troops were banned from it.

The Soviets placed a far greater emphasis on special forces than the West and many Western analysts and journalists accorded the Spetsnaz a correspondingly fearsome reputation. Twenty-five thousand strong, the Spetsnaz were supposed to be used both as shock troops and in SAS-type roles of deep penetration and intelligence-gathering, including the establishment of covert OPs and the capture or kidnapping of military or government personnel. They were also trained to carry out target designation and sabotage, and secure landing zones and dropping zones for other troops.

They were highly specialised and did little of the cross-training in other disciplines that we regarded as essential. Largely as a result of that inflexibility, they operated in larger patrols than the SAS – four to ten men.

They were trained in combat survival and escape and evasion, but because of the relative freedom of movement in the West much Spetsnaz covert infiltration was to be done by conventional means. They were to penetrate every NATO country, travelling in plain clothes, and arriving disguised as merchant seamen, aircraft flight crew, lorry drivers, tourists or students.

To produce 25,000 Russian soldiers capable of maintaining their cover while speaking the colloquial language of their target country would have taken decades and the GNP of the entire Soviet bloc, but the almost mystical belief in Spetsnaz capabilities led some Western journalists and military analysts to credit them with remarkable powers of infiltration and deception.

It was even reported that teams of women Spetsnaz had joined the peace camp outside the Cruise missile base at Greenham Common.[1] Such journalistic credulity may well have been fuelled by disinformation from MI5, aimed at discrediting the peace movement.

The primary tasks of the Spetsnaz were: 'Reconnaissance ... to subvert the political, economic and military potential and morale of a probable or actual enemy ... acquiring intelligence on major economic and military installations and either destroying them or putting them out of action; organising sabotage and acts of subversion; carrying out punitive operations against rebels; conducting propaganda; forming and training insurgent detachments.'[2]

The Spetsnaz were also to seek to assassinate key figures and spread panic among the civilian population through random terror attacks and the use of chemical or biological agents. Ports, airfields, bridges, road and rail junctions and power stations would also be targeted, and specifically military targets would include nuclear installations, command and control facilities, radar and communications, fuel and ammunition dumps.

Under Soviet military plans all this would have taken place before the outbreak of open hostilities. The theory was fine but the practice proved very different. The fearsome reputation of the Spetsnaz was largely based on an enormous misapprehension by those Western analysts and journalists – a large majority – who either believed or were led to believe that the Soviet forces were roughly equal in capability to those of the West.

Before I went to Brixmis, I read every available publication on the Soviet forces. What immediately struck me as strange was that in every single conflict in the Middle East – and there were enough of them – between forces using Western and Soviet equipment, the West had won.

I also found that every 'expert' analysis of Soviet forces, equipment and tactics contained serious misrepresentations of their actual capabilities.

My own view is that all such analysis was driven by hidden agendas. The analysts were keen to secure their future prospects by making themselves experts in fields where no one else was operating. Senior officers in the Western armed forces were delighted to have 'objective' evidence showing the need for ever higher levels of troops and ever more complex and expensive equipment to counter the Soviet threat. It can be safely assumed that the industries supplying that equipment were no less delighted by the analysts' conclusions.

Brixmis was in a position to correct the false impressions, but its staff too had their future to consider. The mission gathered copious intelligence on the Soviet forces' equipment and tactics, but in common with the vast majority of intelligence analysts it did not use the data to make an accurate assessment of the capability of the Soviet forces.

When I began observing the Soviet bloc forces in the field it was immediately evident to me that they could not go anywhere without everything breaking down. I tried to get an analysis done of what percentage of Soviet equipment broke down. No one was interested because it did not fit the prevailing agenda.

Analysts often interpreted intelligence data in ways that amounted to a complete misrepresentation. On one occasion I witnessed a Soviet engineer company attempting a river crossing near Havelburg. They practised it for three weeks. At the end of the three weeks some tanks appeared. The engineer company dropped a bridge into place and within half an hour the tanks were across.

I included that in my report, having already reported fifteen times that they were practising the crossing at the same place. A few months later I saw an analysis from the School of Military Intelligence in Ashford. Under a banner headline it announced that the Soviets had a capability of crossing a major river in thirty minutes. What it did not say was that they could only do that if they practised at the same place for three weeks first.

The Spetsnaz were viewed through the same rose-coloured filters. Analysts – and those journalists and authors who used them as sources – have lavished praise on the Spetsnaz, crediting them with almost superhuman powers.

The truth is that although similar in concept to the US Special Forces, they were nowhere near as well trained. They were conscripts not regular soldiers, lifted from the ranks of the Soviet army and given some extra training. That was enough to make them Spetsnaz.

The fact that they arrived in East Germany in cattle wagons showed that their true status was far from elite and their true capabilities were shown in Afghanistan, where the Mujahedeen wiped the floor with them.

Britain's vulnerability to Spetsnaz-type operations was grossly exaggerated, because during exercises the MoD used the SAS and SBS to simulate Spetsnaz operations. During Brave Defender, a large-scale exercise held in 1985, military, police and civil authorities combined with British and US military forces to defend key installations. The targets, including nuclear weapon stores, missile sites, airfields, command and control centres and nuclear power stations, were then attacked by SAS and SBS patrols. Almost all the attacks were successful, giving the Spetsnaz myth another boost.

While the Spetsnaz was rehearsing for its role in the Third World War, the SAS was preparing for its. While the siege of the Iranian Embassy was bringing the SAS brand of counter-terrorism to the attention of a worldwide audience, the Regiment was also carrying out one of its periodic re-examinations of its role in other theatres of operations. It resulted in a significant shift in our contingency plans for war against the Soviet bloc.

In the event of war, one Territorial regiment, 23 SAS, had the job of organising 'rat runs' to smuggle people out from behind enemy lines. The other Territorials, 21 SAS, had an essentially passive role. In times of acute tension they would deploy to preprepared hides designed to protect them against NBC – nuclear, biological, chemical – attack, and sited overlooking 'choke-points' on lines of communication. They would lie hidden as the Soviet forces advanced over them, and then supply intelligence on troop movements and the deployment of reinforcements.

The only problem was getting the weekend soldiers to rehearse their role. What they really wanted to do was look cool in dark glasses and practise storming the Iranian Embassy. If an exercise was laid on involving a simulated attack or a hostage rescue, every SAS Territorial soldier and most of his mates as well would turn up. If the exercise was to practise what they would actually be doing in wartime – lying up in an OP and carrying out covert surveillance – their instructors would be lucky to get a dozen people attending.

The regular Regiment, 22 SAS, had a more aggressive role in the event of all-out war with the Soviet bloc, with an area of responsibility extending from twenty-five to 250 miles behind enemy lines. Until the late 1970s, however, much of the strategic thinking of the SIS on the use of the Regiment had revolved around the idea of 'stay-behind parties'.

If the Cold War ever turned hot and the Soviets began a push on Western Europe, special forces were to go into the occupied territories and train and arm gangs of civilians to carry out attacks and acts of sabotage. Throughout the Cold War a full SAS squadron was allocated to the task.

The concept was modelled on the Second World War Resistance movements and, in our view, was very outdated. An SAS sergeant at that time would have had a minimum of ten years' training. We didn't feel we needed any help from civilians on the ground. The only useful assistance they could have given us would have been a drawing of the actual target.

I wrote the paper that led to the Regiment's change of strategy in Eastern Europe. The role of the stay-behind parties was altered from controlling special forces to assisting them. Our role would now be the classic SAS strategy: deep penetration and intelligence-gathering.

By bringing the stay-behind strategies up to date we also fostered closer ties with some of our European allies. If the

SAS were involved, the Italians, Germans, Dutch, Norwegians – even the French – suddenly wanted to know.

The Dutch, who have long memories, had never forgiven the SIS for their part in a disastrous SOE operation during the Second World War which the Germans called *Englandspiel* – the English game. With the SAS now taking the active role, Dutch forces joined us in a training exercise, the first joint exercise between British and Dutch forces in forty years.

Despite some successes in intelligence-gathering, my attachment to Brixmis was just a cover for my real mission. I was tasked directly by the British Army on the Rhine HQ at Rheindahlen, and only one other person in Berlin knew what I really did.

In the event of general war, one SAS squadron would be operating on the northern flank in Scandinavia and northeast Russia, one on the southern flank infiltrating from Turkey, one was to be held as a mobile reserve and the fourth would be inserted into Russia and East Germany, operating alone, without civilian involvement.

While ostensibly working with Brixmis, I and a handful of other SAS men were actually establishing potential landing sites, OP sites and targets for that eventuality.

Those tasks would sometimes require me to ask my driver to make unexplained journeys and detours, well away from our normal routes for the mission. He raised an occasional eyebrow, but that was as close as he ever got to questioning me. I never told him anything and he'd been in the forces long enough to know that sometimes it's better not to know.

Some of the targets I was selecting were disarmingly humble ones, but in the event of a war their destruction would have crippled the Soviet advance. Whenever the Soviet forces were on the move, they would put out men they called 'regulators'. Their job was to stand at every road junction and turning, and use black and white striped batons to signal to the Soviet vehicles which way to go.

They were dropped off up to forty-eight hours before a move and, if they were lucky, were picked up again afterwards, but sometimes they had to find their own way back. This laughable system not only indicated the route of the planned advance as effectively as sending a plan to NATO HQ, it also made it very easy to stop it dead. If SAS patrols had killed a few of the traffic regulators, the Soviets literally would not have known which way to turn.

The only time I ever saw a Soviet soldier with a map was when I was observing a Soviet Armoured Reconnaissance Regiment. It was supposedly a crack unit, the very best of the best Soviet armoured units.

The line of about eighteen armoured vehicles was passing our OP along a forest track when they suddenly came to a halt right opposite us. We froze, thinking they had spotted us, but then the turret of the first armoured vehicle opened and an officer got out clutching an enormous map. He spread it across the front of the vehicle but it appeared to be the first time he'd ever seen a map – he was reading it as if it were the *Daily Telegraph*.

After a lengthy pause, he got back into the vehicle and closed the turret. The entire armoured column then did an about-turn and disappeared back the way they had come. If a British officer – or even a private, for that matter – had produced a similar piece of incompetence, he'd have been cashiered on the spot.

I had been in the army for about twenty years by then and in terms of active service was one of the most experienced men in the armed forces. I felt I was reasonably well qualified to pass judgement on the capabilities of other forces and I never rated the Soviet troops as anything higher than Fourth Division quality.

This led me to wonder what the two armed camps were doing confronting each other in Germany. I read in the papers that we were terrified of the Russians, but I could see no justification for that whatsoever; if they had tried to invade us, they could not even have found their way to the Channel ports.

The Soviets rightly feared our armed forces, but their claims to be terrified of an attack from the West also seemed to be years, if not decades, out of date.

It seemed to me just as plausible to argue that all the Warsaw Pact and NATO troops were actually based in Germany to stop the West Germans starting a war. Virtually every resident of Berlin had relatives living in East Germany – occupied territory under Russian control. They would have done anything to liberate East Germany.

I asked one prominent German what he thought would happen in the event of a Third World War. 'The Allies would be in Moscow inside four days,' he said.

'It wouldn't be like that, surely,' I said.

'I think it would. They'd want to stop the Bundeswehr [the West German army] getting there first.'

He could have been right. No one in the West trusted the Bundeswehr and the Soviets were equally mistrustful of the East German NVA, the National Volks Army.

The SAS were not the only ones operating illicitly in East Germany. The Americans also had an Alpha team in West Berlin whose job was to monitor and reconnoitre ways of breaching the Berlin Wall to infiltrate troops into East Germany if war broke out.

Although it was strictly forbidden, I had a number of clandestine briefings from the A-team, without the knowledge of anyone else in Brixmis. It proved very successful, for the Americans were able to show me several ways of breaching the Wall.

From my point of view, it was an insurance policy against the outbreak of a general war. If the air assets to deploy the squadron were unavailable for any reason, we could use the routes through the Wall to infiltrate the SAS patrols.

Although I cannot substantiate it, I had a very strong feeling that the Americans actually infiltrated agents into

East Germany using the same methods. There was at least one recorded incident of an American soldier being arrested by the East Germans while carrying civilians across the inner German border in his car. I strongly suspect that it was part of the same operation.

The RAF also flew regular clandestine missions behind the Iron Curtain, using helicopters and Hercules aircraft. I was in the middle of East Germany one day, miles away from all the air corridors, when I heard the engine note of a Hercules. The next moment it flew overhead, a few feet above me, so low it was almost scraping the hedges. The aircraft was unmarked but I knew exactly what it was. Every time we went anywhere it was in a Herc and what I saw skimming over the East German plain was definitely a Herc.

Like the SAS, the RAF were probing infiltration routes and testing the effectiveness of Soviet bloc defences. It was a risky game, chancing a major international incident, but it was a calculated gamble.

There was every chance that the Herc would complete its mission undetected except by farmers who would assume it was a Soviet or East German aircraft. If the aircraft was not detected it told the RAF something about the Soviet defences; if it was, it told them just as much. It was a win–win situation and the Soviets could not even make much political capital out of discovering the flights.

If the RAF had used a warplane like a Tornado, then the Third World War might easily have broken out, but if a lumbering transport plane was detected, the most the Soviets could realistically do was to lodge a formal protest. That would probably be sent military to military rather than government to government. The crew of the Herc would get an official reprimand for 'straying into Soviet airspace' and a private bollocking for being detected.

Our preparations for nuclear Armageddon began to seem ever more bizarre in the late 1980s when it was increasingly apparent that whatever threat the Soviet Union had once offered had now evaporated. Western commanders still had powerful reasons for talking up the Soviet threat to boost their own branches of the services and secure investment in new equipment, but the view from the ground floor was very different.

With a few exceptions like the MiG 29 Fulcrum – a very fast and capable fighter – Soviet equipment was increasingly outdated, unreliable and poorly maintained. The morale of the Soviet bloc forces was disintegrating almost as fast as their equipment. Their principal preoccupation was to ensure that they were paid.

My own observations of East Germany in the early 1980s led me to conclude that the whole system was close to implosion. Despite being heavily subsidised by the Soviet Union the East German economy could not begin to compete with that of the West, and the Soviet economy was much worse.

Even the most blinkered Soviet bloc apparatchik could also see that and in East Germany all they had to do was look at West Berlin for proof. East German people voted with their feet if they saw the slightest chance of crossing the Berlin Wall, but there was also some evidence that even their rulers might have been looking for a way to dismantle the Wall long before it finally happened.

The members of one of the mission teams on a tour in East Germany were having coffee in a town on the Elbe when they were approached by a man. It was almost unheard of for any East German to speak to them: it was a criminal offence.

He began talking to them in perfect English, claiming to be a minister in the East German Politburo, recuperating from an illness in a nearby clinic. He told them that he could see no reason why East Germany could not come to some sort of accommodation with the West.

They arranged to meet him again, then came back to the mission and checked the files. The only photograph that resembled him was of the East German Defence Minister.

They obtained clearance and went back to meet him again a couple of times, but there was no way of being 100 per cent sure that he was who he claimed to be.

Eventually the Head of Mission and the intelligence analysts forbade further contact with the man on the grounds that he could be a set-up seeking to entrap a mission crew for a show trial that would embarrass the West.

The view of the rest of those of us who knew about it was rather different. We all felt that it should have been allowed to run further. While entrapment was one possibility there were two others: the man really was the Defence Minister and was seeking to defect or, even more interestingly, he was making a genuine approach on behalf of the East German Politburo, seeking a rapprochement with the West.

I was 70 per cent sure that the man claiming to be the Defence Minister was genuine and such a prize was well worth the modest risk to the Brixmis team of continuing to talk to him, but the prevailing orthodoxies in the mission and the West were for continued confrontation, not negotiation.

I am convinced that the high priest of that approach, Ronald Reagan, saw the Evil Empire tottering on the brink and played the Star Wars card to force it over the edge into bankruptcy.

There were a large number of civil disturbances in East Germany at the time, sparked mainly by the failure of its car industry to produce the planned number of vehicles. People there weren't short of money – as Chancellor Kohl later discovered when he made the unwise decision to allow East German marks to be exchanged for West German ones at the rate of one for one – what they were short of were things to spend it on.

There was a waiting list of several years for a car and when the Trabant factories couldn't even meet those soft targets there were riots in the streets. The East German Politburo had to import 10,000 Japanese cars in one year alone just to stop the riots.

The difference between the technology available to the West and that possessed by the Soviet Union was underlined not long after I completed my tour with Brixmis and returned to the Regiment.

I made a couple of trips to the US, one of which was to the Aberdeen testing ground in Baltimore. They could actually analyse a radar signal from a piece of Soviet equipment, reconstruct the equipment that emitted it and then design both a way to defeat it and a superior system. The technology was decades ahead of the USSR.

The US ability to deduce so much from a hostile radar signature may provide an explanation for the downing of the Korean Airlines 747 inside Soviet airspace in 1983, killing 269 people and provoking an international crisis. In day-to-day use, military facilities use ordinary radar systems. To find out what is being held in reserve, you have to provoke a reaction.

Flying a jet in towards the giant Soviet base at Vladivostok would have been one sure way to provoke a response. Using a military jet or a US civilian aircraft would have been too politically risky, which may be why a Korean jet was sent in – or perhaps it really did go off route by accident.

The Americans not only had an unassailable lead in technology, they also had resources that the Soviets could only dream of. On a subsequent visit to America I was shown round Nellis USAF base outside Las Vegas. My security clearance gave me unusually wide access and in one highly secret area I was shown the very latest Soviet fighter-bomber, the Flogger.

I and my Brixmis colleagues had been pounding round East Germany trying to get a sight of one. The Americans had simply gone out and bought one, brand-new, still in its original paint. It was rumoured that bribes totalling $20 million had been enough to persuade a Russian pilot to defect with his jet from an airfield in the territory of a Soviet ally, while radar operators and one or two senior officers looked the other way.

The Soviet Union's growing weakness, blindingly obvious to even the most lowly soldier, remained beyond the apparent grasp of the Prime Minister and her advisers. Mrs Thatcher remained a dedicated Cold Warrior throughout the 1980s and even her personal affinity for the architect of glasnost, President Gorbachev, did not soften her unblinking anti-Communist stance.

She had been right about the Falklands and right about confronting the Soviet Union in the early 1980s, but she was repeatedly wrong in the last years of the decade, though her advisers and the intelligence officers who should have corrected her misapprehensions must share some of the blame.

She backed the wrong horse in Gorbachev, utterly failed to appreciate the importance of the emerging nationalisms within the Soviet monolith and misunderstood the gathering speed of decline and disintegration of the USSR and its East European satellites.

Mrs Thatcher was still adhering to Cold War rhetoric and demanding increases in conventional forces to meet the Soviet threat at the same time that the Berlin Wall was beginning to crumble before her eyes.

She compounded those errors with a stubborn refusal to accept the inevitability of German reunification, which damaged Britain's relations with Germany long after Mrs Thatcher's departure from office. The end of the Iron Curtain also signalled the fall of the Iron Lady.

Within the former Soviet bloc, newly independent states, protected for decades from the harsh realities of capitalist competition, faced a dangerous new era.

The repercussions were also felt beyond the boundaries of the former Soviet Empire. The end of the Cold War was hailed as a triumph in the West but to many Third World countries it came to be seen as little short of a disaster. The end of superpower rivalries also meant that many countries lost most or even all of the little aid – most of it military – that they had previously been receiving.

The 1980s boom in the developed world largely bypassed the rest: Africa, western Asia and Latin America had endured a twenty-year recession ever since the OPEC-fuelled oil price explosion in 1973. Third World debt had rocketed in that time and the World Bank estimated that only seven out of ninety-six national economies it surveyed had debts significantly below $1 billion. Brazil, Mexico and Argentina between them owed $300 billion.[3]

With their industries destroyed or unable to compete, and even subsistence agriculture undermined by the migration to the cities and misplaced 'development' projects, the only alternative sources of income for many countries were in attracting tourism or in growing cash crops for export: exotic fruit and flowers for Western supermarkets – and drugs for Western youth.

The drugs trade provided peasant farmers from Colombia to Burma with an income that exceeded anything they could achieve from staple crops or government-funded development schemes. It also produced a drugs epidemic on the streets of Western cities. The SAS soon found itself thrust into the front line of a war against this new menace to society.

The first skirmishes against drug-runners had come several years earlier, as a by-product of the SAS involvement in Belize, the former colony of British Honduras. For years, Guatemala had made no secret of its ambition to secure a port on the Atlantic seaboard by annexing the southern province of Toledo from Belize.

The grant of independence to Belize merely heightened the pressure. When Guatemala began threatening military manoeuvres, an SAS troop was sent to patrol the dense jungle of the unmapped and largely unexplored border area of Toledo, and carry out hearts and minds work with the Mayan population.

The Regiment continued to use Belize for jungle training for several years, but never fired a shot in anger. The expected confrontation never materialised, for the mere presence of

British troops was enough to give the Guatemalans pause.

Suggestions by one author that the SAS killed several Cuban soldiers while interdicting an arms supply line through Belize to guerrillas operating in Guatemala are untrue. The Regiment would have encouraged such a supply line, not attacked it, since the guerrillas would have been assisting the aims of the SAS by diverting Guatemalan forces from the border areas to meet the internal threat.

Although the SAS border patrols did not lead to confrontations with Guatemalans – or Cubans – they did trap other infiltrators. Colombian drug gangs were using Central America as a land bridge for the shipment of cocaine to the USA.

The drug was carried overland to Belize, then shipped out by sea, either hidden in cargoes of fruit and hardwood from the port of Belize City, or picked up by fast speedboat from the scores of offshore cays lining the coast.

The arrival of the SAS brought the cocaine traffic across the southern border to an abrupt halt, but the Colombian gangs merely switched shipments to other routes. To counter the drug trade more effectively, it had to be tackled much nearer to its source.

In Western terms, the abuse of drugs was a social problem, but the scale of the global drug trade and the resources controlled by its main players made it a problem that required a military solution.

Some of the warlords in the Golden Triangle in the border areas of Burma, Laos and Thailand controlled private armies of thousands of men. In Latin America many of the drug-producing areas had become the fiefdoms of an unholy alliance of drug barons and extreme revolutionary movements. The Shining Path guerrillas in Peru, for example, operated what amounted to a mutual defence pact with the drug lords, offering their armed protection to coca-growing areas and drug shipments in return for supplies, cash and arms.

Although coca leaves were grown throughout the Andes, Colombia was the focus of the drug trade, home to the major cocaine barons, including the notorious Cali and Medellin cartels, and the site of most of the primitive jungle laboratories turning the coca paste into cocaine.

After an appeal for assistance from President Virgilio Barco, Margaret Thatcher offered to send an SAS squadron to train the Colombian National Police. There was a hope – albeit a faint one – that increased anti-drug success by the Colombian police would reduce the flow of cocaine into Britain, but the main dividends from the SAS involvement were once again political. They accrued in Washington as well as Bogotá, for SAS support for the Colombians chimed well with President Reagan's 1988 declaration of an International War on Drugs.

The Regiment already had some experience of anti-drug operations. We had trained frequently with the American Drug Enforcement Agency and the US Coastguard, and had run operations inside Britain to counter IRA attempts to raise funds through drug trading.

The Colombian drug gangs were a much larger problem than the IRA. The private armies of the cocaine barons were equipped with heavy weapons, including rocket-propelled grenades, heavy machine-guns and even ground-to-air missiles, and many of the bodyguards of the cartel leaders had been recruited abroad and trained by Cubans or former Israeli special forces.[4]

Gunfights took place at every level of the drug trade. Street dealers killing rivals for a share of the action, internecine fighting between the cartels and pitched battles with the security forces made Colombia one of the most dangerous places on earth. Drug-related killings were running at 20,000 a year, with 3,000 in Cali alone, and murder was the single most frequent cause of death for Colombian adult males.[5]

The first SAS teams arrived covertly in Colombia in autumn 1988. They began training the paramilitary anti-narcotics police in all the facets of jungle warfare: surveillance and counter-surveillance, aggressive patrolling, OPs, close-target recces and demolitions.

The skill levels of the trainees were not high, but over time the training teams brought them up to scratch. Their main targets were to be the jungle laboratories where cocaine paste was converted to pure cocaine. Like an assault on an enemy airfield, where the aim is to kill the pilots as well as destroy the aircraft, the Colombians aimed to arrest the chemists operating the labs as well as destroying the equipment.

A new lab could be set up and running within days or even hours of a successful raid, but chemists might be harder to find in the Colombian jungle. Killing them would have put them out of the way permanently, but the police were already too scared of reprisals from the cocaine gangs to countenance that. In any event, since many of the chemists were Westerners, killing them would have created political problems.

The initial plan had been for the SAS teams to confine themselves to training, but the corrosive influence of drug money on the security forces – some military helicopters would overfly drug laboratories as an early warning on the way in to raid them – meant that most of the raids by the anti-narcotics police were failures.

The SAS men then took a more direct role, leading teams of Colombians on training patrols. Each one would comb some two square miles of jungle for any trace of laboratories or trails. No prior information was given to any of the Colombian forces and when a target had been located and a raid was called in neither the troops nor the helicopter pilots were told the location until they were approaching the landing zone.

There have been some signal successes in the war against the narco-terrorists. Many labs have been destroyed, many drug shipments have been seized and prominent cocaine barons such as Gonzalo Rodriguez Gacha and Pablo Escobar have been killed in ambushes, but the drug trade can only be restricted, not eliminated. The billions made by the cocaine barons buy a very substantial amount of influence among senior Colombian politicians, judges, and police and army officers.

Begun in 1989, the SAS commitment to Colombia is part of the war against terrorism that the Regiment has waged for thirty years.

In those same three decades, the SAS has fought in three major but very different wars. Operation Storm in the 1970s was a classic counter-insurgency campaign. The Falklands War in the 1980s more nearly resembled the colonial wars of our imperial past.

The last major campaign, fought in the 1990s, was on an even larger scale, and involved the Regiment in a return to its roots of fifty years ago. Half a century of patient evolution of the ultimate strategic fighting force was largely set aside as the SAS found itself – like David Stirling's originals – staging a hit-and-run campaign in the deserts of the Middle East.

15

GULF WAR
1990–91

The trooper was crouching behind a boulder at the side of a shallow wadi in the first grey light of dawn. The rest of his troop lay nearby in their sleeping bags, snatching what sleep they could.

Three Land Rovers were drawn up behind them, bristling with heavy weapons. Two had ·50 heavy machine-guns, the other a complex arrangement of machine-guns and rocket-launchers. Further back, tucked into the side of the wadi, was a Swedish-built Unimog carrying the heavy equipment and the bulk of the troop's rations and water.

The vehicles were covered with a mixture of sand and green paint, and the troop had made a half-hearted attempt to camouflage them from the air with cam-nets, but they were not particularly well disguised. The SAS men knew that the projected threat from the Iraqi air force had disappeared.

The trooper was covered in dust and fine, gritty sand, and his eyes were sore and strained from fatigue. He blinked a few times, trying to ease the strain, and then shifted his gaze forward across the flat plain of central Iraq. In the far distance he could see the main Baghdad Highway, a darker line against the pink-tinged rock and sand. Over the previous nights the troop had repeatedly crossed and recrossed it looking for targets of opportunity.

They planned to rest through the day in their lying-up position before once again starting their quest at nightfall.

Suddenly he stiffened as he heard a faraway, very faint drone. He used his telescope first, then his high-powered binoculars to give him a wider field of vision, and spotted the sun glinting from the windscreen of a vehicle a few miles away. A plume of dust trailed behind it as it sped across the desert, heading towards the wadi.

Shit, he thought, did we leave any tracks? Although the troop was meticulous about erasing any sign as they moved towards the wadi there was always the possibility that something had been missed.

He turned and lobbed pebbles at his comrades. Their sleeping bags wriggled like fat green maggots as the SAS men struggled out of them, instantly awake and alert but grumbling under their breath at the loss of precious sleep.

They grabbed their weapons and moved up to where the trooper was lying and a plan was quickly formulated. An ambush group of four would go to the mouth of the wadi. The rest would man the vehicles, ready for a quick getaway.

The trooper grabbed the ready-bag containing a Claymore mine from the nearest vehicle and picked up his M203, a combined Armalite rifle and grenade-launcher. His three companions carried Armalites, grenades and pistols. They covered the few hundred yards to the mouth of the wadi quickly, assembled the Claymore and then took up an immediate ambush position.

The vehicle was now much closer and the trooper recognised the distinctive shape of a Russian-made Gaz jeep. Through the windscreen he could make out the outlines of four people. Although they did not appear to be following any tracks, they were still heading straight for the wadi. As they came nearer still, he could even make out their badges of rank. They were all officers, which was very unusual.

The engine note swelled to a roar. Everyone released their safety catches and as the Gaz entered the killing area the Claymore was detonated and four weapons opened up with a storm of automatic and semi-automatic fire. The Gaz jumped and bucked, still ploughing forward, though its tyres were shredded and its body was twisted at a crazy angle. The driver slumped at the wheel, the dead weight of his foot revving the engine to a scream.

After emptying half of his magazine into the vehicle, the trooper switched to the grenade-launcher mounted below the machine-gun and loosed off three quick rounds into the engine of the Gaz.

The noise reverberating from the sides of the wadi reached a terrible climax, the cracks and whines of automatic fire drowned in the ferocious concussion of the grenades and the howl of the engine. Then it exploded in a cloud of steam and smoke, and the Gaz stopped dead, its body ripped and torn apart. Three of the Iraqi officers had been hurled out by the blast and lay sprawled on the sand. The driver slumped in the cab, dead at the wheel.

The patrol stopped firing and the din of battle gave way to complete silence, broken only by the hissing of steam, the metallic clicking of the hot exhaust as it cooled and the slow, steady drip of petrol on to the ground. Then there was another sound. Although the trooper's ears were still ringing from the noise of the weapons, he could hear a low moaning.

Two of the SAS went forward, covered by the others. Three of the Iraqis were very much dead but the fourth, wearing the insignia of an artillery captain, was alive and completely unmarked. The shock and the noise had disorientated him, however, and he lay on the sand, mumbling incoherently, his hands clasped over his ears and his whole body shivering and shaking.

The trooper stepped forward, took the officer's Makharov pistol from its holster and tucked it into his own belt.

He fastened the man's hands behind his back, tightening a plastic tie around his wrists with a savage jerk. He searched him for concealed weapons and then removed the map-case slung over the man's shoulder and took a quick glance at the contents.

As he studied the maps, the trooper realised to his surprise that the Iraqi army had much better mapping than the Special Air Service. The maps covered an area to their north-west. Symbols in chinagraph pencil identical to the ones the British army used on their maps showed the position of an Iraqi division.

The rest of the troop had deployed in a semicircle around the mouth of the wadi, waiting for an Iraqi follow-up. None came. They realised that the Gaz had been a solo vehicle, but it was little consolation. They would have to move to another lying-up position and lose their chance of any rest in the process.

They loaded their vehicles and moved off, with two troopers on motorbikes acting as outriders. A safe distance across the desert they drew up in another wadi and held a council of war. The captured maps were vital; to destroy an Iraqi division at such an early stage of the battle would be a tremendous coup.

The signaller set up his 319 Morse set and used his vocab and one-time pad to prepare a message, sent in burst form. They spent an anxious couple of hours awaiting the return signal. The reply, when it came, was what they most expected, but least wanted. The RAF were sending in a Chinook that night to retrieve the prisoner and his maps. The troop spent the rest of the day preparing a landing zone for the helicopter. After last light they laid out the reception area using infra-red light-sticks in the shape of an arrow-head.

The Chinook arrived exactly on time, skimming very low over the desert, invisible to the naked eye but heralded by the thunder of its rotors. It hung motionless over the landing zone, its wheels barely touching the ground as the pilot kept it in the hover to avoid it settling into the desert sand. The rotors whipped up a storm of sand and dust as two of the patrol manhandled the prisoner into the helicopter and passed the map-case to the loadmaster. Within seconds the Chinook had disappeared into the night, the sound of its rotors fading to a faint rumble.

The troop pulled back from their defensive positions to the vehicles, muttering among themselves. 'The bastard Crabs didn't even bring us a loaf of bread.'

They moved on, putting a safe distance between themselves and the landing zone. By first light they had found another lying-up position, camouflaged the vehicles and settled down to rest. One of the troopers glanced around the circle of faces. 'We'll have to go back to the ambush site.'

An argument broke out, even though they all knew he was right, but eventually even the most vociferous objectors bowed to the inevitable. If the Iraqis discovered the Gaz vehicle, they would know that an officer and his map-case were missing and would immediately change the deployment of their troops.

The tension and apprehension grew as they waited for nightfall. No one wanted to return to the site of a previous contact; it was pushing your luck, but it had to be done. The troop formed up at dusk. The two motorcyclists, wearing night-vision goggles, again acted as lead scouts, half a mile or so ahead of the other vehicles.

The troop left their vehicles a mile from the wadi. They advanced on foot, the lead scouts still wearing their NVGs, the others straining to pierce the darkness, using binoculars and telescopes to magnify the ambient light. They paused constantly to look, listen, and scent the night air, every sense strained to the limit.

The lead scouts went forward alone over the last hundred yards. There was an agonising wait before they reappeared out of the darkness. They gave the thumbs-up sign: the wadi was clear of enemy troops.

Half the troop manned a defensive perimeter while the other men went down into the wadi. Nothing had changed. The wreck of the Gaz still lay half on its side, surrounded by the bodies of the dead officers. The troop began the gruesome task they had set themselves, pushing what was left of the Gaz back on to its wheels and lifting the dead bodies into the seats.

Two of the demolitionists packed plastic explosive all round the vehicle. They linked the charges with detonating cord and ran a cable back from the detonator to the side of the wadi. They crouched down behind a rock and fired the charges, blasting the Gaz and its occupants into tiny fragments.

There was now no clue that a ground force was operating in the area. The charges had been placed to simulate the effects of an air-strike, and any Iraqi troops following up the noise of the explosion or chancing across the Gaz would assume that the vehicle had been attacked by one of the coalition's marauding A-10 aircraft.

From what remained of the vehicle and its occupants, even a forensic pathologist could not have established whether three or four bodies had been inside it when it exploded, nor what had happened to the maps they were carrying.

The troop moved back to their vehicles and mounted up, using the rest of the night to put some distance between themselves and the ambush site. Once more, they found a lying-up position just before dawn. Bone-weary, they settled down to rest, still grumbling about the RAF. 'Fucking Crabs. Why can't they get their arses into gear quicker to attack the Iraqis? Why do we always have to take all the risks?'

'Look on the bright side, at least we'll get decent mapping now.'

The Iraqi division was later attacked and virtually destroyed by coalition air-strikes – but the SAS never got decent maps.

A Squadron staff sergeant, Iraq, 1991

On 2 August 1990, 100,000 Iraqi troops poured across the frontier into Kuwait. There was never the slightest doubt that war with the West would ensue if Iraq did not withdraw. Despite pious pronouncements about restoring democracy – a thorny topic in Kuwait and its Arab neighbours – and imposing a new world order, the Gulf War was fought over something much more tangible: crude oil. Almost half of the West's oil supplies came from the fields of Kuwait and Saudi Arabia and what the formidably armed Saddam Hussein had done to one Arab neighbour he could easily do to another.

Led by the US, a coalition to confront Iraq was formed, embracing most major industrialised nations and several of Saddam's Arab neighbours.

There was also a less obvious but no less important rationale behind the US government's enthusiasm for staging a military spectacular in the Middle East. The US has always resented British influence in the region, but has never succeeded in supplanting Britain. The present generation of Middle Eastern rulers are rapidly ageing, however, and the line of succession in most of their states is rarely a direct one.

The Americans undoubtedly hoped to acquire the influence with the next rulers of the Gulf States that they had largely failed to secure with the present ones. In that light, their huge investment of money and manpower in the Gulf War becomes more of a hard-eyed long-term business calculation than a moral crusade against Iraqi aggression or a short-term grab for oil.

Immediately after the Iraqi invasion, G Squadron of the SAS was sent to the United Arab Emirates to begin work-up training for the coming war. They remained in the Gulf for five months but were brought back to the UK for Christmas leave just before the projected outbreak of hostilities. It was an almost incomprehensible decision in itself, but was then compounded by an even more grotesque mistake.

While G Squadron was back in Hereford. A Squadron also returned from a tour of duty in Colombia. They immediately staked a competing claim for the right to go to the Gulf. Their argument had nothing to do with military efficiency and everything to do with office politics and Buggins's turn.

G Squadron had been involved in the Falklands War nine years previously, while A Squadron had been kept in reserve. Faced with the same situation in the Gulf, the OC of A Squadron began an intensive lobbying campaign.

In operational terms there was only one possible decision. While A Squadron had been operating in the Colombian jungle, G Squadron had spent several months training in desert warfare. Yet the lobbying paid off. A Squadron were sent to the Gulf, while G Squadron were held in reserve, one of a series of blunders that were to characterise the SAS involvement in the Gulf War.

A Squadron had only arrived back in England from Colombia on Christmas Eve. They spent two days at home, but were then called into the War Room at Hereford on 27 December for a briefing, and flew out to the United Arab Emirates the next day to begin their hasty conversion to desert warfare.

They arrived in the Middle East to discover the beginnings of a shambles. Equipment that they expected to find was either not there at all or was in a poor state of repair. When they put in requests for additional kit, the only response was the bland assurance, 'It will all be okay on the day of the race.'[1]

It wasn't. The vehicles were not ready, there were not enough weapons, ammunition, Claymore mines or explosives, and the VHF communications equipment supplied for operations in Iraq was equally inadequate. It garbled and swallowed vital parts of messages, and in one case an SAS patrol – Bravo Two Zero – was even given the wrong frequencies.

In addition to the communications problems, there was also no mapping of Iraq other than air-navigation maps, no aerial photographs nor satellite images, and nowhere near enough GPS (global positioning satellite) systems or Tacbes (tactical beacons, also known as SARBEs, search and rescue beacons).

At the briefing prior to their departure the SAS men had been shown good mapping, air photography and satellite imagery of their potential areas of deployment, and promised that it would all be available to them in the Gulf. None ever arrived. As they were later to discover in the ambush of the Gaz vehicle, the Iraqis had better mapping than they did.

The Iraqis do not manufacture their own maps, yet they were able to issue 1:100,000 scale maps to their troops. Iraq was a former British dependency; the maps did exist. I could have walked into a specialist shop like Stanford's in Covent Garden and bought them off the shelf. Yet some SAS staff officer had not bothered to get off his arse and procure them for troops going into battle.

Even if none had been available, both the British and the Americans have a computer-controlled system that can produce a working 1:50,000 map – the ideal map for operations of this type – from air reconnaissance photographs within a couple of hours. The technology is twenty years old. Why it was not used to produce maps for the SAS and the other forces operating in Iraq is a question that has yet to be answered.

In the absence of anything better, the enforced basis of SAS navigation within Iraq was the use of 1:1,000,000 air-navigation charts, which were only accurate to within one and three-quarter miles. Supported by GPS systems, the mapping was just about sufficient in theory, but would only work in practice if every SAS man had a chart and a GPS. That was far from the case: the ratio was less than one for every five men.

GPS systems cost no more than a couple of hundred pounds and can be bought from any decent camping shop. Had the SAS Sabre Squadrons known in advance that there would not be enough, they would have gone out and bought their own. It would be by no means the first time that SAS men had equipped themselves for combat at their own expense, but by the time the shortage was revealed they were already in the Middle East and it was too late to remedy it.

Tacbes are also vital pieces of equipment. They are used for ground-to-air communications, enabling SAS patrols to call in and direct air-strikes, but they also ensure that individual SAS men have a means of calling for rescue if they are separated from their patrol. They are such an essential piece of equipment that SAS men are not allowed to go on training exercises without Tacbes, yet men going into combat did not have them: there was only one for every two men on the Bravo Two Zero patrol, and A Squadron were issued with even fewer, only one to every four men.

Very shortly after A Squadron was committed, D Squadron also arrived and the amount of available equipment was further reduced. By the time a third SAS squadron, B, got to the Gulf a week later, there was virtually nothing left.

A plan that had been based around the use of one squadron was suddenly adapted to encompass three and a half squadrons (for the Territorial R – Reserve – Squadron had also been deployed), who were all trying to operate on one squadron's supply of equipment.

B Squadron was nominally the stand-by, support squadron, but despite that, they were tasked with three patrols without adequate kit. They had rounds for their Armalites, but there were no Claymore mines at all and no grenades for the ·203s. The situation was so bad that the other squadrons took pity and had an equipment whip-round for them; when a comrade is going into combat, it is very difficult to look him in the eye and deny him the kit that might save his life.

The non-combatants back at base did not see the shortages as a problem; those at the cutting edge took a rather different view. With characteristic SAS chutzpah, B Squadron set about improvising Claymores from plastic explosive and empty cartons, but it was a farcical situation for members of an elite force to find themselves in on the verge of a major war.

US special operations forces and their mountains of supplies were based a few miles up the road and could have supplied all the ·203 grenades and Claymores the SAS wanted, but nobody asked.

In the panic to get forces into the field, even the limited equipment that had been delivered to the Gulf often became mislaid. Andy McNab's Bravo Two Zero patrol spent some considerable time searching without success for a consignment of night-vision goggles. In the end the patrol had to leave without them. The goggles eventually turned up; not realising what was inside them, the squadron sergeant-major had been using the boxes to weigh down the edges of his tent.

The SAS command and control were also chaotic. Some HQ elements were in Riyadh, some at the forward mounting base at Victor in Abu Dhabi, some at the forward operating base in north-west Saudi Arabia, and the squadrons were also being controlled from England.

The Regimental HQ – the CO and all his staff – had decamped to the Gulf. The prime intelligence is gathered and collated in the UK, then disseminated to the forces in the field. Instead of remaining in Hereford to fight the political battles and secure every ounce of available intelligence from GCHQ and Northwood, the colonel took himself, his RSM and his entire Head Shed off to Riyadh. It was unprecedented in SAS history; even when Mike Rose went to the Falklands he left the Head Shed in Hereford to co-ordinate the UK end of operations.

The Head Shed based in Riyadh for the Gulf War was powerless to control the flow of intelligence and had to accept what it was given. It was spoon-fed with heavily screened, filtered and edited information that was never an adequate support for the Sabre Squadrons in the field.

DLB had access to strategic intelligence but could scarcely be expected to ensure his former unit was receiving it; his responsibility was to run the whole British campaign, not worry whether the SAS Head Shed was doing its job.

That it was not was further demonstrated by the communications plan prepared by the Signals Squadron. The SAS patrols were supplied with 319 Morse sets with a burst capability. Every signal had to be encrypted and decoded using vocabulary tables and one-time pads, a complex and very time-consuming business. If the Signals Squadron had not anticipated the need for a word in the vocab table – Scud, for example – it had to be even more laboriously spelled out.

Communications went back to the UK, back out to Riyadh and finally to the patrols in the field. The patrols carried sat-coms but were forbidden to use them except to receive signals, including a daily broadcast from the ops room of potential targets or enemy positions within sixty miles of each squadron's location.

The reason for the prohibition on patrols sending signals over the sat-coms was the paranoia felt by the Signals Squadron about Iraqi direction-finding abilities. Yet 'attached arms' of the SAS like the Signals Squadron are purely advisory. They are non-combatants who have never passed SAS Selection and have no experience of SAS operations.

Had they ever gone into the field they would have known that DF is not a problem to patrols carrying out standard operating procedures. You simply send and move. Even if the signal is located, by the time the enemy arrive there is nothing to see but a very empty desert.

In any event, there is always a need to balance a risk against the need to get the job done; the best people to judge the risk of using voice communications were the people actually on the ground, not the signallers back at base.

The communications system devised by Signals Squadron was designed more to demonstrate their own capabilities than to support the operational missions. Such was the complexity of the signals plan that individual vehicles in the SAS mobile columns inside Iraq were not allowed to communicate with each other. They had to use men on motorbikes to carry messages to and fro, a bizarre return to the days of the Second World War.

The Signals Squadron had devised a similarly convoluted system for the Falklands War but were overruled by the colonel, Mike Rose, because the system was unworkable.

No one overruled them in the Gulf; as a result the troops in the field had neither the communications nor the access to intelligence that they needed. If Signals Squadron deserve some of the blame for that, it must be shared by the Head Shed, who did not change the plan.

Even more worrying than the other problems was the fact that there was no defined task for the SAS to perform. General Norman Schwarzkopf had given the US 5th Special Forces Group and the Marine Corps the monopoly on front-line reconnaissance. In any case, he was an advocate of full-scale, up-front, all-out warfare, not behind-the-lines special forces operations. He had seen at first hand the unimpressive performance of the Green Berets in Vietnam and had also been called in to restore some military logic to the shambolic invasion of Grenada. As a result of those experiences he had an understandably jaundiced view of the value of special forces.

Lobbying by Lieutenant-General Peter de la Billiere – who had collected a final dividend from his friendship with the outgoing Prime Minister, Margaret Thatcher, by his appointment as commander of British Middle East Forces – led to a grudging acceptance of a role for the Regiment, but it was not the strategic one that the SAS was trained to fulfil.

The SAS are strategic troops; if there is no specific task for them, they should not be used. The type of mission they would be expected to fulfil in a conflict like the Gulf War would be the marking with LTDs – laser target designators – of high-profile, well-defended targets. Had they been involved in target designation at an early stage of the air war it would undoubtedly have reduced the number of RAF casualties and perhaps the 'collateral damage' to civilians.

The Regiment is always tasked strategically by the theatre commander. In the Gulf that was DLB, yet despite his considerable SAS experience he could not at first conceive of a role for the Regiment. 'Our technological superiority on the battlefield and in the air seemed to be so overwhelming as to leave no gap which Special Forces could reasonably fill.'[2]

The comment is hard to understand. The one absolutely infallible source of intelligence is humint – human intelligence. If a Mark One human eyeball can see it, it is definitely there. The SAS could have been confirming what sigint – signals intelligence – was telling the coalition commanders and they could also have been calling in air-strikes, which would have further magnified the impact of coalition air-power.

The School of Air Warfare accepts that a minimum of 20 per cent of attacking aircraft will not identify a target on the first pass. SAS men marking targets with LTDs would have greatly increased the percentage of first-time hits. Yet at first DLB could not imagine a role for the SAS, and when one was at last found for the squadrons, it was not a strategic but a tactical one: to travel around an area of Iraq beating up targets of opportunity – anything they happened to find.

The only, extremely tenuous, ground on which it could be described as a strategic task was if the mere presence of the SAS in Iraq was considered a strategic asset, a diversion concealing where the main thrust was to come.

The SAS Sabre Squadrons now faced the prospect of going into battle against Iraq without enough equipment, or the proper communications, topographical and intelligence support and, most importantly, without any real targets. The logical, methodical build-up essential for a major campaign simply hadn't happened.

A week before the outbreak of war there was a brief flutter of excitement in the world's media as the Saudis announced that a number of Iraqi helicopter pilots had defected, bringing their Soviet-built MI-8 Hip troop-carrying helicopters with them. There were confirmed sightings of the helicopters, which had been escorted into Saudi airspace by US fighters, and subsequent denials of the story by US officials started a media frenzy.

Reports that the SAS and/or US special operations forces had been involved in a secret mission into Iraq were soon flashing around the world. Explanations of its purpose ranged from the hijack of Iraqi front-line radar equipment to the rescue of Western military advisers trapped in Kuwait or the survivors of a failed attempt to assassinate Saddam.

The reality was rather more prosaic. The Saudis had been offering a bounty to any Iraqi pilots wanting to defect and several of them, realising that the Iraqi forces were in for a pounding in the coming war, had opted to take the money and run.

The only genuine activity the SAS squadrons had been involved in at the time was a move up to their forward mounting base in Abu Dhabi. There they were visited by the Deputy Group Commander. 'He got up on the table in the cookhouse and said, "Iraq is a big theme park waiting to be played in. You'll go there and have a good time, take this, destroy this and destroy that," but there were still no military guidelines or specific targets.'[3]

Before being deployed, the squadrons asked permission to do recces on the border crossing points. They were assured that this was unnecessary because the Force Projection Cell would recce the insertion routes and crossing points and lead the squadrons to them. The FPC is a small cell within the

Regiment, one of a number of departments set up to research specific areas of SAS operations.

It was tasked with establishing ways of putting the right number of people in the right place at the right time. That job description scarcely qualified them to do the recces but because – like everyone else – they were in Saudi Arabia, a job had to be found for them.

Yet again this was a complete departure from established SAS practice. If your neck is the one on the line, you're likely to do a better job than someone who's just going back to a warm, safe base afterwards. In almost any operation, squadrons will do their own recces, inserting a patrol ahead of the main force to establish the lie of the land. It also gives the main force confidence to know that some of their comrades are already operating with impunity inside enemy territory. In the event, the SAS forces were to deploy without any strategic intelligence or advance recces; they were effectively going in blind.

The air war broke out in the early hours of 17 January 1991. Apache helicopters firing Hellfire missiles wiped out Iraqi air-defence radars, giving coalition aircraft two 'black' air corridors through which to attack their targets. Tomahawk cruise missiles and Stealth bombers also pounded command and communication centres in Baghdad.

Iraqi retaliation was directed not at the coalition forces but at Israel. The next night eight Scud missiles hit the suburbs of Tel Aviv and Haifa. By luck the casualties were far less severe than might have been expected, but Israeli anger and threats of direct retaliation led to a political crisis in the coalition and forced an immediate change in military strategy.

Huge numbers of coalition aircraft were diverted from their planned missions to seek and destroy Scud launchers in the western deserts of Iraq. The SAS squadrons were also airlifted to their forward operating base the same night, and moved out in the early hours of the following morning.

General Schwarzkopf and the head of the coalition air forces, Lieutenant-General Chuck Horner, continued to believe that air-power alone would be sufficient to neutralise the Scuds. The SAS was given no briefing on the Scud threat prior to insertion into Iraq; the only instructions were still to cross into Iraq and take on targets of opportunity.

At the same time, one mobile patrol and two foot patrols from B Squadron were inserted to set up OPs overlooking main supply routes in western Iraq. The patrols were of eight to ten men each – too big to hide, too small to fight.

As well as being given the wrong frequencies, Bravo Two Zero were also given a defective sat-coms set and, to symbolise the hasty, ill-conceived way in which they were deployed, as their Chinook flew them into Iraq they were handed an infantry Cougar radio set. They then watched two signallers use masking tape to secure another one to the fuselage, so that the patrol could communicate with the helicopter. The fact that special forces had been communicating with Chinooks for years, using their Tacbes, did not seem to have occurred to the Signals Squadron.

The leader of another Bravo patrol took one look at the exposed, bare rock and gravel terrain of the area in which they had been inserted and flew his men straight back out again on the same helicopter.

The mobile patrol spent twenty-four hours on site before following his example and pulling out. In their way, the decisions were as courageous as that of the other foot-patrol leader, Andy McNab of Bravo Two Zero, who, despite the terrain, waved his patrol's helicopter off into the night.

The other two squadrons parted company at Ar'ar, about thirty miles south of the frontier. D Squadron tracked the oil pipeline north-west to cross into Iraq close to Jordan, while A Squadron swung south-east towards Kuwait. When they reached their start lines, they split again into half-squadron groups and turned north and east to cross the frontier.

The Force Projection Cell gave them zones within which

they were to cross the Iraqi border, but no actual crossing points. Only then did the SAS men discover that no one had recced the crossing points at all.

D Squadron crossed without problem over flat desert, entering hostile territory that night, in the early hours of 20 January, but A Squadron found their way blocked by an anti-tank birm – a sand wall fifteen to twenty-five feet high. Every opening in it was guarded by an Iraqi fort. A covert entry appeared impossible.

For the next twenty-four hours the squadron searched for a crossing point from one end of their zone to the other. Finally they took the least bad option and made a successful crossing. They pressed on into Iraq even though, without adequate intelligence, mapping, aerial photographs or satellite imagery, they never knew what might be in front of them.

The one thing in their favour was the terrain. Unlike the area where B Squadron's patrols had been inserted or the plains to the east where the main coalition assault would be launched, the central and western border areas offered good cover for vehicles. It was high, rocky ground, cut by steep-sided wadis. There were loose rocks and boulders, but very little sand.

Weather conditions were very much worse than they had been led to expect, however. It was the worst winter in the region in living memory and the bleak landscape, mostly over 2,000 feet high, was constantly swept by bitter, freezing winds. They had no proper winter clothing and the mobility troops often had to light fires under their Unimog vehicles to stop the diesel fuel going 'waxy' in the sub-zero temperatures.

The conditions were even more dangerous for the remaining foot patrol, Bravo Two Zero. Compromised and scattered by an Iraqi attack, their ordeal was only just beginning.

The vehicle-based patrols continued to push forward into enemy territory. Contrary to popular opinion, the desert is not an empty place – Bedou goatherders were everywhere –

and one of the principal topics of debate before the SAS squadrons were deployed was how they would deal with the Bedou and the risk of being compromised by them.

Some of the more youthful, gung-ho troopers favoured capturing or killing any Bedou they encountered but, quite apart from the moral considerations, it was never a realistic option anyway. The traditional SAS policy of hearts and minds was certain to pay much better dividends.

Patrols neither abducted nor killed the Bedou. They were respectful to them, offered them food and drink, and if necessary bluffed them.

We told some that we were on exercise with the Iraqi army, and one of them just said, 'Yes, okay.' They are simple people, not simple-minded, and that was a good enough answer for him.

After a few chance encounters with the Bedou, they realised that the patrols were treating them a lot better than the Iraqis. To my knowledge, they never compromised us – we were never followed up by Iraqis after meeting Bedou – they just let life go as it was. They stopped and chatted with us, to pass the time of day. We'd give them some tea, food and blankets, they'd give us information about where the Iraqis were and then they would leave. In the end, if there were Bedou about, we actively let them know we were there rather than trying to hide.[4]

A Squadron had pushed forward about seventy miles and were lying up in a wadi when they ambushed the Iraqi Gaz vehicle. Having captured an artillery officer and the battle plans of his division, they pulled back thirty miles to allow their prisoner and his maps to be lifted out by helicopter. All the positions shown on his maps were later hit by coalition air-strikes.

Although the Iraqi officer had been delivered into their hands by good fortune, the ambush had been carried out with devastating efficiency and the A Squadron OC must have been expecting a few congratulations. Instead he got the sack.

The OC, an SBS officer, was very conscious of his lack of experience of land-side operations and was out of his depth with a lot of the tactics of desert warfare, but he was receptive to advice and content to base his decisions on the expertise within the group. There have been many worse squadron OCs.

It was not enough for HQ. The OC was criticised for the squadron's failure to cross the Iraqi border on the first night of the operation, for failing to pull back to discuss the potential border crossing points with the CO before eventually crossing into Iraq and he was also criticised – ironically – for pulling back to hand over his prisoner.

The regimental sergeant-major flew in to replace him on the same helicopter that had come to extract the prisoner and, as it turned out, the luckless OC. The sacking shocked most of the members of his squadron. They felt that the importance of the intelligence they had obtained fully merited pulling back to pass it on and allow air-strikes to be made, while the problems at the border were not created by the OC but by the failure of the Force Projection Cell to carry out recces. Most of his men suspected that Regimental politics had as much to do with his dismissal as any alleged lack of competence.

The RSM who took over command also brought news of a task – of sorts – for the SAS. The Iraqi Scud missile attacks on Israel had provoked the government in Tel Aviv to fury. If the coalition could not do anything to stop the Scuds, the Israeli forces would do it for them.

Israeli troops were deployed in preparation for a ground assault on western Iraq that could only have been launched by crossing or overflying Arab territory: Jordan, Saudi Arabia or Syria. Intelligence from an American satellite was even more alarming: Israeli missiles armed with nuclear warheads had been prepared for launching at Iraq.[5]

The West's uneasy Arab partners in the coalition – Saudi Arabia, the Gulf states, Jordan and Syria – were already having enough trouble in selling their support of a war against a fellow Arab ruler to their own restive populations. If Israel had joined the fighting at all, the Arab states would have withdrawn from the coalition; if Israel had launched a nuclear strike on Baghdad, a fresh Arab–Israeli war would almost certainly have broken out.

As a result, stopping the Scuds was now priority number one. To prove it, all SAS stations received a signal: 'Preferred prisoners are Scud commanders.' A Squadron could only presume that minnows like artillery officers carrying the deployment plans of an entire division should be thrown back in future.

The US shipped batteries of additional Patriot missiles to Israel 'to counter the Scud threat', but that was at least as much for cosmetic purposes as a truly effective counter-measure. The time taken for US satellites to detect a Scud launch, pass the information and trigger the launch of a Patriot was at least four minutes; the flight time of the Scud was only six.

Scuds continued to get through and even those intercepted by Patriots could still represent a threat. The mid-air detonation of a chemical or biological warhead over Israel would have been almost as great a danger as its uninterrupted flight to its eventual target.

The Scuds' inaccuracy over such long ranges – most of them fell in relatively unpopulated areas away from Tel Aviv – and the deterrent effect of a threatened nuclear counter-strike against Baghdad in retaliation for a chemical or biological attack on Israel were probably greater safeguards. The greatest of all was the destruction of the Scuds before they were launched.

Coalition aircraft had hammered the fixed Scud launch sites in Iraq, but even with overwhelming air superiority they had minimal success in finding and destroying mobile launchers, which were easily concealed from air or satellite surveillance.

Air-power alone had not proved enough to destroy the Scuds. 'The fog of war is present, the picture is not perfect,' General Schwarzkopf said, in explanation of the failure of satellites and pilots to locate more than a handful of the mobile launchers. The SAS squadrons were now given the task of hunting them down in 'Scud Alley' – south-western Iraq – from where the missiles were being fired at Israel. There was never any strategic information or tasking, however, just General Schwarzkopf's new Gulf War mantra: 'Scuds, Scuds, and Scuds again.'

The only intelligence was supplied by the SAS men's own eyeballs. 'Scuds were usually launched at night and gave a huge signature, a great big ball of light. You could see the fireball at the base of the motor from thirty miles away across flat open desert, and that gave us an indication of where to look. The launcher would be moved immediately after firing, but if you looked at the lay-out of the roads and interpreted it intelligently you could generally pick up where the launcher was going to be.'[6]

At first SAS patrols called in air-strikes to attack the Scuds, but the time-lag between locating the launcher and the arrival of the A-10 or F-15E aircraft to destroy it could be as long as an hour and by then the launcher had often been moved again.

The daisy-chain of communications was partly to blame for that. Incompatibility of equipment – a problem that, with a six-month lead-in to war, really ought to have been foreseen – meant that the laser target designators carried by SAS patrols could not be used in attacks by American aircraft. The SAS men could only talk to strike aircraft by using their Tacbes when the jets were directly overhead, and they could not talk directly to the American AWACS (airborne warning and control system) controlling the strike aircraft at all.

The AWACS would not overfly the area where the SAS had been deployed, for no strategic command had been given to do so. Instead, SAS communications were routed all the way back to England, back out to Riyadh and then to the forward operating base. The good news would then go to the US Tactical Aircraft Control Centre, up to the AWACS and finally down to the strike aircraft.

The reliability of the radio sets supplied to the SAS was also a continuing problem. On more than one occasion an SAS group trying to communicate with the forward operating base was forced to use a Tacbe to communicate with an A-10 flying overhead.

The pilot would either relay a message on his own communications, or go round to the SAS ops room after he had landed back at the airfield, where the A-10s were also based.

After a couple of frustrating near-misses because of their communications problems and aircraft delays, the SAS men decided to take matters into their own hands, using Milan anti-tank weapons, general-purpose machine-guns and, on one occasion, rather more primitive weapons. They found an unmanned site and, to conserve ammunition, they just smashed all the bolts on the launch-pad connectors with sledgehammers.

For a week or two the Iraqis had no idea that the SAS were there. Even when it began to dawn on them that they were losing equipment from ground fire rather than air-attack they still held off from major counter-operations because they were under the impression that the troops must have been of at least divisional strength to be operating that far behind Iraqi lines.

When survivors from contacts reported that only a handful of vehicles were involved, the Iraqis finally began to deploy against the SAS groups. A Squadron was chased on three occasions after making attacks, but only one of them developed into a full-scale, rolling contact.

The SAS patrols also forced the Iraqis to change their tactics on their main supply routes. After a few successful ambushes, all vital equipment was sent in ten- to twenty-vehicle convoys with armoured support. These in turn became the target of further large-scale SAS ambushes using bar mines, bulk explosives and mortar bombs fired on pre-set lines.

D Squadron had some immediate successes against Scuds, destroying a couple of launchers and a radar station. They also made a daylight attack on a group of manned watch-towers spread at half-mile intervals along a major Iraqi supply route, like the turrets on Hadrian's Wall. After the SAS men had been spotted a couple of times and chased by Iraqi forces, they took out half a dozen towers, one after the other, which slowed down the Iraqis' reporting procedures.

By now US special operations forces were also clamouring for a share of the action. They had arrived at their forward base after the SAS squadrons had already infiltrated into Iraq, and American analysts told a liaison meeting with SAS staff officers that the flat open nature of the terrain meant that US special operations forces couldn't operate for any length of time in western Iraq.

'That's funny,' one of the SAS officers said, 'we've had two squadrons in there for the last week.'

General Wayne Downing, in charge of US special forces, then ordered US special operations forces to get in there quick and carry out a task, and they were let loose on 'Scud Boulevard', north of the main Baghdad–Amman highway, while the SAS continued to work Scud Alley south of it.

A US special operations forces group was inserted by Black-hawk helicopters with strong fighter support to destroy a large complex, but became involved in a prolonged contact in which three men were killed and a couple more wounded. They had to call in a helicopter to casevac the wounded, and it then crashed, killing everyone on board. The general's task was carried out successfully, but at a heavy human cost.

The US air support for SAS operations could also be two-edged. On one occasion an A-10 fired a Maverick missile at a D Squadron patrol, having mistaken them for an Iraqi group. It was an unforgivable 'blue on blue' incident, since they had laid out Union Jacks on the ground around the vehicles specifically to avoid any possibility of being misidentified. It was pure luck that no one was killed, but it put two vehicles out of commission, though the extent of the damage was limited to burst tyres; the might of air-power is sometimes more myth than reality.

The SAS squadrons continued to do some damage by calling in air-strikes from A-10s on to probable Scud launchers, but the kills could rarely be guaranteed. D Squadron eventually had four confirmed Scud kills, but A Squadron did not have a single confirmed success.

D Squadron were not necessarily better at finding Scuds than anyone else, for their area of operations lay closer to the south-western border of Iraq where the Scud launchers were concentrated. A Squadron was further south and east, and its targets were mainly airfields and communications control systems.

Lateral thinkers to a man, they began to wonder why there were no telegraph lines or microwave relay towers alongside the main supply routes through Iraq. There were drains at the sides of the roads, however, and you don't get much rain in the desert. When they ripped one open, they found fibre-optic cables.

Hitting the elusive Scuds was a major problem but the Iraqis couldn't hide the communications trenches at the sides of the roads. All the Iraqi communications and the data and co-ordinates for targeting the Scuds passed through the fibre-optic links – or so A Squadron were told by the forward operating base. In fact the Russians, who manufactured the Scuds, normally provided survey vehicles to accompany mobile launchers and supply the targeting data.

A Squadron damaged about fifteen major fibre-optic re-broadcasting stations by dropping bar mines down the tunnels, but in one such operation, a daylight attack on the Kuwait–Baghdad highway on 21 February, a huge contact developed with Iraqi forces. The squadron eventually managed to withdraw, but Trooper David 'Shug' Denbury was killed. Why a daylight attack was ordered at all remains another unsolved mystery of the Gulf War.

After regrouping, A Squadron then attacked a Scud co-ordination centre, code-named Victor Two. It was a complex of communications and repair facilities for the mobile launchers, near an airfield about 120 miles behind enemy lines.

Western civilians who had worked there had identified it as an important target and it had already been bombed by Stealth bombers, but the weather conditions prevented an accurate bomb-damage assessment from satellite and aircraft overflies.

A Squadron were sent in to finish off everything – electronic equipment, fibre-optic links or microwave relay towers – that the Stealth bombers had missed. This time it was scheduled as a deliberate night attack, but once again it was not done in true special forces style.

The recce patrol that went to do the initial close-target recce couldn't reach the site because of enemy troop movements around it. None the less the attack went in the following night. The first time anyone from the squadron clapped eyes on the target was when they drove in to attack it. The sixteen-strong party – eight demolitionists and an eight-man fire-support team – arrived in eight vehicles and set up a baseline of rocket launchers, machine-guns and support weapons. Then the assault force advanced through the built-up area surrounding the Scud control complex.

They moved forward on foot using passive night goggles. There were guards in trenches everywhere, but they were either smoking, cooking or sleeping and the SAS men entered undetected through the unguarded main gate.

The complex was already heavily damaged, but the 300-foot microwave tower appeared untouched. Fearing that they would have to blow their way into underground bunkers, the attacking party was carrying no demolition charges, only assault charges, which had to be detonated by firing a percussion cap. The demolitionists packed the explosives around the legs of the tower and fired the percussion caps. They had only one minute of safety fuse to get clear before the main charges went off.

The Iraqis responded to the firing of the caps almost immediately. Thinking they were under renewed air-attack, they first opened up skywards, but when the fire-support group started taking out targets within the complex the Iraqis realised that a ground force was present.

As the SAS assault party reached the main gate they came under heavy fire and were pinned down inside the complex. Realising the only alternative was to wait until sixty pounds of explosives detonated fifty feet from them, they threw white phosphorous grenades and then chanced their arms and ran for it through a hail of fire.

Miraculously they reached the fire-support line without any casualties. There was then a further contact with an Iraqi machine-gun position, but after taking that out the assault force jumped in their vehicles and pulled out.

When they reached the forward RV they discovered a problem. Not for the first time, the VHF voice comms were not working. The fire-support group had split up at the target and although half of them were now back at the forward RV, the other group was still in position, firing at the target, thinking the assault force was trapped in the compound. They were now almost surrounded by the enemy.

One of the SAS men jumped on a motorbike, roared back to the target and led the men out. They regrouped and then moved about seventy miles to lose the Iraqi pursuit.

The following morning a two-man recce patrol went back to a high point with a view of the complex. The microwave tower was down and the target was completely out of commission as a Scud control or communications centre.

A Squadron also brought in air-strikes on two other major targets, a radar station and another electronics complex sited on the Baghdad–Amman highway, but the perennial equipment shortages meant that they had no laser target designators and were forced to improvise. Their only option was to get in as close to the target as possible and then radio the GPS reading from the location back to base. The A-10s responded but their slow flying speed enabled the patrol to get clear before the attack, using iron bombs, went in. Both targets were destroyed.

The SAS vehicles had now covered nearly 3,000 miles over the punishing terrain in Iraq, and were starting to show signs of serious wear. Instead of pulling back the squadrons to resupply them and refit the vehicles across the border, HQ ordered them to be resupplied in a deep network of wadis, the Wadi Tubal, ninety miles inside Iraq.

The SAS was unable to persuade the RAF to fly food and ammunition in to Iraq, however. The aircraft were the special forces' Chinooks of 7 Squadron, but if there was low cloud, or no moon, or the RAF thought it too risky an operation, they wouldn't fly.

Instead, the SAS put together a convoy of trucks, which drove into Iraq in the early hours of 12 February and RVed with the squadrons. You could drive a couple of dozen unarmed trucks ninety miles into Iraq but, according to the RAF, despite the absolute control of the skies that the coalition enjoyed, you couldn't send in a Chinook.

Even if resupply by helicopter was deemed to be too risky, the SAS had two other well-established systems of airborne resupply. One used pods dropped by fast jets. The equipment was on the shelf when I left the Regiment in 1986 and could have been used as a low-risk means of resupply.

There was also a system of stand-off, computer-aided resupply, in which Hercules aircraft, operating at their ceiling of around 40,000 feet, drop supplies under steerable parachutes, computer-controlled by the patrol on the ground. They can be steered in to the chosen site from as far as twenty-five miles away, keeping the Herc far from danger. In the heat of the war the SAS commanders ignored these well-tested and practised advanced techniques and reverted to the safety blanket of old technology: a lumbering convoy of lorries.

Both squadrons had moved south, ready to RV with the convoy, but HQ then sent a signal forbidding them to leave their tactical area of operations unmanned. A Squadron were forced to take a big chance. They went north again, taking D Squadron's emergency fuel and rations – their survival kit – with them.

Had the resupply not arrived for any reason, it would have been physically impossible for them to get out. Even if their vehicles kept running, they would not have had enough fuel. Fortunately the convoy got there and the squadrons were resupplied in turn.

They even found time to convene an ad hoc meeting of the Warrant Officers' and Sergeants' Mess, complete with formal minutes and souvenir photograph, before the empty lorries rumbled south again to Saudi Arabia. There should have been many more important things to do than hold a mess meeting, however, and the charade perhaps says more about the Regimental sergeant-major's desire to build his reputation than to prosecute the war.

A Squadron were then tasked to go further north, above the Baghdad–Amman highway, the previous northern limit of their penetration. One of their targets was an airfield protected by a regiment of Iraqi special forces, but when they reached the area it was already being bombed by B52s.

Once more, it provided evidence of serious failures of communication, command and control. If you turn up at a designated target and find B52s already pounding it, something has gone severely wrong.

A Squadron then moved further west and called in a strike

on another airfield, but as G-Day – Sunday, 24 February, the launch of the ground offensive against Iraq – drew nearer, the SAS squadrons received the baffling instruction to suspend aggressive actions.

The lengthening artillery barrages on the Kuwaiti borders indicated the land war was about to begin, but SAS tasking dried up because the Scuds were no longer being fired. Those launchers not destroyed were keeping the lowest of profiles.

'We started to get signals from the ops room: "Do not, repeat, do not, carry out any offensive action on any enemy target." It was a strange order to receive in the middle of a war.'[7]

On the eve of a ground war, the SAS would normally expect to do more, not less. After six days of inaction, another signal ordered the squadrons to pull back to within easy reach of the border to 'prepare for Phase Two operations'.

They obediently withdrew to within twenty miles of the Saudi border and waited there for another couple of days in a lying-up position, still patrolling and gathering information. Then A Squadron were told to move with best haste back across the border to the forward operating base, leaving D Squadron inside Iraq until B could move up to replace them.

With Union Jacks flying, A Squadron left Iraq at first light the next morning, passing within about a mile of an Iraqi crossing point. D Squadron pulled out a couple of days later, just as the land war began.

Phase Two would have involved the SAS in operations around the oil fields in Kuwait and southern Iraq, and in support of the Marsh Arabs who were trying to instigate an uprising against Saddam, but Phase Two never took place.

'There was a stop, stop, stop, and everyone had to wait while the land war was analysed to see how it was developing.'[8] After two days it was over, too whirlwind fast for anything but retrospective analysis.

While the hot, wham bam, thank you, ma'am, SAS

operations against targets of opportunity inside Iraq had been going on, there had been another, deeper level of SAS activity. It was a much more subtle and focused operation.

Using the SAS Sabre Squadrons training for Iraq as cover, the Regiment set up a training camp and recruited Kuwaitis who were either out of the country at the time of the Iraqi invasion or who had later escaped from Kuwait.

A small SAS team trained them and they were then sent back through Saudi Arabia under the care of Bedou and infiltrated into Kuwait City. Their role was to carry out sabotage missions and intelligence-gathering.

A separate camp was filled with groups of expatriate Iraqis – Kurds, Marsh Arabs and Iraqi nationals – opposed to the regime in Baghdad. Cadres from the various groups were trained in isolation from each other. They learned intelligence-gathering, signalling, sabotage and assassination techniques, and were then infiltrated into Iraq.

The Marsh Arabs were returned to southern Iraq by sea, using fast surface-patrol craft. They started operations immediately in an attempt to tie down Iraqi troops. The other two groups were infiltrated into Iraq by covert means, some using SAS cross-country capability. The Iraqi nationals were dropped close to areas of population with the aim of fomenting general unrest. The Kurds were infiltrated on the Iran–Iraq border where there is a large displaced Kurdish population.

The covert training programme met with mixed success. The Kuwaiti resistance was useful to the coalition, though their activities led to considerable post-war friction with some of their fellow countrymen. Just as it was impossible to find a man in France after the Second World War who hadn't fought with the Maquis, there was no one in Kuwait who had not been a resistance fighter.

The Marsh Arabs also proved partially successful, attacking units of the Iraqi army with some success. After the war had ended, the Shi'ites in the south, including the Marsh Arabs, and the Kurds in the north rose in response to President

Bush's urgings, but then found themselves abandoned by the West. 'When I asked one senior figure in British intelligence about the earlier appeals for revolt, he replied, "We hadn't thought it through properly." '[9]

Both risings were suppressed with Saddam's customary ruthless efficiency. The Kurds faced their traditional fate, persecuted on all sides by hostile populations – Iraq to the south, Turkey to the north, Syria to the west and Iran to the east.

John Major's projected safe havens for the Kurds were a farce. RAF pilots helped to police the no-fly zones in northern Iraq from bases in Turkey, but they operated only with the consent of the Turks and were frequently grounded while the Kurds they were supposed to be protecting were pounded by Turkish forces.[10]

Nothing further was heard of the group of Iraqi expatriates and dissidents. Even as his military forces were being roundly defeated, Saddam's secret police remained more than equal to the task of suppressing internal dissent.

Two tasks that the Regiment might have undertaken – the freeing of the Western 'human shields' and the assassination of Saddam Hussein – both proved impractical. Before the conflict the SAS were asked to investigate the possibility of a hostage rescue operation similar to Delta Force's ill-fated Eagle Claw.

There was nothing to prevent a successful raid deep into Iraq, but the sheer numbers of human shields – hundreds of Britons had been seized in Kuwait and Iraq – and Saddam's dispersal of them to scores of different sites made any rescue attempt impractical. To have rescued some but not all of the hostages would have condemned those left behind to death. In the event, all the hostages were released by Iraq before the war began.

An operation to assassinate Saddam was often rumoured, but never ordered. It would have been far from easy to achieve, mainly because of the training that the forces charged with protecting him had received. Just as the West had been happy to supply arms and even the precursors for chemical and biological weapons to Iraq in the late 1980s, they had also sent military training teams.

Between 1978 and 1980 Saddam's elite forces were trained by a succession of visiting teams. One was German, one American and two were from Britain, composed of former SAS men. The final one, an entire team of ex-SAS NCOs, went in to train Saddam's bodyguards.

That was perhaps one reason why the coalition couldn't assassinate Saddam: they could never find him. They wouldn't. The men who trained his bodyguards were the best in the business. Just the same, the failure even to make contingency plans for an attempt – the ex-SAS men were never contacted to ask what training they had given to Saddam's bodyguards – coupled with the abrupt imposition of a ceasefire when the way to Baghdad lay wide open, suggested that the coalition's political leaders preferred a tyrant like Saddam Hussein to a power vacuum in Iraq.

The ceasefire at eight in the morning of 28 February 1991 was imposed by the US without any consultations with its allies in the coalition. John Major was simply told that the war was over, not asked for his opinion, and whatever DLB or the US military leaders thought of the decision, they had to swallow it.

The largest deployment of troops since the Second World War, and the most massive array of air-power ever assembled, had secured Western oil supplies and ensured a crushing defeat for Iraq, but Saddam Hussein remained, untouched and still in control of his country, while Margaret Thatcher and George Bush both found themselves out of office.

The SAS had been heavily over-committed during the Gulf War. There seemed to be a sense that as it was the only war we'd got, we might as well get everybody there. A lot of people who'd joined the Regiment to wear civvy clothes and do the Iranian Embassy every week suddenly found themselves in Iraq, freezing their nuts off.

The SAS involvement developed into little more than a chase for medals. The squadrons deployed into Iraq were commanded from the ground by their OCs, something I can never recall happening before in my twenty-three years in the Regiment: the OC and the SSM always stayed in the rear.

Back in 1964 the CO of the Regiment, John Woodhouse, had reminded a young squadron OC, Peter de la Billiere, 'I have no objection to you going once on a "special op" (i.e. a cross-border patrol), but it is quite wrong for you to do it more than once. Not necessary, and would be considered hogging the limelight or, far worse, gong-hunting, however pure your motives really are.'[11]

Nothing had happened in the intervening years to change that principle. The squadron OCs in the Gulf should have been back in the ops room, filtering information and directing the attacks, instead of out in the field. It left no one to fight their corner back at headquarters, where all the politics and in-fighting were taking place.

In the absence of the squadron OCs, the SAS men were being controlled by staff officers and intelligence officers who had no idea what the SAS were capable of, nor how to use them to best effect. Just as in the communications plan devised by Signals Squadron, the Sabre Squadrons were being told how to operate by non-combatants.

By watching for the signature of Scud launches in the night sky, chasing the mobile launchers and destroying them with anything from anti-tank missiles to sledgehammers, the SAS were once more showing their ability to think on their feet and improvise. But this belt and braces approach to locating and destroying Scuds in the high-tech world of modern military forces left the staff side of the British army and the whole coalition open to ridicule.

Even successful attacks like the assault on Point Victor by A Squadron illustrated the same problem. It was ludicrous to use an SAS squadron to carry out an attack that could have been done just as efficiently by a well-trained infantry company.

The ideal way for the SAS to have worked in Iraq would have been to split up into four- or two-man patrols, coming together as a larger force only to attack targets. They could not be broken down into their most effective units, however, because there was no way of reuniting them.

The two absolute fundamentals in an SAS patrol, the bedrock on which everything else is built, are navigation and communications. SAS men have to be able to move from RV to RV as a four-man or two-man group or even singly. They also have to be able to maintain radio communications with each other and HQ.

They were reliant on an RV system, but the ground was so flat and open that the only recognisable major features were the Euphrates to the north and the Saudi–Iraq border to the south. The air-navigation maps showed the odd communications tower but there was no guarantee that they were still standing.

In such featureless terrain, with only large-scale maps to guide them, a GPS system was essential. Yet there were only three for each group of sixteen men, travelling in eight vehicles.

I would not have gone into Iraq without a GPS – it runs counter to everything you learn in the Regiment – and I would definitely not have gone in without a Tacbe. Some troopers have admitted that in any potential contact they had half an eye on the enemy and half an eye on the man carrying the GPS. Whatever happened, they did not want to lose contact with him.

If they did, they were hopelessly lost because their maps did not show sufficient detail to identify the designated RVs or emergency RVs, and without a GPS they had no chance of finding them. Their only option was to go into immediate E&E – escape and evasion.

The groups had been left to decide their own E&E plans, but they were all told that Jordan would probably not give them a friendly welcome. It was an astonishing suggestion to make about one of Britain's most dependable allies in the region, whose special forces and Royal Guards had been trained by the SAS.

The deeper the squadrons were operating inside Iraq, the more Jordan made sense on an E&E run. It was a very long way to the Saudi border and the idea that Jordan was a less suitable destination than the only other alternative, Syria, was bizarre in the extreme.

All the E&E plans should have been placed in the ops room so that the ops officer knew the direction the SAS men were taking if anything went wrong, but the lack of co-ordination of the plans meant that no one at HQ knew where men going into E&E were heading for. A great deal of time was spent trying to locate people wandering somewhere in Iraq.

In one famous incident an A-10 pilot actually saw two men from D Squadron exfiltrating across the desert and was able to bring in an SAS group to pick them up. Inevitably the pilot had no means of communication with the ground, but he showed great initiative by overflying one of A Squadron's groups and waggling his wings to show something was wrong. He then repeatedly flew overhead in the direction he wanted them to take and led them straight to the two men.

They had covered about ninety miles towards the Saudi border before they were rescued, an epic feat of endurance, but to have to rely on a chance sighting by a pilot shows what a shambles the E&E plans were.

Yet the planning and co-ordination of E&E are a fundamental part of SAS tactics, giving the troops on the ground the confidence to know that if they chance their arm and things go wrong they will still be able to escape.

The system broke down even more badly with Bravo Two Zero, with tragic consequences. Their E&E plans never reached the ops room, and the officer who listed Bravo Two

Zero's orders did not talk to the ops officer until the patrol were well into E&E. Only then did he realise that the air-search for the missing men had been over the wrong area. They had been searching the desert southwards towards the Saudi border, but the men of Bravo Two Zero were heading north-west towards Syria.

The members of the patrol showed prodigious courage and endurance, covering huge distances in E&E across the mountains of western Iraq. One was shot and killed, two died of exposure and four were eventually captured and horribly tortured before their release at the war's end, but one, Chris Ryan, did the whole run, about 100 miles, to reach the Syrian border.

It was a remarkable feat of human endurance, but much of what he claims to have done during his exfiltration raises serious questions about the level of training that some of the SAS men on active service in the Gulf had received. Ryan was a former member of the Territorial SAS, newly graduated to the regular ranks, and his claimed actions during his E&E run were directly contrary to the standard operating procedures taught to every SAS man in combat survival training.

That is not a dry, academic quibble about someone using his own initiative rather than following set procedures. If an SAS patrol is split up for any reason, members know that they can regroup at a series of RVs and emergency RVs. Some only have a time-window of a few minutes, deliberately short to prevent the risk of compromise by the enemy, but if you miss all of them you know that the last resort is the war RV, a super-emergency RV where the patrol will be waiting.

SOPs instruct SAS men separated from their patrol to avoid all contact with the enemy because if captured and tortured you could not only betray your squadron's war plans, but also the location of the war RV, condemning your comrades to the same fate, or worse. Chris Ryan knew that his prime task was to protect the rest of the patrol by evading capture, yet claims to have invited contact with the enemy by launching attacks on Iraqi sentries. Either he was badly trained, or he deliberately broke SOPs, or we must seek another reason for his version of events.

The SAS men going into Iraq were assured that when they needed air support, all they had to do was shout, but 'Often we shouted and nothing happened. We waited forty-five minutes for aircraft to arrive and give us support when we were going to make a daylight attack on a complex next to the road. We didn't attack it in the end because the aircraft never arrived.'[12]

The SAS were promised that any casualties would be evacuated by helicopter, but there were only three or four Chinooks to support the whole of the special forces in Iraq and the SAS men formed the strong impression that RAF assets were regarded as far more important than men on the ground in Iraq. In any event, the helicopter pilots using passive night goggles couldn't fly if there was low cloud or on moonless nights. This caused some surprise, since helicopter pilots untrained with PNGs had used them to insert SAS patrols in considerably worse conditions during the Falklands War.

The RAF reluctance to commit its assets was no reflection on the courage of the aircrew – doctrine is dictated from the top, not the bottom – but morale was badly affected when seriously wounded men were not moved out for two or three days, or even a week.

In such circumstances it was a tribute to the humanity of SAS medics that they continued to use their scarce medical resources to treat enemy wounded even though, with re-supply so problematic, it reduced their own chances of survival. One or two SAS troopers wanted to take the harder, more pragmatic line and shoot wounded prisoners rather than use the drugs that might later be needed to save their own lives, but they were shouted down and no prisoners were shot.

The RAF's reluctance to use assets in casevacs also impacted on the planning of deliberate attacks. 'The guys would push it a little bit further if they knew that they had good support – fire support and medical support to get you to an aid station if you were injured. But as it went on they began to think, Perhaps I shouldn't push that bit further, maybe we shouldn't do that tonight. You have to put all those things right to keep the guys' morale as high as possible, so that they take the most chances and do the most damage.'[13]

Five SAS men were seriously wounded in action in Iraq and four were killed: Sergeant Vince Philips and Troopers Bob Consiglio, Legs Lane and Shug Denbury. Two died in combat, the other two of hypothermia while making E&E runs. Casualties might have been lower if they'd had GPS systems and functioning communications equipment. Against more resolute opponents than the Iraqi army the Regiment would have paid a far heavier price for its failings.

The combination of poor communications equipment and the lack of mapping, air photography and, particularly, GPS systems and Tacbes prevented the SAS from operating in groups smaller than a half-squadron in Iraq. They were effectively transformed into another infantry company, just another group of soldiers playing follow-my-leader.

The SAS deployment echoed in every detail the first operations of the original SAS fifty years before. Bands of mobile, vehicle-borne troops roamed over the sands, carrying out lightning raids and then disappearing back into the desert.

Such operations may have given the romantics a glow of nostalgia, but they were in no sense a proper use of Britain's most highly skilled and highly trained troops. As the SAS Deputy Group Commander – perhaps forgetting his own earlier description of Iraq as 'a big theme park waiting to be played in' – later remarked, 'The Regiment forgot many of the lessons it had learned over the years.'[14]

That led directly to heroic failures like the Bravo Two Zero mission. The publicity surrounding that mission and the bravery and endurance of the members of the patrol have diverted attention away from the real questions that needed to be asked about the SAS involvement in the Gulf War.

The planning, strategy and tactics were completely awry and there were shortcomings in the supply of equipment and poor communications procedures. The changes introduced in the early eighties, which brought other special forces like the SBS and 14 Int together with the SAS under the umbrella of the Special Forces Group, had now come home to roost. A massive increase in the size of the headquarters in the Duke of York's Barracks in London led to a shortage of suitably experienced officers to man the positions, and a potentially damaging duplication of roles.

Specialist officers were needed to direct the SAS, SBS and 14 Int to maximum effect, but the different groups were now placed in a position where in theory any Special Forces Groups officer could assist in tasking them.

The developing culture in the army that the SAS was now the place to be for a career also led to a number of officers with influence or contacts being posted into Special Forces Group, without ever having served with any special forces.

The system of training NCOs had also been changed at the same time, with similar consequences. The Regiment stopped training its own NCOs and men had to attend a training course at the Infantry Battle School in Wales before becoming senior SAS NCOs. The ideas instilled in them were conventional infantry ideas, not those of special forces, and as a result Regimental plans now tend to have a 'green army' tinge to them.

The Gulf War was the first iron test of the new system and it was found badly wanting. The emphasis had been taken away from the men on the ground and placed far too firmly on the controllers back at base. The ops officer at the forward operating base was the first point of contact, but HQ in Riyadh was pulling the strings. Yet for all the attempts to impose controls, as in every other conflict involving the SAS, it was the initiative, skill and resolution of the men on the ground that produced the results.

Senior NCOs must accept their share of the blame for the shortcomings, for they should have been supporting the officers when they were reaching the right conclusions and reining them in when they were wrong.

The Regiment's increasingly top-heavy administrative structure meant that, for the first time ever, SAS requests for equipment were subject to interpretation by staff officers who often had no experience whatsoever of special forces operations.

If the officer decided that the equipment requested – GPS systems, Claymore mines, ·203 grenades, cold-weather gear and the rest – was excessive or unnecessary, it would not be supplied.

When the Falklands War broke out, the Regiment was equipped with cold-weather gear within three or four days from a civilian shop. Despite a six-month build-up to the Gulf War, SAS men went into it ill-prepared and poorly equipped.

Officers tasking the patrols and half-squadron groups also showed their lack of experience by setting unrealistic times for the completion of tasks. SAS groups were ordered to attack a target eighty or ninety miles' drive across virtually uncharted desert, behind enemy lines, as if they were being asked to pop up the motorway from Hereford for a day out in Birmingham.

In addition to the lack of mapping there was also an almost complete lack of intelligence on the targets. The information given was along the lines of 'There's a target at Victor Two', without any estimates of the strength of the defences or the number of troops guarding it. That made close-target reconnaissance essential but in many cases the squadrons were allowed insufficient time and simply had to hit and hope.

If the SAS had retained a separate headquarters the mistakes would not have been made. The Christmas changeover between G Squadron and A Squadron would simply not have been allowed to happen and it is inconceivable that the Sabre Squadrons sent into Iraq would have been so poorly equipped and badly tasked.

All previous training for major operations and combat experience indicated the most effective roles the SAS could fulfil. A prime task would have been to take the pressure off the RAF by LTD'ing targets. Small SAS patrols, using artillery and fighter ground-attack, not their own firepower, can more than punch their weight in such situations.

Devoting two squadrons to a single task was also a waste of resources. One group should have been doing intelligence-gathering and one LTD'ing targets, and all of it should have been controlled by the OC in the forward operating base, not the field.

The lack of tasking on the eve of a ground war was particularly astonishing. I would have expected more specific, much more intelligence-focused targeting, much earlier. Shortly before the start of the land war, SAS patrols should have spread out across the whole of Iraq, setting up OPs on the lines of communication and reporting on the movement of reinforcements. Instead they were left to twiddle their thumbs.

Where the Director of the Special Forces Group was in all this is yet another unanswered question from the Gulf War. He should have been fighting the political battles with the MoD that DLB had fought and won during the Falklands War. Instead the Regiment appeared to suffer from a form of 'pay-back' from the defence establishment for its successes under the active patronage of Margaret Thatcher.

The public saw the campaign as yet another chapter in the SAS success story. In that they were echoing their new Prime Minister, John Major, who claimed that by destroying the threat from the Scuds the SAS had prevented Iraq from provoking Israel to a retaliation that would certainly have broken up the fragile coalition between the West and the Arabs.

When they visited the Regiment after the conflict, Lieutenant-General Peter de la Billiere, General Norman Schwarzkopf and Lieutenant-General Chuck Horner all added their congratulations to the SAS for their success against the Iraqi Scuds.

Yet if the Scuds were such a serious problem, why were they not recognised as such before the Regiment was committed to Iraq? Western military analysts had had ample time to assess the effectiveness of Scud missiles, for Iraq had used them extensively during the vicious 'War of the Cities' against Iran, when the West was providing Saddam with considerable support.

Analysts ignored or dramatically underplayed the significance of mobile Scud launchers, leading the coalition air forces to the false belief that the missiles could be destroyed on the ground.

That error had been exposed and Iraq's tactics telegraphed six weeks before the outbreak of the Gulf War. On Sunday, 2 December 1990, three Iraqi missiles were test-fired from a site near Basra. The first warning that Western intelligence received was when a surveillance satellite picked up the flare of a rocket. By then the missile had already been airborne for over five minutes and was close to its target, a closed military zone in the far west of Iraq, 400 miles from its launch site.

Two more missiles were launched. On each occasion they were not detected until already airborne. If the missiles' track was extended further westwards, they were aligned directly on Tel Aviv. The Israeli capital lay 250 miles from Iraq's western border, comfortably within Scud range.

The launches blew away any pretension that the West could destroy Iraq's arsenal of missiles before they were fired. Complacent assumptions about the time required to fuel, arm and fire the missiles were also shattered.

Even with the prior notice of a warning to civil airliners to keep clear of that area of Iraqi airspace, the US had been unable to obtain the intelligence necessary to detect the missiles before they were launched or make a pre-emptive strike against them. The Iraqis had used their knowledge of the limitations of American satellite surveillance – the periods between one satellite dipping below the horizon and the next one rising above it – to deploy the missiles from their camouflaged preparation areas and launch them undetected.

The only visible sign that General Norman Schwarzkopf and the rest of the coalition's senior commanders had realised the implications of that warning was a hasty increase in counter-biological and chemical warfare measures for their men. No strategic plan was made to counter the mobile Scud launchers.

Even when the war had begun and the destruction of the launchers was belatedly acknowledged to be vital to the maintenance of the coalition, the allocation of aircraft was never prioritised to the unit tasked with destroying them – the SAS.

The claims about the Regiment's success in the great Scud hunt are also questionable. Firings of Scuds were significantly reduced after the SAS deployment: in the first ten days of the war twenty-one Scuds were fired at Israel and twenty-two at Saudi Arabia; in the next thirty days a further nineteen were launched at Israel and twenty-three at Saudi Arabia.[15]

The rate of firings was cut to about one-third of the opening level, but the reduction was almost as great in the southern firing zones targeting Saudi Arabia, where no SAS patrols were operating, as it was in the west.

DLB's claim that 'no effective launches at Israel were made after 26 January' was also open to question.[16] Among the nineteen firings at Israel after that date was one that injured twenty-five people on 9 February, and another that injured seven more two days later.

A UN Special Commission also cast doubt on coalition claims of scores of Scud launcher kills, claiming that there was no evidence that any had been destroyed at all. That claim seems equally implausible. While aircrew and SAS patrols marking targets at a distance could have been deceived by decoy launchers, it is inconceivable that the SAS men who demolished a launcher with a sledgehammer could have been mistaken.

Suggestions that the 'launchers' could have been articulated lorries or petrol tankers are emphatically dismissed by the men who had eyes on them. Such an error in aerial surveillance might well have been possible but to the men on the ground 'they were unmistakable'.[17]

Whatever the actual total of Scud kills, there is no doubt that the SAS could have been deployed to take them on in a much more systematic way; they were the types of targets the SAS excels in attacking. For General Schwarzkopf to prepare for the battle without taking the Iraqi use of Scuds into consideration shows both political and tactical naïveté of the highest order.

His naïveté was equalled by that of John Major – or his political advisers in the Foreign Office. Immediately after the war he made great play of billing the rulers of the Gulf States for £600 million as a contribution to Britain's war costs.

Yet anyone with the slightest knowledge of the Middle East could have told him that if he had not pressed for payment of that relatively trivial sum in government terms the debt of honour owed to Britain by the Gulf States would have been paid many times over in trade and defence contracts. That act more than any other reveals the damaging extent of the Foreign Office's obsession with Europe to the exclusion of all else.

The Gulf War did show that the spirit of the people within the SAS was as sound as it always had been, but it also showed that an understanding of the use of the Regiment was completely lacking in the staff officers at headquarters involved in tasking them. For this to be the case in a conflict where the senior ground officer was a serving SAS general is surprising to say the least.

DLB had laid down the terms of SAS deployment before the conflict. 'I myself was not prepared to recommend special operations unless two conditions were fulfilled: one was that there must be a real, worthwhile role for the SAS to perform and the other that we must have some means of extricating our men in an emergency.'[18]

As events showed, neither condition was fulfilled, yet the SAS was deployed in greater numbers than in any conflict since Malaya. DLB would not have offered such a hostage to fortune unless he had been misinformed by his subordinates about the level of SAS preparedness, and he would certainly not have tolerated his men going into combat with inadequate mapping and insufficient GPS systems and Tacbes.

The SAS suffered from a lack of leadership at every level from senior NCO upwards, a failure to fight the political battles and, in some cases, a negligent use of manpower. The great strength of the SAS – the smallest number, in the right place, at the right time, using the resources available to the greatest effect – could not be applied. The SAS simply did not punch its weight in the Gulf.

Perhaps the most telling point about the whole operation was the fact that, following the precedent set at the end of the Falklands War, for the second time in the Regiment's history there was no detailed debriefing at the end of a major campaign, merely a short whitewash debrief.

Either SAS commanders felt there were no lessons to be learned from the campaign or they wished to avoid further embarrassment over the unnecessary errors that had been made. One explanation of the spate of books published about the Regiment since the Gulf War may be the anger of men denied any other forum to air their grievances.

The mistakes of the Falklands were repeated and magnified in the Gulf. The next major campaign may find the Regiment even more wanting. If the SAS cannot operate effectively in the deserts of the Middle East, where they have been training and fighting for forty years, where can they now be trusted to operate?

16

THE FUTURE

The Englishman poured himself a whisky from the hotel mini-bar then straddled a chair, facing the television. Apart from the sound of the French commentary, the only noise in the room was the whirr of the air-conditioning.

The slim shape of a space rocket – Ariane 5 – stood poised on the launch-pad, filling the screen. In a few more seconds it would be blasting off, taking its payload of telecommunications equipment into a high earth orbit.

As the final countdown started, the cameras panned slowly back, showing a sweep of beach and ocean, and the dark mass of the rainforest fringing the site.

The count reached zero. There was a microsecond's pause, then a vast cloud of smoke and flame belched from the base of the rocket. It lifted ponderously from the launch-pad, then accelerated upwards to the cheers of the watching crowd.

The camera tracked it upwards, but only a couple of hundred feet from the launch-pad the rocket began to judder and tilt. The nose slid away from the vertical and the clipped voice from the control room began to break in panic.

As the rocket veered further off course, the flight controller pressed the red destruct button. Several hundred million francs of French investment disappeared in a cloud of grey smoke.

The Englishman drained his drink and picked up his case.

He had arrived in South America three weeks earlier on a flight from Heathrow to Caracas. He was travelling on business as a risk-assessment manager for one of the world's best-known insurance companies. He had a British passport and all the necessary documentation and credit cards to support his identity. His only luggage was a suitcase and a shoulder bag.

He spent the next two weeks travelling through Central and South America, visiting a number of clients of the insurance company. He made assessments, gave advice and e-mailed his headquarters in London daily, using his laptop computer.

Two days before the Ariane launch he flew into Cayenne, French Guyana, and visited another client of the insurance company to establish his bona fides. Then he joined a party of tourists on a guided tour of the Ariane launch site at Kourou.

As the group crossed the concrete hard-standing to a viewing platform, he dropped back and then slipped into the trees on the edge of the rainforest.

Once out of sight, he unslung his shoulder bag and took out his laptop. Using a Swiss army penknife, he dismantled the computer, removed a number of components and then reassembled them in a different configuration.

The laptop had become a laser sited on the guidance control portion in the nose of the Ariane. He then set a small explosive device, timed to destroy the evidence of his work immediately after the Ariane's launch.

He wandered back to rejoin the tourist party, and a little while later was back at the airport for the short hop to Surinam. The next morning he watched French hopes of dominating the market in the launch of tele-communication satellites explode in flames.

Ghost Force operative, Surinam, the near future

Ariane 5 did veer off course just after leaving the launch-pad in 1996 and was destroyed in circumstances which at least one distinguished scientist found curious.[1] It was not sabotage – as far as we know – but it very easily could have been; the business of launching communications satellites is worth billions.

Wars now and in the future will no longer be fought over territory. The focus now is industry, communications and technology, and the prize is the creation of jobs and the wealth of nations. The battlefield on which such wars will be fought is global. The opponents are enemies, friends and allies alike, and the forces who will fight against them in the future will be as far removed from the stereotypical British squaddie as the Ariane is from a Morris Minor.

The SAS could once more find itself at the cutting edge of the new warfare – but only if it changes out of all recognition. On the face of it, the suggestion is ridiculous. The SAS is the most feared and fabled fighting force in modern history, a byword for bravery and ruthless efficiency. The name alone is enough to inspire fear; no conventional force in the world nor any terrorist organisation would willingly tangle with the SAS.

Ever since the campaign in Malaya the SAS has also been a substantial indirect contributor to Britain's balance of payments. After the Iranian Embassy siege it became a substantial direct contributor as well. Countries pay, and pay heavily, to have SAS training squads or Sabre Squadrons on their territory. That role has continued since the Gulf War and the Regiment has been heavily involved in setting up and training special forces for several of the Gulf and Far Eastern states.

Every leading nation now has its own equivalent of the Regiment, and most, like America's Delta Force, were not only inspired but also trained by British SAS men. While Delta Force's reputation has – perhaps unjustly – been tarnished by operations such as Eagle Claw, Grenada and the humiliating American intervention in Somalia in 1992, the reputation, prestige and influence of the SAS remains unblemished. It is now at an all-time high.

It's the perfect moment to disband the SAS.

I make that suggestion not as some crank armchair strategist nor rabid anti-militarist, but as one of the Regiment's longest-serving members. I spent over twenty-three years with the SAS and saw active service all over the world.

I'm far from alone in my view that the Regiment needs major surgery, for no one who was in the SAS prior to 1980 – including many former senior officers – is happy with it now. That is not the griping of old codgers complaining that the new generation is not as good as they were; it reflects a growing unease about the direction the Regiment has taken.

The reasons why the SAS operated well below Special Air Service standards of efficiency and professionalism in the Gulf War can be traced as far back as the erosion of standards of entry when G Squadron was formed in 1965. The decline was gradual, almost imperceptible at first, but it has proved irreversible and has been accelerated by more recent changes such as the formation of the Special Forces Group.

Over the years since I joined the SAS, it has evolved from an elite but purely military force to an instrument of covert government policy. I've witnessed the transformation of the Regiment from desert warriors and jungle fighters into today's ultra-sophisticated organisation, and I've been involved in some of the most clandestine SAS operations, known only to a handful within the Regiment itself, let alone the outside world.

Even when 22 SAS was a uniformed regiment, operating openly in foreign theatres of war, there was always a hidden agenda. Virtually every secret contained a darker secret at its core, concealed even from other SAS men. The activities of the Regiment itself became a cover for clandestine operations and undeclared wars.

The secret agendas continued in every SAS operation. Whether training bodyguards for friendly heads of state, countering insurgency in the Gulf, Africa or the Far East, or fighting in the Falklands and the Gulf War, what you saw was never exactly what you got.

The use of the SAS has always been dictated more by political than military considerations. The Foreign Office, not the chiefs of staff, usually decided when and where the Regiment would be deployed and its success as an instrument of foreign policy was based not just on its military effectiveness, but on its absolute secrecy.

Many governments and heads of state around the world owe their survival to the covert activities of the SAS, which instigated or repulsed *coups d'état* and shored up or toppled regimes as British interests dictated. The close relationship between Britain and the Gulf States, which has brought the UK billions of pounds in trade, was fostered by the covert activities of the SAS.

Such operations were only possible when the Regiment and its activities were shrouded in layers of secrecy. The siege of the Iranian Embassy – on the face of it the SAS's greatest triumph – changed all that. It is no longer possible for it to operate in a truly covert way. It is not even possible for operations such as those in which I was involved to be carried out unknown to other SAS men.

The Regiment's involvement in Operation Storm remained a secret for years. Today the SAS barely has time to deploy before a steady stream of information, comment and speculation about its activities begins. Its secrecy is breached from outside, through greater media scrutiny, and from within, through the revelations of serving and former members of the Regiment.

Ironically, Lieutenant-General Peter de la Billiere, one of the Regiment's most famous alumni, has done more than anyone else to bring this situation about. Apart from Tony Jeapes's little-noticed book on the war in Oman, DLB's autobiography was the first major breach in the code of silence that had previously surrounded the SAS.

The only officially sanctioned books until then had been objective histories, telling the story of some of the Regiment's less secret and sensitive campaigns after a decent interval of time had been allowed to pass.

DLB's book recounted some events before the dust had even settled on them. The story of the Bravo Two Zero mission, for example, was first told in his book, based on the confidential SAS debriefings of Andy McNab, Chris Ryan and the other members of the patrol.

Having seen their former commanding officer profiting from breaking the wall of silence around the Regiment, it was unsurprising that his men should decide to follow his lead. The subsequent attempts by the MoD to stop or censor their books merely confirmed their belief that there was one law for some and a different law for others.

A blanket ban on the former SAS men who had written books was later imposed by the CO of 22 SAS, and confirmed and extended by the Director, Special Forces Group, but it compounded the earlier errors. The lack of any distinction between those who had submitted their manuscripts to the MoD for approval before publication and those who had gone straight to print simply encouraged SAS men to publish and be damned. If you were going to be banned anyway, why bother to let the MoD see your book at all?

The banning of DLB – an attempt to show that all SAS men were now being treated the same way – was particularly stupid. DLB had, like Andy McNab, submitted his manuscript to the MoD before publication. He had made all the amendments they had requested, been given the green light to publish and was now being banned for doing so. The loss of an occasional drink in the mess, or a reunion or Regimental dinner, was hardly a crippling blow to most former SAS men, but banning one of the most influential men in the armed forces from all MoD property caused great personal offence to DLB and created a media furore. There was no better demonstration of just how much the Regiment and the MoD had lost the plot, and the bans have, if anything, increased the number of SAS men coming forward to tell their stories.

The Regiment's failure to come to terms with the media fascination with the SAS is only one of its current problems. When it was re-formed, it was seen as a regiment where people gave rather than took. Although officers were promoted on joining the SAS, while other ranks were forced to shed any stripes they held – and with them their extra pay – it was seen as a small price to pay because officers were not allowed the luxury of staying with the Regiment. They did a single three-year tour and then departed.

In the course of time the anomalies of pay and rank had to be addressed, because an elite regiment with poor pay and no career prospects made no sense at all. The SAS battled with the Ministry of Defence for years and finally, at the end of the 1970s, specialist pay was introduced, a massive overnight increase. Although still losing rank, troopers joining the Regiment were now paid an extraordinary amount of money, given that the only thing they had done at that point was to pass Selection.

The SAS now even advertises throughout the armed forces how much you can earn by joining the Regiment. Whether you contribute to it or take from it is down to the individual; unfortunately the majority just take. No longer is it seen as a Regiment in which you give, it is now very much a Regiment in which you can go and get.

A commanding officer trying to tell present-day recruits: 'Rank: forget it, you're not getting any. Career: if you stay here, you won't have one. Pay: if you want money, you'll get none,' would be laughed at.

Over the last twenty-five years more than ten ex-SAS officers have risen to the rank of general and above, including the present Chief of the Defence Staff. He makes much of his SAS credentials, even though he served with the Regiment for just three years as a troop officer in the late 1960s.

I recently saw a CV written by a colonel. On the strength of serving as chief clerk to an ex-SAS general he was able to wangle his next posting into Special Forces Group headquarters. He claimed in his CV that he had spent two years as the officer responsible for 'SAS operations and doctrine'. It was not a job description that any serving SAS man would have recognised.

The changed priorities in the upper echelons of the Regiment were perfectly illustrated by the behaviour of one officer during the Gulf War. He spent two weeks inside Iraq with A Squadron but then left during the resupply in the Wadi Tubal to go back to England for a course at Staff College. Securing the qualification for his next promotion was more important to him than staying in the field with his troops.

At about the same time as specialist pay was introduced, a system of commissioning through the ranks was also started. In itself it was an encouraging development, for many able people had previously been denied the chance of advancement, but it had an unfortunate consequence.

A captain leaving the army after completing his service receives a pension which is more than twice as large as a non-commissioned man with the same length of service, and a gratuity three times as big. Staff officers within the expanded Regiment began using the prospect of a commission for senior NCOs as a lever to help them impose their ideas on the SAS.

Troops on active service in the Gulf War were even threatened by a more direct pressure from officers and senior NCOs: RTU if they did not do as they were told. The Chinese parliament had become a dead letter. It was a complete reversal of direction. The Regiment had always been driven from the bottom up, but now the way of operating was dictated by the top. That may be the way the rest of the army works, but it was not the system that developed the unique qualities of the Special Air Service.

The formation of the Special Forces Group, including 14 Int and the Special Boat Squadron, was also an officer-driven exercise in empire-building. It was not carried out with the best interests of the Special Air Service in mind and has further eroded the Regiment's position.

An integrated Special Forces Group sounds fine in theory, but in practice, to amalgamate such units with the SAS and lay down the same standards and criteria is clearly absurd. Although 14 Int and the SBS are fine organisations in their own right, their requirements are very different from those of the SAS and the experience of their members is not relevant to SAS operations.

Fourteen Int was integrated into the Regiment using SAS rank slots, just as had happened with G Squadron. Serving SAS men missed out on promotions as the slots were filled by people from 14 Int who had never served in the Regiment nor passed SAS Selection. The decision was not even discussed, it was simply imposed.

The mystique that the Regiment has always possessed has been shattered. On the basis of a brief acquaintance with the SAS, or even none at all, groups of officers within the military system now think they should control and dictate the way the Regiment operates.

Prior to the Gulf, when the SAS asked for something they got it. Virtually no one knew what they wanted it for anyway. Now staff officers at headquarters are interpreting requests from troops and patrols, feeling that they know better than the people on the ground what is needed in any situation. They do not, of course, as the litany of SAS errors in the Gulf amply demonstrates.

I played a small role in the introduction of sat-coms to the Regiment. Vital though they were in the Falklands campaign, if I had foreseen the way they would be used to change the way the SAS operates, I would have driven that truckload of sat-coms into the nearest tree.

No tactical evaluation of the impact of sat-coms was carried out after the Falklands War, but their use has progressively emasculated the Regiment's greatest strength, its Sabre Squadrons. Where once they had great latitude and freedom of action in the field, they are now restricted and controlled by superiors who make no allowance for the traditional strategic role of the SAS.

The Sabre Squadrons should have had the freedom to operate in whatever way they felt was strategically necessary. If the Scud threat was going to destroy the unity of the coalition and paralyse the war effort against Iraq, as at one stage appeared possible, Sabre Squadrons would not have allowed the threat of being located by DF – or even nerve-gassed – to have distracted them from using every available means to locate and destroy the Scuds.

Quite apart from its other problems, the Regiment is also grossly overstaffed. In 1960, newly returned from Malaya, the operational strength of the SAS was no more than fifty-five badged troopers in two squadrons, A and D. Thirty-eight years later, when Britain's shrinking global role and the 'peace dividend' from the end of the Cold War has seen the overall size of the armed forces massively reduced, the strength of 22 SAS alone is more than five times that number.

Its present size bears less relation to its operational require-ments than to the need to retain sufficient numbers to keep the present ranking structure intact. The SAS was formerly commanded by a lieutenant-colonel. Now the Director, Special Forces Group, is a brigadier, his deputy is a full colonel, there are three lieutenant-colonels running 21, 22 and 23 SAS, and there has been a corresponding increase in the numbers and ranks of other officers down the line, including a large staff section in the Director's HQ.

To maintain the Regiment's present size requires a flow of recruits that the other forces simply cannot produce. There are not only fewer regular soldiers to choose from, they are less suited to the rigours of the SAS; the standards of fitness of recruits joining the army has never been lower.

The shrinkage of the armed forces as a whole can only continue. Desperately overstretched though all three branches of the services undoubtedly are, that is less a function of understaffing than of over-commitment.

Defence policy has been led by the nose since the Second World War, a prisoner of Britain's continuing obsession with its status as a great power. It continues even today; Tony Blair made reference to it on becoming Prime Minister. Yet it is a fiction. Britain's forces are tiny in comparison to a true modern superpower; the US Marine Corps alone is as big as the British army and has more air assets than the RAF.

Rarely if ever has any post-war British government first considered what defence we can afford and then tailored our military ambitions to fit our means. Instead, successive governments have continued to accept and even seek commitments that we neither need nor can afford. The military expenditure allocated is never enough to sustain even the fiction of British power, but it is always enough to impose an additional heavy drain on resources, further widening the chasm between Britain's self-image and the poverty-stricken reality.

Herbert Morrison remarked as long ago as 1949 that we were 'paying more than we can afford for defences that are nevertheless inadequate or even illusory'. Nothing has changed.

Britain's independent nuclear deterrent remains independent in name only; it is inconceivable that it would ever be used without the express permission of the United States government. Peering into the military future, the only other certainty is that military hardware – including such current science-fiction-to-reality projects as the pilotless Stealth fighter and the million-bullet gun – will only grow more complex and expensive.

The reality of Britain's current world position and the irrelevance of most military commitments to the country's true strategic interests will inevitably ensure further cuts in defence expenditure. Britain's 'moral mission' – in Tony Blair's words – to send troops and RAF squadrons to trouble spots like Bosnia might be admirable to some, but others would find it self-deluding or worse.

The deployment of troops and fighter aircraft to Bosnia was inspired by humanitarian motives, but it was a knee-jerk reaction – send in the troops to keep the warring factions apart – without any real thought to the longer-term aims or consequences of the deployment.

Like Northern Ireland, the festering legacy of generations of mutual hatred between the warring factions almost certainly means that no lasting peace can be achieved in Bosnia. British troops were caught in the middle and the convoluted rules of engagement left both troops and aircrew feeling more like targets than peacekeepers.

Serbs, Bosnians and Croats all fought each other, but also formed temporary, shifting alliances against one of the other factions. All committed terrible atrocities. The Muslim Bosnians – strengthened by Mujahedeen volunteers fresh from the war in Afghanistan and already hungry for another jihad – committed their share, but the worst offenders were the Serb Chetniks and the Croatian HOS troops. During the Second World War even the Nazi SS had jibbed at the barbarism of the HOS.

Troopers from 22 SAS took on the most dangerous tasks, mapping the front line between the warring factions, infiltrating through Serb lines to reach the besieged enclaves of Maglaj and Gorazde – during which one SAS man, Fergus Rennie, was killed – instituting daily foot patrols around the perilous streets of Gornji Vakuf, leading teams of UN observers into villages wiped out by massacres, acting as forward air controllers for air-strikes to prevent further massacres, and on one occasion bodyguarding John Major through 'Sniper Alley' in Sarajevo as he inspected British troops.[2]

The Territorial SAS took on the less arduous and hazardous peacekeeping tasks, though in a region as volatile as Bosnia there was no such thing as a safe area.

The SAS made headlines in the summer of 1997 by

snatching one wanted Bosnian Serb war criminal, Milan Kov-acevic, and killing another, police chief Simo Drljaca, when he tried to shoot his way out of the trap. It provided the peacekeeping forces with a rare success; most of the other wanted war criminals continue to operate with impunity.

The continued presence of British troops in Bosnia is of questionable value, however. It offers little more to Britain than the feel-good factor of occupying the moral high ground in a particular messy and sordid conflict. Unlike the Middle East, there are no real strategic interests to defend in Bosnia and few material advantages in trade or influence to be gained.

The SAS has always been a low-cost, high-value asset to Britain, but that is less and less true as it continues to maintain an establishment whose size bears a dwindling relation to that of the British army on which it draws, or its present level of operations, or its conceivable future tasks.

The Regiment is not only playing the numbers game with its full-time, front-line troops, it is also doing the same with its Territorial wing, and for the same reasons. While the government's post-Cold War review of the forces, *Options for Change*, took a machete to other Territorial units, the SAS TAs were spared. They were deployed in Bosnia, therefore they must be needed. QED.

Yet the reason for using them in Bosnia can only have been to stop them from being thrown on the scrapheap. R Squadron was deployed in the Gulf War – and praised after-wards for its contribution – for similar reasons. If Territorials could be called up for the Gulf War and become successful SAS men overnight, why should any regiment not supply off-the-peg troops to do the same job? And why send weekend soldiers out to Bosnia when full-time, fully trained SAS men were sitting back in Hereford twiddling their thumbs? The answers to those questions lie in the realms of military office politics, not operational needs.

The use of Territorials has also offered a dangerous hostage to fortune the next time cost-cutting politicians or civil servants are casting an eye over the Regiment. If a Territorial – a civilian – can be miraculously transformed into the equal of a fully trained SAS man at the drop of a hat, why do we need a regular SAS at all?

The SAS was reborn in 1950 out of a need to maintain British political and economic influence around the world as we divested ourselves of our empire and colonies. Since then Britain's horizons have grown steadily narrower, to the point where the Foreign Office no longer sees any role for the UK outside Europe. In previous decades the mandarins had rarely hesitated to use the Regiment, but as the Foreign Office became more and more Eurocentric, they became increasingly scared about the possible consequences of SAS operations elsewhere.

The Foreign Office's anxieties have been heightened by the knowledge that the SAS code of silence is no longer so effective or all-pervasive. Many SAS operations are so supersensitive that any public knowledge of its involvement, even after the event, could be politically disastrous.

'What if it comes out in twenty-five years' time?' became a constant refrain. 'What if it does? We might be dead by then' was never going to be a sufficient answer to people who are still denying that the *Lusitania* was carrying munitions when torpedoed during the First World War.

Thatcher has gone, and the SIS and the Foreign Office have developed a collective case of cold feet. Where military training in sensitive areas is still required, it is increasingly steered in the direction of private companies.

Often set up and staffed by ex-SAS men, they operate in trouble spots worldwide. Although much of the business of the more reputable of them derives from their close links with government, they are private companies. If operations go wrong or awkward questions are asked about some of the murkier activities, the Foreign Office can raise its collective arms in horror and deny any knowledge.

It is an extension of the traditional policy of deniability, but the price the government pays for keeping black operations at arm's length is that it no longer exercises any effective control over them. Political accountability has been lost.

The SAS has often operated close to the limits, but we worked under political direction and control. If allegations were made against SAS men, they could be – and often were – tested by formal inquiries or courts of law. The numerous British companies operating in the world's trouble spots may on occasion serve Britain's political ends but, despite their headed notepaper and smart offices in fashionable areas, at bottom they remain mercenaries, accountable to no one but themselves.

The SAS finds itself increasingly marginalised. Its military training role is now the province of private companies, albeit drawing on the expertise of ex-SAS men. Intelligence-gathering is dominated by GCHQ. It is also directed at our friends rather than our enemies, for the Foreign Office's prime need is now information on our allies' negotiating positions, not their military strategies.

The SAS has no part to play in that. As I write, there are a few very limited operations going on on behalf of Her Majesty's Government and the CT team is carrying out its normal training routines. Apart from that, the SAS is currently unemployed.

If the SAS does not evolve, it dies. As it thrashes around seeking a new *raison d'être*, it can only focus on one remaining area of unchallenged expertise: counter-terrorism. The Regiment could continue to serve as a training base and a provider of leaders of excellence in CT but it would be restricted to a purely military role in a very narrow military field. It would also face continuing pressure to hand over its CT tasks to the police, who have always resented the involvement of the SAS in what they see as a purely police matter.

The other reason that the anti-terrorist role is so keenly contested by the police is that it is the one budget that does not have to be justified in detail to the Treasury. Just after coming to power, the new government under Tony Blair asked the Metropolitan Police for a detailed breakdown of their spending on anti-terrorism in 1996–97. The Met came up with an overall figure of £50 million. This excludes what other forces – particularly in cities like Manchester, Liverpool and Glasgow, which have large populations of Irish Catholic descent – are spending on anti-terrorist precautions.

The counter-terrorist budget is paying for large numbers of armed-response police vehicles to cruise around the major cities of the UK, while the public picks up the tab. It is a wasteful duplication of the SAS anti-terrorist provision and it also carries a substantial risk. At some point there will be a terrorist problem that the police will try to solve without using the SAS.

If it all comes apart at the seams, someone – the SAS – will then have to go in and try and pick up the pieces. In the resulting mess, the Regiment could also come unstuck, and if the formidable reputation of the SAS is dented, terrorists other than the IRA will again begin to see Britain as a possible area of operations.

The SAS may resist the police pressure and continue to be the first line of defence against terrorism, albeit as part of a European CT team, but even that is called into question by the EC member states' continuing ambivalence about terrorism. In recent years the government of the Netherlands has refused to extradite ETA suspects to Spain, Germany would not convict IRA terrorists and Italy released the *Achille Lauro* murderer.

Even if the CT team did find employment as part of some European counter-terrorist force, its value would be debatable. To keep a CT team at the peak of efficiency you need a rotation between spells of duty, training and other activities. You also need a flow of fresh ideas and fresh people through the team. Without both, the CT team quickly becomes stale and loses effectiveness.

Whatever its future counter-terrorist activities, the SAS as a whole can no longer find a significant overseas role to play. John Deutch, the director of the CIA, made a speech in November 1995, in which he identified:

the main challenges facing the post-Cold War world:
1 The proliferation of chemical, biological and nuclear weapons...
2 The activities of countries like North Korea, Libya, Iraq and Iran.
3 The growing threat of international crime, terrorism and narcotics trafficking.[3]

There is little sign of new work for the SAS in that list beyond its now traditional counter-terrorist and training roles. There have been periodic reassessments of its role in the past but the situation in which the Regiment now finds itself is very different. I know what the SAS can and cannot do, and I honestly can't see a useful future for it in its present form.

George Robertson, the Defence Secretary in the new Labour government, said in December 1997 that the MoD 'has to be seen to be an up-to-date employer'. That apparently anodyne remark carries the implicit threat of pushing the SAS even further towards the sidelines.

He was in part referring to the right of women to fight in the front line. Few would now dispute it, as long as they are willing to accept the risks that that entails, but though women work as equals with SAS men in specific areas, they can never become part of the regular SAS. They simply do not have the physical strength for the long-range infiltrations, carrying heavy loads, that are central to the Regiment's traditional roles.

Nor, like Delta Force, can the SAS ever be a believer in affirmative action, nor positive discrimination. It is an equal-opportunities employer, but the bottom line is that only the best are good enough, irrespective of what political correctness might require.

Armed forces' recruitment advertisements increasingly stress non-combat activities; the RAF show aircraft flying humanitarian missions to feed the starving of Africa. Such euphemistic advertisements dodge the issue, disguising the hard reality of the armed forces. At root they are there to defend the realm, not carry out humanitarian work. By taking the Queen's shilling, you are accepting that you may be required to die for your country.

The pretence that you can have fighting troops without the inevitable corollary that in combat some will die is breeding a culture similar to that which now exists in the US, where any level of American casualties is enough to create a political storm. As Britain's armed forces come under the same constraints, the Queen's killers – the SAS – will find themselves ever more isolated.

The SAS carried out many covert tasks in the 1980s purely because the American Freedom of Information Act made it impossible for US forces or secret agencies to do so. The British government is now perilously close to introducing its own version of the Act. Some may feel it is long overdue, but by tying the hands of the SAS and preventing covert operations it will greatly damage the interests of the nation.

The Gulf War will almost certainly prove to have been the Regiment's last hurrah. A spell with the SAS may remain a good career move for an officer but, restricted to counter-terrorist duty, it will become a very poor career option for a long-serving trog. Over a period of time the status – and the calibre – of SAS men will inevitably decline.

There is still a wider role that an elite force could fulfil, but it requires the complete transformation of the SAS. Disbanding the Regiment and re-forming it under a new guise happened by accident in 1950 but much time was lost and many mistakes made before it evolved into its modern form.

Working to a coherent strategy from the start, the loss of time and most of the mistakes could be avoided.

Before I left the Regiment I wrote a paper advocating the most radical surgery in its history. Stated baldly, my proposal was to remove it from all operational activities. The paper was rejected out of hand by the vast majority of currently serving SAS men – understandably, since it proposed to abolish the Regiment in which they hoped to serve out their careers.

Yet however unpalatable it may be, the proposal I tabled represents the sole viable future for the SAS, the only means by which it can again resume truly covert operations.

If standing armies confront each other in future wars of mass destruction there will be no role for units like the SAS, but conflicts around the world will increasingly be wars waged by proxy, just as the conflict between Syria and Israel has been fought through their client forces like Hizbollah and the Lebanese Christian militias.

Small groups will also carry out economic warfare, targeting key industries – power, water and information technology, through which virtually every other industry can be brought to its knees.

The combatants in this new kind of warfare are as likely to be allies as enemies. Our 'friends' in Europe, the USA and the rest of the developed world already carry out economic espionage against us. The FBI actually sends out a brochure to US companies listing twenty-two critical technologies at risk from information thieves under the general headings of Materials, Manufacturing, Information and Communications, Biotechnology and Life Sciences, Aeronautics and Service Transportation, and Energy and Environment.

Their caution is well founded. To mention only one example, the French were found to be operating a spy ring in an American aircraft company in 1996. The US and Britain are no more clean-handed, however, for we too spy on our trade rivals. The present and former British Foreign Secretaries have admitted as much in a television documentary[4] and Germany ordered the expulsion of a CIA agent in March 1997, one of 100 still said to be operating in West Germany despite the end of the Cold War.

The man, accredited as a diplomat at the American Embassy in Bonn, had tried to obtain details of German high-tech companies doing business with Iran, and information on German government export loan guarantees to those companies.

As the Berlin-based ex-editor of *Encounter*, 'the intellectual house journal of US Cold Warriors', remarked: 'It's one thing checking out plutonium smuggling. But now they want to know what Mercedes is doing.'[5]

Among the less traditional sources of intelligence are communications intercepted by listening stations like those of the US National Security Agency and Britain's GCHQ and the Menwith Hill Station near Harrogate in Yorkshire, which can eavesdrop on every single telephone conversation in Europe. The German magazine *Der Spiegel* claimed that communications between the European Airbus consortium and Saudi Arabia intercepted by the NSA complex at Bad Aibling in Bavaria helped the US to win a $6 billion aerospace contract with the Saudis.

The US intelligence agencies also lobbied Congress to rewrite draft legislation on the control of the Internet, replacing the right to encrypt data with regulations banning even American citizens from doing so.

The agencies and their political supporters went on to demand that any American whose e-mail could not be deciphered by US intelligence should be liable to five years' imprisonment, and pressed the President to use America's economic and military muscle to force other nations to toe the same line.[6]

The countries of the Middle East and the Pacific Rim countries – the Asian Tigers – also use their intelligence services and armed forces to operate actively against visiting business people. In more than one country every telephone call from hotels used by businessmen is routinely tapped, every fax copied and every waste-basket searched for useful documents. The resulting intelligence is screened by the state and passed to the relevant domestic industries.

Industrial espionage is endemic throughout the world; the step from that to economic sabotage is only a small one. President Clinton was sufficiently concerned by the threat to set up the Commission on Critical Infrastructure Protection in 1996, seeking ways of protecting sensitive US computer systems – over 90 per cent of which are privately owned – and other key industrial infrastructure against potentially crippling attacks by 'cyberterrorists'.

Nervous businessmen wishing to test the security of their computer systems could hire the services of companies such as Hackers for Hire, fronted by ex-CIA agent Robert D. Steele, and including such superstar computer hackers as 'Eric Blood-axe', who was arrested by the FBI in 1990 after hacking into the US government's ultra-secure telephone network.

While everyone is obsessed with protecting the security of their computer systems, however, they tend to ignore the most obvious threat. Computers rely on electricity, and power supplies are even more vulnerable to attack and disruption.

There are two simple ways to interrupt a power supply. You can either throw a cable across the high-tension wires, as kids do with monotonous regularity on electric train lines, or you can remove the drain-plugs from the transformers with a spanner. When the cooling oil drains out, the transformer overheats and explodes. When enough have exploded, the power company will have run out of spares.

The trial of eight men on bombing charges in June 1997 showed that the IRA were not unaware of the damaging potential of such attacks. Their plan to blow up six electricity sub-stations would have blacked out much of the south-east of England, including London. The map of the electricity network on which the plan was based was obtained from a book available at the men's local public library.

Major companies worldwide also now rely on the Japanese system of 'just in time' production. Component and raw-material stocks are held at absolute minimum levels and shipped in from suppliers only as required. Any interruption of that system, at any point on the chain, is a serious impediment to producing goods on time at budgeted cost. The reaction to such failures is usually to move production to another country.

The vulnerability of such companies, suppliers – and countries – to selective attack is obvious. Even hoax bomb warnings can be enough to cause massive disruption to a country's transport and industry, as the IRA has also proved on many occasions.

The skills and capabilities that the SAS has so assiduously developed and practised are largely irrelevant to this brave new world. To wage or counter economic warfare requires the complete transformation of the Regiment; its successor may not be a military force at all.

In the Gulf War and every other conflict in which the SAS has been involved it has operated under the constraints imposed by the other forces' need to protect their ever-dwindling number of assets: aircraft, helicopters, tanks, fighting ships.

At the same time, British Airways and other commercial airlines are flying 100,000 passengers out of Heathrow every day to destinations throughout the world. It is now not merely cost-effective but essential to use those civilian assets for our military purposes.

There will be no more deployments of heavily armed military personnel transiting through overseas bases – how could there be? Britain has very few overseas bases. There will be no military aircraft over-flying other countries. There will be no parachutists free-falling under cover of darkness, no divers in wet-suits, no figures in black balaclavas abseiling down cliffs or buildings. There will be no missiles, no smart bombs, no mortars or artillery, no machine-guns, no grenades, automatic rifles or even pistols. There will be no hearts and minds programmes, no painstaking learning of local languages and dialects, no paramedic training.

The economic warriors of the future will be civilians. They will arrive in civilian clothes, on civilian flights, carrying nothing more threatening than an American Express card. They will be women as well as men, speaking English, the lingua franca of the modern world, and posing as business or salespeople, students or tourists.

Their weapons will be the sort of tools and equipment that can be bought in any High Street hardware shop, but the impact of their attacks will be enormous, causing economic damage running into millions of pounds. The attackers will then leave as they arrived, anonymous air travellers moving on, grey faces in the crowd. The victim nation will probably not even know which country has attacked them.

The new force – an anonymous, faceless Ghost Force – would draw on skills that SAS demolitions experts already possess, but develop, refine and build on those skills in the same way that the arts of bodyguarding and counter-terrorism were revolutionised by the SAS over twenty years ago. We already gather intelligence on our trade rivals. Ghost Force would give the UK government an offensive capability to set alongside its passive intelligence-gathering operations.

You don't need guns or bombs to kill people, nor two tons of Semtex to cause chaos. A Ghost Force team could travel to any country in the world with just a passport, a credit card and a plausible cover story. Using nothing more complex than a £2 spanner you can buy in Woolworths, they could wreak as much havoc as a bombing campaign by the entire RAF.

Water, power and information technology are the vital factors for any industrial society. Take them out and you bring that country's industry to a juddering halt. To defend all the potential targets against highly trained attackers would be impossible.

The conventional way to defend sensitive sites is to surround them with people. Yet that is completely ineffective against the kind of attack that Ghost Force would mount. Computer systems can be breached by hackers operating from anywhere in the world, but even physical targets like power stations and water-treatment plants are indefensible against a determined attack.

The attackers would start from the defensive perimeter around the site but instead of trying to breach it, they would work outwards until they found the weak links. Attacks might come against the water main a few hundred yards down the road or the reservoir up on the moors, an electrical sub-station a few streets away or the electricity generating station 100 miles away.

Arson is another devastating weapon. If a fire is correctly set and sited, currents of air or the chimney effect of a lift shaft will see it spread horizontally or vertically at terrifying speed. Ghost Force saboteurs would be trained to create maximum damage from fire in minimal time.

Arson and sabotage, weapons of the terrorist, have now come full circle. They are the weapons that would allow a country to wage war – even an undeclared war – against its enemies. There would be minimal numbers involved and very few casualties, but the interruptions to production and the damage to the infrastructure of the hostile country would bring it to its knees.

Ghost Force would serve the wider, covert interests of Her Majesty's government in the same way that 22 SAS Regiment has done for the last fifty years. Like its forerunner, Ghost Force would also have an intelligence role, but the target would be commercial intelligence. Our enemies, allies and friends alike all gather it on a massive scale; it is time that we made greater efforts to match their effort, for billions of pounds and hundreds of thousands of jobs are at stake.

Ghost Force is the wave of the future. The SAS, as it is presently constituted, is now firmly of the past. It has lost its way and in a welter of worldwide media interest it has also lost its greatest asset, its secrecy.

The kind of men who made the SAS great have not disappeared. The spirit of the SAS still burns bright among the Sabre Squadrons at the heart of the Regiment, but it is increasingly stifled by the dead weight of bureaucracy, the vested interests of the ever-growing number of peripheral personnel and the critical lack of leadership so tellingly exposed in the Gulf War. One day, perhaps not so far into the future, the spirit of the SAS will be extinguished altogether.

The Regiment cannot reform itself; it is condemned to survive because too many careers depend on it. The only solution is for the SAS to be scrapped – the Regiment that I knew and served with has effectively been disbanded anyway. The pick of its men – the real SAS – and the best of its skills and techniques will be retained, refined and adapted. They will then be used to train a radically different, totally covert and even more potent civilian successor.

A token SAS could remain in existence as a Hereford tourist attraction, but in the tradition of the Regiment there would be a secret within the secret. Its true function would be to act as cover for a force that is deniable, invisible, unknowable and invincible, more deadly even than the SAS at the height of its powers: Ghost Force.

The achievements of the SAS deserve to live for ever in the pages of military history, for 22 SAS Regiment has a glorious past – but it has no future. SAS RIP.

Appendix

Extracts from the Founding Principles of the SAS, laid down by David Stirling

From the start, the SAS Regiment has had some firmly held tenets, from which we must never depart.

1 The unrelenting pursuit of excellence.
2 Maintaining the highest standards of discipline in all aspects of the daily life of the SAS soldier ... a high standard of self-discipline in each soldier is the only effective foundation for Regimental discipline. Commitment to the SAS pursuit of excellence becomes a sham if any single one of the disciplinary standards is allowed to slip.
3 The SAS brooks no sense of class. We share with the Brigade of Guards a deep respect for quality, but we have an entirely different outlook. We believe, as did the ancient Greeks who originated the word 'aristocracy', that every man with the right aptitude and talents, regardless of birth and riches, has a capacity in his own lifetime of reaching that status in its true sense; in fact, in our SAS context, an individual soldier might prefer to go on serving as an NCO rather than having to leave the Regiment in order to obtain an officer's commission. All ranks in the SAS are of 'one company', in which a sense of class is both alien and ludicrous.

4 Humility and humour: both these virtues are indispensable in the everyday life of officers and men – particularly so in the case of the SAS which is often regarded as an elite Regiment. Without frequent recourse to humour and humility, our special status could cause resentment in other units of the British army and an unbecoming conceit and big-headedness in our own soldiers.

NOTES

Chapter 1: Desert Warriors 1941–45
1 Alan Hoe, *David Stirling*.
2 David Stirling, quoted in John Strawson, *A History of the SAS Regiment*.
3 Quoted in Philip Darby, *British Defence Policy East of Suez*.
4 James Morris, *Farewell the Trumpets*.
5 Lawrence James, *The Rise and Fall of the British Empire*.
6 Colin Cross, *The Fall of the British Empire*.
7 Quoted in Paul Kennedy, *The Realities Behind Diplomacy*.
8 Morris, op. cit.
9 Richard Nixon, *The Memoirs of Richard M. Nixon*.

Chapter 2: Malaya 1950–58
1 Anthony Kemp, *The SAS: Savage Wars of Peace*.
2 James Morris, *Farewell the Trumpets*.
3 Donald 'Lofty' Large, *One Man's SAS*.
4 Quoted in Alan Hoe, *Re-Enter the SAS*.
5 Quoted in John Strawson, *A History of the SAS Regiment*.
6 Quoted in Robin Neillands, *A Fighting Retreat*.

Chapter 3: Jebel Akhdar 1958–59
1 Lawrence James, *The Rise and Fall of the British Empire*.
2 *Future Defence Policy*, May 1947.
3 Royal Institute of International Affairs, *The Middle East: A Political and Economic Survey*.

4 E. Shuckburgh, *Descent to Suez: Diaries 1951–56*.
5 I. Clark and N. J. Wheeler, *Origins of British Nuclear Strategy*.
6 Quoted in Hugh Thomas, *The Suez Affair*.
7 James, op. cit.
8 Donald 'Lofty' Large, *One Man's SAS*.
9 Sir Frank Kitson, *Bunch of Fives*.

Chapter 4: Return to the West 1958–63

1 Diane B. Kunz, 'The Importance of Having Money: The Economic Diplomacy of the Suez Crisis'.
2 P. J. Cain and A. G. Hopkins, *British Imperialism: Crisis and Deconstruction, 1914–1990*.
3 Michael Dockrill, *British Defence Since 1945*.
4 F. S. Northedge, *Descent From Power*.
5 *Economist*, 15 February 1964, quoted in Northedge, op. cit.
6 Max Hastings (ed), *The Oxford Book of Military Anecdotes*.
7 Donald 'Lofty' Large, *One Man's SAS*.
8 David Stirling, quoted in John Strawson, *A History of the SAS Regiment*.
9 Large, op. cit.

Chapter 5: Brunei and Borneo 1962–66

1 John 'Lofty' Wiseman, unpublished interview with the author.
2 Ibid.
3 Donald 'Lofty' Large, *One Man's SAS*.
4 John Strawson, *A History of the SAS Regiment*.
5 Robin Neillands, *A Fighting Retreat: The British Empire 1947–97*.
6 Ibid.
7 Peter de la Billiere, *Looking for Trouble*.
8 Large, op. cit.
9 Ibid.
10 *Mars and Minerva*, 1965; de la Billiere, op. cit.
11 Large, op. cit.

12 Donald 'Lofty' Large, unpublished interview with the author.
13 de la Billiere, op. cit.
14 Anthony Kemp, *The SAS: Savage Wars of Peace*.

Chapter 6: The Kennedy Assassination 1963

1 Colin Cross, *The Fall of the British Empire*.
2 George Woodcock, *Who Killed the British Empire?*
3 Lawrence James, *The Rise and Fall of the British Empire*.
4 Cross, op. cit.
5 Woodcock, op. cit.
6 Quoted in Woodcock, op. cit.
7 Eric Hobsbawm, *Age of Extremes*.
8 Nicholas Mansergh, *The Commonwealth Experience*.
9 Bernard Porter, *The Lion's Share: A Short History of British Imperialism, 1850–1970*.
10 Quoted in Porter, op. cit.
11 Sir Patrick Devlin, *Report of the Commission of Enquiry into Disorders in Nyasaland*.
12 Ibid.
13 *Listener*, 31 July 1969, quoted in James, op. cit.
14 Robert Good, *UDI: The International Politics of the Rhodesian Rebellion*.
15 Mansergh, op. cit.
16 F. S. Northedge, *Descent From Power*.
17 Ruth First, Jonathan Steel and Christabel Gurney, *The South African Connection*.
18 Papers of the Commonwealth Secretariat, quoted by Richard Norton-Taylor, *Guardian*, 7 April 1997.
19 James, op. cit.
20 Peter McAleese, *No Mean Soldier*.
21 Cross, op. cit.

Chapter 7: Aden 1964–67

1 Michael Dockrill, *British Defence Since 1945*.
2 Lawrence James, *The Rise and Fall of the British Empire*.

3 Peter de la Billiere, *Looking for Trouble*.
4 *The Times*, 4 May 1964.
5 de la Billiere, op. cit.
6 Ibid.
7 Anthony Kemp, *The SAS: Savage Wars of Peace*.
8 Robin Neillands, *A Fighting Retreat: The British Empire 1947–97*.
9 Donald 'Lofty' Large, *One Man's SAS*.
10 *Daily Telegraph*, obituary, 14 May 1997.
11 Large, op. cit.
12 Neillands, op. cit.
13 Ibid.
14 Philip Warner, *The SAS*.
15 *The Times*, 17 November 1964.
16 Quoted in Dockrill, op. cit.
17 Ibid.
18 Government statement on the Defence Estimates, 1966, quoted in F. S. Northedge, *Descent From Power*.

Chapter 8: Operation Storm: Dhofar 1970–77

1 Robin Neillands, *A Fighting Retreat: The British Empire 1947–97*.
2 Philip Warner, *The SAS*.
3 Max Beloff, *The Future of British Foreign Policy*.
4 F. S. Northedge, *Descent From Power*.
5 Hugh Thomas, *The Suez Affair*.
6 David C. Arkless, *The Secret War, Dhofar 1971–2*.
7 Ibid.
8 Anthony S. Jeapes, *SAS: Operation Oman*.
9 Captain Mike Kealy, quoted in John Strawson, *A History of the SAS Regiment*.
10 Anthony Kemp, *The SAS: Savage Wars of Peace*.
11 Jeapes, op. cit.

Chapter 9: Northern Ireland 1968–97

1 Adrian Weale, *Secret Warfare*.

2 Raymond Gilmour, *Dead Ground: Infiltrating the IRA*.
3 *Daily Telegraph*, 16 March 1979.
4 Peter de la Billiere, *Looking for Trouble*.
5 *Daily Telegraph*, 19 March 1979.
6 de la Billiere, op. cit.
7 Weale, op. cit.
8 Mark Urban, *UK Eyes Alpha*.
9 Ibid.
10 Ibid.
11 'Soldier A', Transcript of Evidence to the Gibraltar Inquest.
12 'Soldier B', ibid.
13 'Soldier D', ibid.
14 Robin Neillands, *In the Combat Zone: Special Forces Since 1945*.
15 Hansard.
16 Michael Paul Kennedy, *Soldier I*.

Chapter 10: Terrorism 1968–98

1 Quoted in James Adams, *Secret Armies*.
2 Ibid.
3 Robin Neillands, *In the Combat Zone: Special Forces Since 1945*.
4 Claire Sterling, *The Secret War of International Terrorism*.
5 Andrew Kain, *The SAS Security Handbook*.
6 Ibid.
7 Adams, op. cit.
8 Charlie A. Beckwith and Donald Knox, *Delta Force*.
9 Adams, op. cit.

Chapter 11: Iranian Embassy 1980

1 Peter de la Billiere, *Looking for Trouble*.

Chapter 12: The Falklands 1982

1 Bernard Porter: *The Lion's Share: A Short History of British Imperialism, 1850–1970*.
2 Nicholas Mansergh, *The Commonwealth Experience*.

3 Lawrence James, *The Rise and Fall of the British Empire*.
4 General Michael Rose, *Advance Force Operations: The SAS*.
5 Peter de la Billiere, *Looking for Trouble*.
6 Ibid.
7 Andrew Kain, *The SAS Security Handbook*.
8 de la Billiere, op. cit.
9 Porter, op. cit.
10 Ibid.
11 Kain, op. cit.
12 Andy McNab, *Immediate Action*.
13 Tim Sebastian, 'Cash For No Questions', *Observer*, 19 January 1997.
14 McNab, op. cit.
15 Mark Tran, *Guardian*, 19 July 1997.

Chapter 13: Afghanistan 1982–89

1 Mark Urban, *UK Eyes Alpha*.
2 Ibid.
3 *Dispatches*, Channel 4, 20 February 1997.

Chapter 14: Cold War 1945–90

1 *Jane's Defence Weekly*, 25 January 1986.
2 *Soviet Military Encyclopaedia*, quoted in James Adams, *Secret Armies*.
3 Eric Hobsbawm, *Age of Extremes*.
4 Robin Neillands, *A Fighting Retreat: The British Empire 1947–97*.
5 Andy McNab, *Immediate Action*.

Chapter 15: Gulf War 1990–91

1 A Squadron staff sergeant, unpublished interview with the author.
2 Peter de la Billiere, *Storm Command*.
3 A Squadron staff sergeant, op. cit.
4 Ibid.

5 Seymour M. Hersh, *The Samson Option: Israel, America and the Bomb*.

6 A Squadron staff sergeant, op. cit.

7 Ibid.

8 Ibid.

9 Mark Urban, *UK Eyes Alpha*.

10 John Nichol, unpublished interview with the author.

11 Peter de la Billiere, *Looking for Trouble*.

12 A Squadron staff sergeant, op. cit.

13 Ibid.

14 *SAS: The Soldier's Story*, Carlton Television, May 1996.

15 Urban, op. cit.

16 Peter de la Billiere, *Storm Command*.

17 A Squadron staff sergeant, op. cit.

18 de la Billiere, *Storm Command*.

Chapter 16: The Future

1 Sydney Alford, 'Space Oddity', *New Scientist*, 22 June 1996.

2 Mike Curtis, *CQB: Close Quarter Battle*.

3 Quoted in Robin Neillands, *A Fighting Retreat: The British Empire 1947–97*.

4 *How to be a Foreign Secretary*, BBC2, 4 January 1998.

5 Mervin Laskey, quoted in the *Guardian*, 26 March 1997.

6 *Guardian*, 18 September 1977.

BIBLIOGRAPHY

Adams, James, *Secret Armies*, Hutchinson, London, 1987

Alford, Sydney, 'Space Oddity', *New Scientist*, 22 June 1996

Arkless, David C., *The Secret War, Dhofar 1971–2*, William Kimber, London, 1988

Barnett, Correlli, *The Collapse of British Power*, Eyre Methuen, London, 1972

Bartlett, C. J., *The Long Retreat: A Short History of British Defence Policy, 1945–70*, Macmillan, London, 1972

Baylis, John (ed), *British Defence Policy in a Changing World*, Croom Helm, London, 1977

Baylis, John, *Anglo-American Defence Relations, 1939–80*, Macmillan, London, 1980

Beaumont, Roger, *Military Elites: Special Fighting Units in the Modern World*, Robert Hale, London, 1976

Beckwith, Charlie A., and Knox, Donald, *Delta Force*, Arms and Armour Press, Ilford, 1984

Beloff, Max, *The Future of British Foreign Policy*, Secker and Warburg, London, 1969

Beloff, Max, *Imperial Sunset*, Eyre Methuen, London, 1969

Bennetto, Jason, 'IRA Plot to Black Out London', *Independent*, 5 June 1997

de la Billiere, Peter, *Storm Command*, Collins, London, 1992 de la Billiere, Peter, *Looking for Trouble*, HarperCollins, London, 1994

Blaxland, Gregory, *The Regiments Depart: The British Army, 1945–1970*, William Kimber, London, 1971

Bowle, John, *The Imperial Achievement*, Secker and Warburg, London, 1974

Cain, P. J. and Hopkins, A. G., *British Imperialism: Crisis and Deconstruction, 1914–1990*, Longman, London, 1993

Campbell, Duncan, 'IRA "Plotted to Black Out London"', *Guardian*, 12 April 1997

Campbell, Duncan, 'Screw the Internet', *Guardian*, 18 September 1997

Chichester, Michael and Wilkinson, John, *The Uncertain Ally: British Defence Policy, 1960–90*, Gower, Aldershot, 1982

Clark, I. and Wheeler, N. J., *Origins of British Nuclear Strategy*, Oxford University Press, Oxford, 1989

Clutterbuck, Professor Richard, *Guerrillas and Terrorists*, Faber and Faber, London, 1977

Cooper, Johnny (with Kemp, Anthony), *One of the Originals*, Pan, London, 1991

Crawford, Steve, *The SAS at Close Quarters*, Sidgwick and Jackson, London, 1993

Cross, Colin, *The Fall of the British Empire*, Hodder and Stoughton, London, 1968

Curtis, Mike, *CQB: Close Quarter Battle*, Bantam, London, 1997

Darby, Philip, *British Defence Policy East of Suez, 1947–68*, Oxford University Press, Oxford, 1973

Darwin, John, *Britain and Decolonisation*, Macmillan, London, 1988

Darwin, John, *The End of the British Empire: The Historical Debate*, Basil Blackwell, Oxford, 1991

Deane-Drummond, Anthony, *Arrows of Fortune*, Leo Cooper, London, 1992

Defence: Outline of Future Policy, HMSO, London, 1957

Devlin, Sir Patrick, *Report of the Commission of Enquiry into Disorders in Nyasaland*, Colonial Office, London, 1959

Dockrill, Michael, *British Defence Since 1945*, Basil Blackwell, Oxford, 1988

Fieldhouse, David, *Black Africa, 1945–80: Economic Decolonisation and Arrested Development*, 1986

First, Ruth, Steel, Jonathan and Gurney, Christabel, *The South African Connection*, Penguin, London, 1973

Frank, Gregory, Imber, Mark and Simpson, John (eds), *Perspectives Upon British Defence Policy, 1945–70*, Proceedings of an MoD conference, Winchester, April 1975

Freedman, Lawrence, *Britain and Nuclear Weapons*, Macmillan, London, 1980

Freedman, Lawrence, *Britain and the Falklands War*, Basil Blackwell, Oxford, 1988

Furedi, F., 'Creating a Breathing Space: The Political Management of Colonial Emergencies', *Journal of Imperial and Commonwealth History*, 21, 1993

Future Defence Policy, HMSO, London, May 1947

Gann, L. H. (ed), *The Defence of Western Europe*, Croom Helm, London, 1987

Geraghty, Tony, *Who Dares Wins*, Little, Brown, London, 1992

Geraghty, Tony, *Beyond the Front Line*, HarperCollins, London, 1996

Gilmour, Raymond, *Dead Ground: Infiltrating the IRA*, Little, Brown, London, 1998

Goldberg, J., 'Origins of British-Saudi Relations: The Anglo-Saudi Treaty Revisited', *Historical Journal*, 28, 1983

Goldsworthy, David, *Colonial Issues in British Politics, 1945–61*, Oxford University Press, Oxford, 1961

Goldsworthy, David, 'Keeping Change within Bounds: Aspects of Colonial Policy during the Churchill and Eden Governments, 1951–57', *Journal of Imperial and Commonwealth History*, 18, 1990

Good, Robert, *UDI: The International Politics of the Rhodesian Rebellion*, Faber and Faber, London, 1973

Hargreaves, J. D., *Decolonisation in Africa*, Longman, London, 1988

Hastings, Max (ed), *The Oxford Book of Military Anecdotes*, Oxford University Press, Oxford, 1985

Hersh, Seymour M., *The Samson Option: Israel, America and the Bomb*, Faber and Faber, London, 1991

Hobsbawm, Eric, *Age of Extremes*, Michael Joseph, London, 1994

Hoe, Alan, *David Stirling*, Little, Brown, London, 1992

Hoe, Alan, *Re-Enter the SAS*, Leo Cooper, London, 1994

Holland, Jack and Phoenix, Susan, *Policing the Shadows*, Hodder and Stoughton, London, 1996

Holland, R. F., *European Decolonisation 1918–81, An Introductory Survey*, Macmillan, London, 1985

James, Lawrence, *The Rise and Fall of the British Empire*, Little, Brown, London, 1994

Jeapes, Anthony S., *SAS: Operation Oman*, William Kimber, London, 1980

Jeffrey, K., *The British Army and the Crisis of Empire*, Manchester University Press, Manchester, 1984

Judd, Denis, *Empire: The British Imperial Experience from 1765 to the Present*, HarperCollins, London, 1996

Kain, Andrew, *The SAS Security Handbook*, Heinemann, London, 1996

Kemp, Anthony, *The SAS, Savage Wars of Peace*, John Murray, London, 1994

Kennedy, Michael Paul, *Soldier I*, Bloomsbury, London, 1989

Kennedy, Paul, *The Realities Behind Diplomacy*, Fontana, London, 1981

Kitson, Sir Frank, *Bunch of Fives*, Faber and Faber, London, 1977

Kunz, Diane B., 'The Importance of Having Money: The Economic Diplomacy of the Suez Crisis', in Louis, William Roger and Owen, Roger (eds), *Suez 1956: The Crisis and its Consequences*, Oxford University Press, New York, 1990

Large, Donald 'Lofty', *One Man's SAS*, William Kimber, London, 1987

Lloyd, T. O., *The British Empire 1558–1995*, Oxford University Press, Oxford, 1996

Louis, William Roger, *Imperialism at Bay: The United States and the Decolonisation of the British Empire, 1941–45*, Clarendon Press, Oxford, 1977

Louis, William Roger, *The British Empire in the Middle East, 1945–51*, Clarendon Press, Oxford, 1984

Mackenzie, J. H., *Propaganda and Empire: The Manipulation of British Public Opinion, 1880–1960*, Manchester University Press, Manchester, 1984

McAleese, Peter and Bles, Mark, *No Mean Soldier: The Autobiography of a Professional Fighting Man*, Orion, London, 1993

McCallion, Harry, *Killing Zone*, Bloomsbury, London, 1995

McManners, Hugh, *The Scars of War*, HarperCollins, London, 1994

McNab, Andy, *Bravo Two Zero*, Bantam Press, London, 1993

McNab, Andy, *Immediate Action*, Bantam Press, London, 1995

Mansergh, Nicholas, *The Commonwealth Experience*, Macmillan, London, 1982

Matloff, M., *Strategic Planning for Coalition Warfare 1943–44*, United States Office of Military History, Washington DC, 1959

Middlebrook, Martin, *Fight for the Malvinas*, Viking, London, 1989

Mohaitis, Professor Thomas M., 'British Counter Insurgency', *Small Wars and Insurgencies*, Vol 3, December 1990, Frank Cass, London

Morris, James, *Farewell the Trumpets*, Faber and Faber, London, 1978

Murray, Raymond, *The SAS in Ireland*, Mercier Press, Cork, 1990

Narias, M. S., *Nuclear Weapons and British Strategic Planning*, Oxford University Press, Oxford, 1991

Neillands, Robin, *A Fighting Retreat: The British Empire 1947–97*, Hodder and Stoughton, London, 1997

Neillands, Robin, *In the Combat Zone: Special Forces Since 1945*, Weidenfeld and Nicolson, London, 1997

Newell, Major Dare and Sutherland, Colonel David, 'SAS Post-War Evolution: The Formative Years, 1954–64', *Mars and Minerva*, September 1987

Nixon, Richard, *The Memoirs of Richard M. Nixon*, Arrow Books, London, 1979

Northedge, F. S., *Descent from Power*, George Allen and Unwin, London, 1974

Overdale, Ritchie, *Britain, the US and the Transfer of Power in the Middle East*, Leicester University Press, Leicester, 1996

Paget, Julian, *Last Post: Aden 1964–67*, Faber and Faber, London, 1969

Platt, D. C. M., 'Economic Factors and British Policy during the "New Imperialism" ', *Past and Present*, 32, 1968

Pocock, Tom, *Fighting General: The Public and Private Campaigns of General Sir Walter Walker*, Collins, London, 1973

Porter, Bernard, *The Lion's Share: A Short History of British Imperialism, 1850–1970*, Longman, London, 1975

Reagan, Ronald, *An American Life*, Hutchinson, London, 1990

Renwick, Robin, *Fighting with Allies: America and Britain in Peace and War*, Macmillan, Basingstoke, 1996

Richie, John, *Inside the Foreign Office*, London, 1992

Roper, John (ed), *The Future of British Defence Policy*, Gower, London, 1985

Rose, General Michael, 'Advance Force Operations: The SAS', in Washington, Linda (ed), *Ten Years On, The British Army in the Falklands War*, National Army Museum, London, 1992

Rosie, George, *Dictionary of International Terrorism*, Mainstream, Edinburgh, 1986

Rotberg, R. I. and Mazrui A. A. (eds), *Protest and Power in Black Africa*, Oxford University Press, Oxford, 1970

Royal Institute of International Affairs, *The Middle East: A Political and Economic Survey*, London, 1958

Royle, Trevor, *The Last Days of the Raj*, Michael Joseph, London, 1989

Royle, Trevor, *Winds of Change: The End of Empire in Africa*, John Murray, London, 1996

Runciman, Steven, *The White Rajahs: A History of Sarawak 1841–1946*, Cambridge University Press, Cambridge, 1960

Searight, Sarah, *The British in the Middle East*, Weidenfeld and Nicolson, London, 1969

Sebastian, Tim, 'Cash For No Questions', *Observer*, 19 January 1997

Shaw, Jennifer, et al., *Ten Years of Terrorism*, RUSI, London, 1979

Shuckburgh, E., *Descent to Suez: Diaries 1951–56*, Weidenfeld and Nicolson, London, 1986

Slessor, Sir John, *Strategy for the West*, Cassell, London, 1954

Smiley, David and Kemp, Philip, *Arabian Assignment*, Leo Cooper, London, 1975

Smith, Dan, *The Defence of the Realm in the 1980s*, Croom Helm, London, 1980

Sterling, Claire, *The Secret War of International Terrorism*, Weidenfeld and Nicolson, London, 1981

Stockwell, A. J., 'British Imperial Policy and Decolonisation in Malaya, 1942–52', *Journal of Imperial and Commonwealth History*, 13, 1984

Strawson, John, *A History of the SAS Regiment*, Secker and Warburg, London, 1984

Stubbs, R., *Hearts and Minds in Guerrilla Warfare: The Malayan Emergency 1948–60*, Oxford University Press, Singapore, 1989

Thomas, Hugh, *The Suez Affair*, Weidenfeld and Nicolson, London, 1967

Traynor, Ian, 'CIA Agent Fuels German Fury', *Guardian*, 17 March 1997

Traynor, Ian, 'Bridge of Spies', *Guardian*, 26 March 1997

Urban, Mark, *Big Boys' Rules*, Faber and Faber, London, 1992

Urban, Mark, *UK Eyes Alpha*, Faber and Faber, London, 1996

Waddy, Colonel J., 'Response to SAS Post-War Evolution', *Mars and Minerva*, April 1988

Walker, General Sir Walter, *The Bear at the Back Door*, Foreign Affairs Publishing, Richmond, Surrey, 1980

Warner, Philip, *The SAS*, William Kimber, London, 1971

Weale, Adrian, *Secret Warfare: Special Forces Operations from the Great Game to the SAS*, Hodder and Stoughton, London, 1997

Wiseman, John 'Lofty', *The SAS Survival Handbook*, Collins, London, 1986

Woodcock, George, *Who Killed the British Empire?*, Jonathan Cape, London, 1974

Woollacott, Martin, 'Brass Hats Get Down to Brass Tacks', *Guardian*, 24 May 1997

INDEX

A Squadron 32–3, 41, 55, 71,
    81–5, 95, 109, 127, 130,
    326
  Aden 188, 209
  Gulf War 463, 465, 484, 489,
    496
Abdullah, King 62
abseiling tactics, Iranian
    Embassy 349
Abu Dhabi 117, 161, 466, 470
Acheson, Dean 94
Achille Lauro 410, 517
Action Directe 306
Aden 116, 130, 155, 175, 225,
    232, 254, 325
  see also Yemen
  (1964–67) 110, 180–218
  overview 184–8
Afghanistan, (1982–89) 415–
    26, 441
Africa 167–79, 206
Aggressive OPs 287
Ah Hoi 49, 50
Ah Niet 50
Aid to the Civil Power Act 348
airborne operations, WWII 12
aircraft 65, 73, 245, 420–1
  see also helicopters
  A-10 461, 477, 480, 483, 491
  B-52 484

Boeing 707 322
C130 252, 336–40, 381, 411
Canberra bomber 394
Caribou 246
Chipmunk 432
FB-111A 218
F-15E 477
Flogger 449
Harrier 371, 373, 381, 390
Hercules 322–3, 374, 378,
    395, 446, 484
hijacks 227–9, 318–20, 409–
    14
Hunter jet-fighter 181, 189
Korean Airlines 747 449
MiG fighters 323, 416–7, 447
Mirage 373
Pucara 371, 385
Shackleton 81
Skyhawk 373
Skyvan 246
Stealth bomber 471, 481, 512
Strikemaster ground-attack 3,
    5, 246, 250
Super Etendard 356, 373, 376
Tornado 85, 446
VC10 380
Venom 77, 81
aircraft-carriers 217, 361
airfields, Gulf War 484

al-Nahas, Mustafa 62
Al Yammamah arms sales 85
ambushes 35, 40, 200, 280
Amin, Idi 321–4
ammunition 32–3, 52, 250
Angola 177
Angry Brigade 306
animal tracks 35, 137
animal traps 36, 137
Anne, Princess 154
anonymity *see* secrecy
Arabs 16
Argentina
    cattle story (Northern
        Ireland) 267
    Falklands War 356–414
armaments
    see also nuclear weapons
    anti-tank missile 435
    Armalite 53, 119, 126, 181,
        429, 457, 465
    Blowpipe missile 422
    Bren 181–3
    Browning 9mm pistol 292,
        299, 310–11
    Browning machine-gun 74,
        77, 80
    Claymore mine 457, 463,
        466, 496
    Exocet missiles 356, 373
    flash-bang grenades 310, 325,
        349
    fragmentation grenades 349,
        457, 496
    heavy machine-gun 453, 456
    Heckler-Koch submachine-
        gun 262, 310, 331
    Hellfire missile 471
    Kalashnikov AK74 rifle 427–
        9, 434
    M10/11 submachine-gun 310
    M203 rifle/grenade-launcher
        257

Makharov pistol 458
Maverick missile 480
Milan anti-tank weapon 478
million-bullet gun 512
mortar shells 78, 120, 250,
    372
Patriot missile 476
phosphorus shells 78
phosphorus-tipped bullets
    201
pistol 102, 156, 457
Remington repeater shotgun
    310
remote-controlled bomb
    289–92
rocket-launcher 183, 456
rocket-propelled grenade
    (RPG) 421, 453
sales 85
sawn-off shotgun 53, 126
Scud missiles 467, 471, 475–
    6, 485, 489, 497–8, 500, 511
self-loading rifle (SLR) 53,
    119, 126–7
shooting training 101–5,
    223–4, 307–9
Stinger ground-to-air missile
    378–81, 385, 394, 422–3
Tomahawk cruise missile
    438, 471
armour, T-64 429–30, 435
'arms for hostages' deal 413
arson 525
Artists' Rifles 13
Asian Tigers, economic warfare
    521–2
assassination ideas, Saddam
    Hussein 487
Athens 410
Atlantic Conveyor 387, 397–8
Attlee, Clement 15, 60
Auchinleck, Claude John Eyre
    10, 12

AWACS 478
Azahari, Sheik 124

B Squadron 32, 42, 45, 49, 139, 193, 199, 209, 250, 326, 348
   Botswana 407–8
   Falklands War 374, 376–7, 395
   Gulf War 465, 472–3, 485
Baader-Meinhof gang 321, 326
backup, importance 263
Baker, Paddy 190
Balcombe Street siege 320
Balfour Declaration (1917) 60
Baluch mercenaries 1–8
Barco, Virgilio 453
BBC 321, 341, 342, 344
Beckwith, Nathan 'Charlie' 110, 328–40
Bedou 473–4, 486
Beirut 409, 413
Belize 451–2
Bembridge, Trooper 83
Bennett, Bob 42
Bentine, Michael 307–9
beret (beige) 109, 210, 213, 223, 230
Berlin Wall, breaches 445–6
Biafra 167–8
Biggin Hill 303–6
Bishop of Birmingham 98
Bisley Ranges 14
Black September group 312–13
Blair, Tony 512, 517
Bloch, Dora 323
Blue Light 329
Boat Troop 106, 366–7, 371
body language, BG protection 157
bodyguards (BGs) 153, 170, 222–3, 235–6, 309, 333
Boese, Wilfrid 321

born-again Christians 333
Borneo (1962–66) 119–48
Bosnia 513–14
Botswana 407–8
bottom-up methodology 509
Boyle, John 283
Bradbury Lines 95, 114
Bradshaw, Bob 250
Bramall, Lord 393
Bravo Two Zero 464, 466, 472–3, 491, 494, 507
Brecon Beacons 45
briefings 353
Brigade of Guards 209, 527
Briggs, Harold 30
Brighton bombing 288
Brixmis 430–50
Brooke, Oliver 45
Brown, Poet 125
Brunei 95
   (1962–66) 119–48
   overview 124
Buckley, William 409, 410
'buddy system' methodology 96
Bundeswehr, mistrust 445
Burma 16, 21, 452
Bush, George 487, 488

C Squadron 48, 175
Calvert, 'Mad' Mike 12–14, 29–33, 44–5, 105
Cambodia 328, 424–6
Careless, Jack 96
Carlos the Jackal 307
Carter, Jimmy 329, 334–40
Carter, Trooper 83
censorship, publications 507
Ceylon 16
Chapman, Roger 250
Charles, Prince of Wales 154
Chelsea Chindits 32, 41
Chiang Kai-shek 19

Chile 357, 374, 382, 394
Chin Peng 26–7, 51
China 19–20, 26, 123–4, 206, 232, 240, 425
Chindit warriors 213
Chindits 25, 29, 31–3
Church, Frank 414
Churchill, Winston 9, 15–19, 46, 62, 65
CIA 61–2, 414, 431, 518, 521
civilians, economic warriors 520–6
Clinton, Bill 522
clock tower memorial 107
close-quarter battle (CQB) training 101–5, 223–4, 307–9
clothing 23, 24, 103, 125, 223, 327
  beret 109, 210, 213, 223, 230
  CT team 311
  flak jacket 311
  Gulf War 496
cocaine crisis 451–5
Cold War 417, 424, 426
  (1945–90) 427–55
  emergence 164
Colombia 450–5, 463
combat training, CQB 101–5, 223–4
command structure 11, 97, 511–12, 527
commercial intelligence 525–6
Commission on Infrastructure Protection 522
Commonwealth 166, 169
communication skills 36, 98, 99, 129
communications equipment
  current importance 510–12
  Falklands War 382–90
  Gulf War 463, 490
  interceptions 521–6

radios 4–5, 33–4, 181, 190, 369, 432, 466–7, 472, 478, 481, 491–5
satellites 382–4, 464, 467, 472, 477, 499, 502–4, 521
Communist Terrorists (CTs), Malaya 26–55
community relationships, Hereford 113
compensation payments 300
computer systems, protection 520–1, 524
concept, SAS 10–12, 527–8
Condon, Harry 139
Congo 167, 408
conscription 17, 90
Consiglio, Bob 494
Contras 413
Cooper, Johnny 193
counter-insurgency role 13–14, 29, 46, 53, 94, 116, 153, 223, 455
counter-interrogation techniques 54, 98, 99
Counter-Revolutionary Warfare (CRW) Wing 307–15, 333
counter-terrorism 25–55, 153
  see also terrorism
  (1968–98) 302–40
  CT team 309, 314–20, 326, 516–17
  Iranian Embassy siege 261, 340, 341–55, 441, 504
  Northern Ireland 262–302
covert operations 85–6, 102, 125, 133, 193, 222–3, 355, 425–6, 434, 438, 505
creation of SAS (July 1941) 10
criticisms
  Falklands performance 367
  standards 505, 511, 518, 525
Croatia 513

Crooke, Ian 377, 405–6
CS gas 305, 310–11, 349, 403
CT team 309, 314–20, 326,
    516–17
Cuba 407, 452
Cubbon, John 191–2
Curzon, George 15
Cyprus 63, 259–60

D Squadron 48, 49, 55, 71–85,
    95, 101, 109, 116, 130,
    174, 203–4, 215, 326
  Falklands War 365–8, 368,
    371, 381, 383, 387
  Gulf War 465, 472–3, 479–80,
    484, 491
  Northern Ireland 267
  Oman 237–9
Daily Telegraph 281, 444
Davies, Barry 324
Dayan, Moshe 66
de Gaulle, Charles 166
de la Billiere, Peter 188, 281,
    316–17, 364, 373, 376,
    395, 400, 467–501, 506–7
Deane-Drummond, Anthony
    71, 84
debriefs, importance 398–9,
    501
declining standards 505, 511,
    518, 525
Dellow, John 348
Delta Force 260, 329–40, 354,
    378–9, 393–4, 406–7, 504,
    518
Delves, Cedric 368, 371
demolition skills 11, 54, 97,
    222, 461, 481
Denbury, David 'Shug' 481, 494
Denmark 100
Der Spiegel 521
desert warfare 73–85, 116, 180–
    218, 219–261, 456–501

Deutch, John 518
Dhofar 1–8, 199, 433
    (1970–77) 219–60
    overview 222–6
Diana, Princess of Wales 316
diplomacy, usage 21, 94
direction-finding (DF) 467, 511
disbandment suggestion 518,
    526
discipline 11, 41, 72, 77, 108–
    9, 113, 327
'discomfort allowance' 240
disguises 195–6
Distinguished Conduct Medal
    264
diving skills, SBS 391
dog-tags 134
dogs
  Hard Dog Section,
    Metropolitan Police 303–6
  Northern Ireland 271
domino theory 186
donkeys, Jebel Akhdar 78
Downing, Wayne 479
drains, Gulf War 480
drill square 110
Drljaca, Simo 513–14
drugs crisis 450–5
Duffy, Patrick 281
Duke of York's Barracks,
    London 495
Dye, Jack 205

18 Troop 76
economic plight (post-WWII)
    17–18
economic warfare 520–6
Eden, Anthony 62, 64–8
Edgecombe, Greville 199–200
Edwards, Robin 190
Egypt 58, 62–3, 186, 194, 197,
    410–12
Eisenhower, Dwight D. 66

electricity supplies 522
Elizabeth II 154, 315–16, 407
empire, disintegration 14–21, 54, 89, 94, 164, 361
endurance training 45
English language, universality 520
Enniskillen Remembrance Day outrage 297
Entebbe 321–4
'Eric Bloodaxe' 522
escape skills 98, 100–1, 491–2, 494
Escobar, Pablo 454
ETA 297, 306
European Economic Community (EEC, later EC) 165, 218, 373, 517
Euston Station drill hall 14
evasion skills 98, 100–1
exercises
  Brave Defender 441
  Salisbury Plain 87, 107
exports, SAS services (post-1980) 357, 503

14 Int 269, 275–7, 280, 495, 509–10
Faisal, King 69
Falklands War 90, 238, 356–414
Farouk, King 62
Farran, Roy 12–14
Farrell, Mairead 290–9
FBI 378, 520, 522
female soldiers 267–8, 275–6, 518
Ferragher, Joe 409
Ferret Force 31, 36, 105
Fianna Fail 272
field hospitals 244
firqats 1–8, 241–60
first-aid skills 11
fitness training 102

flak jackets 311
Flavinius, Marcus 211–12
food 78, 88, 271
  jungle 39, 134–5
Force 136 25, 29, 31
Force 777, Egypt 411
Force Projection Cell 470–1, 472–3, 475
Ford, Gerald 414
Foreign Office 90, 94, 115, 153–4, 159, 218, 224, 362, 506, 515
Founding Principles of SAS (extract) 527–8
Four Square Laundry 268
Four-Power Agreement 430
France 59, 65, 67, 93, 166
  Exocet missiles 356, 373
  terrorism 307, 315
Franks, Brian 281
Freds 268
Free-Fall Troop 106, 232
Fury, Wayne 427–30
future prospects 502–26

G Squadron 139, 203–11, 216, 231–2, 250–1, 279, 326, 368, 370, 383–90, 462–3, 496, 505, 510
Gacha, Gonzalo Rodriguez 454
Galtieri, Leopoldo 362, 389, 393, 396
Gambia 404–6
Gandhi, Mahatma 15
Gaz jeeps 457–61, 474
GCHQ 399–400, 431–2, 466, 516, 521
Geary, Graham 435
Germany 307, 310, 313, 321, 352
  East Germany 341–4, 427–50
  mistrust 445
Ghalib ibn Ali 70

Ghana 176
Ghost Force concept 525–6
Gibraltar, IRA incident 289–99
GIGN 318, 405
Glubb, John 62, 65
'Golden Triangle', drugs crisis 452
Gorbachev, Mikhail 422, 450
GPS systems 464–5, 483, 490, 494, 501
Greece 18, 410
Green Berets 468
'Green Slime' 257
Greenham Common 438
Greenwood, Anthony 167
Grenada 407, 504
Grey, Nicol 27
GSG-9 318, 324, 330
Guards battalion, Falklands War 392
Guards Independent Parachute Squadron 209
Guatemala 451–2
Gulf War 13, 52, 212, 241, 486–501, 505, 509
Gurkhas
   reputation 138
   Victoria Cross 146
Gurney, Henry 46

hackers 522, 525
Haig, Alexander 379
Hamilton, John 388
Hard Dog Section, Metropolitan Police 303–6
Harding, John 30
Harry, Prince 316
Hastings, Max 388
Hauf 199
Hawkins, Herbie 75
Healey, Denis 133, 140, 144, 191, 217–18
hearing, jungle warfare 29

'hearts and minds' strategy 43–5, 125–6, 247–8, 258, 272, 333, 451, 524
Heath, Edward 234, 314, 317
helicopters 7, 46, 49, 53, 137, 142, 205, 232, 243, 250, 356, 474
   Agusta 109 393
   Apache 471
   Blackhawk 332, 479
   Chinook 370, 459, 472, 483, 493
   Falklands War 356–361, 365–414
   Hind 435–6
   MI-8 Hip troop carrier 470
   Scout 202
   Sea King 257–61, 382, 383
   Sea Stallion 336–40
   Sycamore 37
   Wessex 180–3, 366
Henderson, George 186
Hereford 95, 110, 113, 162, 210, 223, 239, 360, 525
hijackers 227–9, 318–20, 409–14
Hitler 9
Hizbollah 413, 520
HMS Antelope 382
HMS Antrim 367
HMS Conqueror 363
HMS Eagle 205
HMS Endeavour 365–8
HMS Endurance 90, 361–3
HMS Fearless 199, 364
HMS Glamorgan 371
HMS Hermes 46, 361–3, 371, 383, 392
HMS Intrepid 364, 383
HMS Invincible 361–2, 364, 392
HMS Plymouth 367
HMS Sheffield 371, 382
Hollingsworth, Yogi 130

holsters 103
Hong Kong 19
Hopkinson, Henry 165
Horner, Chuck 472, 498
hostages 307, 335–40, 341–55,
    405–6, 410–12, 413
Houston, 'Fablon' 368
Howe, Geoffrey 293, 402, 408
HQ Squadron 32
'human shields' 487
humility 528
humint 431, 469
humour 528
Hungary 45, 98
Hunt, Rex 362
Hussein, King 62, 65, 163, 227
Hussein, Saddam 13, 157, 462–
    501

Iban tribesmen 35–6, 42
Ibn Saud 59
illness 37–8, 48, 51, 137
India 15, 17, 21, 166
Indonesia 119–48
industrial espionage 522–6
infantry
    Gulf War 490
    Northern Ireland 280
infiltration skills 106, 222, 438
inflatable craft 53, 230, 267
informers 278
inner motivation 96
insurance claims, Malaya 27
intelligence work 9, 30, 48, 95,
    140, 155, 248, 257, 267,
    274–80, 431, 469, 516,
    521–6
Internet 521–2
internment 278
interrogation 437
    terrorists 353
    training 193
IRA 262–302, 306, 453, 517

Iran 60, 225, 253, 320–1, 322,
    423
    'arms for hostages' deal 413
    Embassy siege 261, 340, 341–
    55, 441, 504
Iraq 58, 60, 68–9, 116, 230, 344,
    456–501
Ireland 172
Israel 60–8, 151, 203, 208, 225–
    6, 280, 313, 471, 475–6,
    498, 520
    counter-terrorism 321–4
    Gulf War 486–501
Italy 203, 215, 373

Japan 25, 26, 28, 30, 53, 523
Jawara, Dawda 404
Jeapes, Tony 237–9, 243–4,
    258–60, 506
jebalis 232–60
Jebel Akhdar 225, 239
    (1958–59) 56–85
    overview 58–60
Jeeps 32
Jews 60, 410
    see also Israel
jihad 241, 333
Johnston, Jim 193
Jones, H. 387
Jordan 58, 62, 84, 163, 253, 476,
    491
journalists 284, 388, 438
jungle warfare 22–55, 106, 119–
    48, 451–5
just-in-time production system
    523

Kealy, Mike 250
Keenan, Brian 413
Kennedy, J.F. 93, 109, 153–9,
    161, 327, 354
Kenya 159–61
Kenyatta, Jomo 159–61, 166

Keynes, John Maynard 17, 218
KGB 432
Khaled, Leila 227, 323
Khmer Rouge 424–5
Khomeini, Ayatollah 225, 334–40
Khuzestan 344
Killing House 106
Kingston, Bob 329–30
KISS philosophy 336
Kitson, Frank 72, 85
Kohl, Helmut 448
Korean Airlines 747 disaster 449
Korean War 19, 32, 98, 101, 164–5, 168, 327
Kovacevic, Milan 513–14
Krocher-Tiedemann, Gabrielle 321
Krushchev, Nikita 94
KSK 327
Kurds 486–7
Kuwait 116, 462–501

Labalaba, 'Lab' 249–51
Land Rovers 107, 456
Lane, Legs 494
language skills 2, 39, 97–8, 129, 220, 524
Laos 452
Large, Lofty 77, 142, 201
Laser target designators (LTDs) 468, 477, 497
Lawrence of Arabia 208
lawyers
    CIA stations 414
    Northern Ireland 281–2, 295
    operation briefings 353
Learmont, John 434
Lebanon 59, 407, 413
leeches 23, 35
left-handedness 102
Libya 58, 288, 423

Lie Ton Ten 26
Lillico, Eddie 'Geordie' 141–2
Lloyd, Selwyn 65
local community relationships, Hereford 113
Lock, Trevor 344, 348
Long-Range Desert Group 9
Lusitania 515

M19 116
McCann, Daniel 289–99
McCarthy, John 413
McKenna, Sean 272
Maclean, Mac 244
McLeod, Hugh 427–30, 434, 437
Macmillan, Harold 66, 89, 93–4, 164–5, 171
McNab, Andy 285, 408, 466, 472, 507
Mahmoud, 'Captain' 325
Mahsood, Ahmed Shah 418–19
Major, John 487, 497, 500, 513
malaria 38
Malay Scouts (SAS) 31–3, 105
Malaya 105, 123, 197, 260
    (1950–58) 22–55, 71, 126
    overview 25–6
Malvern 95
Mao Tse-tung 26, 232–3, 244
maps, Gulf War inadequacies 494, 501
marksmanship skills 198
Mars and Minerva (Regimental journal) 15
Marsh Arabs 485–6
Marshall Plan 19
Masirah 73
'Master, The' 105–6, 308
Maunsell, M.S. 310
media 281, 321, 341, 342, 344, 353–4, 444
medical skills 38–9, 43, 97–8, 239, 247, 258, 493, 524

memoirs, publications 507
Menendez, General 389, 393
Menwith Hill Station, Yorkshire 521
mercenaries 178, 194
Mention in Despatches 142, 147, 251, 393
Merebrook Camp 95
Metropolitan Police 303–6, 517
MI5 275–8, 293, 296, 439
MI6 (also SIS) 61, 275–8, 416, 431
  Afghanistan 415
  Falklands War 363
Middle East 1–6, 19, 56–85, 117, 161, 455, 462–501
Military Cross 136, 147, 301
Military Intelligence Centre, Ashford 433, 440
Military Medal 142, 301
Military Reconnaissance Force 268
Min Yen 26
Mindszenty, Cardinal 98–9
Ministry of Defence (MoD) 90, 113, 210, 374, 392, 507
Mirbat, Battle 248, 251
Mitchell, Colin 'Mad Mitch' 203–4
Mobility Troop 106
Mogadishu 325
Mohammed, Oan Ali 347–55
monsoon weather 1–2
Moore, Jeremy 364, 386–90, 398
Moores, Steve 245
moral courage 214
morphine syrettes 134
Morrison, Alastair 324
Morrison, Herbert 512
Morse code 34, 130, 459, 467
mosquitoes 23
motorbikes, Gulf War 468, 482
Mount Kenya 101

Mountain Troop 106, 243
Mountbatten, Lord 90
Mozambique 177–8
Mubarrak, Said 241–2
Mugabe, Robert 178–9
Mujahedeen 416–26, 441, 513
Munich Olympic Massacre 309, 312, 314, 324
Muscat 69–70
Mussasdiq, President 61

19 Troop 76, 365
Nairac, Robert 263
nante sikkit thorn 35
napalm 114
Nasser, Gamel Abdul 62, 64–8, 186, 197
National Security Agency (NSA), US 521
NATO 64, 91–2, 93, 430, 435, 438, 444–5
naval power 20
navigation skills 11, 29, 33–4, 490
Nehru, Pandit 171
Netanyahu, Jonathan 323
Netherlands 443
New Zealand 48
Nicaragua 413
Nidal, Abu 410–12
night-vision goggles (NVGs) 315, 358, 437, 460, 466, 481, 493
Nixon, Richard 19, 224, 259
Nkomo, Joshua 178
Norry, Keith 107
North Africa 9
North, Oliver 413
Northern Ireland 224, 240, 262–302
  IRA 262–302, 306, 453, 517
  military solution option (1970s) 301